Thieves in Court

From the seemingly insignificant theft of some bread and a dozen apples in nineteenth-century rural Germany, to the high courts and modern-day property laws, this English-language translation of Habermas' *Diebe vor Gericht* explores how everyday incidents of petty stealing and the ordinary people involved in these cases came to shape the current legal system. Habermas draws from an unusual cache of archival documents of theft cases, tracing the evolution and practice of the legal system of Germany through the nineteenth century. This close reading – relying on approaches of legal anthropology – challenges long-standing narratives of legal development, state building, and modern notions of the rule of law.

Ideal for legal historians and scholars of modern German and nineteenth-century European history, this innovative volume steps outside of the classic narratives of legal history and gives an insight into the interconnectedness of social, legal, and criminal history.

REBEKKA HABERMAS holds the chair in modern European history at the Georg August University, Göttingen. She is an editor of the of the journal *Historische Anthropologie* and of the book series *Historische Studien.*

KATHLEEN MITCHELL DELL'ORTO has, in the course of her career, held positions in university teaching, private industry, and the United States government. As a professional linguist for many decades, she has translated documents and books on subjects from science and technology, the humanities, and law.

Publications of the German Historical Institute

Edited by

SIMONE LÄSSIG
with the assistance of David Lazar

The German Historical Institute is a center for advanced study and research whose purpose is to provide a permanent basis for scholarly cooperation among historians from the Federal Republic of Germany and the United States. The Institute conducts, promotes, and supports research into both American and German political, social, economic, and cultural history; into transatlantic migration, especially during the nineteenth and twentieth centuries; and into the history of international relations, with special emphasis on the roles played by the United States and Germany.

Recent Books in the Series:

Adam T. Rosenbaum, *Bavarian Tourism and the Modern World, 1800–1950*
Hartmut Berghoff, Jürgen Kocka, and Dieter Ziegler, editors, *Business in the Age of Extremes: Essays in Modern German and Austrian Economic History*
Lars Maischak, *German Merchants in the Nineteenth-Century Atlantic*
Thomas W. Maulucci, Jr., and Detlef Junker, editors, *GIs in Germany: The Social, Economic, Cultural, and Political History of the American Military Presence*
Gerald D. Feldman, *Austrian Banks in the Period of National Socialism*
Eric C. Steinhart, *The Holocaust and the Germanization of Ukraine*
Alison Efford, *German Immigrants, Race, and Citizenship in the Civil War Era*
Cathryn Carson, *Heisenberg in the Atomic Age: Science and the Public Sphere*
Michaela Hoenicke Moore, *Know Your Enemy: The American Debate on Nazism, 1933–1945*
Yair Mintzker, *The Defortification of the German City, 1689–1866*
Astrid M. Eckert, *The Struggle for the Files: The Western Allies and the Return of German Archives after the Second World War*
Winson Chu, *The German Minority in Interwar Poland*
Hartmut Berghoff and Uta Andrea Balbier, *The East German Economy, 1945-2010: Falling Behind or Catching Up?*
Roger Chickering and Stig Förster, editors, *War in an Age of Revolution, 1775–1815*
Monica Black, *Death in Berlin: From Weimar to Divided Germany*
John R. McNeill and Corinna R. Unger, editors, *Environmental Histories of the Cold War*
Christof Mauch and Kiran Klaus Patel, *The United States and Germany during the Twentieth Century: Competition and Convergence*

Thieves in Court

The Making of the German Legal System in the Nineteenth Century

REBEKKA HABERMAS
University of Göttingen

TRANSLATED BY KATHLEEN MITCHELL DELL'ORTO

GERMAN HISTORICAL INSTITUTE
Washington, D.C.
and
CAMBRIDGE
UNIVERSITY PRESS

CAMBRIDGE
UNIVERSITY PRESS

One Liberty Plaza, 20th Floor, New York, NY 20006, USA

Cambridge University Press is part of the University of Cambridge.

It furthers the University's mission by disseminating knowledge in the pursuit of education, learning and research at the highest international levels of excellence.

www.cambridge.org
Information on this title: www.cambridge.org/9781107046771

First published 2016

Printed in the United Kingdom by Clays, St Ives plc

A catalog record for this publication is available from the British Library

Library of Congress Cataloging-in-Publication Data
NAMES: Habermas, Rebekka, 1959– author.
TITLE: Thieves in court : the making of the German legal system in the nineteenth century / Rebekka Habermas.
OTHER TITLES: Diebe vor Gericht English
DESCRIPTION: New York : Cambridge University Press, 2016. | Series: Publications of the german historical institute | Includes bibliographical references and index.
IDENTIFIERS: LCCN 2016025908 | ISBN 9781107046771 (Hardback)
Subjects: LCSH: Theft–Germany–History–19th century. | Criminal law–Germany–History–19th century. | BISAC: HISTORY / Europe / General.
CLASSIFICATION: LCC KK8648 .H33 2008 | DDC 349.4309/034–dc23 LC record available at https://lccn.loc.gov/2016025908

ISBN 978-1-107-04677-1 Hardback

This work was translated by Kathleen Mitchell Dell'Orto

The translation of this work was funded by Geisteswissenschaften International –

Translation Funding for Humanities and Social Sciences from Germany, a joint initiative of the Fritz Thyssen Foundation, the German Federal Foreign Office, the collecting society VG WORT, and the Börsenverein des Deutschen Buchhandels (German Publishers & Booksellers Association).

to Hepp
for everything

Contents

Acknowledgments

I have many friends and colleagues to thank for having allowed me to put forward parts of the book in various stages for discussion: Michael Werner and Jacques Revel (Paris), Martina Kessel (Bielefeld), Lucian Hölscher and Regina Schulte (Bochum), Jakob Tanner (Zürich), and Alf Lüdtke (Erfurt). I also want to thank the Einstein Forum (Potsdam) and especially the Historic Anthropology Work Group, which had to discuss many versions of this book. I profited greatly from those discussions.

I would likewise like to thank Susanna Burghartz (Basel) both for suggestions just dropped into telephone conversations in passing and for much reading. Maria Rhode (Göttingen) also contributed a great deal without slowing her running speed. For reading I am especially grateful to Philipp Müller (London), Richard Hölzl (Göttingen), Alexandra Przyrembel (Göttingen), and Gerd Schwerhoff (Dresden), all of whom had to deal with everything in very rough form. I found the reading by Sylvia Kesper-Biermann (Bayreuth) particularly helpful – for that I owe special thanks.

For what was probably the most important information, calling my attention to the Marburg Main State Archives, I would like to thank Joachim Eibach (Berlin).

Without the work of Alexandra Ortmann (Göttingen/Berlin) I would be suffering from even deeper, and especially even longer-lasting, desperation. She did much more than edit the manuscript. She wrote comments ranging from friendly to annoyed in the margins, made suggestions for shortening and putting in commas, and especially tried to recreate the context that had sometimes gotten away from me.

I owe Adalbert Hepp thanks for commenting on chapter drafts in such an unusually friendly way that it instantly became clear to me: that must not have been it yet. Because of her first impression (gained from reading only one page) and her comment, "That is too boring for me...," Toni helped bring about the result that not everything stayed quite so boring.

Finally, Tanja Hommen (Campus Publishers) was likewise subjected to painstaking reading of the manuscript and spared me several bloopers, not only of a stylistic kind. For that and for the judicious management of the manuscript and then the relatively quick publication of the German edition I wish to give thanks.

Without the work of Mrs. Walter, who attempted to keep the worst university demands from reaching my desk, and the work of a great number of former research assistants in Bochum and Göttingen, the book would never have gotten finished. In the last years they have had to suffer many tribulations with the thieves: Bettina Brockmeyer (then Bochum, today Bielefeld), Lena Steilen, and Eckart Schörle (Erfurt), who found every Hessian town, no matter how small; Wiebke Jensen (Göttingen), Alexandra Ortmann (Göttingen/Berlin), Christina Nawa (Regensburg), who developed what is probably the most extensive database of nineteenth-century thieves, and Ole Münch. Christin Templin and Sandra Michaelis also searched one last time for errors – and found an endless number. In cases of doubt, I was the one who smuggled in the ones still present.

They transcribed and corrected; they created databases; they sought to bring order to the murky Electoral Hessian administration and to track down important, and less important, jurists. More than anything else, however, they showed me repeatedly that universities involve more than administration of outside funds and of real and fictive significant details: they are places of intellectual curiosity.

For that I am grateful.

Introduction

Questions Regarding Thieves, Reformers, Jurists, and Others

In May 1854, Maria Scherrer filed charges against a day laborer by the name of Anton Zimmermann for having allegedly stolen bread and a cap from her thirteen-year-old son and his eight-year-old friend. The two boys, for their part, had obtained the bread, a loaf and a half in all, by begging.

In 1857 two children, eight and fifteen years old, were accused in Gelnhausen of having first sought to beg from a ten-year-old boy who was walking home through the forest completely laden with purchases, and then having threatened him. One of the children supposedly approached the boy and said, "I want the bread." At the same time the child, a girl, "stepped right up close to him. He declared that he hadn't any bread. In response, she allegedly said, 'Then we'll take the rolls.'"

A few years later, more precisely in 1859, the servant Johannes Bernstein was accused of having stolen, or taken with him, an ownerless hat that lay in the village wood yard. Of course the hat was not ownerless, but had been forgotten there by a certain Brandeis, a day laborer by trade.

At first glance we appear to be looking here at three harmless offenses. After all, the objects in question had little material worth; the cases involved conflicts between neighbors, and sometimes it is not even certain whether oversights, absentmindedness, or simply misunderstandings may have been the cause. And yet, these are stories that were recounted in court and in each case resulted in charges of theft, leading to legally binding convictions. For in the eyes of the men and women of those times, theft was by no means a trivial or even harmless matter. Instead, it was an offense that drew serious attention from victims, jurists, literati, and journalists alike.

THE INTEREST OF JURISTS, CRIMINOLOGISTS, LITERATI, AND JOURNALISTS

Jurists devoted considerable energy to such offenses, conducted research with unrelenting meticulousness, and exhibited extraordinary persistence in pursuing every little bit of evidence. Never before had the need to describe thoroughly what constitutes a theft and who plays what role in it appeared so great. This enormous interest in property offenses is all the more remarkable because, as a rule, relatively worthless objects were involved. Neither the cap nor the bread, obtained by begging no less, was valuable. Indeed, most of the other thefts that were the focus of intensive interest by the state authorities revolved around articles with little material value, for example, socks, shirts, hats, vegetables, or daily-use articles such as pots. The overwhelming majority of thefts in the nineteenth century involved this kind of petty larceny in which relatively worthless items were taken. Nevertheless, entire armies of jurists delved into the question of what belonged to whom and how the stolen article was acquired. Senior and junior state procurators – precursors to state prosecutors – judges, defense attorneys, junior attorneys, and even law professors focused on the offense with an intensity not to be seen in either the eighteenth or the twentieth century, even after the most thorough search.

Jurists were not the only ones interested in property offenses during the nineteenth century. A separate science arose, dealing remarkably often, if not exclusively, with property offenses. At the latest with Lombroso's 1876 work *L'Uomo delinquent*, criminology took shape in Germany as well. The new field researched the habitual criminal – and he/she was usually a thief. Criminologists wanted to know who thieves were, where they came from, and what they looked like. The science that developed set about applying precise measurement instruments to investigating in detail the criminal's nose, mouth, forehead, and eye position, and mapped him as exactly as only landmasses had been previously.

Literature also turned theft into a topic. Just think of Friedrich Schiller's *Verbrecher aus verlorener Ehre*[1] or Wilhelm Raabe's *Horacker*.[2] Indeed, an unprecedented increase in works on crime could be observed in the burgeoning literary market of the nineteenth century. New crime genres evolved and gained an audience: Eugène François Vidocq published his adventurous crime stories, which were quickly translated into German.[3] Ernst Dronke was one of the first to write so-called police stories which sometimes reproduced complete interrogations.[4] The stories about criminals and judges by the writer and liberal jurist Jodocus Temme[5] were crawling with thieves. Then the first crime novellas were published, usually as serials in widely circulated papers such as *Die Gartenlaube*. Finally, the crime genre par excellence, the detective novel, developed in the nineteenth century; as seen in Sherlock Holmes, it moved the focus to detective work, to the act of discovery, and thus to the detective rather than the criminal. All these stories found an audience. Even more, the new genre was a great success, as the following 1866 commentary by Paul Féval on the situation in France illustrates: "Crime is booming; it sells....France has one to two million consumers who want nothing but crime served up to them, if possible, done to a turn."[6]

Worth mentioning is also the genre likely most popular in nineteenth-century middle-class reader circles, although frequently overlooked today: the travel description. There, too, thieves turned up in droves, especially when the journey passed through inhospitable regions. For example, the Caucasus was home to true "masters of the art of thievery."[7] Indians were considered "rapacious,"[8] and in Texas, according to the author of one travel report, no one went out in the evening without a knife because there were so many thieves.[9] When the "thief" became one of the central figures in children's literature toward the middle of the century, he was then a fixture in middle-class nurseries.

Finally, a fourth group should be noted that discovered its interest in criminals (although not primarily thieves) at about the same time: journalists, or more precisely, the new subspecies, the court reporter. In addition to court reporting, which detailed significant, and not so significant, court cases,[10] another genre appeared. Still very popular today and devoting particular attention to criminals, so-called "miscellaneous items" or *faits divers* reported frequently, if incidentally, about thieves. The two genres originated in the nineteenth century and quickly kindled the enthusiasm of readers for criminal matters.

This massive interest gives rise to a number of questions: What was the cause of the interest and what consequences did it have? I want to start with the first question. Why were jurists, writers, journalists, and criminologists, as well as an increasing number of newspaper and magazine readers, suddenly so intensely interested in thieves? What aspects made these cases so interesting to them? What exactly did the jurists want to find out from repeated interrogations? Did the violence in theft cases, or primarily the character of the simple thief or perhaps rather of the female thief, arouse their curiosity? Were the court and the investigative proceedings of interest, or was it possibly even mostly the legal issues that captured their attention? – after all, the nineteenth century is the century of great legal reforms. What interested the men and women readers? Did people want to learn more about the individual figures within the process, about investigators, judges, and defense attorneys, or was it instead a matter of establishing whether the new public jury trials actually delivered what their proponents had so vehemently promised? Was it thus perhaps not even a matter of the particular details surrounding the theft, but rather of fundamental questions regarding justice? Or did the fascination lie neither with the thieves nor the judges and defense attorneys, but instead with property issues that people actually wanted to explore in reading crime novellas, court reports, or even only brief items in the "miscellaneous news items" column? Why did the police and criminologists spare neither time nor effort, using constantly refined measurement procedures and precisely preserving even the most insignificant evidence through sketches and in evidence rooms, to get the goods on delinquents?

Certainly a number of factors played into the massive interest in theft. The increase in literacy and the advent of the popular press made a great deal now possible; the development of new fields such as criminology expedited some things; the self-conception of professionally evolving jurists and even new bureaucratic techniques played a role. However, of particular significance – as argued in the following pages – were the property and legal systems, which were changing fundamentally in the nineteenth century. It was the explosiveness of these changes that gave rise to the robber stories, the "miscellaneous news items," the criminological treatises, and the legal studies on property crimes and shifted them to the center of attention.

BACKGROUND: PROPERTY AND LAW

In the nineteenth century, the meaning of "property" changed. The modern notion of absolute property with the distinction, obvious today, between possession and ownership took clear shape in a manner significant for many people. Now for the first time a scholarly debate long associated with the names Adam Smith and John Locke became reality, even impacting everyday life. At the latest when the reforms of the so-called peasant liberation took effect, it became clear even to the man and maid servants in the most remote corners of Electoral Hesse, the focus of this book, that new rules now determined the value of property.

Furthermore, property was not just being redefined; its relevance also grew considerably. This greatly increased significance is evident from many indicators, for example, from the fact that property determined whether a person had the right to vote, or that the right to own property appeared prominently in the American, French, and Frankfurt constitutions.

That the new prominence and significance of property contributed to the rise of theft as an important topic seems obvious: When everyone is talking about property, property crimes also attract increased attention. However, it is important that the change in the property system played at least as great a role for the thieves and their victims as for the jurists; at the same time, the meaning of the new property concept for the two groups could not have been more different. As representatives of the middle class, the jurists, not without self-interest, became proponents of the modern property concept and saw it threatened by even the most innocuous theft. The thieves and their victims, who in both cases came from the lower classes, were by no means as strong supporters of the new property system; after all, they had little to gain from it, at least in the short term. In fact, for them the very finely drawn distinctions between "ownership" and "possession," "lent" and "used for the time being," were, as before, fluid, because their everyday make-do economy functioned on the basis of multiple possibilities, not the unambiguousness of property concepts. Yet – as will be seen – the day laborers and maids who showed up at police stations to report the loss of a hat or a piece of fabric were also sometimes able to use these new absolute property concepts to their advantage, and not just because in the best case they got their hat or pipe back.

The modified concept of property in the nineteenth century thus undoubtedly played a role in the new interest in theft, but this new interest must secondly – as I have asserted – be viewed in the context of a legal system that had itself been fundamentally restructured. After long and intensive debates, the legal system of virtually every state of the German Confederation was radically transformed in the middle of the nineteenth century. Codes of criminal procedure that provided for public instead of secret court proceedings and furthermore subscribed to the new fundamental principles of equality before the law, uniformity of procedure, and certainty of the law created a new foundation for the legal system. This new foundation – as interpreted not only in legal circles – was the exact opposite of the Early Modern Period's inquisitorial process, which now seemed to epitomize arbitrariness and torture. In the new legal system, a special role was assigned to the publicly held jury trial. Many saw this as the emergence of an institution that realized on a small scale what middle-class society promised on a large scale: a society in which the public was assigned the central role of guardian, ensuring adherence to rules that, once agreed upon, applied to everyone regardless of class, status, or property.

The legal reforms were thus strongly politicized and had come to represent *pars pro toto* reform of society as a whole; they received so much attention because they were regarded as an important part of the great transformation from an estates-based system of social stratification to a modern constitutional state. Precisely this politically charged new legal system – I will argue – was a further factor underlying the increased interest in theft. As the focus was always on the big questions about achieving a better society, the jurists devoted inordinate meticulousness and persistence to examining every little property crime, and criminologists never tired of pursuing every bit of evidence with unrelenting zeal. As a result of the interest in these big questions of the nineteenth century, the newspapers, too, were full of court reports and people read crime novellas and socially critical novels about judges. After all, questions about the ideal organization of social existence, about justice and injustice, could be vividly discussed in multiple dimensions on the basis of actual legal cases. Every thieving novel hero, every court report and criminological investigation provided an opportunity to consider the small but also the big questions of justice, the relationships between top and bottom, and consequently, the problems of good, and better, societal models.

Of course here, as in the new property system, differences in viewpoint are evident. Very few day laborers shared the all-too-optimistic perspective of the liberal legal reformers. In fact, there were many who viewed the new legal system with open skepticism. The differences were so great that some maid-servants interpreted actions labeled by jurists as theft to be emergency responses essential to survival. At times, it was perhaps just this difference in perspective regarding the legal system and the associated societal models that further heightened interest in property cases.

RESULTS: PROPERTY AND LAW

The background of the remarkable interest in theft, treated only briefly here under the heading of changes in the property and legal systems, is important in order to understand why cases such as those of Anton Zimmermann and Johannes Bernstein mentioned at the beginning so intensively engaged jurists, journalists, criminologists, and many others. At least as significant is a second aspect: The results that this interest produced, the meticulousness with which the jurists sought to explain the thefts, and the sheer volume of crime representations with which authors and journalists confronted their growing audience did not remain without effect. The actual procedures in theft proceedings, their representation practices, and the debates they touched off in themselves changed the legal and property systems.

The central focus of this book is the results that emerged for the legal system. (The results for the property system will only be mentioned secondarily.) These results, I maintain, were momentous. At the point when every single theft of a piece of bread had to be researched – dozens of interviews conducted even in cases of almost worthless trousers; evidence secured at great expense; or complicated residential searches performed, requiring production of crime scene sketches and write-ups of exact physical descriptions, just to locate an old pipe – the procedures for finding the truth changed. Furthermore, every little theft that was investigated judicially with such excessive attention led to development of additional methods for evidence production, refinement of crime scene sketches, and modification of criminological considerations – just as every court report could shift the perspective on the offense or offender.

Precisely this altered legal system, the way in which law was established or truth produced anew with each theft proceeding, is the focus of my interest: the gradual creation of the modern state of law (*Rechtsstaat*) from hundreds of thousands of legal negotiations, illustrated by the example of the crime of theft, which is especially important for many reasons. Thus, neither the special characteristics of thieves in the nineteenth century, nor theft and its portrayal in crime novels, court reports, and criminal treatises are central to this book. Instead, a detailed examination of theft proceedings will show how the legal system changed from trial to trial in the course of the nineteenth century. The question arises as to what direction these changes in establishing justice took. Did the changes in the production of truth – to use a term of Michel Foucault's[11] – seen at the latest by the mid-nineteenth century really result in greater equality and uniformity as maintained by both contemporaries and by the mainstream in current research? And did the public, acting as a new control authority monitoring whether greater equality and justice had been attained, play the principal role in the new legal system, as so frequently emphasized? Or had the legal system been transformed instead into a system of class justice as a smaller number of contemporaries believed? Did a great deal remain unaffected, as had long been thought? Or, a further possibility: Is it necessary to describe the changes in completely different terms? Or was it perhaps the case that, although questions of class (and of gender as well) were doubtless important and we certainly cannot speak of a simple increase in equality and uniformity, the public still had an important function that was not just limited to guardian of the laws?

"DOING LAW"

A description of the changes in the legal system that neither considers them the creative act of a few extraordinary jurists nor views the political system, social structures, or the economy as the single determining cause has moved beyond models based on the history of ideas or social history. Both models have in fact lost their persuasiveness in the last decades. Classical legal historiography is increasingly less likely to assume that the source of all law is jurists and their pronouncements alone. In fact, no one has more sharply criticized the all-too-narrow history-of-ideas perspective that justice results from laws, is applied by judges, and is changed by legal reforms than classical legal historians themselves.[12] Likewise, other models, for example, the social history model of the 1980s, which assumes that law was conceived in well-organized economic circles or government offices bent exclusively on maintaining their own power, no longer seem plausible.[13] In the meantime, there have been a whole series of attempts to find a nuanced answer to the difficult question of how law is made and changed. The most interesting come from the "anthropology of law."[14]

In keeping with these studies from cultural and social anthropology and with considerations from the "Doing Gender"[15] and "Doing Culture"[16] debate, I assume that changes in law, as in other areas, cannot be explained monocausally or by simply adding on various causes – that is not the case only because everything is much more complex than it appears at first glance. More important, in my view, than this always accurate insight is recognition that such a perspective conceals the dynamics among forces contributing to alteration of the legal system instead of placing those dynamics at the center of consideration. Developments in the legal system result in fact from the constantly changing interaction of norms, actors, and institutions. Thus, the idea that justice is "set" or "established" is replaced by the concept of a dynamic process involving a multitude of entities, which, endowed with varying degrees of power, repeatedly renegotiate justice.[17]

I wish to describe that particular concept with the term "doing *Recht*," that is, "doing law." "Doing law" combines a distinctly English-language gerund with an equally distinctly German concept "*Recht*," rendered for these purposes as "law." The concept means, first, that the definition of what constitutes law and how violations of law are to be punished is a process of negotiation involving many participants rather than a process of assignment. Thus, as a negotiation process, "doing law" should not be confused with the well-known "labeling approach" of criminology in the 1980s, nor should law be considered a two-figure model in which antagonists – for example, justice or the state versus the criminal – confront each other. Neither the "social crime" narrative, long popular in research studies, which constructs the criminal as a powerful figure who through crime is rebelling against the state and its ideas, nor the social discipline model, which casts the state as the powerful force educating the delinquent, does justice to the complex interaction among widely varying forces and actors. Instead of only two characters, a multitude populates the stage: persons filing reports, criminals, witnesses, persons defamed though innocent, on-lookers, administrative employees, investigative officials, judges, defense attorneys, journalists, politicians, and jurists. But not only actors in an all-too-narrow sense shape the way in which law is produced. In addition, there are "actors" in a broader sense. The norm framework, the procedural structure, the patterns of interrogation methods, the methods of making written records, the juristic training, the experts' habitus formation, and the judges' self-conceptions play just as important a role, in fact determine which events may be brought before the court at all, which persons decide the topic of discussion, and according to what rules.

Second, viewing law as a process of negotiation with many participants means keeping in mind that the many forces and actors operate on different levels. The meaning of a criminological study is on a different plane from that of the defendant's testimony. The principles governing the judicial production of knowledge, what is defined in each case as an offense – and what is not – and the rules according to which policemen prepare reports and thus determine what is available to the court in writing, for example, regarding the crime scene or the items taken, have different weight in answering the question of how law is determined and how a legal system is changed. Likewise, the effects that the attorneys' linguistic code or the symbolism of the court architecture has on judgment of the crime are on different levels, to be compared to one another only with great care.

Third, "doing law" in not a process of negotiation outside the reaches of power; in fact, power plays a considerable role, of course with quite variable effects. The power of the procedural system to establish rules for speaking and silence strengthens, weakens, or undermines any chance of exerting influence that the state procurators and judges may have as their habitus or on the basis of their social position. Court reporting's ability to present interpretations can in turn be more significant than the power deriving from a plea. Likewise, the jury may mean less than the power of a certain procedural step for the decision on whether someone will or will not be found guilty. In short, all that and much more determines with ever-varying weight the form of a legal system and its transformation.

The thought figure of "doing law" derives not just from the idea of negotiation among many varyingly powerful entities and many entities on different levels with unequal degrees of power. Also important, fourth, is that the performative dimensions are taken into account. Or as stated loosely by Foucault himself, "People know what they are doing; often they know why they are doing it, but what they don't know is what their doing does."[18] For example, the effect the physical descriptions of persons (*Signalements*) has in the process of establishing norms and producing criminal stereotypes only becomes gradually apparent and has precious little to do with the intentions that originally prompted generation of a physical description. That court reporting does much more than report the events in court, that is, actually contributes to structuring events, also belongs to the performative dimension, just as does the fact that women who murdered their husbands played, much to their advantage, to the gallery as "hysterical madwomen," with the result, for example, that the hysteria discussion in psychiatry produced a surprising effect.[19]

Fifth, and even more important: Law is not simply made and then realigned at some random date to then function in a certain way for a particular period. In so saying I do not intend to recall the always correct simultaneity of the non-simultaneous, but to point out that inherent to establishing justice/producing truth is process, which tends never to stand still. Establishing justice/producing truth is not to be investigated, as the structure of most criminological studies suggests, by treating the procedural code and norms of criminal law in the first part under the heading "general framework," followed in the second part by the results according to this "general framework," as they ostensibly emerge, new and immediately, in every proceeding. Actually, the "general framework" itself also changes in every proceeding – after all, even strengthening can be change. Not only does the general framework give structure; it is itself repeatedly re-structured.

Of course, none of this happens without conflict – to mention a sixth point that is of considerable consequence for the "doing law" concept.

Conflicts, for example, about whether a textbook or a higher appeals court has more authority in deciding right and wrong, are daily events and structure legal practice in their own right. It is always a matter of "jurisdictional politics," as Lauren Benton puts it, that is, of "conflicts over the preservation, creation, nature, and extent of different legal forums and authorities."[20] In these conflicts, something new often comes about, changing the finding of truth. If the dynamic character Benton stresses is taken seriously, it becomes obvious that setting the boundary between the old estates-based system and modern legal system, so important for development of the latter, was an act of self-empowerment by eloquent and influential criminal law reformers of the liberal movements prior to the March Revolution who thus placed themselves in the thoroughly glorious position of all-powerful innovators. Thus, these boundary demarcations, too, are part of "jurisdictional politics" and anything but objective descriptions of structural changes in the legal system.

MARIA SCHERRER, JOHANNES BERNSTEIN, AND SEVERAL CHILDREN BEFORE THE COURT

Although the notion of law as having many participants and changing constantly in dynamic proceedings may appear entirely plausible at first glance, analysis of this process for the nineteenth century quickly reveals difficulties.

A central problem, that is, the lack of sources, has been overcome by chance, luck, and prior work of other researchers.[21] Although court records were not generally retained in the nineteenth century, especially for widespread crimes such as theft, the Hessian archivists made an exception to this rule, keeping a considerable number of such records. Unfortunately, however, much less was recorded or saved by Hessian historians and archivists than would be desirable for a scholarly historical study in the early twenty-first century. To mention only one example, a great deal remains unsaid, especially in record books that would be of interest for quantitative questions. Detailed information about the five thousand accused persons listed there is often missing; the occupation of the accused is seldom given in the brief record summary. Direct statements about possible prior convictions or confessions – both are information noted in any witness statement – are usually missing.[22] Consequently, the comprehensive record books created by the courts are above all the basis for complex data collection by the justice apparatus, which mainly sought, using quantitative recording procedures, to "fence in" the actors of the state apparatus[23] rather than the "criminals"[24] and thus to make the former subject to control.[25]

Even the detailed records, the interrogation and court protocols, are limited sources and at times remain silent, with the result that a great deal must be added from broad regional research, and numerous other documents must also be consulted, for example, various legal journals, studies and treatises, law and regulation texts, administrative provisions, articles from the Electoral Hessian provincial press, crime novellas, and criminological treatises.

A further problem for analysis in the context of "doing law" is on the level of representation: How to describe complex dynamics with their many ramifications on various levels without ending up with an exhausting enumeration, a boring list, or even a technical explanation of legal rhetoric or case histories? How, when faced with the contrast to legal jargon, to capture the rural world of almost illiterate thieves and their statements, which have been modified in protocol records, without succumbing to the all-too-tempting language of "authenticity" and social romanticism? How to escape the trap of wanting in the end effect to be the better and particularly the more just judge? How to lay out the logic of criminological treatises without just copying their style? How to bring out central interconnections without wanting to connect everything to everything else? How to make connections clear without endorsing simple cause-and-effect models?

The structure of the book has been determined by the effort, if not to resolve these and numerous other difficulties, at least to address them. Part I takes up the question of how an event becomes a criminal case. The focus is first of all on the living environment of the thieves and that of their victims. Many facets of this world, for example, the perception of the social and economic changes so central in the mid-nineteenth century, can only be briefly mentioned. Nevertheless, it will hopefully become evident that both offenders and victims alike viewed questions of law and property in different contexts from those of jurists and criminologists, producing tension – the thesis of this part – which contributed decisively to the result that thefts of even the most worthless articles were tried in court. While the jurists believed that every stolen piece of bread confronted them with highly significant questions of a new social order, the male offenders and the few female offenders possibly only wanted to clarify who had say in the matter. In any case, the victim filed a complaint not only to get back some piece of bread and thus to set right the modern property system, but also because it was for him or her a question of honor, raised with great vehemence just at this time of marked change and many new uncertainties.

Part II examines how these conflicts about honor, property, social reforms, or just about pieces of bread could develop into a preliminary investigative record of several hundred pages even before the beginning of the actual public court trial. Was this preliminary investigation really as meaningless as the new codes of procedure would have people believe, or was the actual place where law was made there, in long interrogations and during complicated evidence gathering, only then to be presented in court to a marveling public? The preliminary investigation was – to reveal that much – of considerable importance for the question of who was or was not a thief, and how that thief was to be punished. But the preliminary investigation was also of great significance in other regards. There the new techniques for evidence gathering, report writing, preservation, and sketching discussed prior to this in criminology, statistics, and the many police treatises were applied, and at the same time completely new methods were developed for necessarily separating truth from untruth. Of course, the new methods did not conform primarily to the guidelines for legal equality and uniformity asserted by contemporary reforms and broad sectors of research but rather to other logical approaches geared toward the legal procedure of decontextualization and the statistical procedure of quantification. Thus, the approaches to establishing justice were by no means only of a legal nature; in fact, criminology and statistics played a decisive role.

Although the power of the statistical, criminological, and police techniques that to some extent dominated the preliminary investigation was very great and consequently considerable weight was given to events before the public court trial, the latter remained important – as Part III intends to show. In this part, events in the courtroom are scrutinized: What did the public trial, as introduced in 1848, change about the way in which justice was established? One answer is that the events in court for deciding in concrete terms how an offense was to be assessed, although far less important than those of the preliminary investigation, had enormous weight. The significance lay much less on the level of actually establishing justice than on the level of legitimizing the entire legal process. The new public, as well as further reforms such as the introduction of the jury, a public audience, and defense attorneys, lent increased legitimacy to the legal process. The courtroom was the place where a play about establishing justice was staged, not necessarily bringing with it more justice but in any case commanding a higher degree of legitimacy.

That not being enough, the public negotiation produced a second, perhaps more important effect: a public, actually more than one, that had little to do with the "public" as understood by contemporaries. The public that could be reduced to the role of a guardian and protector upholding laws was not significant. Significant instead was the public – as it appeared, for example, in the form of the press – to which no specific role could be assigned and which saw to it that judgments were made according to common sense criteria, at times with regard to social justice and at times according to the logic of moral concepts specific to class or gender. The criteria according to which the public passed judgment took different forms, depending on which conception of justice and also on which public power held sway. Sometimes the public criteria stood in direct contradiction to the letter of the law; sometimes they did not conform to the spirit of the law. Of even greater import, the circumstance that the public, or rather the various publics, would not allow itself to be assigned the role of guardian and protector but instead acted according to its own rules made law a matter to be negotiated publicly. Precisely this possibility is perhaps the most important characteristic of the modern state of law. More equality and uniformity may have been goals; what in fact was achieved was the new and momentous possibility of discussing publicly which method of establishing justice was just and which unjust.

Notes

1 Friedrich Schiller, 1999 (First edition, 1786).
2 Wilhelm Raabe, 1876.
3 Eugène François Vidocq (1775–1857) reports primarily about the criminal milieu and less about the act of discovery. See Hans-Otto Hügel, 1978. For an overview, see Jörg Schönert, 1983b.
4 Ernst Dronke, 1846. See also Erich Edler, 1977, 129ff.
5 On Jodocus D.H. Temme, see Erich Edler, 1977, 157ff.
6 "Le crime est en hausse, il se vend, il fait prime; au dire des marchands, le France compte un ou deux millions de consommateurs qui ne veulent plus rien manger, sinon du crime, tout cru," quoted in Dominique Kalifa, 1995, 29. See also Jörg Hennig, 1991.
7 Wilhelm von Freygang and Friederike von Freygang, 1817, 45.
8 Joseph Friedrich von Weech, 1831, 89.
9 Wilhelm Steinert, 1850, 105.
10 See Jörg Hennig, 1991; Klaus Marxen, 1991; Joachim Linder and Jörg Schönert, 1983b; Philipp Müller, 2005; Eric A. Johnson, 1995.
11 Michel Foucault, 2003.
12 For example, the history-of-ideas orientation is central to the criticism of Michael Stolleis, 1985 and 1997.

13 See Hans-Ulrich Wehler, 1989, 183.

14 This area of work from ethnology and anthropology developed out of the early studies of Laura Nader in the 1960s. See Laura Nader, 1969, 1990, and 1997; Jonathan Aleck and Peter Sack, 1992; Jane F. Collier and June Starr, 1989; Reiner Schulze, 1990; Francis G. Snyder, 1993.

15 Central to this subject, Candace West and Don H. Zimmermann, 1987.

16 See Karl H. Hörning and Julia Reuter, 2004.

17 For details, see the initial reflections in the literature overview of Rebekka Habermas, 2003. The pioneering work is still the collection of Andreas Blauert and Gerd Schwerhoff, 2000; a very stimulating work on the nineteenth century is that of Claudia Töngi, 2004.

18 Quoted in Hubert L. Dreyfus and Paul Rabinow, *Michel Foucault. Jenseits von Strukturalismus und Hermeneutik* (Frankfurt, 1987), 219; quoted in Michael Maset, 2000, 239.

19 Ruth Harris, 1988.

20 Lauren A. Benton, 2002, here 11.

21 I owe the information about the holdings of the Marburg State Archives that I used to a chance meeting in the hallways of the Frankfurt State Archives; Joachim Eibach (today in Bern) was performing research for his dissertation there at the end of the 1990s, and I was preparing my edition of the child murder trial of Susanna Brandt when Joachim Eibach, in response to the question of whether he knew of good holdings for the nineteenth century, casually mentioned Marburg. Without that valuable information, this book could not have been written.

22 See Marburg State Archives (STAM), 273 Marburg 324. The archival holdings quoted in the following pages all come from the Marburg State Archives, unless another source is explicitly cited.

23 The notes entered under the heading of "Comments" in the record books are especially indicative of that situation. In that column, there are many completely illegible references to the work of the justice system.

24 The references to other offenses provided under the heading of "Comments" made it possible to furnish information about prior convictions of and suspicions about the person in question from recent court and police inquiries.

25 An extensive form bundle results; it introduces the investigative record and includes the "List of persons charged," the "Subject of the complaint," a column with the heading "Offense," and two other columns – never filled out – intended for entry of the dates when the individual was placed in investigative detention and when released. A further column is provided for entering the name of the official in charge, the state procurator. Yet another column follows for the "Status of the matter," generally listing very exactly which agency sent records to which other agency, and especially, when that occurred. On the basis of this column, the path of a record can be tracked exactly. At the end of the form is a "Comments" column. The hand-written entry here usually reads "Completed" or "Completed (Accident)" (273 Marburg 324). However, not all record books were so detailed; see, for example, 268 Marburg 97.

PART I

WHAT IS THEFT

Questions Regarding Thieves and Jurists – Questions Regarding Honor and Property

In mid-May 1854, Maria Scherrer from Ockershausen filed charges against a certain Anton Zimmermann, a twenty-two-year-old day laborer from the neighboring village. He was accused of having stolen bread and a cap from her thirteen-year-old son and his nine-year-old friend. The bread had been obtained by begging and was valued at six or seven silver pennies.

At about ten o'clock in the morning of the same day in Ockershausen, the two boys had set out – according to the statement of Engelberg's mother – "to come up with some bread."[1] As had usually been the case before, they were quite successful; they received bread from a total of twenty-three residents in the surrounding villages of Cyriaxweimar, Haddamshausen, Hermershausen, Weiershausen, and Allna. When they were on the way home again (they had obtained about two loaves of bread by begging), they met Anton Zimmermann not far from their home village. He warned them, as they were after all guilty of begging, which was not allowed, that they should be on the lookout because he had seen policemen. What is more, he did not leave it at that but demanded that they give him the remaining[2] one-and one-half loaves of bread. When they did not do so – according to the statement of Heinrich Scherrer[3] – "Zimmermann grabbed me, threw me to the ground on my back, and took the bundle of bread ... away ... from me ... with one hand, then smacked me a couple times with his crop." He also "boxed" Engelberg's "ears" and snatched the bread.

Barely four days later, the junior state procurator in Marburg, Meibom, had Anton Zimmermann arrested. In September of the same year, the state authorities sentenced Zimmermann in the Marburg

Schwurgericht to a five-year sentence of imprisonment with an eight-pound chain on his right foot.

The theft was an ordinary one, as occurred daily by the hundreds, even thousands, in the nineteenth century – theft was by far the most common crime. Yet despite the minimal value of the stolen goods, the little significance of the persons involved, and the almost banal – at least at first glance – motives (if it seems simply to have been a matter of hunger), the offender was prosecuted for months at great expense, and his case documented with hundreds of pages. The question of why so much energy was expended on such a case arises with good reason. The answer, as I asserted, points out the new conception of property that was interpreted differently by the actors who participated in the criminal proceedings – jurists on one side versus thieves and victims on the other. But how much did the paradigms of the judges and state procurators with which they determined what was a theft and whether it was a "qualified" or "simple" theft differ from the conceptions of rural society about what was actually stealing and how it was to be handled? Were these different assessments at all meaningful or was an increasingly dominant legal interpretive authority at work, gradually erasing other perspectives? And why did Mother Scherrer bring charges against the day laborer at all if she had different notions of property and theft from those of the authorities? Or put in another way, why was there such an intensive investigation by the authorities if jurists were operating under conceptions of property different from those of the rural population?

To answer these questions, the men and women involved and their living circumstances in Electoral Hesse in the mid-nineteenth century must be examined more closely.

Notes

1 268 Marburg 91, Statement of Eva Engelberg, May 19, 1854, 16.
2 In the meantime, the two boys had already eaten half a loaf.
3 268 Marburg 91, Statement of Heinrich Scherrer, May 24, 1854, 8.

1

Who Are the Thieves and Who Are the Victims?

1.1 LIFE AND SURVIVAL "ON THE MARGINS"

Who were the thieves, where did they come from, and what social and economic changes did they have to contend with in the mid-nineteenth century? Let's look at Anton Zimmermann again: Starting with the simplest data, he was a man and still quite young – thus pretty typical, and not only for thieves in the Marburg region. If the hand-written record books of the Marburg High Court District[1] are consulted, the data from more than six thousand defendants indicate that crime in general was an overwhelmingly male phenomenon.[2] Likewise, for property crimes, we are dealing in most cases with men, although there the proportion of women, at a substantial 20 percent[3] both in Electoral Hesse[4] and elsewhere, was somewhat higher than for crime overall.

Most property crimes were thus committed by men, and in fact by fairly young men; the thieves were as a rule between twenty and thirty years old.[5] In this respect, too, the twenty-two-year-old Zimmermann proves to be typical. This age is associated with a particular social status, that of the single man.[6] None of the scant twenty-five property crime records examined more closely report a man with children, much less a married man. That also means that these men had not yet had an opportunity to obtain the financial basis for establishing a household.[7] The situation looks the same for the few recorded female thieves; they were for the most part between fifteen and thirty years old and the majority were single.[8]

Anton Zimmermann's occupation – he was a day laborer – also proves to be typical, not only for thieves, but for Electoral Hessian male offenders in general.[9] From the standpoint of overall crime, the majority of all offenders were day laborers or artisans;[10] less often they were plowmen[11] or messengers.[12] Educated middle-class citizens[13] were almost completely absent. These findings tend to be confirmed for the subgroup of thieves.[14] Crime in general and theft in particular was a lower class phenomenon in the mid-nineteenth century, in contrast to the eighteenth century.[15] Poverty seems to have been a characteristic of thieves – the dry figures reveal that much. That may not be very surprising.[16]

Yet the indication of poverty raises more questions than it answers. What did it actually mean to be poor in the mid-nineteenth century? In the case of Anton Zimmermann, it meant – as written in the records[17] – that he was not only a day laborer but, what is more, "without property." "Without property" means here in concrete terms that he did not have his own household and lived with his mother. She had herself once come into contact with the law enforcement authorities; in 1853 she was in court for "various abortions." She was also of ill repute but nevertheless not entirely without property; she owned the house in which she lived with her two sons and her sister's widower (and his new wife). This kind of cohabitation with relatives was usual in the Hessian countryside. That fact is evident from comparison with other villages where more than a quarter of the inhabitants frequently lived together with other family members outside the nuclear family.[18] With five people, the house was fully occupied, which probably worked because the brother-in-law was employed elsewhere and did not commute home every day. This living arrangement probably provided a cost-free, or in any case low-cost, place of residence that Zimmermann, in his precarious circumstances, thoroughly appreciated.

Zimmermann thus came from a poor family, but by no means from the lowest class of the population. As a day laborer, he belonged to that large segment of the population that always lived on the edge of poverty without being poor in the official sense. He was not so needy that he could apply for poor relief, but had so few means that he had developed a poverty-stricken life style. In contrast, the people who received poor relief[19] differed from day laborers like Zimmermann mainly in that they were structurally unable to make a living on their own over the long term because they were too old, infirm, disabled, or perhaps mentally ill. They were supported by the local poor relief commissions – be it with alms or by assigning to them small jobs such as night-watch duty or field protection.

Zimmermann, as he was capable of working, thus had scarcely any prospect of relief and therefore lived in hard-pressed circumstances. Day laborers like Zimmermann – after all, a rather large group that encompassed approximately one-quarter to one-third of the rural population in Upper Hesse[20] – were classified by the authorities as without property and earned so little that they were only able to get by after a fashion. The average daily wage was 4.3 silver pennies which, compared to the value of the bread Zimmermann stole, six or seven silver pennies, was really not very much. They were thus forced to always look around for additional sources of income if they did not want to go begging.[21] Sometimes they had their own piece of land available, but generally it was not any larger than a hectare, that is, 2.471 acres.[22] They possibly earned a small supplemental amount as cloth-makers, iron-workers, or smiths; went as seasonal workers to farms on the fertile plain of the Amöneburg Basin in the summer months or to Holland; or hired themselves out short term for railway construction. For example, Zimmermann had already worked for a stocking-maker, engaged in construction work – on the very day of the crime –, taken brooms to Marburg to sell, and helped mow the meadows.[23]

Many of the recorded thieves shared this life style, which was not characterized by deep poverty or acute need but threatened to quickly slip into just that situation, if the affected individuals did not have flexible recourse to a wide variety of social and material resources. Another theft suspect, a certain Balthasar Mengel, claimed to be a cloth-maker's assistant, which implies that he had completed an apprenticeship. But he earned his money through other activities. For example, he repeatedly worked in railroad construction, where he could earn up to twelve silver pennies a day. Of course, that was not a long-term job; after all, completion of the Kassel-Marburg-Frankfurt railroad line took only a few years. He had housing – as stated in the records[24] – with his sweetheart, a certain Catharina Prinz, who in turn lived in the house of her brother-in-law.[25] Mengel had lived for a time "from the poverty of [his] mother,"[26] meaning the poor relief that his mother received in Marburg because she could no longer work.[27] For a time, he had also been supported by his sister, who also had a checkered work history. She had entered service as a maid in Frankfurt, returned home because of an illness of her mother, lived from "sewing and knitting," and sometimes in addition did washing.[28] Overall she lived in precarious financial circumstances.[29]

People thus lived almost from hand to mouth and did not have one but several jobs at the same time, depending on the season and their age. The existence of a day laborer, a tradesman, and a landowner was frequently combined in one person. Other people ran through these occupational stages several times in the course of their histories.[30] In addition, people did not live from their own work alone but were part of a household that had many resources available: work, land, honor, connections, or even state support. Jürgen Schlumbohm and Laurence Fontaine characterize the life style of the day laborer and other members of the lower classes in the country and small towns as "life on the margins of subsistence."[31] In addition to as many income options as possible, an important factor was cultural and social capital, which – as Dennis A. Frey[32] emphasizes – also took the material form of certain consumer goods, as the latter were in turn an investment in social capital. Important was a flexible family economic approach that permitted rapid reaction to changes and identification of new methods appropriate whatever the circumstances to dealing with permanent existential insecurity – be it that individuals could fall back on living in their parents' house or could borrow money from their brothers or sisters, or that such individuals received produce from their mothers or fathers or had a job arranged by uncles or aunts.[33]

The presence of family ties and thus of family economies explains why many of the day laborers entered into the official crime records were only active within a small perimeter. Balthasar Mengel always remained within a radius of twenty kilometers from Marburg.[34] Zimmermann stayed in an even smaller area.[35] Still another thief, Georg Quehl born in the Oberaula District, managed to get beyond Ziegenhain to Marburg.[36] But all in all, he did not get further than eighty kilometers from his home community. The thieves thus usually came from the Marburg High Court District in which they were also charged. If the offenders had left their home villages at all, they had not gone far.[37]

These facts identify another characteristic of thieves in nineteenth-century rural society. The overwhelming majority of property criminals were by no means strangers or uprooted beggars, vagabonds, or victims of the migrations triggered by industrialization – as many middle-class contemporaries very alarmed by social conditions in rural areas would have people believe.[38] In fact, the property criminals were residents of Marburg, Ziegenhain, Schwälm, or like Anton Zimmermann, Cyriaxweimar. That fact is revealed by exact analysis of the record books, which always cite place of residence.[39]

The majority of thieves, like most of the people from the rural lower classes, were integrated into a close family and village network that facilitated their complex form of economy. Just how extensive and close-knit these social networks were is evident in the case of Anton

Zimmermann. He had so many relatives in the village that many witnesses, when asked about possible familial relationships with the accused, were able to explain in detail through which aunt they were related to which side of the Zimmermann family. Others, like the mayor, indicated that he was "very distantly related to the accused, so that he could not give any degree."[40] Even to the people who were not related to him he was a known figure. Thus, Eva Engelberg from the neighboring town Ockershausen, a Marburg district with eight hundred residents, called him simply "the Cyriaxweimar resident with the fat cheeks."[41] Other people knew him only as "the Dinges"[42] – that is, he had a nickname, which always implies deep roots in a social community. Even in neighboring towns many people knew him by name, as inquiries indicated.[43] Thus, for example, a maid from Hermershausen claimed to know him well because she was confirmed with him.[44] Mengel, too, despite his temporary absence because of his work in railroad construction, was so firmly socially rooted in Marburg that many people knew him.[45] This high level of familiarity also appears in some cases to have been the reason that offenders could be identified quickly.[46]

1.2 THE VICTIMS: GOOD OLD ACQUAINTANCES?

If the thieves were thus generally not strangers[47] and furthermore not necessarily socially isolated in their immediate environment, the question of whom they robbed proves particularly thorny, because under the circumstances described they knew their victims, at least by sight. And indeed, the situation is such that almost all the property crime records, which permit an in-depth look at the events based on the detailed witness statements, interrogation records, witness lists, and other documents contained therein, relate to crimes that were committed among friends or acquaintances. Thus, thieves robbed people they knew.

What else can be said about the victims? Were they socially higher placed than the men and women thieves,[48] did they belong to another religion, did they have more or even fewer rights, were they socially integrated or outsiders – what was the nature of the relationship between the offenders and their victims? Anton Zimmermann knew his victims, at least in passing. The two boys, as mentioned, came from neighboring Ockershausen, a town with a relatively large percentage of Jews in its population.[49] The boys were known, according to the statements of a large number of people, for "often" being out and about to beg. As a rule, they begged for bread and were quite successful with this acquisition technique.

The boys were poor – as can be concluded from this method of obtaining food – and probably were entitled to poor relief; however, it was evidently not granted to them. Probably their mother was not considered a "worthy poor person." In the case of Mother Engelberg, her Jewish religion (her son was generally known as "the Jewish boy"[50]) could have had the effect that the local commission did not feel responsible for her, even though the Jewish population had been officially covered by local poverty law since 1833.[51] The members of rural Jewish communities were as a rule poorly situated financially in the mid-nineteenth century, generally living from so-called irregular trade (*Nothandel*), that is, from buying and selling frequently used articles and from livestock trading.[52] Although there were no pogroms in the Marburg region in the mid-nineteenth century and an improvement in legal status had been achieved with emancipation legislation, as begun under French rule in Electoral Hesse under King Jérôme[53] and never completely rescinded, the living situation of the Jewish population in the hard-pressed financial circumstances of the small villages around Marburg was nevertheless difficult.[54] Robert von Friedeburg speaks of a prevalent "communal anti-Semitism."[55] In any case, there was a status difference between Christians and Jews that set the tone of their dealings with each other.[56]

The social status of the two mothers also contributed to their financially and socially difficult situation. They were mothers raising children alone and even single at that. In the rural society of the nineteenth century, that did not necessarily mean that the person would have to play the role of a social outsider, but as a rule it implied an economically straitened situation, as the possibilities for earning money were limited by the child. Moreover, Mother Engelberg was ill and her condition was so serious that she had to be taken to the Marburg hospital. Given the state of hospitals at that time, this was for everyone the last resort – that is to say, hospitals were scarcely more than makeshift holding facilities for the poorest of the poor and were consequently administered, not only in Marburg, by the poor relief commission.[57] Furthermore, one of the boys, Heinrich, was physically handicapped with a leg condition known at the time as "crooked legs" (*Scheibe Beine*).

In the case of Zimmermann, the victims thus lived on the margins of society, but without being socially isolated. If anything, they were poor, one was a Jew, and their ethical-moral circumstances left something to be desired – at least from a middle-class perspective. And yet, the two boys were socially integrated and acknowledged members of rural society.

That is clearly evident when the material support they received from the village society is considered; a total of twenty-three people, almost exclusively women, from the surrounding villages had given the begging children bread. Among them were the wives of two mayors. Furthermore, the witnesses stated that the children often begged and always got something.[58] None of the people questioned denied the boys their alms. This fact is all the more remarkable as both begging and giving alms were officially forbidden and were also actually punished[59] – strict state procedures can be observed, especially in the case of Jewish beggar boys.[60] The open support for boys begging despite the prohibition, when one of them was Jewish besides, speaks for the fact that the two victims were poor, but by no means outsiders.

Thus, in the case of Zimmermann, the offender and victims knew each other (even if Zimmermann was to deny that later) and came from comparable, economically difficult situations, but were by no means socially isolated, being firmly rooted in their family and village networks. In this regard, too, the Anton Zimmermann case appears to be typical. The overwhelming majority of petty thefts – and most generally fell into that category – was committed against persons whom the thieves knew.

One case that occurred in 1859 in Weichenbach was quite similar.[61] In mid-October, the forty-nine-year-old day laborer Johann Friedrich Brandeis appeared at the home of the mayor, Jordan von Weichenbach, and reported Johannes Bernstein, who had already been legally convicted multiple times of property crimes,[62] that is, for theft. Bernstein was said to have taken a hat that Brandeis had left lying at the wood lot not far from his house. The loss of the hat was publicly announced after Brandeis had noticed it, and still Bernstein did not come forward. Brandeis and Bernstein did not know each other well; they both worked as servants for a certain Johann Müller. A very similar case, already considered notorious, is that of the thief Johann Heinrich Bloh, a youth who had already committed several offenses. He, too, knew all his victims, not only by sight, but some quite well. His first victim, a shoemaker's assistant, lived in the same house. From him the youth stole boots, which he wore the next Sunday to church.[63] He knew his next victim, a servant, even better; after all, he went in and out of his house. He committed a third theft from a school friend with whose family he had lived a few years earlier. The social and economic situations of offender and victim were not identical, but were still comparable because Bloh, as the son of a day laborer, could also expect a future as a servant, or in the best case, as a shoemaker's assistant. Other thefts looked exactly the same: Many, if not most, of the simple thefts occurred between people who knew each other,[64] and who lived in the immediate vicinity[65] or at least in the same village.[66] In those cases, too, victim and offender did not seriously differ in their social, economic, or legal circumstances.[67]

Two exceptions to this type of theft among equals can be identified: first, and legally considered separately, low-class thefts that took place within relationships that were close but characterized by considerable social and economic differences.[68] For example, that is the case for one of the few female thieves, Charlotte Birk, who worked as the shop girl for a merchant in Gelnhausen. Although she was the daughter of a policeman and her circle of friends also comprised representatives of the lower class – the wives of a field guard and of a shoemaker belonged to it – the employer whom she robbed was quite wealthy.[69] A similar case occurred in 1850 in Hanau; the sales clerk Peter Hartenstein[70] – who was not actually without means – was accused of having stolen considerable sums from his employer Guckemus.[71]

The second type of exception to the usual theft pattern encompasses the few property crimes between complete strangers. Although such thefts apparently were still the order of the day in the eighteenth century,[72] they happened only rarely in rural society at the mid-nineteenth century. These rare cases usually involved very different amounts and special forms of theft.[73] One case was a mail coach robbery,[74] another, the crimes of a convict in irons who was on the run,[75] and finally, a very brazen theft that was associated with massive insults to officials and assumption of false identities, almost with the qualities of Thomas Mann's character Felix Krull.[76]

All the other property crimes, which were much less colorful, followed the usual pattern: They were committed against people who were known to the offender and who came from the same circle of young, still unmarried men with limited means.[77]

1.3 HETEROGENEOUS RURAL SOCIETIES

Analysis of the social composition of the offenders and victims is enlightening, because the results contradict the notion widespread among contemporaries that the thieves were detached, even rootless creatures who sought refuge in big cities and enriched themselves there from socially and materially better-situated city dwellers. At the same time, analysis raises a whole series of new questions. What did it mean for a young day laborer to live in the rural society of Electoral Hesse in the mid-nineteenth century, and especially, to remain there? What was life in this rural society like? Are possible reasons for the thefts to be found there? The questions are more complicated than they appear at first glance because *the* rural society did not exist. It was an invention of contemporaries, more precisely of the middle class, of figures like Wilhelm Heinrich Riehl and the representatives of the local conservation and historic preservation movement (*Heimatschutzbewegung*) that formed toward the century's end. They had sought, and found, an undeveloped, primordial state and idyll in the rural countryside, and in the process made the case for a homogeneity which does not stand up to empirical scrutiny[78] – but which was nevertheless reproduced in research studies for a very long time.[79]

As complicated as the search is for signs that might perhaps shed light on the background of the thefts, it is worth the effort – as I intend to show in the following pages – because in the tangled, very diverse rural living conditions at mid-century evidence can indeed be found, illuminating at least a few aspects of property crime. First of all, a more detailed look must be taken at the region from which the thieves and victims came. What did the Marburg High Court District look like?

The Marburg High Court District[80] covered an area that extended from Marburg in the west to Frankenberg in the north and Ziegenhain in the east. It was a region that from 1852 on was connected by a railroad line to the Frankfurt economic network in the south and to the seat of the Electors and later the most important Prussian administrative institutions in Kassel in the north. And yet the Marburg region was anything but well connected, let alone centrally located. The Marburg region was far removed from the Thuringian and Saxon industrial centers in the east and from the booming coal regions on the Rhine and Ruhr in the west, which were not least of all hard to reach because of the mountainous Westerwald.[81] This strip of land was veritably cut off from the centers of modernization, but the same applied to a great many, if not the vast majority, of the German regions in the second half of the nineteenth century. Pomerania, Posen, parts of Bavaria, northern Germany, Mecklenburg, the Palatinate, and the Southwest were also located outside the developing industrial centers.

Marburg itself, with barely six thousand residents, was the largest town in the region and dominated the fertile Lahn Valley. Marburg had a small university that was, however, rather unattractive in the mid-nineteenth century; the town was the region's administrative center and hosted its central marketplaces. Marburg was characterized by a relatively high proportion of middle-class families,[82] and yet, as in all the cities of the mid-century, agriculture played a considerable role.[83] Finally, Marburg was surrounded by a row of so-called house villages (*Hausdörfern*), which were quite large, having in some cases more than five hundred residents. The Marburg District, that is, the small area around the town itself, was not well-to-do, but it was by no means poor, either. The proportion of the poor was not 20 percent, like the average for Upper Hesse, but in mid-century just barely 10 percent.[84]

To the north lay a region that was somewhat hilly and not very fertile, extending through Wetter to Frankenberg, a town with more than three thousand residents. An 1842 description calls this region "harsh and scarcely bearable."[85] As the woolen cloth weavers there also "had not been reduced in numbers but certainly more so in significance" toward the middle of the century[86] – once again, according to a contemporary – this northern part was among the poorer regions. Thus, the northern part of the Marburg High Court District, the Frankenau locality, was considered "a little old town at a low cultural level."[87]

Immediately to the east was the Kirchhain Court District. Here lay the fertile plain of the Amöneburg Basin, which, having previously been territory of Electoral Mainz, was partially Catholic, in contrast to the largely Protestant regions of Electoral Hesse. The Catholic center was the town of Amöneburg, which had about one thousand residents.[88] Neustadt and Kirchhain were larger, with populations of just two thousand in 1900.[89] Further to the north lay Treysa and Ziegenhain on the Schwalm River. Along the Schwalm toward the north in the direction of Fulda was a region that in 1840 had already had a special local character ascribed to it because it "lived in the full splendor of its own folk customs"[90] – which was supposedly also evident from the fact that "coffee had not yet become comfortably familiar."[91] But economically, this was also a prospering region, shaped by agriculture.

Even this superficial overview of the Magdeburg region makes clear how differently living situations developed, even in such a relatively small, manageable space. There could be considerable variation not only between city and country but also between individual villages. Robert von Friedeburg emphasizes that, even in a small region such as the Schwalm, the living circumstances differed markedly, depending on whether the localities possessed good soil or mountainous and therefore mostly unproductive land.[92]

1.4 THE MANY SMALL DIFFERENCES IN THE VILLAGE

Back to the search for evidence: by more closely examining the Marburg region's rural society, what hints can be found of the many thefts that occurred there among individuals who lived on the margins of society? There is a great deal of evidence, which of course can only be detected by looking a level deeper. Particularly on the local level many differences, large and small, become apparent, and it is precisely those differences, or rather the intensification of those differences observed particularly at mid-century, that help to clarify why so many thefts occurred. This intensification – I intend to argue further – pitched the people who had long been living in a precarious situation into even more difficult circumstances. Of course, those circumstances were not primarily difficult because many people who lived on the margins were in worsening straits economically, but because the social and material differences within this class became more pronounced. One person might profit more, another less, from the distinctions to be examined more closely in the following pages. It was not need that led to theft, but rather the increasing distinctions within the class of individuals who had already lived quite flexibly on the margins for a long time, distinctions that caused the tensions within this group to increase. The tensions could also have led one person to accuse another of being a thief. What were the differences in the microcosm, on the level of the village, that were perceived especially clearly by the people who had so little?[93]

Let's take as an example the small hamlet by the name of Cyriaxweimar, which was Anton Zimmermann's hometown. Cyriaxweimar is located less than five kilometers from Marburg and in 1838 had 110 residents. By the end of the nineteenth century only twenty more had been added. There were no Catholics, only a few Jewish men and women, and two members of the Reform Church; the rest of the residents were Lutherans. Thus, the village was one of the many places in the Marburg region that almost exclusively espoused one religion, usually Lutheranism.[94] However, there were also regions with a mix of religions. For example, ten thousand Protestants, an almost equal number of Catholics, and almost six hundred members of the Jewish faith lived in the Kirchhain District in the second half of the nineteenth century.[95] There, as in the other regions with mixed religions, the conflicts among the religious groups increased noticeably in the course of the nineteenth century – even before the *Kulturkampf* ("Culture War").[96]

In addition to religious distinctions, which were probably not very pronounced in Cyriaxweimar, there were economic differences between individual residents. The differences had to do with the economic situation: Six families lived from agriculture, seven were tradesman families, and another six were day laborer families. Unfortunately, we do not know how large the particular farms were.[97] However, it can be assumed that that there was at most one landholder with a relatively large land parcel (*Vollbauer*), who in addition to at least ten hectares of land also owned several horses and cows and had servants and maids.[98] The other five peasant farmers will have had only had a narrow strip of land and only owned a few or no farm animals, but instead will have worked as weavers, masons, or distillers, or hired themselves out as day laborers. The wives earned a bit extra by sewing or perhaps by selling eggs or vegetables. The differences among the seven Cyriaxweimar families that lived predominantly from manual trades will also have been considerable. Rural trade generally meant that, in addition to blacksmithing or tailoring activities, artisans dealt in used clothing or scrap iron, and also worked a piece of land or hired themselves out seasonally outside the village. Very few rural artisans could afford to have only one source of income.[99] That the living and work circumstances of day laborers could also differ a great deal is already known from the Zimmermann family. In short, the economic situation of the residents within a village varied significantly.

The internal differentiation within village society was not just considerable; it intensified even more over the nineteenth century in a manner that worked to the advantage of a few people and to the disadvantage of many. In addition to a whole series of economic and demographic causes – among them, the end of proto-industrialization,[100] the decline of skilled crafts and trades,[101] and population growth[102] – the numerous agrarian reforms in particular, which are lumped together under the misleading generic rubric "peasant liberation," were of central importance. As a result of the sweeping elimination of rents, leases, and other feudal relationships still remaining between those who owned the land and those who worked it, the agrarian reforms led to a fundamental change in the property culture. The complex web of tenure, interrelationship, property, lease, and rent structures was reduced to a single form, absolute ownership.[103] This modern form of ownership was characterized above all by a lack of differentiation between right of use and right of disposition and by replacement of a whole palette of possible relationships between persons and things (or land) by a single possibility, that is, the total, all-encompassing ownership of a thing, a piece of land, or an animal.

Of course, it took a long time for this so-called peasant liberation to take hold in Hesse.[104] By mid-century, only half the estates had passed to those who worked the land.[105] The reforms were especially advantageous for peasants with large holdings, as they could redeem their land more quickly and purchase additional new land because they possessed the required financial means.[106] In contrast, the small and smallest landholders were not in any position to raise the large sums needed to purchase a piece of land, even though separate credit institutions had been established for such purposes. The smallholders frequently overextended themselves, resulting in forced public auctions.[107] The result was a complete restructuring of rural society, not only economically, but also with regard to the legal situation.

After all, closely associated with the agrarian reforms were legal changes in the status of the residents. Whether a person was a "full citizen" (*Ortsbürger*) or a "citizen with limited rights" (*Beisasse*)[108] determined the extent to which that person could participate politically. Full citizens were the economic upper class, and at the same time, had full political rights as well as, traditionally, complete access to the common areas (*Allmende*, that is, the forest, the meadow, or the lake that belong to a village).[109] All other residents were citizens with limited rights. They had little or no rights to the common areas, could not participate in the poor relief commission,[110] and were excluded from other village committees. In 1834, a third category was created, that of the "persons entitled to use," who now also had access to the common areas.[111] They could allow their cows to graze, fetch wood, and get straw for their stables. The entitlement to use enabled precisely those individuals who owned little or no land to keep one or perhaps ever two animals.[112]

The most important consequence of this reorganization for our context was further differentiation of village society into the people with and those without access to the common meadows, forests, and waters – even though it would take a long time before this change had been translated into practice.[113] Martin Kukowski speaks of a regular "devolution of peasant culture" in the second half of the nineteenth century.[114] It must be kept in mind that rural society increasingly grew apart, into peasants and the land-poor;[115] there were thus an increasing number of large farms and likewise an increasing number of tiny farms that could no longer guarantee subsistence. Rough estimates have shown that after the mid-century only a third of the rural population in Upper Hesse still lived exclusively from agriculture.[116]

All these factors – confessionalization, economic changes, introduction of the right of use, and agrarian reforms accompanied by a new property culture – accentuated the differences within the village, and not in Cyriaxweimar alone. Many researchers even speak of a "growing social polarization of rural society."[117] A number of studies have shown that it was increasingly a class society that, because of the ties between the landless and land-owning classes, still retained elements of traditional peasant society, as Jürgen Schlumbohm characterizes the situation.[118] In any case, it was a rural society in which the economic and social resources were visibly distributed in an unequal manner even within the group of people who lived at the very edge of the minimum for subsistence. Thus, it was also a society that changed radically, in fact, was undergoing a downright meteoric transformation, not least of all because of agrarian reforms, proto-industrialization, emigration, railroad construction, and demographic shifts. A great deal – land distribution, political rights, trade – changed at an enormous speed.

This transformation must have been seen very clearly by those who lived on the margins of society. In the villages changing rapidly and on multiple levels, the young men who became thieves (but also their victims) seem, to overstate the situation, to have been the only thing that remained unaltered. While everything around them changed, and worsened for many,[119] the poor, but not entirely impoverished young men were characterized by a remarkable inertia. They neither immigrated to America, nor moved to the economically prosperous areas of German-speaking territory. Before this backdrop of radical change, the thieves appear to be surprisingly immobile, at least in terms of geography. They stayed and maintained their flexible life style that shifted among various income sources, without having to become mobile. They developed various "survival strategies" and practiced the "economy of makeshifts" described by Olwen Hufton.[120] In this situation, however, immobility was a central element. Besides the family, with its manifold economic, social, and cultural resources, friends' use entitlements and the poor relief support of relatives in their home towns were two important reasons for remaining, precisely for people who lived in difficult circumstances. The precarious survival economy was dependent on the multifaceted networks most likely to be provided by long-standing contact and family ties.

Thus, we are usually dealing in a rural area of the Marburg region with property crime in which the offenders and victims were members of the lower class who knew each other. Their living conditions at mid-century became increasingly precarious, in part because the social and economic differences within the class intensified. Of course the term "lower class" is imprecise. Within this class there was a range that extended from people who lived right on the edge of poverty to those on the threshold of the middle class, for example, artisans.[121] Furthermore, the concept is imprecise because in the second half of the nineteenth century over half the population can be considered part of this lower class. Besides, the term is inadequate because it obscures small but important differences. It is therefore more appropriate to speak of a group of people who stole and were stolen from, lived together in a small space, knew each other, and lived in economically precarious circumstances, but who might have considerably differed from each other in details – they were primarily circumstances that became more pronounced from about the mid-century on, with the result that the many small differences in access to material and social resources became increasingly significant.

1.5 THEFT FROM NEED OR THEFT IN ADVERSITY?

Although the villages from which the thieves came have now been delineated, at least in broad outlines, and the relationship structure joining the offenders and victims has become somewhat clearer, the possible motives are still only at best conjecture. Even the evidence of increasing tensions within the group of those living on the margins, to be detailed later, still does not at first provide a plausible explanation. What do gender and age, living conditions, and the relationship structure within which the property crimes were committed really say about the thieves and their motives? Does the attempt to take a closer look at the lives of the thieves actually bring to light useful evidence that gives some indication of motives?

Contemporaries considered this evidence helpful; they used it to proclaim that property crimes resulted from material need and were therefore simply acts of self-help. Wood thefts in particular were interpreted as crimes of need.[122] Everyday petty thefts were also considered by many jurists, welfare officials, statisticians, and early national economists to be purely the product of hunger in this "pitiable class of people."[123] Karl Marx himself made this connection, as can be read in his contributions to the *Rheinische Zeitung*, published during a *Landtag* debate about wood theft.[124]

Marx and other contemporaries are not the only ones who assumed that theft in the nineteenth century was the direct result of poverty. This particular interpretation is shared by large numbers of historical researchers. For example, Dirk Blasius, the pioneering historian of crime in the nineteenth century, reaches the following conclusion, "The minor violation of law was often the *ultima ratio* in the restricted world of the rural lower classes stuck without property or work income in towns still barely affected by the industrialization process."[125] This historical interpretation, carried forward from contemporary explanations, is initially convincing, and I do not wish to entirely dismiss the motive of economic need. However, the closer this explanation is examined, the greater the doubts that arise, at least about the interpretation's credibility as an all-encompassing explanation. First of all, determining the economic situation of individuals is quite complicated. Although historical researchers (much like contemporaries)[126] for a long time measured poverty on the basis of grain prices – the higher the grain prices, the higher the poverty level and thus the number of property crimes – it has become clear in the meantime that the economic situation of the population was too complex for that situation to be understood by calculating grain prices.[127] Such a procedure is based on a much too modern conception of the nineteenth-century economic world; this view overlooks the fact that in rural society there were many ways to get around official grain prices, at least in the short term. Only a very few members of the lower class obtained grain or flour through official market channels. People made ends meet by using complex strategies from the varied repertoire of the makeshift economy. The repertoire ranged from barter to processing of basic raw materials and money-lending systems within families, thus providing, especially in times of need, an often smoothly functioning informal social network that guaranteed a degree of independence from market prices, at least temporarily. As already shown, the rural lower classes were involved in what modern economists call an "informal economy" – an economy that is "unregulated by the institutions of society, in a legal and social environment in which similar activities are regulated" and is dependent on "kinship-based economic structures."[128] Alternation of various jobs that might last for weeks or only for days, and family support, furnished in the form of produce or free housing, were typical for Anton Zimmermann and many of the people who lived in similarly precarious situations. Indeed, for many thieves, and for their victims as well, this life style was downright characteristic. Consequently, the assumption that a correlation exists between grain prices and theft is not a solid basis for assessing the social situation of the lower classes or the actual poverty level of a thief.

Second, and far more fundamental, E.P. Thompson in his 1971 essay on the "moral economy" of the English lower classes uses the example of the eighteenth-century food riots to point out that behaviors are never only "simple reflex reactions to economic stimuli."[129] Instead, the actors' powers of interpretation are decisive. Depending on how an economic crisis is perceived, it may lead to apathy, to rebellion and tumult, to small violations of the law – such as theft – or to experimentation with new and old forms of makeshift economy. Therefore, no path leads inevitably to rebellion or theft. That, however, is what Marx and others claimed when they explained theft solely by pointing to material need.

Third, the interpretation that people steal purely from necessity, that is, to satisfy elementary needs, is based on a problematic definition of what elementary and less elementary needs are. This dichotomization results from the notion, by no means obvious, that there is a clear boundary, firmly fixed for all time, between "natural" and "superfluous" needs; precisely this differentiation between "necessities" and "decencies" had been the subject of a very contentious debate about luxuries at the end of the eighteenth century.[130] The supposedly very obvious differentiation between elementary and less elementary is questionable because it assumes that there are "goods that sustain life and health and others that service the mind."[131] In contrast, Mary Douglas and Baron Isherwood argued that such a sharp distinction is illusory because goods do not have any value expressible in objective terms; instead, their meaning is relative and therefore historically changeable. It thus becomes clear that goods, besides ensuring subsistence or luxury, whose definitions vary widely, can always have other symbolic or cultural meanings,[132] for example, that of making social boundaries evident. In the words of Douglas and Isherwood, "Forget that commodities are good for eating, clothing and shelter, forget their usefulness and try instead the idea that commodities are good for thinking, treat them as a nonverbal medium for the human creative faculty."[133] Applied to stolen objects, this means that the latter point to more than the necessities of life, or hunger and cold – especially as we do not know what the actual necessities were, for example, for Anton Zimmermann in the second half of the nineteenth century. In any case, he was hardly concerned with hunger when he stole the bread from the youngsters: He had just eaten a cake himself and had furthermore earned some money from temporary work in construction.

The theory that property crimes are purely crimes of need is thus not convincing. Certainly need plays a role, sometimes even an important one, but it does not explain everything. Another, frequently proposed interpretation, that property crimes are "acquisitive crime[s]"[134] – that is, have enrichment as their goal – likewise falls short. This explanation is unconvincing, if for no other reason, because most of the thefts involved objects of very little value. Cases like the burglary at the Marburg bookstore of Elwert, an honorable member of the Marburg middle class, in which a rather large sum, totaling over 211 thaler, jewelry, and watches were taken, were the exception. The same is true of the pharmacology student Friedrich Arnold, who had 170 thaler stolen from a drawer.[135] The rule was Zimmermann's bread theft.

Likewise, the theory that property crimes are "social crimes" or, what Foucault rather imprecisely called "popular acts of lawlessness,"[136] only explains a small, perhaps sometimes even relevant aspect, but does not provide a central cause. A "social crime" is defined as a crime in which a conflict exists between differing conceptions of the law and through which the offenders are also protesting against the state's attempts to impose order.[137] Furthermore, the "social crime" is described as a crime which very few people commit but many silently endorse "because it serves to bolster the peasants' self-esteem."[138] Finally, it is characteristic of "social crimes" that they touch "deeper levels of the collective consciousness," or keep alive the "memory of an injustice suffered, of humiliation and oppression, in the symbolically liberating counteraction."[139] Although contemporaries such as Karl Marx were already convinced that the majority of property crimes, particularly wood thefts, were to be designated as just such "social crimes," the Electoral Hessian findings yield no evidence for the validity of this theory.[140] In any case, what the robbery of beggar boys has to do with "peasants' self-esteem" is not clear, nor does it become so from the pilfering of a hat. Handworkers who stole from each other can hardly be called social rebels. Their actions cannot be considered acts of revenge by the lower class against the developing state or even against capitalistic companies. To the contrary, it had to do with relationships within the poorer parts of rural or small-town society.

Precisely this central aspect is addressed by Josef Mooser when he interprets wood theft as part of a struggle against agrarian modernization on one hand, and – important in this context – as an expression of tension within peasant society on the other.[141] According to Mooser, the thefts had to do with conflicts within the lower class of rural society. Thus, he in a sense turns the "social crime" theory right side up, from its head onto its feet, and introduces a new perspective for analysis of property crime. Applied to the circumstances at mid-century in the Marburg region and the property crime there, the meaning is as follows: the conflicts within the population's poorer class that were closely associated with the new property concepts – which in rural areas primarily took form in agrarian reforms – were also expressed in the thefts by one part of the rural poor from another part of that class.

1.6 THE MEANING OF THINGS

What was the nature of the conflicts? What was contentious when, viewed superficially, there were in essence only a few pieces of bread and a used hat involved, and when need played a role but is not in itself an adequate explanation? To learn more about the conflicts and the previously mentioned tensions which may have been associated with the offense, and thus to verify the validity of Mooser's theory, the articles stolen must be examined more closely. Jurists in particular subjected the stolen objects to this kind of precise examination at the middle of the nineteenth century. In doing so, they were primarily interested in the material value. The value was calculated exactly because it was crucial for the sentence. If articles valued at less than five thaler were stolen and if there were no aggravating circumstances – for example, theft at night or with illegal entry – the incident was considered a "simple petty theft." The overwhelming majority of all thefts were such "petty thefts."[142] In Prussia, for example, we know that petty thefts and wood thefts[143] were by far the most common forms of theft.[144] In other places, too, articles of very little value were stolen.[145]

However, stolen articles have more than just a material side. According to Appadurai, there is a "social life of the things,"[146] a social and symbolic significance of things. What social, symbolic, and emotional significance can be determined for the stolen goods? Roughly two types can be differentiated here: stolen goods that were unusual and not commonplace, at least to rural society's lower class in the middle of the nineteenth century, and things that belonged more to the everyday life of rural society.

The unusual type of stolen articles played a secondary role in nineteenth century Electoral Hesse. According to the theory to be developed in the following pages, such stolen articles served primarily as a means of marking social position and establishing social distinction. That is evident in the case of the shop girl Birk as well as in the case of the sales clerk Hartenstein. Both stole from their respective bosses, to wit: coffee, sugar, raisins, soap, rice,[147] and "silk watch chains," brown cotton gloves, white cotton crocheted change purses, cigars, wine, "hair combs," letter paper, and raisins again.[148] Coffee and sugar no longer had the ostentatious luxury character still evident in the eighteenth century, when these semi-luxury items were colonial goods with which the middle class in particular could display its financial power and present itself as competitive with the nobility on the level of consumer goods. And yet, before the wide distribution of domestic sugar refineries, sugar was not an inexpensive, everyday foodstuff. Coffee, too, had after all become so common after 1800 that a mother living "in poverty" could bring her incarcerated son coffee every day,[149] but it was still a special beverage because it represented material prosperity and life style improvement, most particularly in rural areas. Just how much coffee was considered something special with great luxury character is evident from the fact that many middle-class observers of rural society branded coffee drinking an indication of ethical and moral decline in rural areas.[150] Raisins had to be imported from Italy, Spain, or even Syria and were important on one hand for medical uses and on the other as spices. They, too, were definitely not an everyday food that was cheap and easy to obtain.[151] Nor can soap, at least when it was not produced at home and consequently cheap, be regarded as an everyday consumer good. That crocheted change purses and combs clearly were not everyday articles of the rural population is obvious; after all, they were not among the gewgaws that peddlers, for example, carried with them. These exceptional stolen goods are thus indicative of articles with both significant material and symbolic value. The stolen goods were among the things that could serve as marks of social distinction and signs of an elevated social position. A person who lived on the margins of society, drank coffee, had access to raisins and fine soap, and furthermore possessed elegant crocheted purses was undoubtedly an unusual phenomenon.

What is more, great emotional significance was associated with these conspicuous goods – as again illustrated by the example of the penniless Charlotte Birk, who, like her friends and acquaintances, came from the lower class.[152] She stole the luxury items cited neither for just her own consumption nor only as a mark of social distinction; instead, she also used them to structure her social and emotional relationship network. She in fact passed these special goods on to her father, her brother, and the wife of a shoemaker. She also settled her mother's debts with the money stolen from her boss. Precisely because the articles, as upscale colonial goods, had a particular symbolic value, they served as gifts to create or strengthen bonds, be it within the family or to acquaintances.[153]

Stolen goods not of the everyday type also indicate an emotional dimension on a second level – that becomes clear particularly in the case of the not entirely penniless sales clerk Hartenstein, who, as described, was accused by his employer, the merchant Guckemus, of having stolen tobacco, wine, raisins, change purses, cigars, combs, and buttons.[154] Hartenstein denied the accusations and claimed to have had permission to take a bit of tobacco and occasionally a cigar. Furthermore, he stated the following to explain the theft, "I took the wine once when I was annoyed because of harsh treatment by Mrs. Guckemus .... I thought that I would get myself a bottle of wine as revenge for the swallowed annoyance."[155] In addition, he stated that the lady boss, Mrs. Guckemus, "... didn't like me from the beginning and always ... treated me like a dog."[156] Furthermore, he was "treated very badly [by his] boss."[157] The theft was revenge or a means of consoling himself for emotional rebuffs. Both the Hartenstein case and the background of the Charlotte Birk case show signs of emotional problems in the relationships with the bosses who were robbed and their wives. Specifically, Birk stated that she was locked up by her boss and abused, in fact struck and thrown down the stairs, just to make her confess.[158] Likewise, in the case of a major theft in which a nephew robbed his uncle, emotions seem to have been involved. The stolen money served to kindle a romantic relationship between the nephew and his girlfriend and to restructure the relationship between the uncle and the nephew into a father–son relationship.[159]

In short, the thefts of unusual and very valuable articles also had symbolic and emotional motives, not just material objectives. (After all, Charlotte Birk could have just as well stolen beans, potatoes, or flour.) Thus, relationships played a role; they were perceived to be disturbed, as is blatantly obvious in the cases of the thefts by underlings, or they were supposed to be improved with the help of the stolen goods.

The second, much more frequently encountered type of stolen goods involved things of little value that differed considerably from luxury goods not only in their material insignificance but also their emotional and symbolic worth. Did these stolen objects also have dimensions other than the material one? Did they also indicate a relationship level? To answer these questions, the objects must be examined more closely. They were things from everyday life, very ordinary food, tools, shoes, and clothing or fabric. Once again, Anton Zimmermann is illustrative; as his 1854 offense was not his first, but his third, he could look back on a small collection of stolen goods belonging to the category of everyday necessities. He had already stolen a total of twenty-six bean poles, twenty-two of them already "stuck in the ground and surrounded by beans and four not yet stuck in the ground,"[160] potatoes worth twelve silver pennies, one lost object of little value with no further description, and that loaf and a half of bread the boys had obtained by begging. Even if we include the house slipper also mentioned by Mother Scherrer and the cap that were supposedly stolen in the robbery, the amount is still a few silver pennies, the equivalent of one day's work for a day laborer – of course without the meals that the laborer also received, frequently the most important part.[161] For other thieves the booty was similar: The son of the Widow Richter heisted two pieces of satin cloth fifteen and twenty-eight ells long, respectively.[162] Georg Blum stole three used shirts and a pair of stockings.[163] Johann Heinrich Bloh amassed a haul, relatively: six thaler, a pair of boots, and fourteen kreutzer.[164] Conrad Raab appropriated four used shirts.[165] The Ebert children, on the other hand, did not even manage to acquire a couple of rolls.[166] More successful were the attempts of various other thieves to steal washtubs, potatoes, used pipes, bread, and "beat-up wood."

Articles of little value, especially food and clothing articles, were also typical for thefts outside Electoral Hesse.[167] In Baden during the early nineteenth century, fruit thefts – which are not explicitly treated here because they are legally defined as a separate category – and especially thefts of clothes, shoes, and cloth were entered into the official records.[168] Female thieves in Bremen stole mostly clothes and fabrics, followed by food, money, and household implements.[169]

These articles were not only common, they literally constituted the core of everyday life. Bread, beans, and potatoes were, together with cereal porridge, the region's classic fare of the poor; most nourishment came from these three sources alone. Almost everyone in rural society needed agricultural and household implements. The situation was similar for clothing, which usually consisted of used everyday clothes: used shirts, hats, or fabrics from which clothing articles could be made. These were articles that, in contrast to "luxury items," neither lent themselves to producing social and cultural distinction nor were to the same degree helpful in creating and structuring relationships. They represented objects of everyday banality which people relied upon in a very basic way, whether for economic, social, or cultural reasons. The victim felt their loss directly, regardless of whether they were valuable materially or not. Indeed, without these articles, managing everyday life was rendered considerably more difficult: bread obtained by begging and agricultural implements indicate fundamental aspects of work life. They were not articles that only marginally brushed existence but instead struck at its core. Other articles – such as used shirts, stockings, fabrics, hats, pipes, and boots (those of a shoemaker's assistant at that) were less indicative of the work core but were instead intimate personal items that fit close to the body and were in their own turn central (of course on a different level) to the personal identity of a person, or better said, of a man.

The second type of stolen objects thus encompassed things that had little value from a strictly economic (or keeping the contemporary view, national economic) and legal perspective. For the person robbed, however, they were most probably of considerable importance: things from everyday life that bespoke intimacy because of their everyday character and whose theft was in any case painful far beyond the material loss.

The reasons why mostly young men of the lower classes stole articles of little apparent value from other people generally known to them are therefore more complex than it might at first appear. For the people involved, even the most ordinary appearing goods could have had great economic, emotional, or symbolic meaning. The material aspect that interested jurists concealed a broad range of motives on the part of the offenders, and the victims as well. Just how great the emotional significance of these everyday objects must have been, becomes clear from the efforts made by the victims to get their things back. After all, individuals took the risk of conflict before a state institution, even though the parties could perhaps have just as well, or sometimes even better, agreed informally on compensation or return, given that the people usually knew each other.

Closer examination of the stolen articles has thus brought to light a relationship dimension inherent to the stolen articles and undetected before now. Beyond that aspect, an additional question arises: Why were such everyday thefts of materially insignificant goods reported? It was clearly not because of the material value of the articles. That consideration leads us from the thieves and their motives to the victims who reported these offenses.

Notes

1 The following analyses only consider the complaints that were entered into the record or in some cases led to trials – more specific distinctions become evident in connection with the individual record books. Unreported crimes are not considered. For more detailed information see the appendix in the original German edition of the book.

Unless otherwise stated, all of the data cited in the following sections are derived from analyses of three Upper Hessian court record books. The record books are those kept by the particular courts. They list the name of the accused and the crime in question. Many entries also include information on the age, occupation, place of origin, and family status of the accused. For the present study, three record books of varying size were evaluated using a database. I owe great thanks to Christine Nawa (Göttingen) for the time-consuming preliminary work relating to the analysis.

The following record books were analyzed:

1 Record book 268 Marburg 97, with the title "Marburg Criminal Court – Record book – the Investigative Records from 1840 to 1863, Inclusive." In actuality, it includes entries from 1849 on. Data from a total of around five thousand people who stood trial in Upper Hessian criminal courts are contained in this record book.
2 Record book 273 Marburg 324, which does not have any meaningful title. All the information comes from 1867. The record book pulls together all reports received that have to do with police offenses and other events (for example, a report regarding discovery of a body).
3 Record book 268 Marburg 96, listing the approximately 250 *Schwurgericht* cases from the years 1849–1859.

2 In the Marburg region, only about 13–18 percent of all the people listed in the official records were female in the 1840s to 1860s. Compare 268 Marburg 97, 273 Marburg 324, and 268 Marburg 96.

This statistical determination has already been made for other regions of the German Federation in the nineteenth century. In the first third of the nineteenth century, the proportion of women in the entire criminal population of Prussia was 25.6 percent; see Dirk Blasius, 1978, 80. In the Grand Duchy of Hesse, only 16 percent of all people convicted were women in the middle of the nineteenth century; see "The Civil Tribunals in the Grand Duchy of Hesse," in *Hitzigs Annalen*, 35, New Series (1853), and "Criminal Statistics for the Grand Duchy of Hesse," in *Hitzigs Annalen*, 36, New Series (1854). In Austria, too, the proportion of crimes by women in the last third of the nineteenth century was around 15 percent; see Hugo Hoegel, 1900, 233. In Tirol and Vorarlberg, it was even only 10 percent; see Elisabeth Dietrich, 1995.

Nothing about this picture changes for the more common, less serious offenses usually tried in police courts or settled by the police with fines and without trials; see Stefan Brakensiek, 1999, 130ff; Andreas Roth, 1997; and Ralph Jessen, 1991. Although research in this area is still in its infancy, women, with a proportion of 10 percent, seem to have played a lesser role in these crimes; see Ralph Jessen, 1991, 244.

If we consider the crimes at the top of the police offense list, the proportion of crimes by men is approximately two-thirds to three-fourths of the total. For a summary of crimes by men and women, see also Otto Ulbricht, 1995a.

3 Eric A. Johnson, 1985, 154.

4 Thus we know, for example, that thirty of the hundred thefts that were reported to the Marburg junior state procurator in 1867 had been committed by women; see 273 Marburg 324.

For simple thefts, the proportion of female thieves was 26.7 percent; see 268 Marburg 97. Around 17 percent of the serious thefts that were tried in a

Schwurgericht were committed by women; see 268 Marburg 96. Of the 106 property crimes to which a gender status can be assigned eighteen were committed by women.

5 For the eighteenth century, see Joachim Eibach, 2003, 295, who talks about an average age of thirty. See Eric A. Johnson, 1995, 197, who states that the age of the perpetrators for the total number of crimes by men is twenty-one to twenty-five years old; thefts were generally committed by eighteen- to twenty-one-year-old delinquents. Similar results are cited by Dietrich Oberwittler, 1997, 203; the average age in this case is twenty to twenty-nine.

6 Still, the illegitimacy rate in Electoral Hesse at mid-century rose to over 10 percent; see Konrad Vanja, 1978, 98ff. The rate was also related to the limitations on marriage, which ensured that only individuals who could prove property ownership and "adequate food" received permission to marry; see Konrad Vanja, 1978, 97.

7 See Andrea Hauser, 1994, 361, who emphasizes the importance of matrimony and the household as the basic financial requisites.

8 See Martina Käthner, 1988, 38. Female thieves were thus apparently considerably younger than other female criminals; Eric A. Johnson, 1995, 197, states that the average age of women for all crimes was thirty to forty.

9 Such a calculation is not particularly easy, given the numeric material available. The most extensive record book (268 Marburg 97) only provides information about occupation for less than a fifth of all cases, the two others (268 Marburg 96 and 273 Marburg 324), for about a third of all persons. The following percentages thus only cover those cases for which occupational information is given. For this computation, all the other cases were taken out of the basic total.

10 See 268 Marburg 97: 17.9 percent of the offenders were day laborers and 29.2 percent were artisans. See 268 Marburg 96, the period 1849–1859; in this source, 20.6 percent were day laborers and 33.6 percent were artisans.
See 273 Marburg 324. The proportion of artisans in this record book for 1867 is 30.5 percent; artisans constitute 10 percent.

11 See 273 Marburg 324. In this record book (for 1867), the proportion of plowmen is 12 percent. See also 268 Marburg 96, with 6.5 percent plowmen.

12 273 Marburg 324. In this source, the proportion of servants is relatively high at 8 percent.

13 None of the three sets of statistics indicate a proportion of the educated middle class higher than 3 percent; see 268 Marburg 97. In this source, 1.4 percent of the offenders belong to the educated middle class; in 268 Marburg 96, the proportion is 2.8 percent.

14 In the statistics for 1867 (273 Marburg 324), artisans are represented with 35.7 percent of all thieves, compared to 30.5 percent of all offenders. These results, available for only one year, are also confirmed by 268 Marburg 97.

15 See also the examination of the eighteenth century by Michael Frank, 1995b, 268.

16 The finding is confirmed by a series of studies on other regions. Regula Ludi, 1999, 524 and 525, reaches the following conclusion for the first half of the nineteenth century in Bern, "Eighty to ninety percent of all property crimes are

committed by people from segments of the population whose material existence is endangered and who in the daily struggle for survival always find themselves on the margins in need of support." See Elisabeth Dietrich, 1995, 120; she speaks of "thieves without property." See also Dirk Blasius, 1990, 223, who quotes the assessment of the authorities in this regard, expressing agreement. Martina Käthner, 1988, 42, reaches the same conclusion for female property crime in Bremen.

17 268 Marburg 91, Statement of Anton Zimmermann, May 26, 1854, 10.

18 Robert von Friedeburg, 1997, 74.

19 In the Marburg region, this group constituted about 2.5 percent; see Cameron Munter, 1983, on the poor and poor relief. In her conception of the "Marburg region," Munter includes a somewhat smaller area than the territory here based on the high court district. See the calculations for the city of Marburg in 1847; Jürgen Bohmbach, 1973, 340, estimates recipients of relief at 20 percent.

20 Martin Kukowski, 1995a, 56. The first "scholarly" study of Hessian day laborers was published already at the beginning of the twentieth century, showing, among other things, how great the interest in scholarly research on this type of rural laborer even at the end of the nineteenth century; see Adolf Nebel, 1909. The work is based on an extensive survey.

21 In this context, it should be noted that begging was allowed in one's home town.

22 In any case, not more than five hectares – with more than five hectares, the person was considered a smallholder.

23 All the information is taken from the crime document 268 Marburg 91.

24 At another location, Mengel is also referred to as a "pimp"; see 266 Marburg 72, Kirchhain Electoral District Gendarmerie to the Marburg District Court, April 5, 1849.

25 Like Anton Zimmermann, Catharina Prinz had a fixed location in the form of a co-residence from which Mengel could also profit; see 266 Marburg 72, House search at Catharina Prinz's, April 6, 1849.

26 266 Marburg 72, Interrogation of Mengel, February 12, 1849.

27 Regulation of the welfare system as provided for in the 1831 civil rights law had the result that people remained in their home locations; see Susanne Grindel, 2000, 144ff. People only received support where they had lived for years. That did not change until 1897 when new rural community regulations adopted the Prussian right to freedom of movement. Furthermore, only local citizens were entitled to relief. At the same time, poor relief was tied to specific honor categories.

28 266 Marburg 72, Interrogation of Margaretha Mengel, May 24, 1849.

29 They thus belonged to the group that was designated "needy" in an 1847 survey of district offices and police headquarters; see Jürgen Bohmbach, 1973, 341. Life was hard, especially in the winter months, when weaving baskets and binding brooms at home, forest work, and stone breaking were difficult or were completely abandoned because of weather conditions; see Konrad Vanja, 1978, 142ff, on day laborers in Electoral Hesse.

30 For example, see Konrad Vanja, 1978, who also showed an example of this internal differentiation in a village study of a place located in the north of the Marburg District.
31 Laurence Fontaine and Jürgen Schlumbohm, 2000, 2.
32 Dennis A. Frey, 2000. See also Andrea Hauser, 1994, 215ff.
33 Vivid examples of the day laborer existence in Electoral Hesse in Konrad Vanja, 1978, 50ff.
34 266 Marburg 72.
35 268 Marburg 91.
36 268 Marburg 62.
37 In addition, analysis of the record books of the Marburg High Court shows that crime was distributed relatively evenly across the high court district, but that there was something of a concentration around Marburg. Furthermore, it can be seen that people in towns located on important travel routes were more frequently enticed into criminal activities than others: For example, Cölbe had only something more than five hundred citizens and nevertheless produced fifty-four offenders in barely two decades. A similar situation can also be observed in Langenstein and Gossfelden. Most scholars advocate the theory that a connection exists between urbanization and crime; Dirk Blasius, 1976, 33. A critical opinion on the subject in Peter Wettmann-Jungblut, 1997, 295.
38 Unfortunately, studies on the origins of property offenders in the nineteenth century are lacking. Instead of their being researched, the very popular image in contemporary literature of the thief who is at the same time a vagrant or simply a foreigner was just given further shrift. As an aside, note the moralizing discourse of the Inner Mission, for example, which can similarly be observed in the pauperism debate of the time conducted in the liberal middle class. In that context people liked to make connections between poverty, rootlessness, and moral decline. For the eighteenth century, assuming that the offender was foreign seems to have been entirely correct. Joachim Eibach, 2003, 299, was able to show for Frankfurt that almost 50 percent of the thieves were foreigners and can also be placed in the lower class (Joachim Eibach, 2003, 305).
39 Thanks here to Eckart Schörle for the detailed analysis of the town data.
40 268 Marburg 91.
41 268 Marburg 91, Interrogation of Eva Engelberg, May 29, 1854.
42 268 Marburg 91, Statement of Ludwig Schadt, *Schwurgericht* record, September 27, 1854.
43 Zimmermann was also known in Haddamshausen, a neighboring village to the south with about 200 residents; see 268 Marburg 91, Interrogation of Anna (surname unknown), maiden name Müller, mother-in-law of the miller Ludwig Will from Haddamshausen, June 8, 1848.
44 268 Marburg 91, Interrogation of Elisabeth Becker, June 8, 1954.
45 266 Marburg 72, Interrogation of Elwert, April 13, 1849. This is probably attributable to the political events of 1848 and 1849 in which Mengel apparently actively participated. Mengel had a training suit made for himself – a clearly political article of clothing. Furthermore, he was involved in political protests, so-called cats' concerts; see Walter Kürschner, 1934, 223. He

apparently also participated in the so-called Vilmar protests. On the protests in front of the house of the *Gymnasium* director Vilmar, see Walter Kürschner, 1934, 218ff. It is also stated there that the bookseller Elwert (the bookseller robbed in the crime for which Mengel was charged) rushed to Vilmar's aid during the "cats' concerts."

46 Thus, the neighbor of the Schneider family that was robbed was able to state immediately after the theft was discovered that the son of Friedrich Hißerich Wilhelm had entered the house that very morning and consequently had to be the thief; see 269 Marburg 196, Report.

47 Of course, there were cases in which the thieves came from outside the village or city. Although quantification is not possible, such cases frequently appear to be thefts actually involving articles of significant value and were therefore not really typical.

48 Joachim Eibach, 2003, 305ff, sketches just that picture for the eighteenth century: 53 percent of the people robbed belonged to the Frankfurt middle class; thus, they were not necessarily prosperous, but in any case had more than "adequate food," while the majority of the thieves came from the lower class.

49 Ulrich Reuling, 1979, 226ff.

50 Ockershausen had a high percentage of Jewish population. Paul Amsberg, 1972, 49, indicates 31 in 1835 and 40 in 1861, with a total population of just 800 residents in 1838. See also the study of Konrad Vanja, 1978, on the village of Halsdorf where there was also a very large percentage of Jewish population, 25ff.

51 Robert von Friedeburg, 1997, 183, mentions conflicts that developed for just such reasons.

52 In Electoral Hesse in 1852, 95 percent of the cattle trade was supposedly in Jewish hands; see Avraham Barkai, 1988, 52.

53 Electoral Hesse was part of the Kingdom of Westphalia.

54 Robert von Friedeburg even speaks of a precarious situation, "Because of the pauperization of the Jews and the majority [status] of their Christian neighbors, the politicizing of the emancipation question, and the growing direct and indirect participation of the lower classes, which were especially fearful on account of their part in the baseness, the concrete material cause of the conflict among variously entitled corporate groups finally merged out on the flat land as well ... with other, already existing resentments against Jewish neighbors, giving rise to general resentment against the Jewish minority ..."; see Robert von Friedeburg, 1997, 180ff, here 188. See also Dorothee Schimpf, 1994, 17ff, on the legal situation of Jews, which worsened with the 1816 act because the people who worked as peddlers (*Nothändler*) and minimally as cattle traders were not on the same level as the Christian population with regard to civil rights. In 1833, discrimination against population groups living from peddling continued unchanged; otherwise, fundamental equality was provided for. Not until 1869 was all legal discrimination eliminated.

55 Robert von Friedeburg, 1997, 191.

56 Heike Wirthwein, 1994.

57 Cameron Munter, 1992, 159.

58 268 Marburg 91, Interrogations on June 8, 1854.

59 In the Marburg Court District, such crimes constituted about 10 percent of all the crimes tried before the court in the decades between 1849 and 1869; see evaluation, 268 Marburg 97. Of course, it should be mentioned that the frequency with which the edict prohibiting begging was repeated indicates that this edict could not be, and perhaps was not meant to be, implemented as effectively as the social discipline theory wanted for a long time to have everyone believe; Cameron Munter, 1983, 179 argues in this direction. See Susanne Grindel, 2000.

60 Heike Wirthwein, 1994, 82, describes the situation for the Duchy of Hesse in this way, and it is equally applicable to the Electorate.

61 268 Hanau 29. The case took place in the Hanau Administrative Court District. This district is adjacent in the south to the Marburg District and is, from the standpoint of rural district social structure, quite comparable to the Marburg region.

62 268 Hanau 29, Schwarzenfels Justice Office, October 21, 1859: Sentenced once to police detention for theft, then for begging, and finally for three petty thefts, embezzlement, and fraud.

63 266 Hanau 145, Interrogation of Andreas Wenzel, May 22, 1850.

64 For example, this is clear in the case of the twelve- and fifteen-year-old siblings Friedrich and Friederike Ebert, who tried in vain to pilfer rolls from a barely ten-year-old boy. Furthermore, they came from a wainwright's family without assets; 268 Marburg 111. The schoolboy Christian Euler, who took or stole the pipe left behind by a carpenter, knew his victim; 269 Marburg 16. Both also came from similar social groups.

65 That was so in the case of the Hoffmann brothers, who came from economic circumstances similar to those of their victims; 266 Hanau 236.

66 For example, in the small village of Oberzell, where a piece of linen was stolen in a May night; 266 Hanau 302.

67 Ultimately, the relationship between the person committing the theft and the person robbed is characterized by its gender-specific structure; as a rule, young men stole from other young men or even boys. While women played a secondary role as offenders, they were also seldom victims. Women usually only turned up as part of a household that was robbed. Of course, this almost exclusively male-dominated relationship between the thief and the person robbed may be the result of a male-dominated property culture – still, this male dominance is not explained solely by the legally, socially, and economically conditioned discrimination against women.

68 For thefts from homes, see also the study of Otto Ulbricht, 1995b. This work treats servant thefts of the conventional type, that is, by maids who stole from their masters. Ulbricht, who only analyzes numbers for the beginning of the nineteenth century in the Duchy of Schleswig-Holstein, shows that such thefts are statistically insignificant. For Bremen, see Martina Käthner, 1988. According to this study, property crimes are dominated by offenses that are connected with the employer.

69 See 268 Hanau 8, Interrogation of Maria Großmann, March 4, 1853. A sergeant's post was one of the positions that communities preferred to award in place of poor relief.

70 His parents were "good, upright middle class people," and he owned a house with his sister; see 266 Hanau 203, May 10, 1850, Information from Mayor Hoon von Dorndorf.

71 266 Hanau 203.

72 There are not yet comparable studies for the nineteenth century; for the eighteenth century, on the other hand, we know from one study that the offenders and victims in the majority of property crime cases were not acquainted; see Joachim Eibach, 2003, 301, who speaks of 59.8 percent.

73 For the legal distinction between "petty and major thefts," see the second part of this work.

74 266 Marburg 123.

75 266 Marburg 98.

76 268 Marburg 62.

77 Regula Ludi, 1999, has produced one of the few studies on crime in the first half of the nineteenth century; it also considers the question of who the victims of property crime were. Ludi reaches a different conclusion for the urban society in Bern. She writes on one hand that "the victims came surprisingly often from social circumstances similar to those of the offenders" (529), only to then explain that three-fourths of the thefts were from people who were better situated. Ludi devotes special attention to thefts in the work place which were "often symptoms of long-smoldering conflicts between the two parties" (530). Peter Wettmann-Jungblut, 1990, reaches the following conclusion for 1779–1801, "The overwhelming number of people bringing charges probably came from the poorer classes of the population" (163). He goes on to say in this regard that the people in question were probably the victims or their representatives.

78 Not only the socio-topographical reports and the early ethnographies from the pens of middle-class teachers, ministers, physicians, and some attorneys, but also contemporary statistics with significant claims to being "scholarly," which it was hoped would provide objective information, contributed to constructing rural society as a homogeneous entity. The *Statistical Reports on Electoral Hesse's Economic Conditions* by Bruno Hildebrand, 1853, for example, only distinguishes between "rural" and "urban" real property; a further table is needed to represent the "skilled trades," and a third for the "day laborers," creating the impression that these groups led separate lives. Criticism of this approach was already voiced very early by Ian Farr, 1986. Still groundbreaking: Wolfgang Kaschuba and Carola Lipp, 1982. See also Clemens Zimmermann, 1998.

79 Earlier research on agrarian history must accede to the charge that it fell for the romantic social projections of the late nineteenth and early twentieth centuries, for example, the fantasies of a Wilhelm Heinrich Riehl, to mention only the best known of the Hessian folklorists.

80 *Electoral Hessian Court and State Handbook for 1850*, Cassel, 1850, 104ff.

81 The same argument about the representative nature of "backwardness" in the region was made especially forcefully by Cameron Munter, 1983, 61ff.

82 The university was also the reason that Marburg, with 40 percent of the households classified as "prosperous," was far ahead of the Marburg District,

where only 22 percent of the households were prosperous; see Jürgen Bohmbach, 1973, who quotes from the government office reports for 1847, which was of course an especially severe famine year.

83 At the middle of the nineteenth century, they were still affected to a surprisingly great degree by agriculture. At that point, more than 40 percent of the population often lived from agriculture; see Martin Kukowski, 1995a, 79.

84 Jürgen Bohmbach, 1973, 343.

85 Georg Landau, 1842, 367.

86 Georg Landau, 1842, 400, reports 140 masters, only 100 of whom had work and "only 6 had several workers."

87 Georg Landau, 1842, 403.

88 Bruno Hildebrand, 1853, 63.

89 Cameron Munter, 1983, 70ff.

90 Georg Landau, 1842, 435.

91 As coffee consumption was considered an important criterion for modernity, that means that contemporaries viewed this area as especially conscious of tradition.

92 Robert von Friedeburg, 1997, 38ff.

93 A number of works on agrarian history have very emphatically pointed out these distinctions in recent years. The work of Rainer Beck, 1993, is an illustration: Using the village of Unterfinning as an example, he clearly shows the heterogeneity of rural society in the Early Modern Period, and especially the great complexity of the property circumstances and legal relationships.

94 In Marburg, for example, there were fewer than three hundred Catholics and not even one hundred Jews among the approximately ten thousand residents.

95 Bruno Hildebrand, 1853, 63.

96 Whether for that reason it must be called a "second religious age," as Olaf Blaschke does, is questionable. See the collective volume by Olaf Blaschke, 2002. The thesis of the second confessionalization suffers from the problem that we would then have to speak of the "third confessionalization" for the twenty-first century – however, today "fundamentalization" is assumed. In my view, the concept does not explain and analyze the particular meaning that religiosity, or rather reference to religious models, had specifically in the various epochs but instead blurs that meaning. In addition, the multifarious forms of parallel and interacting religions that structure daily life are disregarded.

97 Occupational differences were of importance beyond economics. People still used to marry primarily within their own circles long after the turn of the century, thus further accentuating the social boundaries. Robert von Friedeburg was able to show in his study of Upper Hesse that in 1860 more than 80 percent of the farmers had sons-in-law from the same social group. The closedness of the social groups was just under 50 percent for smallholders and 45 percent for artisans, at the least. Likewise, 57 percent of laborers married in their own circles. See Robert von Friedeburg, 1997, 58.

98 Basically, in Hesse at the time landholders with more than ten hectares of land (*Vollbauer*), who could live well from their farms, could be differentiated from smallholders and parcel owners, who always needed supplementary earnings.

The proportion of *Vollbauer* was – with all of the differences in details – very small; they seldom constituted more than a third of rural society; see Martin Kukowski, 1995a, 62.

99 See the statistics of Bruno Hildebrand, 1853.

100 The most important factor was the decline of the linen weaving industry, the classic income source of proto-industrialization. With the decline, an important supplementary line of work gradually disappeared, especially for day laborers like Anton Zimmermann, who had been able to hire himself out for a short time to a stocking weaver (268 Marburg 91, Interrogation of Mrs. Clötz, May 29, 1854). In some regions of Hesse, proto-industrialization had been of enormous importance – for example, in Frankenberg; see Georg Landau, 1842, 400. But Hessian thread exports were already past their peak by 1800; see Susanne Grindel, 2000.

101 Of course, research on the trades has qualified the assessment shared by many contemporaries that the trades experienced one of their greatest crises at mid-century as the result of free enterprise and approaching industrialization. Researchers have pointed out that the trades definitely profited from industrialization and furthermore that free enterprise was considerably longer in coming than previously assumed; see the groundbreaking work of Friedrich Lenger, 1986. However, studies that also consider the situation of the rural trades are for the most part non-existent. With regard to rural society, it can be assumed that the worsening condition of the agricultural sector also affected those people who pursued trade activities in addition to agriculture.

102 Not until after mid-century did considerable emigration make the effects of population growth less evident. The population had increased more than 15 percent between 1830 and 1850; see Konrad Vanja, 1978, 30ff.

103 The starting situation, that is, the discourse and practices of the Early Modern Period regarding property, were altogether multi-faceted, especially for real estate. In any case, it cannot be assumed that ownership and possession were generally the same thing, as Christopher M. Hann, 1998, 7, maintains, "In most pre-capitalist societies property relations seem to be inchoate, only vaguely defined in law, and leaving much scope for interpretation." In any case, in the Early Modern Period a distinction was made between the *dominus directus*, the "top owner," and the *dominus utilis*, that is, the person who worked the land; see the comprehensive description in Stefan von Below, 1998.

But even beyond land, the term "ownership" covered much more in the nineteenth century. For example, the Prussian Civil Code recognized a wide variety of "ownership" types: the fief, the hereditary tenant farm, and the family entailed estate were the three most important. That also meant that disposal, use, and ownership rights did not have to be the same thing. That is, ownership was understood to be a "bundle of entitlements" and not the "right to disposal, control, and use unrestricted in time and content . . .," as was advocated in the eighteenth and nineteenth centuries, at least in many debates; Hannes Siegrist and David Sugarman, 1999b, 23.

104 The abolition of serfdom and all privileges provided for in the 1807 Westphalian constitution was gradually limited; the 1809 redemption law also

failed. In 1832 a new redemption law was passed that made acquisition of land possible for everyone. At the same time, serfdom was abolished. Of course, this law was not as successful in Electoral Hesse as comparable reforms in other regions, because consolidation and distribution of the common areas was neglected until 1870, being instead carried out half-heartedly.

105 On this subject, see Eihachiro Sakai, 1967; Susanne Grindel, 2000; Manfred Bullik, 1972; Martin Kukowski, 1995a.

106 See Eihachiro Sakai, 1967. He states that the personal dependency relationships in Hesse were minimal and consequently "peasant liberation" was not particularly important.

107 The end of the 1860s marks a peak of such forced court-ordered procedures; see Susanne Grindel, 2000, 26.

108 According to the 1831 Electoral Hessian municipal code, the legal status designations of "full citizen" (*Ortsbürger*) and "citizen with limited rights" (*Beisasse*) applied in every town.

109 "Full citizen" referred to people who owned a house, farmed with their own draft teams, were masters of a guild trade, or had a fortune or a profession that brought in at least 100 thaler; on this subject, see the overview description by Konrad Vanja, 1978, 40ff.

110 That meant that the "respectable" part of the community decided about relief, as Cameron Munter, 1983, strongly emphasizes.

111 At the same time, village society was further differentiated on the legal level. Membership in the group entitled to use was not identical with the sub-classification as a "full citizen" versus a "citizen with limited rights," a distinction that continued to exist. In Cyriaxweimar there were five "persons with rights of use," as opposed to eleven "persons not entitled to rights of use" and three "citizens with limited rights"; see Ulrich Reuling, 1979, 327.

112 Many full citizens lost their previous rights of use, while other citizens with limited rights were able to obtain use rights. However, it can be stated in general that it was clearly simpler for full citizens to obtain rights of use. On the average, less than one-third of the citizens of a village now held rights of use. A regulation was thus rescinded that had still been usual in the eighteenth century and had provided that all full citizens had rights of use, but citizens with limited rights did not. As in the eighteenth and the beginning of the nineteenth centuries many people still had full citizenship rights, the new 1834 regulation worsened the situation of a large number of the residents; see Konrad Vanja, 1978, 93. For access to wood in particular, see Susanne Grindel, 2000; Brigitta Vits, 1993, 49ff; Jürgen Bohmbach, 1973, 339.

Of course, it was by no means the case that none of the poor had rights of use. Rights of use, full citizenship rights, and land ownership are categories that are not mutually dependent; see Robert von Friedeburg, 1997, 109, Note 213. Of course, as a rule the landholders with at least ten hectares of land enjoyed the greatest advantage from the new rights of use regulation – although the high court of appeals found in 1838 that full citizens were entitled to their share of wood as a civil right, this could never be put into practice; Robert von Friedeburg, 1997, 105. Consequently, it is not surprising that it was the full citizens who, in the 1870s with the annexation by Prussia, demanded from the new authorities that the areas which had until then been common use areas for all those with rights of use be transferred to private ownership. That is precisely what happened toward the end of the century, marking the end of the slow development of private ownership in rural society that had been launched with the agrarian reforms.

113 For the very reason that a radical break was to be made with the traditional sharing of the common area, it must be assumed that it took years, if not decades, for the detailed provisions of these rights of use to be implemented. However, as long as they had not been implemented – this process was not complete legally until the rights of use had been transformed to private ownership toward the end of the nineteenth century – ties to land previously accessible to many day laborers remained very strong. The ties became even stronger, as dependence on access to that land grew for economic reasons.

114 Martin Kukowski, 1995b, 176. In my view, the term implies too great a homogeneity in the period before the reforms.

115 See the comprehensive study of Robert von Friedeburg, 1997.

116 Although it can be said that the farms in Upper Hesse were tiny to small until the middle of the nineteenth century, the size of almost 30 percent of the property holdings was already thirty to fifty acres in 1854. In the Marburg High Court District, around 50 percent of the rural population owned less than ten acres, and for that reason the people in question required additional income sources to make a living; see Martin Kukowski, 1995b, 178.

117 See Susanne Grindel, 2000, 27.

118 Jürgen Schlumbohm, 1994, 615ff.

119 See Konrad Vanja, 1978, 94ff. In Halsdorf, the proportion of servants, day laborers, and their families was 19 percent in 1785; in 1867, it had risen to 44 percent.

120 Olwen Hufton, 1974.

121 In turn, the problem with the poverty concept is also that poverty is a question of stage of life. The elderly and children were especially threatened with poverty, especially when they had few ties to relatives.

122 Thus, Grand Duke Leopold von Baden issued an amnesty for all wood offenses committed in the winter of 1829–1830, because it was a very hard winter; see Peter Wettmann-Jungblut, 1997, 287.

123 Quoted as in Christina von Hodenberg, 1996, 216.

124 Karl Marx, 1975. On this subject, see also the argumentation of the Augsburg magistrate; in Wolfgang Weber, 1985, 265ff.

125 Dirk Blasius, 1990, 223: "There is no question that the poverty of wide segments of the population led to enormous growth in the criminal population." Dirk Blasius, 1976, 30, speaks of a connection between the growth rate of property crime in 1845 and 1847, and the last economic crisis of the "old type." Regula Ludi, 1999, 523, also states, "Property crime in the nineteenth century is for a long time and to a high degree conditioned by need." Monika Weinfurt, 2001, 220, says, "The most important motive for property crime ... was existential need."

126 Georg von Mayr proceeded in exactly the same manner in his *Statistics on the Court Police in the Kingdom of Bavaria*, published in 1867.
127 Eckhard Formella, 1985, 29, made this criticism of Blasius.
128 Manuel Castells and Alejandro Portes, 1991, 11–37.
129 Edward P. Thompson, 1980.
130 See Neil McKendrick, 1997.
131 Mary Douglas and Baron Isherwood, 1979, 72.
132 See the survey article of John Brewer, 1997.
133 Mary Douglas and Baron Isherwood, 1979, 62.
134 George Rudé, 1985.
135 269 Marburg 171.
136 Michel Foucault, 1976, 352.
137 Hobsbawm defines a "social crime" in the following manner: "when there is a conflict of laws, e.g., between an official and an unofficial system, or when acts of law-breaking have a distinct element of social protest in them, or when they are closely linked with the development of social and political unrest"; see Eric Hobsbawm, 1972, 5. On a similar note, Dirk Blasius, 1990, 234, says: "Doubt about the justice of the existing order, often justified, was part of the mix contributing to thefts and wood thefts."
138 Norbert Schindler, 2001, 27.
139 Ibid.
140 See the brief but comprehensive examination of research in Andreas Blauert and Eva Wiebel, 2001, 77–79.
141 Mooser views the conflict as "polarization of the social classes and emancipation of the rural poor and the unpropertied lower classes from the peasant village, indicating mass poverty during a crisis-ridden transition period of the entire economy"; see Josef Mooser, 1984, 82.
142 In Prussia, the category refers to objects with a value of less than five thaler; Dirk Blasius, 1990, 221.
143 However, there was an average of almost ten times as many wood thefts per year as petty thefts. Figures for the period after 1882 are provided by Eric A. Johnson, 1995, 136ff.
144 Dirk Blasius, 1976, 141, tables for 1830–1850. There were generally five times as many petty thefts as grand thefts. See also Andreas Roth, 1997, 72, who shows the clear prevalence of simple theft for Duisburg in the eighteen nineties.
145 There are no detailed studies for the eighteenth century; for the eighteenth century, see Fritz Verdenhalven, 1974, 117ff. See Michael Frank, 1992, 1995a, 1995b; Peter Wettmann-Jungblut, 1990, 1996, 1997; Joachim Eibach, 2003, 332, seems to reach a different conclusion, when he speaks of stolen goods consisting of approximately 20 percent noble metal/jewelry and 22 percent cash. Of course, it must be taken into account that he focuses almost exclusively on grand larceny.
146 Arjun Appadurai, 1986. For the meaning of things, see also Tilmann Habermas, 1999.
147 The articles were taken by Charlotte Birk; 268 Marburg 8.
148 The articles were taken by Hartenstein; 266 Hanau 203.

149 266 Marburg 72, Report of the prison guard Scheldt, May 18, 1849.
150 See also the characterization of the Electoral Hessian Schwalm region addressed above as tradition-conscious because coffee was not consumed; Georg Landau, 1842, 63.
151 I owe thanks to Christian Hochmuth, Dresden, for this information; his tips regarding relevant passages in Zedler were very helpful.
152 A tanner, among others, belonged to her circle of acquaintances. Tanners were considered artisans who had no honor. David Kalbfleisch was such a tanner, and he had a power of attorney from C. Birk to act on her behalf in court; see 268 Hanau 8. She was also a friend of the wives of field guards and shoemakers.
153 Gifts create and structure relationships – Marcel Mauss emphatically pointed out that phenomenon in his "Essay on the Gift," published in 1925; in Marcel Mauss, 1950. On Mauss recently, see Beate Wagner-Hasel, 2003, 141–170.
154 266 Hanau 203.
155 266 Hanau 203, Interrogation of Peter Hartenstein, June 1, 1850.
156 Ibid.
157 266 Hanau 203, Public session of the criminal chamber, testimony of the defendant, August 20, 1850. Of course, defense claims are involved here; they were legally relevant because the sales clerk could count on mitigating circumstances if he had been treated badly by his employer. And yet, the claims are not merely strategic, as the course of this and other comparable cases proves.
158 268 Hanau 8, Testimony of Charlotte Birk, May 27, 1853.
159 269 Marburg 218. The nephew bankrolled himself and his fiancé with the stolen goods on the one hand; on the other, the case was such that the uncle adopted his nephew after he had retracted his complaint. On thefts from homes, see Regula Ludi, 1999, 530.
160 268 Marburg 91, Copy of the decision of July 21, 1852.
161 Jürgen Bohmbach, 1973, 335.
162 266 Hanau 302.
163 261 High Court of Appeals Index 7/Criminal Records III.
164 266 Hanau 145.
165 266 Hanau 297.
166 268 Hanau 111.
167 Dirk Blasius, 1978, 54. Andreas Roth, 1997, 72, shows the clear prevalence of simple theft for Duisburg in the 1890s.
168 Peter Wettmann-Jungblut, 1990, 162: Clothes, shoes, fabric, and yarn, 23–32 percent; food, cattle, and fruit, 31–36 percent; money, 9–14 percent.
169 Martina Käthner, 1988, 47. On Bern, see also Regula Ludi, 1999, 511. She writes that it is a question of "objects being stolen that are for everyday needs."

2

How Does a Person End Up in Court – Why Does Something Go on the Record?

Did conflict-laden encounters such as that between Anton Zimmermann and the two beggar boys – and such incidents were anything but uncommon – always have to be decided immediately in court? Why couldn't the parties settle the matter much more quickly and inexpensively among themselves? Was it really so unusual for a man like Zimmermann, who was older and physically stronger, with more social capital than the two sons of single mothers, to try noisily to gain respect and a little bread? Above all, did official action really have to be taken instantly for this behavior? The conflict in itself, jostling and theft of bread obtained by begging, was not especially important, new, or even unusual. How and why did a more or less everyday conflict actually become a crime on the record that, for good measure, was labeled "theft?"

What is unusual about the case, indeed, what is surprising and demands explanation is not Zimmermann's behavior, but the fact that the mother of one of the boys reported that behavior to the mayor, the police, or the district administrator's office. After all, without such a report, the entire matter would never have gone on record, and a rather harmless incident would not have become a property conflict that was transformed with costly legal resources into a lengthy court proceeding ending in a multi-year sentence of incarceration in irons.

Why weren't all other means of settling the conflict exhausted first? Why did new rules suddenly take hold in Electoral Hesse in mid-nineteenth century? The consensus among resarchers on the Early Modern Period is that, at least as late as the end of eighteenth century, going to court had been the last resort of those seeking to resolve a conflict.[1] Why it seems had out-of-court settlement, at least in cases of theft, suddenly become the exception rather than the rule?[2] Were the conditions for such out-of-court solutions as identified by Francisca Loetz for Early Modern Period societies missing in the Electoral Hessian villages? Was it no longer possible to facilitate the "capability of the opposing parties to reach an agreement" (it could be said the "desire to reach an agreement"), or to achieve "ritual forms of reconciliation?" Was the necessary "tolerance on the part of the authorities" lacking?[3] Only if the conditions for an out-of-court settlement were not present, or if the desire was to actively use the court as a forum for conflict resolution[4] because someone expected more resonance for his or her position there, did people go to the justice system in the Early Modern Period.[5] Recent studies have established in the meantime that exactly the same situation can still be observed in nineteenth-century rural society. Going to court in conflicts with potential for criminal prosecution was by no means taken for granted but was instead the result of a "complex assessment of the chances of winning or losing."[6] Filing a complaint with the authorities even in Cyriaxweimar thus required an active decision to deliberately bring about court proceedings in order to use the justice system for individual purposes, a form of "use of justice."[7]

Maria Scherrer was no isolated case. Theft reports piled up everywhere. As a rule, the material objects were rather inconsequential and young men were involved who, because they knew each other, would have had every opportunity for informal conflict resolution,[8] especially as the state restrained itself almost completely.[9] In only one case in thirty did a policeman take the initiative and report an alleged theft in Electoral Hesse during the second half of the nineteenth century.[10]

2.1 A CONSEQUENCE OF LEGAL REFORMS?

Why did people turn to government authorities that were not always particularly understanding? Why did they tolerate sometimes long journeys and in any case complicated interviews to settle a conflict which they would have routinely resolved on their own a few years before and which furthermore involved objects of no great material value? One answer to this question may lie in the court organizational reforms instituted at the beginning of the nineteenth century and designed – according to the declared objective of the legal reformers – to make it easier for all justice-seekers to make their case before the court by enhancing the presence of the rule of law at the local level. As crimes were reported to the local police and officials rather than to the court even before the reforms, an increase in court density was at first irrelevant to just filing a report. However, actually going to court was greatly simplified because the responsible offices were no longer a day's march away. In addition, it could be assumed that the courts' greater proximity would lead to greater familiarity with them, reducing fear of entering the courtroom. And in fact, taking into account just the sheer mass of reforms intended to increase court density, it might seem that the density actually did lead to an enhanced court presence, making it easier for even a Maria Scherrer to bring suit, and that, consequently, charges really were brought as a result of the reforms.

But – stating the answer right at the outset – this kind of enhanced presence of the state of law was not what was going on in Electoral Hesse; in this case, the impression of better court accessibility created by reform rhetoric is deceptive. Reforms that were meant to increase court density and thus facilitate court access for the rural population in particular were most certainly carried out in Electoral Hesse. The Edict on Organization of June 29, 1821, "regarding reorganization of the previous state administration" and then the 1831 constitution already attempted to structure the court districts such that they were all the same size and were responsible for approximately the same number of residents. In reality, the court districts still differed considerably. That was due primarily to the fact that the new districts were not organized strictly according to the abstract category of uniformity but that historical relationships were also taken into account.[11] Instead of an improvement with regard to the ratio of courts to residents,[12] the reforms resulted in a change for the worse. Nor did the separation of administration from the judiciary apparatus bring about greater court density.

TABLE 1 *Court Density before and after the 1821 Reforms*

	Residents per office	
Court district	**Before July 1821**	**1823**
Marburg	10,766	19,066
Frohnhausen	3,679	5,743
Kirchhain	5,625	10,141
Wetter	11,673	11,455
Average for Upper Hesse	5,000	8,300

Source: Author's calculations on the basis of the *Handbook of the Electoral Hessian Military, Court, and Civil State* and the *Electoral Hessian State and Address Handbook, 1823–1854*.

TABLE 2 *Development of Court Density, 1821–1879*

Year	Jurisdiction	Population size	Number of justice offices	Average number of residents per office
1821	Upper Hesse Province	55,000	11	5,000
1823	Upper Hesse Province	100,000	12	8,300
1831	Upper Hesse Province	108,000	12	9,000
1833	Upper Hesse Province	113,837	15	7,600
1850	Marburg High Court			8,200
1854	Marburg High Court			7,950
1862	Marburg Criminal Court District	95,837	12	7,987
After Nov 1863	Marburg High Court District	120,193	15	8,013
1879	Marburg Regional Court	184,961	20	9,249

Source: Author's calculations on the basis of the *Handbook of the Electoral Hessian Military, Court, and Civil State* and the *Electoral Hessian State and Address Handbook, 1823–1854*.

On average, an office before the *Edict on Organization* was responsible for barely 5,000 people; a justice office after 1821, for something more than 8,300 residents. As the number of people employed in each office remained the same,[13] the resident-to-court ratio must have gotten worse rather than better.[14] Furthermore, because the particular court districts had gotten bigger, the way to court had become more inconvenient and in cases of doubt also more expensive. Court density did improve in the following years because of additional reforms, but remained significantly lower than before the 1821 reforms.

In 1848, the court districts, especially the individual courts' jurisdictions, were once again reorganized. But these reforms still did not cause all the courts to become more accessible and complaints to be handled more quickly. To the contrary, in many ways the situation worsened.[15] The change for the worse was largely due to substantial expansion of the responsibilities of the lower courts to include civil disputes and matters of voluntary jurisdiction.[16] Moreover, after elimination of the police[17] and forestry jurisdictions, the lower courts had to deal with by far the most common crimes[18] – the cases of so-called petty crime, including simple theft.[19] As a consequence, the lower courts were presented with a whole series of offenses that they previously had investigated but did not have to adjudicate.[20]

While the lower courts were only able to do rudimentary justice to their own requirements for finding truth due to the increased work load, the situation in the upper courts and thus for serious crime, which was almost insignificant quantitatively, was another matter. In fact, exactly the reverse course of development can be observed there. Upper courts had their workloads noticeably lightened, and they had ever greater amounts of time to spend on serious criminal cases.[21] The concomitant enhanced presence of the state of law was consequently limited exclusively to major crime matters.[22]

In short, numerous reforms aimed at extending the rule of law locally and increasing access to courts. However, it was precisely that accessibility that was not achieved when it came to everyday crimes,

TABLE 3 *Court History before and after the 1848 Reforms*

Year	Jurisdiction	Number of residents	Number of justice offices	Residents per office
1847	Upper Hesse Province/ Marburg High Court District	121,685	14	8,100
1848	Upper Hesse Province/ Marburg High Court District	115,303	No information	No information
From March 1850 on	Upper Hesse Province/ Marburg High Court District	115,306	14	7,380
1853	Marburg Criminal Court District	95,125	14	6,795

Source: Author's calculations on the basis of the *Handbook of the Electoral Hessian Military, Court, and Civil State* and the *Electoral Hessian State and Address Handbook, 1823–1854*.

among them petty theft. To the contrary, court density deteriorated, despite any reform assurances.

The question thus remains why Maria Scherrer and others suddenly turned to the authorities in cases that a few decades earlier would have been settled out of court.

2.2 EMOTIONS AND HONOR

The answer that I would like to propose in the following pages goes back to the stolen articles. If the morsel of bread and the used shirts were significant emotionally and symbolically, were the opposing parties before the court perhaps fighting about something emotional or symbolic? At least in the Scherrer case – thus returning to the increasing tensions among those who lived on the margins – it appears to have been less, or at least not primarily, a matter of clarifying property issues; the protection of property as the justice system saw it, or restitution for the stolen articles, does not appear to be the only, or the primary, goal. Maria Scherrer clearly had a much broader conception of protection or restitution, and perhaps only of the support that she wanted to obtain through the court. Her concern was not to have the value of the bread and cap calculated exactly. If it had been a matter of getting back the bread obtained by begging, there would have been possibilities to achieve an out-of-court settlement, even for a single mother. People knew each other and could have found a forum to resolve that conflict, for example, could have turned to the clergyman or another village authority figure to serve as mediator.

But Maria Scherrer did not do that, because she was concerned with more than restitution for property. After all, Zimmermann had not stolen just anything, but rather an item key to the everyday life of the children, even if materially of little importance: the result of their day's work. Consequently, for her son it was about a fundamental aspect of his existence, that is, about his right to obtain food in that manner – the mother claimed precisely that right by reporting the incident. Begging was not actually an officially recognized right but instead was the basic problem of "work-averse individuals,"[23] to be combatted by any means, no matter how ineffective, in a very slowly evolving modern state. That fact makes Maria Scherrer's logic even clearer: she was exploiting the state of law's institutions while still not accepting the state's content. For her, the report was evidently about clearing up who was allowed to engage in what conduct toward whom and how the laws of social behavior were to be determined – not about enforcing property rules of whatever kind.

Does that describe a generalizable pattern important for explaining the many petty thefts, or rather why they were reported, or is Maria Scherrer an individual case? Were petty thefts also reported because they were not considered just stealing but also encroachment on relationships? Could the offenses, precisely because of the symbolic and emotional significance of the stolen articles, be regarded as insults,[24] or – as Paul Cassia writes – as "accusations," "expressions of suspicion," or "metaphors" for whatever?[25] Should such an offense sometimes be interpreted as an offer for a relationship – as anthropologists have found for the thefts committed by Cretan shepherds?[26] If the victim's action is thus ascribed a further – possibly even central – significance, what does that mean regarding the motivation for reporting a theft? Did the victim respond with the full force of a report, which necessarily involved public justice, in order to have the opportunity to articulate individual social demands with the help of the new state of law's instruments?

Let's turn our focus back to the Electoral Hessian conflicts. The 1849 case of the theft of a wagon ladder along with the wagon shafts and draft pole, involving distantly related neighbors, arouses at least some suspicion that this was not just a simple property theft. In that case, too, the articles were of very little value, and there was every opportunity for an out-of-court settlement. And yet the theft victim, the forty-two-year-old peasant Johannes Imhoff, did not take advantage of the opportunity to resolve the matter informally. Upon following tracks in the snow at night after discovery of the theft, he immediately suspected that the offenders were members of the neighboring miller's family. The obvious reaction would have been to confront them at once or the next day. It also would have been obvious for him to do so, because he was a peasant who owned enough land that he was to all appearances adequately supplied with food[27] and thus was probably on about the same level socially as the neighboring miller. The social and physical proximity as well as the course of events give rise in this case, too, to the following question: Was the incident reported because it was about more than just things? Did Imhoff get police help because he wanted to make sure that a conflict of this significance was tried in an official forum?

The relationships were even closer in the next case. The local citizen Raab accused a servant, previously convicted several times, of having induced the twelve-year-old son of Raab's widowed sister-in-law to steal the used shirts of his deceased brother and give them to the servant.

The servant in turn sold them.[28] Four shirts were involved; the local appraiser estimated their value at twenty silver pennies apiece – on one hand a really small amount, but on the other, they were the shirts of Raab's deceased brother, the son's own father. In this case, a twelve-year-old boy had thus committed a theft within the family, and precisely that fact was made public by the boy's uncle because he reported the person who had allegedly seduced the child to act. Formulated differently, Raab's own nephew had to go to court even though very small amounts were involved; in this case, too, an out-of-court settlement would have been the obvious solution.

One of the most confusing cases in this regard is the theft from the day laborer Brandeis already mentioned. As was said later, Bernstein's lover supposedly claimed to Brandeis' wife that Bernstein had stolen Brandeis' hat in July 1851. However, it should be recalled in this context that "theft" is perhaps too strong a word for the fact that Bernstein had taken a hat that Brandeis had forgotten while chopping wood at the wood lot and that was still lying there late in the evening. The lover, a thirty-seven-year-old single tailor's daughter, was thus the person to whom the original report could be traced. As became evident in the course of the investigation, she had denounced her former boyfriend Bernstein. But it was Brandeis who filed the report. He knew the defendant well; they worked together and they both came from the same class of day laborers.[29] The difference in his social position from that of Bernstein's former lover, who was after all responsible for the original report, was only a matter of degree – however, there was a considerable age difference of at least fifteen years between the single tailor's daughter and Bernstein. In the court proceedings, the situation became so confused that Brandeis and Bernstein in the end offered each other the hat – or as the record of the proceedings reports, "The defendant was brought forward and declared regarding the ... hat that he was not satisfied that the hat would be given back to Brandeis .... Brandeis declared that he wanted to give up the hat. The defendant declared that he did not want the hat, either."[30] The former lover then claimed that Bernstein had tried to convince her to testify in the court that the hat was a gift from her. However the story played out, the case was about something more than and different from restitution for property. It was about a relationship structure that was to be decided by indictment before the state judicial institutions, before the public in court, to "obtain justice." However, "justice" in this case, too, did not just mean acknowledgement of certain conceptions about property. Instead, in the Brandeis case, questions regarding male–female relationships appear to have been the object of the trial, or rather the accusation of thievery seems also to have had a thoroughly defamatory intent. The public court venue was just the right place to put forward that insult.

In the Mengel case, too, much indicates that charges were not filed just to resolve property issues. Central to the case was a serious theft from the bookseller Elwert. After a long period of searching in vain for suspects in the course of which the Marburg police authorities had quite unsystematically targeted a series of suspects with relevant prior convictions,[31] a tailor by the name of Daniel Götting spread the rumor almost a year after the crime[32] that a certain Mengel was the perpetrator. How could this rumor surface over a year after the offense? In this case as well, relationship problems seem to have been the main issue. Mengel and Götting had known each other well long before the theft. One was a tailor's assistant and the other was a cloth-maker's assistant; both had prior convictions and had probably served their sentences together in Marburg. In addition, they were distantly related to each other.[33] Mengel came under suspicion because of an incident that initially had nothing to do with the Elwert theft. To start, Balthasar Mengel had initially accused Daniel Götting of having stolen from him. On that basis, the house of Götting's girlfriend was searched.[34] However, the accusation proved baseless. A short time later, charges were brought again. This time, Götting claimed that Mengel had burglarized the bookseller Elwert's establishment. Mengel denied everything and stated without hesitation for the record, "Götting filed completely false charges against me to take revenge."[35] He made this accusation at every interview and repeatedly maintained that he had found new evidence for this claim. He stated, for example, that Götting told his brother that, "He wanted to pin one on me; I was supposed to get sent to the castle, even if I didn't get anything more than having to sit [in jail] for a while."[36] (The prison was located in the Marburg castle.) Then he said, "... [F]alse charges were brought against me."[37] The case was drawn out for a long time, and Mengel and Götting repeatedly accused each other of being thieves. Nothing could be proved – to stay with legal terminology – beyond the shadow of a doubt. This case, too, makes abundantly clear that in the eyes of the offenders and victims, property crimes could to all indications be about more than acknowledgment of certain property rights.

In summary, people from the lower class who knew each other accused one another before state institutions of stealing things that were of less material than emotional value. Thus, they sought out state authorities to settle conflicts that they would have settled on their own a generation or two before – that was the case even without state authorities having on their part encouraged such conduct by organizationally expanding their presence. These were thus cases of "use of justice" as described by Martin Dinges for the Early Modern Period: The public venue of the court was actively sought out to frame a conflict that in fact did not necessarily conform to the juristic viewpoint regarding either the conflict's definition or ideas for its resolution.

2.3 A QUESTION OF HONOR?

At least from the perspective of offender and victim, it was thus less a question of property, as the jurists firmly maintained in the countless pages of the investigative records, than of recognition, of relationships, at least of "personal matters." What exactly does that mean? As I intend to maintain, at issue was perhaps the most important things a person had: in contemporary terms, honor, rights of individuals who feel wounded, demands for recognition of social position, and restoration or re-establishment of relationships. That should not mean that there were not questions of property or negotiation of property rights, not least of all because property more than anything else in the nineteenth century defined people's social and political position – for example, the right to vote. Furthermore, the "acquisitive crime" aspects could be significant – especially in the case of major theft. Sometimes the "survival crime" aspect may have played a role – for example, in the case of the two children who tried to snatch rolls away from another child on a forest path.[38] But – as Josef Mooser indicated – these petty thefts, when charges were brought, also expressed conflicts between people who lived at the lower margins of society and were fighting for acknowledgment of their rights. The material and the emotional, property and honor were (and are) more closely related than is apparent at first glance.[39] This phenomenon is especially familiar from divorce proceedings in which exhaustive disputes about cups, chairs, bed linens, and stoneware pitchers went on endlessly when the issue was really emotions, relationships, and identities.[40]

While the complaints focused on the loss of hats, washtubs, and bread, relationships and personal negotiations were also on the agenda. Furthermore, the real or supposed theft of a used hat was brought before the court because the hat itself, in its non-material meaning, represented an essential element of personal identity.

But why did people seek out the court to fight about their honor, and why did people do so by accusing someone of theft? There are many reasons why the nineteenth-century theft trial presented the opportunity to argue about personal identity. One reason derives from the specific situation in which both victims and offenders lived in rural society around 1850. As stated, the situation was shaped by intensifying social differentiation and social tensions in a very small geographical space. People especially seriously affected by such conflicts because of their precarious situation were involved in the theft proceedings before the court. They filed charges for the most insignificant theft, perhaps even for some property conflicts that were the result of a simple misunderstanding. People who had their backs to the wall but stayed anyway and did not seek the solutions that many others in their situation would have sought – emigration – viewed the conflicts with neighbors, distant relatives, or even just day laborers from the neighboring town as disputes which would be resolved most effectively by state institutions. In a situation involving living circumstances that had become precarious, they no longer chose the informal way of fighting back. They went to court, but unlike the situation previously in the Early Modern Period, not because they lacked the "ability to reach agreement" or possibilities for "ritual forms of reconciliation." They brought charges so that they could negotiate before a public forum about their own position and their position in relation to others in this broad group that lived on the margins. They used the courts "as a settlement authority, a kind of counter-public or public supplementing that of the tavern or the street."[41] They did so because they were all the more dependent on strengthening their own position in a situation – as shown – of strongly intensifying differences within a class of people living on the margins. When material and social resources, as well as legal and religious differences, gained importance, social positions had to be defended with all the means available.

The mention of personal identity in the context of trials for theft also reflects a change in the legal treatment of crimes against honor introduced at the beginning of the nineteenth century. The theft cases treated here dealt with conflicts that a few decades earlier would have been approached as defamation conflicts, indeed, would have led to a defamation lawsuit. In the Early Modern Period, defamation conflicts had at their core – as Nils Minkmar established – "debates about a person's identity." The identity of a person was publicly called into question, and the struggle for restoration of honor was at the center of the trial.[42] That also meant that people attempted "to secure a place in society ... by using abusive language."[43] The struggle over position and thus personal identity in Early Modern Period defamation trials was of course not conducted in the abstract terms of identity construction but very graphically, if not to say extremely concretely. In the typical defamation trial of the Early Modern Period, one person or another was typically accused of being "a whore," "a knave," or just "a thief." The overwhelming majority of accusations that then led to a defamation trial were couched in these three terms.[44] Unfortunately, the investigations that analyzed these charges in greater detail are missing. Consequently, we do not know why, for example, in a region such as Lippe during the eighteenth century almost a third of all defamation cases involved thievery charges.[45] In the nineteenth century as well, abusive names such as "knave" and "commons [*Allmende*] thief" apparently sometimes continued to play a significant role in honor conflicts.[46] Basically, however, it is evident that these accusations could be heard less and less frequently in the general courts of the nineteenth century, for one simple reason: the possibilities for pursuing a suit regarding honor were radically reduced. The court was no longer to be the stage open to all equally where battles regarding personal identity were to be fought.

While persons from all classes could fight for their honor before the court in the eighteenth century, that changed in the nineteenth century, especially because the concept of honor had changed. Instead of matter-of-factly assuming, as in the eighteenth century, that every person – aside from representatives of so-called dishonorable occupations – potentially had honor, it became a matter of common sense, at least in the nineteenth-century middle class, that honor was very unequally distributed, being class-dependent, and thus was very unequally actionable. Essentially, according to that logic, only men from the middle class and nobility possessed the scarce resource "honor," and only they could claim it.[47]

This revaluation of the honor concept was also reflected in the new legal system. Thus, in the General National Law for the Prussian States – which of course was not considered exactly the most modern of the reforms – it was held that defamation suits between "persons of low class" were to be handled in abbreviated civil proceedings and without appeal. In addition, the severity of the penalty was to be determined by the class of the persons involved, that is, the lower the social position of the injured party, the less the chance that the defendant would be convicted.[48] In Hesse, "private defamation," that is, defamation that was not directed against representatives of the authorities, was to be followed up only with "considerable fines" and only at the "request of the injured party."[49] However, injuries of this kind in particular had constituted the vast majority of defamation suits; precisely in such cases had the question of a person's social status been relevant. Now only injuries directed against "persons of authority" were considered "qualified injuries."[50] Thus, a completely different offense structure was defined, i.e., disputes with the state or city authorities, that is, conflicts that were more likely to have occurred in the course of disturbances, food revolts, or bread riots.

A similar devaluation of the traditional defamation charge can be seen in the 1849 draft of the Hessian Criminal Code. That draft proposes that "honor grievances" only be punished with a maximum of four months in prison. Furthermore, Article 264 states, "The severity of the penalty depends [on] ... the seriousness of the charge ..., the kind and extent of the dissemination ... the personal circumstances of the injuring and the injured parties, and the magnitude of the damages incurred."[51] The light penalty here compared to that of the Early Modern Period is striking and amounts to devaluation of the crime. In addition, given the changed honor conceptions in the nineteenth century, the clear indication that the personal circumstances of the parties involved were a factor raises a flag; it means that persons from the lower classes had to reckon with a lesser penalty than representatives of the nobility and the middle class. A consequence of this revaluation was that the lower classes had little prospect of success in defamation suits because their honor had been for the most part denied.[52]

In fact, honor complaints did actually decline rapidly in the nineteenth century. After the mid-nineteenth century, the number of defamation complaints in Electoral Hesse handled by the general courts fell continuously.[53] Furthermore, crime statistics show that there was a strange parallel between theft and defamation offenses.[54] Property crimes in the nineteenth century rose in inverse proportion to the decrease[55] in defamation complaints listed in the crime statistics for the Early Modern Period.[56] This trend can be very clearly seen in rural areas; for example, in the Landgraviate of Klettgau during the seventeenth century, 13 percent of the crimes reported were property crimes and 45 percent were verbal injuries. At the end of the eighteenth century, 59 percent of all convicted criminals had been charged with theft and only 3.4 percent with defamation.[57] For the Marburg Court District the numbers are likewise unambiguous. During 1849 there were still eighty-four property crimes as opposed to sixty-nine defamation suits, while in 1862 there were ninety-four property crimes and just eight defamation complaints.[58] Of course, in this context it cannot be overlooked that these supposedly unambiguous numbers frequently conceal the fact that defamation suits were no longer admitted to general courts but instead were subject to action under administrative criminal law[59] – but even this change is indicative of a redefined honor concept. In short, in the nineteenth century, theft seems, in both quantitative and especially qualitative importance, to have superseded defamation as the central – and especially the most common – crime, one that demanded reporting.[60]

The preceding pages have provided at least one answer to the question of why materially worthless objects, which nevertheless had great emotional and symbolic meaning, led to court proceedings. The court provided the necessary stage for addressing questions of honor; the court guaranteed the public venue required to establish honor. Furthermore, questions of honor had a dimension that really was very difficult for the opposing parties alone to unravel; for this, resort had often been made to superior authorities even in the Early Modern Period.

At this point a further new question arises: Why were conflicts about questions of honor, personal identity, and recognition of subjective rights now, in the middle of the nineteenth century, negotiated in property crime trials,[61] apparently with great frequency, and not in trials for immoral behavior, brutality, or fraud?[62] I already emphasized that an affinity existed between defamation and theft in that the most common defamation charge brought in court between men in the eighteenth century was the accusation that one party was a thief. Obvious is also that property could often be emotionally charged, and an injury to such property – especially in the case of very personal articles – could have been quickly interpreted as a personal attack. Yet it is still necessary to explain why the accusation of theft in the eighteenth century led to a defamation proceeding, while the same accusation in the nineteenth century could end in a property trial.

Notes

1 Harriet Rudolph, 2001, in her study on the embarrassing state of criminal justice in the Bishopric of Osnabrück during the eighteenth century, points out that in addition to a "pretrial waiver of sanctions" the trial itself might also be waived, that is, there was willingness not to try minor offenses. A further possibility, especially in the case of minor offenses like simple theft, was to tighten up the trial (243).

2 That is the case especially for complaints regarding provision of subsistence, but also for honor offenses. Certain forms of property crime undoubtedly belong to

this category. See also Barbara Krug-Richter, 1997; Joachim Eibach, 2003, 300, even explains the fact that in Frankfurt during the eighteenth century almost 60 percent of the victims and offenders in property crimes did not know each other by asserting that non-strangers were reported less often, "Personal relationships between the antagonists encouraged searching first for conflict settlement possibilities outside the courtroom."

3 See the overview study on infra-judicial practices (*L'Infrajudiciaire*) by Francisca Loetz, 2000.

4 To find such solutions, the attempt was made to "formally establish public openness" and to bring in third parties; see Barbara Krug-Richter, 1997, 227.

5 In terms of a paradigm, the handling of complaints regarding provision of sustenance should be mentioned. See Ulrike Gleixner, 1994, 115; such cases were always submitted if no other option for a solution was found.

6 Claudia Töngi, 2004, 48. Scholarship for the nineteenth century assumed for a long time that intervention of the justice system was a matter of course; this assumption was based on the notion that the modern state is omnipresent and allows no option for a decision by the general public in a positive or negative sense.

7 In using this term, Martin Dinges, 1993, is referring to the circumstance that the public exploited institutional offers to make courts available to deal with disputes, in exchange for or in combination with other non-institutional possibilities for conflict resolution. Central to the process is the proposition that intervention of the court did not necessarily result in an accepted ruling but instead had as its goal enhancement of its power in the actual conflict. The justice system, or rather the executive authority itself, was not in a position in terms of personnel or even the institution to assert a legal monopoly in preference to the public's practices.

8 Only if family dependency relationships literally or figuratively played a role was there any hesitation about deciding a conflict before the state authorities – for example, in the case of real or symbolic father–son relationships in which the son supposedly robbed the father. In the legal sense, they were generally so-called family thefts that might occur between relatives but also between a sales clerk and a merchant. Furthermore, so-called simple family thefts, involving goods of little value, were not subject to reporting, or were only pursued further if a "request for punishment by the injured party" was present; see Law on Procedure, 1848, Article 7. (The 1877 Code of Criminal Procedure and Implementation Act, Second Book, Third Section, Article 156 makes a similar statement.) Thus, the merchant Friedrich Guckemus definitely attempted before making a report to confront his sales clerk Peter Hartenstein, who was ultimately convicted of theft; 266 Hanau 203, Report of the police administration, May 1, 1850. There was a similar constellation in the case of the schoolboy Bloh. In this case, the teacher had taken the first step toward carrying out independent sanctions, and only when those sanctions did not prevent the boy from committing further thefts was he reported; 266 Hanau 145.

9 There are no studies on this subject for the nineteenth century, aside from a few peripheral analyses such as that of Otto Ulbricht, 1995b, who comes to

the conclusion that few thefts from homes were reported. For Lippe at the end of the eighteenth century, Michael Frank, 1995a and 1995b, describes a similar process of increased willingness by the public to file complaints, while the number of *ex officio* complaints dropped.

10 See 268 Marburg 11. In that case, seventeen-year-old Louisa Fisher, by occupation the daughter of a day laborer, was stopped by gendarmes on the way to Frankenberg, a small town north of Marburg, and asked what was in her basket. She opened the basket and a sheepskin came to light – which immediately made her suspect of having stolen the sheep and killed it. Just days later, a shepherd reported the loss of a sheep. No case other than this one has survived in which the constabulary played an active role in a property crime report.

11 The division into districts (*Kreise*) was thus in no way identical to the division into justice offices; in fact, a district variously encompassed one to three justice offices. In addition, the offices in Lower Hesse were divided up very differently from those in Upper Hesse, so that a uniform number of people per district was not achieved, either – resulting in a varying number of people per district. Originally, none of the justice offices was to cover more than ten thousand souls, but this could not be consistently realized everywhere; see Reinhard Wulfmeyer, 1971, 178.

The newly created Province of Upper Hesse now encompassed a larger area than the previous Upper Principality, and the population therefore increased from fifty-five to one hundred thousand. In addition, the Mainz offices and the Earldom of Ziegenhain had previously been added to the territory. All subsequent calculations were based on the *Handbook of the Electoral Hessian Military, Court, and Civil State*, 1821, and the *Electoral Hessian State and Address Book*, 1823ff. The specific territorial shifts were taken into account in reforms. At the top was the Marburg High Court, which was subdivided into a senate for civil matters and a senate for the criminal jurisdiction. In addition, disciplinary matters for officials were handled here, and it was also the court of second instance for lower courts; F. Oelzen, 1867, 15. On the level below, eleven justice offices and one regional court were created. Before 1821, in addition to the government of Marburg, which had been equally responsible for administration and justice, there had been a whole series of institutions concerned in part or exclusively with legal matters: the College of Trustees (*Pupillen-Kollegium*), among its responsibilities guardianship matters of nobles directly subordinate to the overlord; the Consistory Court (*Konsistorium*), among its responsibilities impregnation complaints; the "Criminal Court," which had taken over special inquiries into "awkward matters"; and the "Fiscal Office." Below this higher level of government on one hand and "Special Courts" on the other there had been nineteen offices in the separate areas of the Upper Province, each headed by a senior official. These senior officials had lower and voluntary jurisdiction, were responsible for investigation of petty offenses, and acted as administrators.

12 On this subject, see Monika Wienfort, 2001, who posed precisely that question for her study on patrimonial jurisdiction.

13 Before 1821, there was a senior official, an office secretary, and usually an assistant for each office; after 1821, there was a justice official, an office secretary, and an assistant.

14 See the calculations for Lower Hesse in Stefan Brakensiek, 1999, 51ff. At that location there were 4,240 residents per senior official in 1822; compared to the numbers provided by Brakensiek for the Westphalian period – 1813 – the 1822 numbers represent a decided change for the worse.

15 On October 31, 1848, the "Law Concerning Creation of New Administrative Districts" was issued. The result of the reform was, among other things, that the administrative and justice districts were no longer identical. The only change in the division into justice offices was that the Rauschenberg Justice Office no longer belonged to the Marburg High Court District. Just as important was a further law of October 31, 1848, which heralded "establishment of courts and state agencies at the courts." But the law did not actually go into effect until March 1850. The law stated that there should only be high courts, justice offices (or lower courts), *Schwurgerichte*, and the high court of appeal in Kassel. The regional courts were dissolved; only the Kassel Municipal Court was to remain. The "special courts" such as the university court and the military court were also to be retained; see the 1848 Law on Establishing Courts, Article 1.

The Marburg Regional court was finally dissolved by a regulation of March 21, 1850 (1850 Dissolution Regulation), and its responsibilities were assumed by three newly established justice offices.

While the justice offices were responsible for an average of 8,300 residents in 1823 and for 9,000 in 1831, there were 8,100 residents per court in 1847 and 7,380 in 1848. Furthermore, on July 7, 1851 – we are now in the restoration period when much of what had been considered good and proper in 1848 was abolished again because it was considered all too revolutionary – the dissolution of the provinces was reversed. Marburg was reinstated as the capital of Upper Hesse. As at the same time the lower courts were divided into criminal court districts, and the boundaries of the Marburg Criminal Court were not identical to those of the high court, the revision of the reform again led to changes in the lower court boundaries. The basis for the calculations is the 1854 *Electoral Hessian Court and State Handbook*.

16 As the voluntary jurisdiction in particular made up a considerable part of the justice business – also in rural areas – a large additional work load must be assumed.

17 A course of development in the "police system" (*Policeywesen*) had thus come to an end, a course which had begun at the end of the eighteenth century with the debates about the responsibilities of "good" police practice. At that time, criticism was directed at the police for being an institution that had responsibilities from all three different power areas. Indeed, the police of the eighteenth century were equally responsible for administrative, judicial, and executive tasks. Limitation of police tasks to the realm of ensuring safety had been an especially important requirement of numerous liberal legal reformers. They viewed the comprehensive police concept of the Early Modern Period as a relic of the absolute state. See Karl Härter, Lothar Schilling, and Michael Stolleis, 1996.

18 In 1848, that applied to offenses punishable with a fine of up to fifty thaler or three months of confinement. In a new 1851 revision, the jurisdiction of the lower courts for these crimes was expanded once again in that their area of discretion was no longer to be limited by any maximum sentence guideline; see the 1851 Law on the Administration of Justice.

19 With the 1851 law revision the responsibilities of the lower courts were expanded for a fourth time. It was now stated that all the offenses requiring punishment of up to two months in the workhouse should be tried by the lower court. See the 1851 Law on the Administration of Justice, Article 3. However, with regard to property crimes, it did not say that second theft offenses were to be handled by the lower court, because they were in any case to be brought before the criminal court. Regarding sentencing for a second theft offense, see Wilhelm Koch, 1855, 4.

20 The 1821 Edict on Organization clearly stated in Article 46 that the criminal senate of the high court was to be responsible for "findings on offenses which were investigated by the regional courts and justice offices and which [were] not to be punished either by the police or with torture."

21 A clear hierarchy of crime types thus became established unofficially. The few cases of murder, high treason, grand theft, and robbery could be handled in depth, while mass crimes had to be dispatched with increasingly reduced efforts. This development becomes clearly evident from a glance at the changes in the ratio of residents per high court or criminal court. Comparison of the situations before and after the justice reforms shows that the ratio of responsibilities was clearly improved by the successive size reductions of the high court districts. With the October 1848 law, the division of the Electoral court system into four high court districts was changed such that there were now to be six high court districts (1848 Law on Establishing Courts Article 24). A new revision followed in 1851, so that now there were only two high courts, one with its seat in Kassel and one in Fulda. At the same time, the function of the high courts was again redefined, leading to their devaluation, because a considerable number of their responsibilities were assumed by the newly created criminal courts. Criminal courts were established at the same locations where high courts had previously existed. In the new Kassel High Court District there were six courts of this type: in Kassel, Eschwege, Rotenburg, Fritzlar, Marburg, and Rinteln. In the new Fulda High Court District there were only three: in Fulda, Schmalkalden, and Hanau. The criminal courts were responsible for about the same crimes as the high courts had been previously. Furthermore, they were equivalent to the high courts in that they were administratively comparable units. Thus, there was a total of nine criminal districts, and those criminal districts corresponded approximately to the justice offices that had previously been combined to form a high court district. At the same time, there were changes. In general, it can be stated that the criminal court districts were smaller than the high court districts.

An exact comparison of the 1851 situation to the 1854 situation (in 1853 the Frankenau Justice Office had been located in the Marburg Criminal Court District) shows that in 1854, four fewer justice offices belonged to the Marburg Criminal Court than had three years earlier to the Marburg High

Court District. The following justice offices had been eliminated: Frankenau, which was merged with Frankenberg; Neukirchen; Ziegenhain; Marburg III, which was for the most part merged with Marburg II Justice Office; and Treysa. The Oberaula Justice Office was added. In 1851, the Marburg High Court District encompassed sixteen justice offices; in 1854, there were still only twelve. That means that in 1848 there was definitely a slight improvement in the ratio of residents to high court or criminal court; however, compared to the considerable improvement that the revision of the 1848 laws brought about in 1851, the 1848 improvement was of little consequence. In other words, the ratio of residents to high court or criminal court did not change permanently until the 1948 laws were once again revised.

22 Moreover, a further easing of the high courts' burden can be observed when their number increased. The number rose already in 1851 when criminal courts were introduced, assuming many of the high court functions. With the 1851 legal changes, the high courts had become entities which now, divided into chambers, were supposed to monitor the course of preliminary investigations and trials, and to organize those activities. See the 1851 Law on the Administration of Justice, Article 4. The jurisdiction of the criminal courts was exercised by a presiding judge and two further court members. These criminal courts were to be responsible for complaints regarding offenses against the sovereign, insurgency, press offenses, second and third theft offenses, and dangerous thefts. In those cases, they had to lead the investigations and to adjudicate. They also served as the appellate body for the justice offices of the particular criminal court district.

23 According to the terminology of the repeatedly reissued prohibitions on begging.

24 See Yves Castan, 1998.

25 Paul Sant Cassia, 1998, 193.

26 See Michael Herzfeld, 1998.

27 The circumstance that his daughter was already married to a twenty-six-year-old man implies a certain level of prosperity, which would allow provision of a dowry. It was obviously also guaranteed that the couple could feed themselves; otherwise consent to marry would not have been given. Imhoff also speaks of a "courtyard," arguing for property holdings in the middle range; see Brigitta Vits, 1993.

28 266 Hanau 297.

29 Still, Brandeis had enough income that he was married. At least at the point when he got married, he was judged to be in a position to find income. However, that fact also implies that the social and economic differences between the two were not fundamental but rather a matter of degree.

30 268 Hanau 29, Hanau session record, April 10, 1860.

31 266 Marburg 72. Thus a thrice-convicted cloth-maker's apprentice without property was suspected, then an Elisabeth Schmidt, who had been convicted multiple times of theft and vagrancy, and finally, a typesetter with money for emigration from an unknown source.

32 This had happened in July 1848; Götting filed his complaint in April 1949.

33 266 Marburg 72, Interrogation of Daniel Götting, April 30, 1949.

34 266 Marburg 72, Interrogation of Balthasar Mengel, April 12, 1949.
35 Ibid.
36 266 Marburg 72, Interrogation of Balthasar Mengel, April 5, 1949.
37 266 Marburg 72, Interrogation of Balthasar Mengel, April 12, 1949.
38 268 Hanau 111.
39 Claudia Töngi, 2004, 114, shows that even when it was a matter of things of little value force was quickly used, because possession had such great symbolic importance. Or as Chris Hann puts it, "... [T]he ways in which people relate to the objects in their environment play a vital role in forming their social identities," Christopher M. Hann, 1998, 2.
40 See Sylvia Möhle, 1997. See also Claudia Töngi, 2004, 115ff; she states emphatically that the "social significance of conflicts about possession" was not "exhausted in safeguarding material property" (115).
41 Peter Wettmann-Jungblut, 1997, 255.
42 "In defamation conflicts, it was a matter of debating about the actual identity of a person: Had the defamatory statements sullied the person, as the accusers said, or accurately labeled and thus exposed him/her, as the accused sought to demonstrate[?] In very rare cases, the court confirmed the defamatory statements that were actually infamy. As a rule, words spoken without discretion were nullified by the decision of the court." Nils Minkmar, 1996, 323. See also Michael Frank, 1995a.
43 Michaela Schmölz-Häberlein, 1999, 143, "In that way an individual could express that he/she was someone, that he/she had a justified place in society which was to be respected." See Albert Schnyder-Burghartz, 1992, 335.
44 See Nils Minkmar, 1996; Laura Gowing, 1993. Women were as a rule slandered as "whores"; Michaela Schmölz-Häberlein, 1999.
45 Twenty-six percent of the insults involved calling a person a "knave," whereby "knave" could mean many things, among others, that the person was a thief. See Michael Frank, 1995b, 325ff. He continues, "The accusation of theft clearly dominated in defamation cases in Heiden. There the accuser alleged that the person in question had stolen the property of others; the desired objects ranged widely from wood, articles of daily use and work implements such as knives, rakes, and plows to horses, geese, sheep, flax, food such as bread, meat .... (327)." See Bernd Plaum, 1990, 177, who writes that the criteria for defamation were satisfied when someone said "thief."

Nor can Ralf-Peter Fuchs provide an explanation for "how significant the concept of property was for honor and criminal justice. Among slanderers, accusations of property crimes quite clearly predominated in comparison with other relevant matters of criminal law." Ralf-Peter Fuchs, 1999, 292f.

See Joachim Eibach, 2003, 228: "The frequent use of defamation indicates the universal condemnation of property crime in urban society."
46 See Claudia Töngi, 2004, 117.
47 See Ute Frevert, 1991, 225. Accordingly, a specific kind of honor associated with physical and sexual integrity was attributed to women. In the nineteenth century, offended female honor was restored within the middle class and nobility by men, for example, in a duel. On female honor, see Susanna

Burghartz, 1992. Unfortunately, there are no detailed studies on honor in the nineteenth century that also distinguish between different levels of honor.

48 ALR II, 20, 10th Section. See Reinhart Koselleck, 1967, 97.

49 Heuser, 1853, 70.

50 Ibid.

51 Published in Ernst Schubert, 1993, 50ff. This is the 1849 "Draft of a Criminal Code for Electoral Hesse," which of course remained a draft.

52 Illustrative of the denial that a feeling of honor existed among members of the lower classes is the statement of a Prussian district judge: "With rare exceptions, defamation trials only occur here among the peasants and the serving classes. Only in the rarest of cases can it be assumed that the basis for the complaint is the intention to obtain legal satisfaction for offended honor, because the majority of the parties have almost no concept of honor and only press charges to hurt the other person with court and extra-court costs." Quoted according to Christina von Hodenberg, 1996, 193.

53 From 1849 to 1851 there were more than fifty defamation complaints annually; after 1851, there were generally less than ten such complaints annually.

54 Gerd Schwerhoff, 1991, 458, table, shows the following for the late sixteenth and early seventeenth centuries: 17 percent property, 20.9 percent violence, and 3.6 percent verbal abuse. It should be noted here that what was classified as violence was frequently defamation.

55 The proportion of defamation cases had already begun to fall in the eighteenth century but was still larger than that of thefts. Not until the nineteenth century, when theft became a mass crime, did defamation complaints slowly slip to the edge of insignificance. Peter Wettmann-Jungblut, 1997, 121ff; similarly, see also Ulinka Rublack, 1998.

56 For example, it can be shown for Freiburg that defamation was the most common offense: over 30 percent of the complaints in the sixteenth and early seventeenth centuries involved verbal injuries; see Peter Wettmann-Jungblut, 1997, 104.

57 Peter Wettmann-Jungblut, 1997, 143.

58 See the analysis of record book 286 Marburg 91 in the appendix of the German edition.

59 Thanks to Sylvia Kesper-Biermann for this information.

60 Peter Wettmann-Jungblut, 1990, 151, table 6; in this case, the development does not appear until about 1840 for the crimes tried before the Baden offices. In contrast to the other mass crimes of the eighteenth and nineteenth centuries such as field and forest crimes, both crimes were reported by the public itself, if at all.

61 On this subject, see the discussion of Lawrence Stone's theories in Michael Frank, 1995b, 240, "In feudal society, honor and estate reputation were the highest values, and consequently crime was particularly directed against people. In contrast, money and market relations were the basis for social organization in middle-class society; for that reason crime increasingly targeted property."

62 A conclusive answer cannot be provided, if only because all the crimes would have to undergo a precise analysis. That cannot be achieved, nor are there studies that provide a commensurable analysis.

3

The Theft Happens – from Act to Crime

3.1 THE "TRANSLATION PROBLEMS" IN REPORTING A CRIME

One of the reasons why theft involving both need and personal conflict understood by contemporaries primarily in terms of honor was handled on the level of property has to do with a "translation problem."[1] The translation problem between the rural world of the day laborer and the legal sphere of the radically reforming state is evident in a variety of circumstances. One such circumstance is the situation associated with reporting a crime. At that point, another actor came into play: the gendarme. According to Article 142 of the Code of Criminal Procedure, it was the constabulary (*Gendarmerie*) that received the crime report and thus put down the statements from the general public in written form. Beside the gendarmes – and police headquarters in large towns like Marburg [2] – it was frequently the mayor who received the report.[3] On rare occasions, an intermediary, for example, a school teacher, might be brought in.[4]

Who were these police employees and how did they record the report? We know little about the social composition, mental disposition, or even the financial circumstances of the police in rural areas during the second half of the nineteenth century.[5] Research has only been able to shed light on a few aspects so far. What is certain is that most of the operational staff were former soldiers until deep into the last third of the nineteenth century, and that, as already usual in the Early Modern Period, individuals who otherwise would have been entitled to poor relief were allowed to continue performing low-level police services.[6] It is agreed that until the *Kaiserreich* was founded the actual police presence was limited.

Furthermore, because of the enormous population growth beginning at the latest at mid-century, police density decreased relative to population size.[7] With regard to the quantity and the quality of police training, equipment, and duty scope, modernization was a long time in coming. Professionalization of the police forces, that is, systematic training, compensation not in the form of doles, standard uniforms, and clear service guidelines, was slow to set in.[8] Thus, at mid-century the relevant manuals still stated that police employees were very susceptible to corruption and that it would be helpful to introduce denunciation payments because police employees would then perform their work more conscientiously. In addition, they were expressly admonished to confront even "poor, helpless citizens" "without partiality."[9] Likewise, they were urged to conduct themselves with "correctness, strict regularity, and prompt obedience."[10] It was also still emphasized that "being able to read and write"[11] – apparently not a given – was a requirement for police service. Finally, in addition to the task of ensuring safety, the police had responsibility for the old "police task" of providing social services.[12]

Well-trained police employees in the modern sense only existed in large towns like Marburg, where four field wardens, four police sergeants, six night watchmen, and one senior night watchman were in service at the middle of the nineteenth century.[13] Not until almost the end of the century was a special criminal police unit introduced; in Marburg, two officers in criminal service were appointed for the first time in 1906.[14] In the rural areas, there was usually no police force, as the localities were too small to maintain their own police sergeants.[15] There, in a great reform effort, the attempt was made instead to establish a special group of police employees: gendarmes organized as in the military and housed in large groups. They changed their deployment area often so that they did not become too familiar with the population and were thus protected from corruption.[16]

The gendarmes or policemen were thus in most cases the people who recorded the reports. What did "recording a report" involve, and what happened with accounts about persons accused by someone of being a thief?[17] What methodologies for creating records guided transformation of the description of an experience into a report? How did writing down reports structure, construct, and organize the definition of what happened, and thus also of what was to be the central focus of the legal process to be initiated?[18] How was it possible for the "translation problems" cited to arise? As important as the answer is for my purposes, it must remain an approximation, because not the account but only the report has survived. Nevertheless, I will attempt an approximation.

The report that was created in May 1850 from the account of the merchant Friedrich Guckemus by the Hanau police administration through the efforts of Police Commissioner Kunz is typical for many reasons. It is entitled, "Report Filed against the Sales Clerk Peter Hartenstein from Dorndorf for Breach of Trust."[19] For other proceedings the titles were very similar, "Report Filed against...,"[20] because people generally did not go to the constabulary just to report a theft but to report a suspect. Very rarely – usually when a high-value theft was involved – was a report against an unknown party enough. In the majority of cases, the person filing the report, as a rule the theft victim, believed that he or she knew who had committed the offense. Consequently, the investigation had a clear direction from the outset and an exact determination of the actors' and actresses' roles in the crime; both the person robbed and the suspect were named. The crime – mostly theft, in this case "breach of trust" because it was theft by a subordinate – was also captured right in the title. There was no ambiguity here, either with regard to the offender or the offense.

How was the content of a report prepared? How was a likely complex event, perhaps having a long history and under some circumstances also including completely different people, transformed into a clear, succinct report? To understand this transformation, it is important to know that the actual goal of a report was the translation of complex accounts into legally defined terminology. This translation was the responsibility of the police employees. Through this act, the investigation was guided in a particular direction, a possible perpetrator and offense named, and a potential result of the investigation prefigured. Furthermore, the reports constructed a relationship setting that organized the entire legal negotiation process: an offender, who was a thief; a victim, who was a person robbed; and an offense, which was theft. Whether the merchant used the charge "thief" to strip the apprentice of his honor; whether the apprentice appropriated things to settle a conflict with the merchant's wife (it appeared so in the further course of the investigation); or whether it was about ambiguous instructions that led to mistakes – all of these uncertainties were translated into the unambiguousness of a theft offense.

Crucial was that such a translation remained plausible. This plausibility in particular, without which a report would never have led to a preliminary investigation, much less a main trial, was created by means of a series of techniques that taken together contributed to underscoring the truth and objectivity content of the basic statement captured in the title – a certain offender committed a theft. "True" and "objective" were understood to refer to that specific piece of reality which was of importance for the legal definition of theft.

What were the techniques that produced truth and clarity and were designed to make a complex translation effort invisible? They were techniques to produce authenticity, consisting for example in recording the report in the first person singular to give the impression that the report giver had portrayed the facts in just that manner, that it reproduced an account verbatim, or that it was an eyewitness report. Of course that was definitely not the case; in the end effect, it was certainly not a stenographic word-for-word record, but an account that had considerably changed its form though a textualization process in which not just the eyewitnesses had participated. Such reports could not be verbatim reproductions of accounts if for no other reason than that the text version was not completed until the report had been completely communicated orally.

If a report had attained the required degree of plausibility, it did not take long for the court to take action. The court rules of procedure established that after such a report had been recorded it was to be disclosed to "the responsible public prosecutor,"[21] that is, the state procurator, who immediately had to launch a preliminary investigation, provided that he saw "substantial suspicion [of a crime]."[22] This record thus constituted the basis for the decision about whether or not to initiate a criminal proceeding. In the case of Peter Hartenstein, the process moved forward quickly. On the actual day of the report, State Procurator Hille started an investigation proceeding against Hartenstein and appointed an investigating judge who interrogated the suspect, likewise on the same day, and ordered a certificate of character from his hometown. Even in cases about things of little value, the state procurator reacted promptly to being sent a record and initiated a proceeding without delay.

When an event was translated into a report, a construct claiming objectivity and thus truth took shape; the construct included victims, offenders, a defined crime, and an institution that established a true interpretation of the scenario. At the same time, other possible accounts dropped from the radar. The fact that the one interpretation of events had first come about in the interaction between the victim and the gendarme during the act of textualizing the report was inconsequential. Just as unimportant was the circumstance that complex factual information having to do with relationships and emotions, perhaps with questions of honor and recognition, or with a status problem, were reduced already at this stage of the process to simple questions of property and theft.

At the same time, the police sergeants, gendarmes, and field wardens, who had been able to read and write at the middle of the nineteenth century but still had never completed a training course in such subjects as police records services, forensics, and fundamental legal concepts, had acquired the most basic essentials of modern police work. Taking down a record that was correct in a legal sense was thus a first step on the path to assuming a new identity as a policeman. These new policemen were defined not only by new uniforms, a regular pay structure, and independence from doles; the modern professionalism now required also evolved from preparation of these and similar records, producing a new police outlook. The more practiced this police outlook, the more smoothly the translation of an account about thieves, everyday articles, and people from the immediate vicinity could be transformed into a theft report.

Whether "translation problems" were concealed behind the report thus produced, or whether the resulting report should instead be called only a reformulation or even clarification of the facts, may vary from case to case and can no longer be determined because the sources are missing that might provide information about the "true course of events." The answer also depends on the way in which this segment of the legal process is viewed. Given my suspicion that here, too, questions of honor were transformed into questions of property, indications of translation problems can definitely be discerned in any case.

3.2 WHAT IS PROPERTY – WHAT IS THEFT?

Why were the local gendarmes and policemen apparently so quick to declare these conflicts about property if honor was also involved? How was it that they no longer considered the conflicts described to be disputes about relationships and identities but instead to be robbery and theft? It would be too simple merely to point out the gendarmes' lack of legal training or even to criticize them for not being up to the demands of the as-it-were professionalized state of law then evolving. To the contrary – as already shown – they complied very precisely with the form requirements and the criminal code standards. After all, from the manuals and the research instructions of the state attorneys and the investigating judges they gained detailed information on how jurists trained in the field saw the handling of such cases. As I will argue, it was instead the contemporary debates within the middle class, and especially among jurists, that caused these "translation problems." But what issues could generate such a powerful effect that people only heard "theft" when it was perhaps also a matter of more complex questions of honor, personal identity, and social position?

This question leads back to one of the central debates of the nineteenth century, to the property debate. But it is also a question that leads back to rural society and thus to the point of departure, Anton Zimmermann. As already indicated, questions of property occupied nineteenth-century contemporaries like almost no other topic. For example, property questions were of central importance for Immanuel Kant, who linked the existence of middle-class society with a new property concept, and even for Johann Gottlieb Fichte, who viewed property and contract theory as closely connected. Many less well-known contemporaries grappled with the question of what property was, how it was connected to law and contracts, and how the necessity of private property could be justified. Views on the subject definitely cannot be called consistent, and many points were the subject of vigorous debate. For example, the Frenchman Abbé Morelli disputed the value of private property and argued in favor of communal sharing of goods. Morelli's position is not far removed from Pierre-Joseph Proudhon's catchy formulation, "Property is theft." Contested was furthermore whether the issue was not the right to use or "usufruct" rather than the right to property.[23] No less hotly discussed was the question of whether every natural person should have an equal claim to property. The debate, on one hand surprising in view of the fact that the most important principle of contemporary property theory was specifically the right to acquire property, appears on the other hand entirely logical, considering that slavery was *de facto* and even to some extent *de jure* practice in the colonies.

In addition to philosophical discussions on an abstract level, some very practical debates developed on questions of property during the previously described agrarian reforms, which mainly focused on fundamental restructuring of property relationships. In this process, a multilayered, graduated property concept that did not consider possession and ownership as one and the same and that differentiated separate use rights was transformed to a uniform, comprehensive "modern" property concept.

Central to this modern property concept, however, was not only that right of use and disposition were regarded as one but also that property was linked to the likewise new constructs of "citizenship and personal identity."[24] At the latest in the moment when the human being, in the wake of John Locke, was defined as a being that in his natural state had property in the form of his own person, a connection was established between the right to property and the right to self-determination – to use a modern concept. That insight was accompanied by a moral and natural revaluation of the absolute property concept. Just as the right of all people to unrestricted personal development was declared to be a core element of middle-class society, the right to own property was defined as a central concern of the new middle-class society. Such a middle-class society considered its most important task, after protection of life and freedom, to be protection of property. People not granted this protection, or denied the right to this protection by middle-class society, were accordingly defined as being outside that society. Just recall colonial policies that denied "natives" both the right to protect their own lives and the right to own property, not only legitimizing appropriation of their land but virtually forcing that on them.[25] Bear in mind, too, the gender system inherent in the liberal property system; women were also denied the same protection.[26]

As with the Bill of Rights and the Declaration of Rights of Man and Citizen (both 1789), the right to own property was codified. At least in law, a process had come to an endpoint where a multi-layered property concept was replaced with an absolute one viewed as being directly related to the core conceptions of middle-class society. Now only the relationship to things, to a piece of land or animals, was called "property"; encompassing all facets of use and complete availability, the relationship was understood to be a legal title allocatable to the individual, thereby associating it with personal freedom.

Thus, according to the liberal tale of progress spun by many contemporaries and broad portions of present-day historical scholarship, the private property system, civilization, and middle-class society had become an indissoluble whole that was, moreover, morally and also economically superior to all other systems.[27] Precisely this form of private property system appears to have gained acceptance in Electoral Hesse as well; after all, the 1852 constitution there states, "Property or other rights and authorities can be used for purposes of the state or of a community, or of such persons as exercise the rights thereof only in cases and forms determined by law and with full compensation in advance – to the extent that compensation after the fact is not legally prescribed for emergencies."[28]

Of course, if we leave the normative level and look more carefully at practice and other discussions outside jurisprudence, both the theory of an indissoluble whole of the private property system, civilization, and middle-class society and the notion that such a modern absolute property concept had gained acceptance in the nineteenth century prove erroneous. Only consider the living circumstances of the people who lived "on the margins of subsistence." They could only survive because they practiced many forms of borrowing, leasing, shared housing, and barter of social capital for money or natural products, in short, because they were integrated into a network of informal economies that determined everyday life in rural society, economies in which the barter principle was frequently coupled with relative property concepts.[29] Thus, in nineteenth-century rural society and in many parts of urban society, use of equipment was exchanged for conveyance of goods; a book was given as a present and an increase in social capital was expected in return.[30] People were also entangled in complicated property networks through various family credit systems,[31] making it impossible to determine property relationships that were unambiguous in the modern sense. As a consequence, there can be no talk of the absolute property concept prevailing in the nineteenth century, much less of that concept being linked to a certain quality of civilization or even to middle-class society.

But the fact that many of philosophers, jurists, and members of the public with literary interests were intensively occupied with questions regarding property cannot be ignored. They were convinced on the one hand that the modern property concept must prevail, and on the other, that the concept was closely linked to certain standards of civilization. The debates about property were ongoing and persistent. In this context, John Brewer and Susan Staves speak of the "rhetoric of absolute private property."[32] Naturally, these debates changed the concept of property, for the long term, of course not in the sense that programs once planned were carried out but in the sense that the programs were repeatedly re-negotiated and their form thus slowly transformed.

What do these debates and property practices have to do with theft? A great deal – because property, middle-class identity, and freedom were not just debated in contemporary discussions. In trials as well, where plaintiffs claimed that something had been stolen from him or her, it quickly became a question of property and the discussion very soon turned to how close the relationship was between the things and the people. In that way, the process of negotiating law was a place where property was discussed. Or, putting it another way, the process was a "legal model for assigning things to people."[33] Regardless of whether that was the central issue of interest to the accuser and the accused, regardless of whether also at issue was perhaps the problem of who took what position with regard to which object and which people, the simple question of property ownership always quickly became the main focus of interest in the court proceeding. Property was considered a guarantor for middle-class society and civilization, and consequently, that property was quickly threatened. What was therefore more obvious than to regard a complaint about theft of an article brought by a member of the lower class to be primarily a property issue?

Moreover, against the backdrop of the highly charged nineteenth-century property debate, a complaint in which someone maintained that he had been robbed would almost necessarily have been reduced to what it really might be: a question of property. When the central meaning of an absolute property concept for middle-class society was being discussed, the interpretation that the theft of bread obtained by begging was primarily a question of property literally thrust itself into consideration. That issues regarding social relationships and social positioning could be connected to the complaint about the loss of a hat, and that the property language was only a code, as in the case of Early Modern Period honor conflicts in which someone was reviled as a thief, was readily overlooked. Such was all the more the case, as I will show in the following pages, because during the nineteenth century a second important change took place in this context.

The second important change was the slow, imperceptible shift in the legal definition of theft, which is admittedly not easy to trace because of its numerous ramifications. In particular, the legal definition of theft changed such that here, too, all relationship aspects gradually disappeared and the monetary value of the article was given priority. An offense in which many circumstances, and relationship components as well, had played a role ultimately became a crime devoid of any interpersonal dimensions. In the same manner as has already been seen in the case of the property concept, the shift in meaning within the legal discourse forced a complex social event – the encounter of Anton Zimmermann and the beggar boys is undoubtedly representative – to be reduced to a property issue. Thus, not only the debates about property and middle-class society but also the legal discussions about theft contributed to the lasting change in the treatment of robbery complaints in rural areas during the nineteenth century.

What did the changes in the legal definition of theft look like?[34] In the first half of the nineteenth century there were two main categories of theft: so-called simple theft and qualified theft. "Simple theft," that is, stealing an article without violence and other aggravating associated actions or circumstances, was in turn subcategorized first, as "small"(petty) theft,[35] second, as "large" (grand) theft, or third as "repeated" theft.[36] Important for adjudicating the "simple thefts" was the value of the article stolen and the frequency of theft, that is, the extent of repetition.[37] Added to these as a further criterion was the "malice displayed and the extent of criminal intent."[38] The length and form of the penalty were supposed to be determined on that basis.[39]

Although the "simple theft" category changed little in the nineteenth century, very substantial changes can be observed in the second theft category, the "qualified theft" – changes that contributed to the disappearance of the relationship dimensions of an offense and thus in no small measure to the "translation problem." This category encompassed property crimes that were considered dangerous "to people or property"[40] and also morally reprehensible.[41] Included were special offenses which had taken place at particular crime scenes[42] and at particular times,[43] for example, at night, or in which the stolen article had a special character, for example, was classified as a sacred object.[44] Also included were thefts in which there was a "special relationship of the thief to the person sustaining damages."[45] Thus, for example, thefts among heirs, thefts within families,[46] or thefts in the home were considered "qualified."

All these dimensions of the offense were no longer supposed to play a role in judging a property crime after mid-century. In various reform steps, aspects of an offense such as relationships and all the quality definitions relating to the stolen article,[47] aside from its material value, were declared irrelevant. Thus, in 1851 the category of articles stolen from various trusted locations[48] no longer appeared; the bleaching meadow, the marketplace, the fair, the public street, the field – none of them had a role any longer in precisely defining the meaning of a theft. Other significant offense circumstances, for example, time point, were dropped from the 1871 criminal code.[49] The particular reprehensibility of thefts from children and "the feeble-minded" and the relationship framework in which such offenses occurred likewise now only played a minor role, or none at all.[50]

Reduction in the criteria according to which thefts were judged was at the expense of many previously important elements, such as relationships, place, and time. Now it was no longer the sum of article, relationship framework, place, and time that decided the severity of the penalty and therefore structured the legal system. Now things were no longer to be part of a complex relationship framework within which their significance could be repeatedly regenerated. Instead, they were objects which had a value that had been established once and for all, devoid of any symbolic attributes. That explains a little better why Maria Scherrer's account, which was probably multi-faceted, already had all the elements that did not revolve around the value of the articles stripped away during the first textualization process as the complaint was recorded, and why very little was necessary to produce a "translation problem." The legal perspective caused all the personal dimensions of the conflict to disappear.

The change also explains why many records after mid-century were exclusively interested in determining the exact value of the stolen articles and why many case descriptions consisted only of a list of value estimates and exact information on the height, depth, and width of doors, walls, or other hurdles that may have been breached. Anything else, for example, the relationships of victims and thieves, was entirely omitted. The contexts of the offenders and of the things were no longer mentioned. The words that people hurled at each other, and the misunderstandings that became apparent in the process, were legally irrelevant. Making off with an article was reduced to what it could only still be, a theft.

3.3 THEFT, HONOR, AND PROPERTY

What did this narrowing of the property concept on one hand and the theft definition on the other – as can be observed in the nineteenth century – mean for the question of why people stole and why the offenses were so intensely deliberated in court? As to the question of why people stole, discussions about changes in property and theft concepts only provide indirect answers, or they give rise to the heretical question of whether the thefts were thefts at all and whether it makes any sense to continue speaking of an increase in thefts during the nineteenth century. However, for the question of why the state offices devoted themselves so intensively to investigating the whereabouts of articles that were relatively worthless in material terms, the discussions are of considerable importance.

When Maria Scherrer went to court and stated that her son and his friend had their bread stolen, people thought around 1850 that they knew exactly how this event was to be interpreted legally: simple theft, or – on the basis of the violence threatened by Zimmermann – robbery. To determine the severity of the punishment, all means available had to be used to ascertain the exact value of the stolen articles, and umpteen persons had to be interviewed to learn precisely how much bread the boys had obtained by begging, because the value of the stolen bread could only be established in that manner. Just that, the value, was decisive in determining the sentence for the alleged property crime: Not place, time, or relationship, only the value of the article was among the legally relevant facts that had to be worked out. That other factors were involved in the confrontation between Zimmermann and the boys – and that the mother's complaint was more about protection of her social position, which due to numerous changes in rural society during the nineteenth century had become precarious – was not recognized by the state criminal prosecutory offices called in. That was the case for the simple reason that they considered all the interrelationships illuminating the circumstances of the offense to be irrelevant and therefore paid no attention to them. Furthermore, the fact that perhaps other property practices still existed and that Zimmermann, the boys, their mother, and all their relatives and friends lived with different property concepts was not of interest; or precisely because of the disregard for all the circumstances surrounding the offense and offenders, that fact was erased. In addition, Scherrer's defense of the children's illegal begging practices was likewise ignored. The jurists and gendarmes concerned with the case saw the conflict against the backdrop of the new property system and the changing theft definition.

Maria Scherrer and Anton Zimmermann for their part probably still did not know very much about the legal attempts to reorganize the handling of theft and property. From their perspective, these debates may have had little relevance, at least with regard to the offense or to the question of whether to file a report or not. But other circumstances were also only of secondary importance. The prosaic fact of hunger may have been present, but it did not necessarily drive a person to steal a piece of bread when that person had just eaten. In particular, it would not drive a person to be involved in a lengthy, expensive court proceeding. In any case, Zimmermann appears not to have stolen from need or because he wanted to initiate a redistribution process. Above all, he and his likes probably did not steal any more than his predecessors. In all likelihood, negotiating such conflicts in court had just become more common, because in the eyes of the offenders and the victims, questions of social identity were also being negotiated, and because for offenders and victims the original recourse, defamation charges, was scarcely available anymore. But there were other reasons as well. One has to do with the new significance of property and its new definition, or rather the need to establish that definition, as well as the fact that jurists and gendarmes who heard of a theft had to quite automatically believe it was a property crime. Another reason relates to Anton Zimmermann and the beggar boys. They lived in a precarious situation in which a great deal had begun to totter, and only they, young men on the margins of rural society, remained in their ancestral place, their village in Electoral Hesse, so they needed to affirm their social position more urgently than ever. The less they had to lose in material terms, as indicated at least by the low amounts from a legal standpoint they were bickering about, the more was at stake with regard to honor – at least so they believed.

An injury in the everyday framework of relationships (and that includes in particular those things which were stolen in cases of petty theft) was enough to ask questions in court about a person's own position. That Scherrer and the many others who filed complaints were not only negotiating the terms of their personal identity but were also, through their complaints, making possible initial development in court of new property concepts is another story, to be told in the next chapters.

Notes

1 Willibald Steinmetz, in his study on the English labor court system, shows that the decisive hurdle in implementing particular court goals was the transformation of experiences into the terminology of jurists; Willibald Steinmetz, 2002, 496–498.
2 Marburg had police headquarters in 1853.
3 It is also often said that the administrative district office received the report. As in 1851 the administrative district offices also housed the police department, the latter was probably meant.
4 266 Hanau 145. The suspect was a schoolboy.
5 Research on police in the Early Modern Period has increased in the last few years, not least of all thanks to the large-scale project of the Frankfurt Max Planck Institute for European Legal History; see Karl Härter, Lothar Schilling, and Michael Stolleis, 1996. Research has also been advanced by the debate initiated by Schlumbohm on the laws that were not implemented; see Jürgen Schlumbohm, 1997; Peter Nitschke, 1990; and André Holenstein, 2000. Since the pioneering work of Alf Lüdtke, 1982, research on the nineteenth century has largely emphasized police work's disciplinary character, giving rise to the perception of a smoothly functioning police force that closely regulated the citizenry and supported the authoritarian state; also see the works of Albrecht Funk, 1986, who speaks of a "internalization of the state power monopoly" that can be observed in the nineteenth century, and of "forced civilization primarily of classes other than the middle class" (315) by the police. This image was called into question by more recent works on police practice when it became clear how "less-than-professional" the police still was in the nineteenth

century; see Bernd Wirsing, 1991 and 1992. For Electoral Hesse, there are no solidly researched analyses that examine the police as a social group. Ralph Jessen, 1991, provided such a study for the last third of the nineteenth and the start of the twentieth century in the Ruhr region and pointed out, among other things, that recruitment changed. While in the middle of the nineteenth-century policemen were predominantly former soldiers, from the last third of the century on they came primarily from the worker class. See also the study of Andreas Roth, 1997.

6 In Marburg this remained usual for night watchmen, for example, until the beginning of the twentieth century; see Bruno Schmidt, 1982, 81.

7 This also means that the military remained important as the actual power keeping order, for example, in strikes or disturbances, until the beginning of the twentieth century. Ralph Jessen, 1991, 62, shows for the Ruhr region, for example, that the density of the police was decreasing.

8 See Andreas Roth, 1997, 122, who, using the example of the Hamburg police, vividly portrays the situation, which was not reformed until the 1870s.

9 Gustav Zimmermann, 1849, 1119.

10 Gustav Zimmermann, 1849, 1124.

11 Gustav Zimmermann, 1849, 1147.

12 Ralph Jessen, 1991, 99.

13 Walter Kürschner, 1934.

14 Bruno Schmidt, 1982, 82.

15 Under the 1848 Law regarding Police Administration, which went into effect on October 29, 1848, the communities were responsible for police administration, and according to Article 4, were supposed to "provide from their own resources the personnel, equipment, and facilities ... that [were] generally required for proper management of the police." Of course, the constabulary was also present in cities. Thus, for example, Frankfurt, a city that in the middle of the nineteenth century had about seventy thousand residents had at its disposal a constabulary force of fifty-five men; see Kurt Kraus, 1997, 41.

16 They thus represented the reverse image of the policemen of the Early Modern Period, who came from the lower classes and were ill-prepared for service, never mind being adequately paid and having a conception of duty in which varying, situation-driven activity consistently outweighed strict application of abstract standards. According to the report of a Württemberg court, the new policemen were supposed to provide for the enforcement of law and order more effectively than the previous forces, "in keeping with their uniforms ... and military organization in general, and ... by performing their duty promptly, of course with the result that they effected reporting of more violations of the existing police imperatives and prohibitions than was the case for earlier policemen and court body guards (*Hatschiere*)." Quoted as in Bernd Wirsing, 1992, 65.

17 Only in recent years has the interest of historical scholars in the formal and material contents of administrative and justice records begun to grow. Willibald Steinmetz, 2002, 182ff, still limits himself to a large extent to description and analysis from the standpoint of how the records can be evaluated; Claudia

Töngi, 2004, in her work about Uri, treats in detail the formal and material side of interrogation and of records overall. From the standpoint of literary scholarship, see Michael Niehaus, 2003 and 2005. From the perspective of recent administrative history, the collected volume by Peter Becker and William Clark, 2001a, is informative, as are the recent overviews by Peter Becker, 2002 and 2005.

18 History scholars have grappled with this question in recent times, after a more documentary manner of reading the sources had prevailed for a long time; on this subject, see the criticism of Dominick LaCapra, 1987, regarding Ginzburg's pioneering study *Cheese and the Worms* (Carlo Ginzburg, 1979). Researchers then deliberated with increasing intensity about the constructed contents of the criminal records, but attempted to read them through a truth filter to "cleanse" the authentic witness statements of possible additions by the scribes. Making the sources' constructed contents themselves the point of departure for the analysis is still a rather rare endeavor.

19 266 Hanau 203, 1850.

20 266 Hanau 297, 1850; see also 268 Marburg 91, 1854.

21 1848 Law on Criminal Procedure, Article 143.

22 In cases involving theft of articles with little value, a preliminary investigation was not performed; instead, the case moved immediately to trial in a lower court. In 266 Hanau, 297, 50, it took two days to initiate a proceeding, which in this case, because it was about things of little value, was conducted by the justice office itself.

23 See the informative encyclopedia article by Warnkönig, 1860.

24 Christopher M. Hann, 1998, 22.

25 See the informative study by Nils O. Oermann, 2003, 171–184, on the physical punishment practices in the German colonies. Recently, see Lauren Benton, 2002. See also the very stimulating collection of John Brewer and Susan Staves, 1995a.

26 Just recall wives' limited right of disposal and guardianship of women. For an overview of the subject, see the still relevant work of Ute Gerhard, 1997.

27 It should at least be pointed out in passing that this construct did not remain uncontested. Marx countered with a different construct in which the abolition of private property went hand in hand with the end of alienation, disenfranchisement, and poverty. He predicted this state to be a later stage of society's development. However, the people who assumed positive connotations for private property and asserted that this new ownership concept had already taken effect *de jure* in the nineteenth century were dominant. See Hannes Siegrist and David Sugarman, 1999a, 20; their collection is an attempt to contribute to description of ownership cultures beyond these two tales by the masters.

28 1852 Constitution, Article 22.

29 On this subject from a historical perspective, see Laurence Fontaine and Jürgen Schlumbohm, 2000.

30 See the more expansive essay of Beate Wagner-Hasel, 2003.

31 Andrea Hauser, 1994, 247, describes this phenomenon from another perspective: "The deficiencies and limited space demanded new ways of dealing with

things. An example is the use of a washing kettle by three parties, but also sharing housing in a very close space. The common use of material goods was more than necessary for survival; it required a particular form of solidarity and cooperation."

32 John Brewer and Susan Staves, 1995b.

33 Hannes Siegrist and David Sugarman, 1999b, 11.

34 Basically, a property crime was considered to be an offense which involved not only disruption of ownership (*ablatio* [carrying away]) with the objective of gain, but also the intent to appropriate the property for oneself, if the offense "went beyond the means to satisfy momentary hunger" – of course, that was only the case until 1851; Hermann Kersting, 1853, 664. That is to say, there was in the case of theft, too, a so-called act of necessity, as already recorded in the *Constitutio Criminalis Carolina* (1532), the first German criminal code (*Carolina*, Article 166). The act of necessity referred to the theft of food verifiably committed to urgently avert starvation (Otto L. Heuser, 1849, 206); this category of petty theft of food was eliminated in 1851. At that point, the difference between theft and fraud was unambiguously established and a process begun in the Early Modern Period came to an end. See *Carolina*, Article 160; on this subject see also Heinrich Janßen, 1969, 1–51. In the handbook of common German criminal law by Temme, theft is defined as follows: "Theft (*furtum*) is the illegal removal of someone else's moveable object from that person's safekeeping, with the intent of appropriating it for oneself and achieving unlawful gain from doing so"; Jodocus D. H. Temme, 1876, 340. Kersting collected similar definitions for the Electoral Hessian region; see Hermann Kersting, 1853, 659ff.

35 A "petty theft" was defined as a theft that was characterized by the pronounced material insignificance of the stolen object; see *Carolina*, Article 157. In Electoral Hesse, petty thefts involved articles valued at less than three thaler. Until mid-century, they were usually punished with fourteen to twenty-one days incarceration; see Hermann Kersting, 1853, 664.

36 Paul J.A. Ritter von Feuerbach, 1836, 292–313 also differentiates "common" (on one hand in the first, second, and repeated form, and on the other, in the large and small form) from "qualified" theft.

37 In Electoral Hesse, repeated theft was supposed to be punished with not less than two months in the workhouse; see Hermann Kersting, 1853, 673. In cases of more than three thefts, a considerable qualitative jump occurred; now higher level courts came into play that could extend up to the high court of appeals; see Otto L. Heuser, 1849, 286. In cases of more than three thefts, other criteria besides the value of the stolen goods were relevant in assessing the penalty: the number and severity of sentences to date, the length of the interval between punishment and the new crime, and the "characteristics of the recently committed crime"; see Wilhelm Koch, 1855, 18.

38 Wilhelm Koch, 1855, 26.

39 After all, there were various forms of penalties. They extended from being placed in irons to jail, the workhouse, or prison. Prison could consist of simple arrest or intensified arrest. One year in jail and any sentence in irons were severe ("painful") penalties. The workhouse never counted as one of the

severe penalties. One 1853 treatise states regarding public humiliation penalties still found in many edicts, that is, the pillory, jougs, and moving the criminal around, that they had fallen into disuse; see Otto L. Heuser, 1853, 40. As is generally known, their abolishment is considered a milestone on the way to the modern state of law.

40 Jodocus D. H. Temme, 1876, 348.

41 A moral explanation relating to the character of the offender was given here. Thus, at least the more severely punishable case of pickpocketing was decided in 1845 by a ruling of the Electoral Hessian High Court of Appeals; see Otto L. Heuser, 1849, 254f. Moral arguments were also used with regard to a more severe penalty for theft: [theft] with the "zeal and dangerous cast of mind of the thief"; see Otto L. Heuser, 1853, 105. A further argument for a more severe penalty in the case of qualified theft was that "the person whose property was injured by the thief was compelled to place particular trust in the thief or in state protection, and that the penalty had to be all the more severe if protecting and safeguarding the property appeared to have been rendered more difficult"; Wilhelm Koch, 1855, 27.

42 The topography of qualified theft was primarily characterized by the fact that in certain places, such as bleaching meadows, marketplaces, and fairs, theft "represented injury to trust in public safety" because the articles stolen there would have had to be given over to public trust; see Hermann Kersting, 1853, 665. In older German law, such public places were considered areas that had been enclosed to prevent intrusion and were therefore protected by special penalty measures. German law followed the basic principle from Roman law which held that the less possible a crime was to avoid, the more severely it had to be punished. Farm implements stolen from an open field belonged to this category; see Hermann Kersting, 1853, 676.

43 In Roman law punishment was already especially likely to be imposed for property crimes committed at night. Thefts during "an unusual emergency (fire or water danger)" should also be mentioned in this context; Jodocus D. H. Temme, 1876, 353.

44 Special qualities were attributed to sacred objects; i.e., church theft was already mentioned in Roman law and in the *Carolina* (Article 171); see Otto L. Heuser, 1849, 260–263. Other articles – only mentioned here in passing – were of such a nature that their theft was punished less severely or they constituted a special category. Examples are wood and fruit theft.

45 Hermann Kersting, 1853, 678.

46 Family theft, including theft among heirs, was documented with milder penalties. There was a common law tradition according to which theft was not even possible among blood relatives and spouses. Thus, the *Carolina* states that cases of a family theft "should not be officially prosecuted or punished"; see *Carolina*, Article 165. In an 1876 commentary, the following statement is made on the subject: "Imposition of penalties only on request and in less severe form is undoubtedly justified because the sanctity of family ties is involved"; Jodocus D. H. Temme, 1876, 354.

47 The only exception is sacred objects.

48 This category never went into effect in Electoral Hesse because of supplementary provisions, but it appeared in the 1851 Prussian criminal code and its 1859 third edition, which was authoritative for Electoral Hesse. Just recall the washing on the bleaching meadow or the animals in the pen. In the 1871 criminal code, a new reduction of complexity is evident in the description of the offense specifics.

49 For example, Article 218, 9, stating that theft in the case of "fire and water emergencies" should be judged especially aggravated, was abolished. However, theft at night was still treated as distinct.

50 Of these, only kinship and employment were still taken into account. The guest who was under protection in his own house had disappeared, just as had the factory worker who was to be punished especially severely for thievery when he had stolen in the factory. Conversely, however, a special "private" space protected from state interference was created within the family. Thus, thefts and misappropriations by "parents or grandparents committed against their children or grandchildren, or by spouses against the other spouse" were regarded as immune from punishment. In Roman law, the provision had been the reverse; the son had been able to steal articles from his father without penalty.

The 1871 Prussian criminal code thus created a protected space for married couples and parents or grandparents. Electoral Hesse made a qualitative step forward in 1863 (1863 Law on Criminal Procedure, Article 6) by still stipulating only that no official complaint could be filed in the case of family thefts; that provision replaced the regulation that only the *pater familias* was entitled to file a complaint. In turn, the precursors for that regulation had as their central focus persons who were closely related for purposes of inheritance law. The possibility of being exempt from punishment was transformed to mandatory immunity from punishment in the case of theft within a marriage or of theft by parents from their children.

In reality, the meaning of this new intra-familial space was different for women than for men, a development that was not reversed again until the end of the twentieth century, when rape within marriage was made actionable. On this subject, see Isabel Hull, 1996, 333ff.

Admittedly, thefts in which considerable obstacles had to be overcome or force was used continued to be subject to more severe penalties. However, unlike previously, the danger to the victim rather than the moral "inferiority" of the offender was the central focus. "Whether the offender encountered many or only a few difficulties has no effect; buildings and walled spaces are instead to be placed under special protection." Quoted as in Christian F. Müller, 1851, 129.

In addition, the potentially trivial character of simple theft went by the wayside. If at the same time the simultaneous trend toward increased penalties for repeat offenders is considered, it can be demonstrated that theft was constructed as a more serious crime even without any change in criminal law. The category of petty theft of food disappeared completely, and so-called simple theft was upgraded so that it could no longer be handled in the police court system. There was no longer any property crime of a trivial nature, aside from field, meadow, and wood theft, which meant criminalization, expansion of the statutory offense, and toughening of the penalties. The relatively severe penalties for repeat offenders also show that thefts were in no way viewed as trivial offenses, but as crimes to be severely condemned. However, at the same time, it can be observed that the severity of the penalties changed little or not in any clear direction. As is certainly well known for every type of crime, the kinds of penalties did change.

PART II

HOW LAW IS MADE

Evidence Production

Since the end of the eighteenth century, jurists and other representatives of the middle class had concerned themselves intensively with legal questions to achieve the greatest possible public effect, whether the subject of discussion was the social background of female child murderers or rumors of witch-burning. In the first half of the nineteenth century, the brutality of torture, the horrific conditions in prisons, and a penal system denounced in some quarters as disproportionately cruel upset the public. People also actively discussed the course of the secret written court proceedings conducted in most of the German states up to the mid-century.[1]

By contrast, questions relating to the preliminary investigation preceding the trial were of little public interest. Consequently, it was only logical that demands for reform took aim at criminal law, the prison system, and the manner in which justice was achieved in court. Furthermore, in many of the German states criminal law reforms and prison improvements were already occurring during the first half of the century, and finally, in 1848, trial reforms were implemented almost everywhere. The preliminary investigation, however, was not on the reformers' radar.[2] Certainly the preliminary investigation changed to some extent with the 1848 codes of criminal procedure; a tripartite division into the court investigative proceeding, the intermediate proceeding, and the main trial was established. Before then, there had only been a rough subdivision into preliminary investigation and main trial.[3] The tripartite division sought to make cross-checks possible among the individual stages of the process. Furthermore, cross-checking was supposed to be facilitated by introducing a series of new positions – state procurator and investigating judge (*Instruktionsrichter*), to name the most important – that were intended to correct each other.[4] By contrast, in the inquisitorial process of the Early Modern Period the preliminary investigation and the main trial were often directed by the same person.[5]

In short, individual procedures in the preliminary investigation had been changed by the court system reform; however, the structural basis had apparently remained the same. As before, the goal was to identify the offender and the circumstances of the crime, and as before, that was not supposed to happen publicly, nor could a defense attorney be brought in.[6] In this segment of the proceedings, the defendants thus had to shift as completely for themselves after 1848 as they had before in the inquisitorial process.

And still – according to the argument to be developed in the following pages – while no reforms worth mentioning took place in this area and the public debated enthusiastically about all kinds of legal matters, just not about the preliminary investigation, the latter changed fundamentally. The preliminary investigation was transformed so radically at about mid-century that Maria Scherrer and Anton Zimmermann became familiar with a legal system in the preliminary investigation which had not existed only a few decades earlier, and that was the case, even though no law to reform the preliminary investigation had been passed. What the changes were that apparently took place almost unseen and without being set in motion by a change in the code of criminal procedure is to be the focus of this part. How they can be explained and what background is important in this context must be briefly outlined in advance.

The manner in which justice was established in the preliminary investigation changed so markedly because the emphasis was no longer on exhorting a confession from the suspect or finding two witnesses to the crime who were of good reputation. In the inquisitorial process of the Early Modern Period, the focus of the preliminary investigation was to obtain a confession[7] or to find two eyewitnesses because only with a confession or two witnesses was a conviction possible and was the function of the preliminary investigation thus fulfilled.[8] Other evidence was purely of secondary importance.[9] A far-reaching improvement was introduced in the 1848 Code of Criminal Procedure; now, if sufficient other evidence was present, charges could be brought without a confession or witnesses to the crime.

The consequence of the significantly increased importance of evidence was that, although the preliminary investigation was still about the confession and witnesses, the search for evidence became just as important, if gradually not considerably more so. Furthermore, as evidence gained enormous significance, the entire preliminary investigation underwent changes more radical than any conceivable reform could have accomplished. New types of evidence were devised, new interrogation forms were developed, and new criminological types of evidence production were tested. At the same time, new types of texts were developed in which the new evidence could be captured; the "visual inspection report," the "house search report," and the "crime scene sketch" are only a few examples. Other, older procedures for evidence production, such as the "lookout description" (the *Signalements*, a special kind of personal description) were modernized.

But how significant were these new procedures for the question of how justice was established? Was it not, as contemporaries thought, simply a matter of better methods by which more certain knowledge of the crime or the possible perpetrator could be learned? That was not the case, more recent research maintains, emphatically pointing out that no procedure and no form is merely a "tool of knowledge."[10] Every procedure and every kind of textualization is, as the argument goes, an "assumption of power."[11] In the case of the preliminary investigation, this "assumption of power" consisted in creating new parameters to distinguish "true" from "untrue."

The new parameters created by which true was separated from false, cannot be read about in well-formulated new paragraphs of the code of criminal procedure – nothing on that subject is there. So in the following pages the individual improvements must be traced step-by-step in practice to establish what exactly they looked like and how they changed the process of establishing legal findings. It will become apparent that implementation of these new methods for describing and investigating possible perpetrators and crime courses was very closely associated with the methods that developed in the sciences of statistics, criminology, and jurisprudence. In fact, the new methods in the sciences cited and in the preliminary investigation went hand in hand, were intimately connected to each other, and cannot be viewed independently of one another; they were part of a much broader change in knowledge formation and types of knowledge production. Exactly what the new methods of evidence production were and what specific procedures of selection, description, combination, and representation they were based on will be examined in the following pages. At the same time, I will develop the theory that these procedures conformed to a principle of decontextualization and desubjectification that had a substantial claim to objectivity.

In the end, however, something else also changed in the preliminary investigation at the middle of the nineteenth century. At this point, considerable efforts contributed to the so-called professionalization of the actors involved, whether jurists or gendarmes. That being said, the concept of "professionalization" is just as inadequate (as will be shown in the following pages) as the concept of "disciplinization" – both only describe partial aspects of a process in which the characteristic that should distinguish a jurist or a gendarme emerged: a new outlook.

Notes

1 For extensive details relating to the legal reforms in the German federal states, see Sylvia Kesper-Biermann, 2007, 13ff.

2 Until today virtually no modern studies have appeared on preliminary investigations; see Andreas Roth, 1997, 18, who complains about that lack in particular and for his part concentrates on the investigative procedure. A debate about the preliminary investigation already criticized how frequently decisions that actually belonged in the main trial were made at the preliminary investigation stage; the debate did not begin to heat up until toward the end of the century. Of course, legal professional circles had already begun discussing the preliminary investigation at mid-century, but those debates did not have any great public value. I owe thanks to Alexandra Ortmann for this information. See Lothar Nagel, 1935, Otto Meiners, 1922; Helmut Haug, 1930.

3 Until that point, the inquisitorial proceeding had generally been directed, carried out, and completed by a judge or the presiding judge of the interrogation office. A distinction was made between a general inquisition and a special inquisition; the latter focused on a particular suspect, while the former more broadly investigated the crime itself and possible suspects. Of course, this formal distinction often blurred in practice and had already been completely dropped from many of the codes of criminal procedure in the eighteenth and early nineteenth centuries. See Heinrich A. Zachariae, 1868, 57.

4 According to this new division of tasks in Electoral Hesse, a state procurator was in charge of the proceeding in the case of crimes that were tried before a *Schwurgericht,* and the investigating judge on site had to seek instructions from the state procurator for important decisions, while the court to adjudicate later was not yet involved at this stage. The division of tasks between the state procurator, the investigating judge, and the review chamber is taken up in the 1848 Hessian Code of Criminal Procedure in Articles 150–156 and then Article 158f (see 1848 Code of Criminal Procedure). See also 1863 Law on Criminal Procedure, Article 107. This regulation was changed in 1863 to the disadvantage of the state procurator in that the investigating court was given a greater scope of action. See 1863 Law on Criminal Procedure, Article 110.

5 Another new feature was that the investigating judge on site ended the preliminary investigation with a final interview and an "organized summary of events" and sent the records to the state procurator in charge of the proceeding. The

latter then drafted the charging document on the basis of the final report and then sent it to the court with jurisdiction. See the 1848 Code of Criminal Procedure, Article 172, and the 1851 Law on Administration of Justice, Article 38.

6 On the position of the defender according to the Carolina and according to the 1848 reforms, see Johann F. Henschel, 1972; Alexander Ignor, 2002, goes into the weak position of the defender in the reformed criminal trial and explains that position as the result of the reform's goal, which was to achieve legal certainty for the individual and containment of crime.

7 The goal of the interrogations had been this confession, which in certain cases could also be induced by torture. See Harriet Rudolph, 2001, 123, on the restrictions and conditions for torture in the Bishopric of Osnabrück.

8 Insight into the practice of the preliminary investigation in the eighteenth century is provided by Harriet Rudolph, 2001, 120–130, and Rebekka Habermas and Tanja Hommen, 1999.

9 See Andrea Griesebner, 2000, 64, who restricts herself to this rather normative viewpoint. She says of the Ferdinandea (1656) that there were definitely convictions without a confession. As Griesebner argues, the *corpus delicti* was also important.

10 Peter Becker and William Clark, 2001b.

11 Robert Descimon, Jean-Frédéric Schaub, and Bernard Vincent, 1997, 14.

4

Techniques for Finding Truth – the Slow Production of the Modern State of Law

4.1 WHAT IS EVIDENCE?

The more important evidence became, the more unclear it was what exactly evidence actually was, when evidence was evidence and when it was only a false or even a bogus. Although the preliminary investigation concentrated increasingly on searching for evidence, only indirect indications can be found in the 1848 Code of Criminal Procedure regarding what is to be understood as "evidence."[1] Only a single paragraph referred explicitly to what was to be accomplished in the preliminary investigation.[2] Article 157 of the 1848 Electoral Hessian Code of Criminal Procedure, stated that the "objective facts of the case" were to be ascertained, the "proof of the perpetrator's guilt" was to be provided, and "collection of the [information] on circumstances that were the basis for assigning the penalty were to be carried out." There was not a word about how "collection" was to proceed. A Law on Criminal Procedure that took effect in Electoral Hesse in 1863 did not describe the task in any more detail.[3] Likewise, in the 1877 German Code of Criminal Procedure scarcely a word was lost on the substance of the work to be performed in the preliminary investigation.[4] Textbooks emphasized the "great importance . . . of the court preliminary investigation,"[5] but its exact form and thus the definition of what evidence was remained obscure.

Furthermore, instead of clear definitions of evidence or perhaps even guidelines for evidence collection being issued, the few instructions usual until then for evaluating evidence were rescinded. In contrast to the inquisitorial process of the Early Modern Period – and this is a second important difference – the so-called free consideration of evidence now applied, that is, there were no clear rules that determined once and for all what evidence was substantive and what was not. The *Constitutio Criminalis Carolina* (1532) defined not only just two possible types of proof of guilt, but also clear rules on how various types of evidence were to be assessed. For example, it was specified there that the statement of a low-class person was less substantive than that of a higher-class person.[6] Thus, an evidence hierarchy existed that was of course administered flexibly in individual cases but still did not provide *eo ipso* a great deal of room for interpretation. The elimination of rules of evidence was meant to facilitate judgment of a case outside the estates-based rules system that was at that point considered problematic, and in that way to contribute to greater equality of the law. However, as I would like to assert, this free consideration of evidence definitely did not necessarily lead to "individualization of the case,"[7] as contemporaries believed it would and some researchers today still do, and thus to a more just judgment of the individual suspect. Such an interpretation overlooks the fact that assessing the credibility of statements does not become more objective because there are no explicitly formulated rules that codify unequal treatment according to class, gender, or religion. Many rules regarding social, gender, and religious discrimination do not have to be written out at all and are still followed as a simple matter of course, as numerous studies from the anthropology of law have documented for present-day court events.[8] Such indirect, unspoken, and unwritten rules obviously existed in the nineteenth century as well.

Furthermore, the elimination of rules of evidence led to an absolute explosion of methods with scientific authority; the methods were to be used to check which evidence had what validity.[9] The result was development of technical departments for criminal investigation. At the same time, an ever-increasing number of evidence types emerged. Fingerprints are the best-known but by no means the only new evidence type that took shape in the course of the nineteenth and early twentieth centuries. As a consequence, the preliminary investigation was gradually transformed into an ongoing succession of new evidence compilations and increasingly elaborate means for checking the validity of the arduously prepared evidence. Sometimes the impression is that the preliminary investigation merely consisted in the uninterrupted production of new evidence that was to be prepared with the most scientific methods possible.

Who decided how these many new types of evidence were to be assessed, and what was true and what was false evidence, when the legal codes were silent and silence alone was no guarantee of a just evaluation of the evidence? In this context, the many new sciences that now proved useful must be mentioned: forensic psychology, which found the human body to be an almost inexhaustible gold mine of evidence, and criminology, which developed a regular catalogue of personality types that was supposed to give some indication of who possessed greater or lesser credibility, for example, as a witness, or who more or less had the capacity to impute a man or woman in a crime. Statistics, as well, made available important techniques for measurement of evidence. Emerging police science, with its special emphasis on precise observation, furnished gendarmes with new methods for evidence collection, and many more or less scientific methods proved helpful. Before these sciences and the criteria for evidence evaluation they developed are elaborated, the numerous new evidence types that emerged in the course of the nineteenth century must be examined more closely.

What was the evidence that now played such a great role in the preliminary investigation, especially in cases of property crime? A great deal that now was considered evidence had already played a role, if a somewhat secondary one, in trials during the eighteenth century. Much that was new was added; in addition, greater meaning was now attributed to all forms of evidence. Roughly five different forms of evidence production[10] can be distinguished: first, material that was produced using the knowledge resources in the investigators' own administrative office and that contained information about the suspect or other people. Criminal records, certificates of character, and lookout descriptions should be mentioned in this context. Second, in the course of house searches and crime scene investigations sketches and reports were prepared that had the character of evidence, and third, seizure lists and inventory lists were often associated with visual inspection, as were objects collected in evidence rooms that were meant to provide information about the perpetrator or crime course. Fourth, expert opinions had the character of evidence, and fifth, witness statements or confessions with probative force were obtained in interrogations.[11] These evidence types are to be examined more closely because they constituted the framework of criteria that decided whether the view of things formulated in a complaint was true or untrue in a legal sense.

4.2 EVIDENCE: CRIMINAL RECORDS, CERTIFICATES OF CHARACTER, AND LOOKOUT DESCRIPTIONS

Material which was produced using the knowledge resources of the investigators' own administrative office, and which contained information about suspects or other persons had already been usual to some extent in preliminary investigations during the eighteenth and nineteenth centuries, whether requests were made for certificates of character,[12] research was conducted in the archives, or lookout descriptions[13] were provided. The more data the administrative office had archived and the more informative this material was, the more promising these methods proved to be. The quality of the data depended both on the archiving methods and the communication possibilities. As both of the latter expanded in the nineteenth century, the documents in question were increasingly easy to access, and their importance grew as evidence in its own right was ranked higher.[14] What did these criminal records, certificates of character, and lookout descriptions look like in the middle of the nineteenth century and how did they structure the process of establishing justice in the preliminary investigation? Did they become "highly disciplined," that is, more objective and neutral, as Andreas Roth has maintained for the era of the *Kaiserreich*, or German Empire,[15] with the result that a more solid basis for establishing legal findings was found, completely as desired by the liberal reformers? Or can the development of these evidence types be described somewhat less positively, perhaps in less unambiguous terms, or simply as different?

Generally the most important documents, which the investigating judge acquired from other agencies, were the "Excerpts from Existing Judgments against the Accused" and the information about "Reputation and Financial Circumstances."[16] It can be said that these documents were routinely requested, even when a simple theft was involved, as can be seen in the case of "two pieces of narrow satin fabric twenty-eight and fifteen ells long" which were stolen in May 1849.[17] Certificates of character and criminal records were even obtained for children.[18]

At the request of the investigating judge, a so-called crime list was prepared using the "Excerpts from Existing Judgments against the Accused."[19] In addition to the crimes of the suspect, the list contained a series of other data that were usually listed individually, distinctly separated from each other by numbering: an exact designation of the crime, which in the case of thefts usually implied naming the article stolen, the sentence, and the particular court. At the same time, judgments rendered abroad were also mentioned. For example, in the crime list for the suspect Wiedersum, a goldsmith, the information that he had been sentenced "to four weeks in prison for embezzlement, [is based on] information from the Grand Ducal Municipal Office in Carlsruhe on October 17, 1839."[20] This indicates that the crime list was not just a carefully compiled personal document from the Electoral Hessian holdings but that the administrative office worked actively on the document and attempted to keep it up to date.[21] Furthermore, the collections of personal data were expanded in the second half of the nineteenth century.[22]

The certificate of character, which was likewise requested from the appropriate administrative offices and often not separated from the crime list, was likewise usually short and schematic. The introduction was a sentence about the person's financial circumstances, which rarely had to be listed specifically because they could usually be adequately described with the laconic comment "no assets." A brief sentence about "reputation" followed; in the best case, it indicated that the person in question had "earned a reputation" for being "loyal, diligent, and honest."[23] As a rule, it did not go beyond a list of two or three adjectives. In the case of women, the comment was now and then added that they "conducted themselves morally" and "never incurred reproach."[24] The negative attributions, which by far predominated, were rarely any more detailed. In that vein, it was said that the suspect had "abandoned himself to idleness ... and a dissipated life; complaints were lodged about him everywhere for misdeeds."[25] Only when the particular mayor, chief mayor, or justice official who had to provide information about reputation and assets knew the individual personally was there any deviation from this style.[26] In that case, "the parents, too, were good, honest people" was recorded here.[27] Or the reporting individual might have believed that a negative judgment required justification, as in the case of thirty-two-year-old Heinrich Fach. Fach did "not have a good reputation" because "his parents" had "neglected his upbringing."[28]

All these documents used dichotomic constructions like diligent versus dissipated, honorable and honest versus shiftless, frivolous, and untruthful. For females, morality tended to refer to sexual behavior, while men often had to prove their morality as defined by alcohol consumption, that is, in terms of moderate living.[29]

In this way, themes known from various contexts were recalled. They came from the "middle class value system,"[30] discussions of so-called social questions, and police discourse. In the middle-class value system, categories like "diligence and integrity," here often still used as the opposite of "aristocratic falseness" and thus in the sense of "authenticity and naturalness," and female "morality" as well as male "moderation" played an important role.[31] These attributes were known from the debate about the material and moral situation of the lower classes carried on heatedly in Electoral Hesse. In this arena, the "rabble," the

"Lumpenproletariat," but also the "peasantry" (*Landvolk*), in the words of Wilhelm Heinrich Riehl, were labeled with those terms, be it with cautionary or sympathetic undertones. Questions of alcohol consumption and prostitution were also of great significance in this debate.[32] In police discourse as well, for example, in the relevant manuals, the same terminology appears. The police authors had had their attention focused on hedonism and sensuality, and like the Berlin criminologist Merker, did not shy away from directly linking prostitution with alcohol and property crime.[33]

Certificates of character and crime lists also entered into this discourse and kept it going. At the same time, they lent the interpretations new authority because they made use of a specific narrative structure that was considered objective and impartial. What is meant by structure is the frequent numbering, the to some extent almost graphic subdivision into separate units of meaning, and the succinct style that were typical for the administrative culture of the nineteenth century. This ductus corresponds exactly to what Peter Becker and William Clark have described as characteristic of bureaucratic knowledge: "impartial, disinterested engagement of subjects and objects."[34] A special characteristic of this administrative language was the redundant use of the same adjectives whose meanings were like codes and an impersonal style that suggested objectivity by its impersonality.

As effective as this procedure may have been to gain authority in the contemporary situation, the texts are no more or less objective than the input from the context of the debate about the social question, where identical attributes were used.

Naturally, despite the self-styled view of contemporaries and many research theories to the contrary, the authors of these certificates of character were by no means just objective administrative officials but also proponents of genuinely middle-class values who described themselves as persons endowed with very special capabilities: the capability to "exactly" and "neutrally" observe and analyze suspects.

I will come back later to these new police force inventions, which can be observed indirectly in documents, but for now the immediate subject is the attributes used here that contributed to suspects being transformed irrevocably into figures of a very strange sort. The objects of police observation were not simply captured in the crime lists and certificates of character; instead, the suspects underwent a regular metamorphosis, changing into shadowy outlines of suspicious forms. Because the certificates of character and the crime lists only recorded data that the administration regarded as important, day laborers, school boys, shop girls, and cowherds became either simple prototypes of the lower class or the equivalent of what many contemporaries saw as criminals. In the certificates of character and crime lists, a "specific manageable reality" was thus created, as Stefan Haas worked out for other types of records in his study on the Prussian administrative culture.[35]

What exactly distinguishes these figures, which in so many ways recall the types from contemporary middle-class discourse, becomes clear from the records that deviate from the pattern. An illustrative example is a certificate of character that had not been written by a mayor, judge, or gendarme but instead by a man who was not socialized in the administrative culture of nineteenth-century Electoral Hesse, a certain Reverend Richter from Praunheim.[36] Richter prepared a certificate of character for a thirteen-year-old boy who was suspected of theft. Not that the youth was described in particularly positive terms in the certificate of character; to the contrary, he was characterized as "frivolous, stubborn" and inclined to commit "all kinds of pranks." Nor can it be asserted that the minister was any stingier with stereotypes than the representatives of the administration; indeed, he speaks of "drink" and of an "indolent, frivolous, and dishonest person." However, and herein lies the crucial difference, the two latter descriptions referred not to the youth who was the focus of the investigation but to his mother and father; the clergyman thus placed the youth in his family context and explained his character in that way. Through references to his school conduct and other biographic details, the youth was represented as part of a relationship structure within which he perhaps did not lead an exemplary life, but still was portrayed as a being of flesh and blood, with relationships, connections, experiences, and even hopes. This image was not necessarily more accurate than the report of a mayor would have been, but it was more nuanced; taking into account different levels produced a more complex figure. Consequently, in the clergyman's description, the youth assumed the form of a child who was "gifted with a certain astuteness, and sly," yet was inattentive and a "constant disrupter of peace and order, and therefore far behind in all fields of learning," and who had a weak-willed mother and an alcoholic father who would have most preferred to have his wife arrested at the same time.[37] The contrast to the clipped, impersonal speech of the administrative office's certificate of character could not be greater.

Whether against this backdrop the representational form of the administrative office's certificates of character can be described in terms of "disciplinization" is doubtful. Furthermore, if the contemporary requirements for "professionalism" are applied, the minister's outlook was in any case "more professional." After all, the minister's text had considerably greater information density, and according to "reputation research," that is precisely what was certificates of character were supposed to achieve. They were to be detailed regarding "class and nature" and to provide information on "social circumstances, personal characteristics, and possible connections to the crime in question."[38] The clergyman accomplished that in greater detail than the administrative official who wrote one or two lines, in the best case stating only that someone was "honest and diligent."

Although the certificates of character and crime lists – as the comparison with the observations of the Praunheim clergyman has shown – were by no means an expression of disciplinization, they nevertheless claimed the status of a "disciplined" administrative text. They were also perceived as such and thus had an effect that cannot be underestimated. The new figures created appeared at many points in the records compiled by the investigating judge and became fact to everyone who read those records – and all the jurists appearing in court were supposed to do just that. The figures found their way into the so-called summary, which in turn constituted the basis for the charging document. In the case of a bad reputation and many prior convictions, the information from the certificate of character served as an important argument for a more severe penalty, in the case of a good reputation and no prior convictions, for a lesser sentence. The figure created in the certificates of character and crime lists then played a direct role in court in that a summary version of the crime list and certificate of character was read aloud at the very beginning of the public trial and the defendant was asked whether he agreed with this shortened description of his sentences served and his reputation.[39] Only with his agreement was life finally breathed into the figure created in the files. In short, at various points in the process, the documents appeared, were referred to, and were quoted verbatim; as a result they were lent increasingly great significance. In other words, the attributes used in the certificates of character and criminal records requested during the preliminary investigation rapidly transformed the suspects into shadowy figures which bore little resemblance to human beings; the attributes therefore also decisively determined the perception of the accused in court and thus the establishment of justice.

Along with the certificate of character and crime list excerpt, other documents served as evidence, contributed to determination of the accused's position in court, and were at least in part produced from the resources of the administrative office's archives. They included the lookout description and the police wanted notice, printed in the wanted bulletins created for that purpose or in the local press. In these documents, too, suspects were gradually transformed into shadowy outlines of suspicious figures that had little of the human being about them. What did these wanted notices and lookout descriptions look like, and what was their part in evidence production and thus in the new methods for differentiating true from untrue?

Lookout descriptions and wanted notices were no more inventions of the nineteenth century than certificates of character. Wanted profiles and so-called trickster and thief lists already existed in the eighteenth century; they attained public character because they were printed in intelligence bulletins.[40] Andreas Blauert and Eva Wiebel have shown that these lists and wanted profiles had more the "character of a collection of materials or database than of a card file set up for special search purposes or a collection of wanted profiles."[41] They also pointed out that the effect of the lists and profiles lay in the standardization of personal description methods. According to this view, in the eighteenth century these text types served more to establish new language usages and techniques within administrative offices than to conduct searches for wanted persons. As will be argued in the following pages, they did not primarily serve the purpose of conducting searches in the nineteen century, either; or rather they were virtually worthless in that regard. Their meaning in the process of producing truth, and for legal personnel, was on another level. In the nineteenth century, too, they made a language and technique available for assessing and describing suspects; but not until then could they, because of new communication possibilities, decisively help structure the perception of criminals.

What did lookout descriptions look like in the second half of the nineteenth century?[42] A model for the personal description in lookout descriptions had been established in Electoral Hesse at mid-century; the model was already mentioned in the 1828 recommendations of the Prussian Ministry of Internal Affairs.[43] Each lookout description was supposed to contain data on age, height, hair color, brow shape, eye color, eyebrow color, nose shape, mouth shape, tooth condition, chin shape, beard, face shape, facial coloring, body stature, religion, and so-called distinguishing characteristics. To some extent, language was also included; in German-speaking regions, this usually meant that the dialect was noted. Sometimes a description of clothing followed, including everything from cap to shoes. As a rule, these lookout descriptions were structured such that the particular body parts to be described were listed at the left and three or four adjectives for selection at the right: thick lips, low brow, and oval face were typical attributes. Because the possible descriptive categories were limited, a certain uniformity was supposed to result or to be guaranteed so that the person described in this manner would be identifiable, or as written in the statement accompanying the lookout description, so that "this person is identical to someone."[44]

Though the lookout description actually contributed little to anyone recognizing when "this person is identical to someone,"[45] it nevertheless influenced finding truth, and not just because it was published directly or in modified form in wanted bulletins provided specifically for that purpose, as in the *Police News* that appeared around mid-century in Marburg,[46] in the *Eberhardt General Police Gazette*, or in bulletins and newspapers, thus influencing the public perception of criminals.[47] More than that, lookout descriptions structured the image of criminals in the legal negotiation process, from the very beginning on. The suspect's very first appearance in the justice records was determined by the view of the lookout description; the suspect already emerged in the complaint report as a figure reduced to the central perspectives of the lookout description. In other words, even when the initial report was filed the questions about the suspect focused to some extent on characteristics that would be asked about in the lookout description – particularly if the suspect was already a fugitive. It can in fact be observed in many cases that the report generally recorded by the gendarme reappeared almost verbatim in newspapers and wanted bulletins.[48] Consequently, the description not only structured the perception of broad segments of the population and the lookout and identification forms, but even the narrative organization of the original report, thus constituting an essential element already from the outset of the search for truth, imparting to the suspect a face and a figure, likewise from the beginning on.

What kind of a figure was it? Did it resemble the figure in the certificate of character? In the report about Erich von Lippe, the figure appeared as follows: twenty-one years old, "medium height, pale face, with a small black moustache" – only that much regarding physical characteristics. He was dressed in a "very long blue-black cloak of uniform color," with a "fuzzy overcoat, black jacket and trousers," and with a "black, dented-in, high felt hat." Then it was indicated that he could possibly be accompanied by a woman.[49] This report was printed almost verbatim in the Kassel gazette.[50] The *Eberhardt General Police Gazette* expanded these meager facts with the information that the woman was his lover, a certain Catharina Ebert, who was a prostitute by occupation.[51] Compared with the impression that Lippe made in the interrogation record, he appears in the lookout description to be a downright colorless figure. According to all the interrogation records, Lippe was a very lively and imaginative, not to mention adventurous young man, but mutated in the lookout description into a normalized figure that lacked any form of individuality and thus any characteristics which would have made it possible to recognize him. This form of disindividualization was not an isolated case, but the product of the specific structure of the lookout description. The body became the ultimate ineluctable truth, as it were, recreated and standardized by measurement procedures, and in the process disindividualized to such a degree that everything human and familiar was stripped from him.[52] The lookout description made the person into an almost chimera-like being, a figure removed from any context, dissected, and reduced to physical characteristics and his clothing shell, who thus mutated to "the other" per se. All social information, for example, about origin, generally also about occupation, religion, and class was lacking; such information was regarded as less important than eye or ear shape.

A large number of these lookout descriptions were often immediately published in their own categories, with another result: the impression that this being, describable by measurement units, colors, and shapes, could be assigned to one and the same special species solely on the basis of identical categories used to describe him/her. At the same time, because even in a publication like the *Upper Hessian Weekly Bulletin* almost half a dozen of these figures were publicized week after week, the impression arose that there must be many, very many, of them. The lookout description, in the form made public, consequently produced a special species of criminal that seemed to be present in huge numbers.

Disindividualized, robbed of any context, and devoid of everything human, the figure seemed curiously alien and lifeless. It was shaped by what Wolfgang Bonß in his study on the history of empirical social research calls the "factual view," produced by "desubjectification, decontextualization, and quantification."[53] Thus a criminal emerged who was diametrically opposed to the criminals who possessed many highly individual characteristics, as could be found in great numbers at the end of the eighteenth and beginning of the nineteenth centuries, both in Schiller's works and in Feuerbach's case histories. The latter criminals, for example, in Schiller's *The Criminal of Lost Honor* but also in the early legal case collections from the beginning of the nineteenth century, were figures who invited identification because they often were plagued by moral scruples, had frequently suffered dramatic blows of fate, and were often solitary bundles of psychological agonies, that is to say, humans of flesh and blood. They will be sought here in vain.

4.3 EVIDENCE: HOUSE SEARCHES AND CRIME SCENE PROCESSING – THE SEARCH FOR CLUES ON SITE

In addition to certificates of character, crime lists, and lookout descriptions, produced by comparable decontextualization procedures using the knowledge base of the investigators' own administrative offices, there was another type of evidence collection: house searches and crime scene investigations that entered the process of establishing justice in the form of "visual inspection reports" and sketches, and indirectly, through inventory lists. These documents also worked with decontextualization and quantification procedures that now led to strange metamorphoses not of persons, but of things. The central focus of house searches and crime scene investigations was things, which were captured so precisely in extensive reports and sketches that they almost took on a regular life of their own there, a life that helped structure the process for establishing justice no less decisively than the figures from the certificates of character and the lookout descriptions.

The "visual inspections"[54] were not as a rule conducted immediately after discovery of the crime but in the course of the preliminary investigation. Sometimes evidence collected in a house search was the sole basis for initiation of a criminal trial.[55] While house searches served the particular purpose of securing stolen goods, that is, evidentiary material, and according to relevant textbooks, of locating "the defendant or investigating clues, objects, tools, and products of the crime,"[56] visual inspections were primarily intended to help determine the background of the crime, which was important for deciding the severity of the penalty. How did someone get into which house; what effect did that have on judging the crime; what was the nature of the obstacles that possibly had to be overcome; did force have to be used; and many other questions had to be clarified according to the criteria of simple and qualified theft. Notwithstanding contemporary doctrine, house searches evidently did not necessarily take place under the direction and by order of the investigating judge.[57] Instead, they were conducted at the request of simple gendarmes,[58] chief gendarmes,[59] chief mayors, [60] or state procurators.[61]

Striking in the case of this sometimes very costly form of collecting evidence is the fact that the value of the stolen article apparently played no role in the decision of whether or not to carry out the procedure. It could just as well have been bread obtained by begging[62] or an old hat[63] as expensive jewelry pieces. Visual inspections were a very costly matter for the justice system,[64] which nevertheless believed that it must conduct them and document them thoroughly, even obsessively.

The only limitation on house searches, which was of course stated repeatedly, was that they required "justifying grounds" as they were not permitted to encroach "on the private sphere" or offend the "honor of particular persons."[65] In the case of house searches in connection with property crimes, such a limitation generally had no meaning, as the suspects usually scarcely had anything like a private sphere;[66] moreover, as members mostly of the lower classes, they were conceded the benefit of honor only in the most attenuated form – at least by the jurists. Nor can a single case be observed in which the process went forward with special regard or in which any hesitation to conduct the search was exhibited out of a desire to protect the person affected or that person's private sphere.[67]

Although the visual inspection reports differed slightly in form, content, and style, depending on whether they had been written by local mayors, gendarmes, or justice officials,[68] common narrative techniques can nevertheless be detected.[69] The exact place, date, and time were always recorded. Who had participated in the visual inspection, what was searched, in what manner the search was conducted, and what was found were precisely noted. Finally, the articles found were described exactly. A separate list of the objects found was frequently appended to the report. The statements of the witnesses or suspects about how the articles came to be in the house were likewise noted.[70] Then the crime scene, generally a house, was described in detail, starting with its external location and moving to the distribution of rooms and the exact layout of cupboards and chests from which something had been stolen.[71]

As was the case for the certificates of character and the lookout descriptions, a veritable metamorphosis gradually took place in these reports, not of persons but of things. This phenomenon is especially clear in the case of Daniel Fischer, a forty-four-year-old day laborer from Frankenau, who already had multiple convictions for theft and was suspected in 1852 of stealing a sheep. The case was set in motion because an alert gendarme stopped Fischer's daughter on her way to the neighboring town of Geismar and asked her what she had in her basket. He was not satisfied with her evasive answer, so he searched the basket and found a sheepskin. The gendarme connected this sheepskin with her father, Fischer, who already had previous convictions for theft, and the gendarme lost no time in initiating a house search.

The quickly ordered search of Fischer's house brought to light "a pot of rendered sheep fat" in the hallway on top of a cupboard and "three pieces of boiled mutton which were wrapped in an apron" in the neighbor's garden. "Several lentils were stuck to the mutton,"[72] the gendarme recorded. Even though the report is not very systematically organized, it still contains many nuggets of information and precise observations. Included there is the comment that the chief gendarme, after enquiring, stated for the report that there was a pot on the stove in which "so-called fat globules which came from meat were found, [and] that it was very likely that the meat in question had been taken out of the pot. Daniel Fischer's wife stated that she purchased the ... fat discovered from a Jew she did not know." The report closes with the comment, "read aloud and approved with the addition that Fischer and his wife appeared embarrassed during the house search, but the former trembled violently, presumably when the meat was found in the garden adjacent to the house."[73]

The gendarme thus noted very exactly what the consistency of the meat and the fat were, whether both possibly contained clues regarding the stolen object and thus represented evidence. He therefore wrote that the meat probably was taken out of the pot in which lentils had just been cooked. He also made exact observations regarding the suspects' physical reactions and interpreted them psychologically. While the investigating judge did not pay these observations any further attention, the junior state procurator, to whom the records had been sent, insisted that the gendarme's observations be followed up.[74] He wanted to know exactly to whom the apron and the plate belonged and whether perhaps someone else from the house had cooked lentils on the day in question, or whether the provenance of the mutton found in the garden could be determined in any other manner.

This case, as well as investigative records from other property crimes, shows two things: the enormous meticulousness with which the fat globule information was detailed in writing,[75] apples were taken as evidence,[76] and stolen goods were listed. To achieve that meticulousness, not only were visual inspection reports used, but so-called inventory lists, crammed with an almost endless enumeration of real and alleged stolen goods, were also prepared.[77] The lists contained precise descriptions of the goods, and in the case of foreign currencies, reference to their value, all exactly numbered and divided into alphabetically designated subcategories. However, the inventory lists and visual inspections not only demonstrated great meticulousness; at the same time, they established an order of things that helped structure the course of the entire process. Because of the "exhibit list" and the "visual inspection report," the specific objects cited therein reappeared in almost every interrogation record; it had to be determined which object belonged to whom. Even in the main trial, reference was made repeatedly to these detailed object descriptions.

What was the order of the things; how were they described? What things appeared there; how had their form and thus their significance changed by being put in writing? Cataloging, assessing, and preparing reports reduced the things and actions to what was legally essential. In this case, that means that the things were reduced to the aspects which were significant for the legal definition of theft – aspects whose number became increasingly limited in the course of the nineteenth century, as has already been shown. In this manner, the things and actions were, so to speak, robbed of their subjective and emotional or even cultural and symbolic meaning. They were no longer part of a relationship structure but were decontextualized exactly like the suspects in the lookout descriptions and were only still characterized by just three attributes: first, by their material value; second, by their ownership status; and third, by the obstacles that had been overcome when they were stolen.

The reduction to the legally essential and the associated altered representation of things and actions can be observed just as consistently in the reports and inventory lists as the transformation of suspects into chimera-like figures can be in the certificates of character and lookout descriptions. In both cases, the documents function so well because they are characterized by a style that evokes objectivity. Just as in the case of lookout descriptions and crime lists, the house inspection reports and inspection lists are texts that have an enumerative style, suggesting completeness, objectivity, and detachment, and thus seem to guarantee the absence of emotionality or subjectivity, of the superfluous or embellishment.

Exactly the same thing can be observed for another kind of evidence that was produced in connection with visual inspection: the crime scene sketch. Let's go back to the investigation of the sheep theft. References to fat globules and the trembling of the suspected married couple named Fischer was by no means the end of evidence collection. To the contrary, on the basis of this report the junior state procurator had ordered additional house searches, which led to new reports and then to preparation of sketches as well. A female neighbor stated that Louisa Fischer had thrown the mutton out the window in an unobserved moment during the house search. As the corpus delicti had been found in the garden, this denunciation was entirely plausible. The renewed visual inspection was intended to verify the statement made on the occasion of the first house search and in so doing assumed increasingly grotesque forms.

The Fischer house was located in the immediate vicinity of two other houses and was adjacent to three gardens. The houses and gardens were intensively searched and described; the ultimate purpose was to check whether Mrs. Fischer could have thrown the mutton out the window during the house search. In the descriptions, exact measurements had to be taken, angles measured, and a series of calculations made. That was not only reported but precisely captured in a sketch that was labeled exactly as "a" to "k."

Such sketches were often appended to the visual inspection reports. As a graphic medium, the sketch itself was as a rule a visualization of the crime scene before crime scene photography existed. Noteworthy is that the same set of visualization strategies was always used. No houses, gardens, streets, or room furnishings were drawn, but only the outlines of houses, the site plans of villages, or plans reminiscent of architectural drawings showing individual furniture pieces from which something was stolen. The objects, indicated here with such limited graphic means, were always marked with letters of the alphabet. The letters of the alphabet were explained on the lower edge of the sketch in a key with the heading "Comments": a = house, b = street, etc. Unlike the crime scene photographs established toward the end of the century, these sketches did not produce an abundance of new data.[78] To the contrary, the sketches reduced the empirical reality once more – when compared to the already reduced narrative description of the crime scene effected in the visual inspection report.

Finally, because these plans and maps were tagged with separate letters of the alphabet that were explained in a key, the sketches recall cartographic representation techniques. In the nineteenth century, maps were means for the scientific rendering of space (promoted not least of all by the institutionalization of geography), so to speak creating new national and thus also new colonial spaces and changing the perspective on them, as recent studies such as that of David Gugerli and Daniel Speich have pointed out.[79] Cartographic procedures suggest one-to-one depictions of empirical reality and derive their legitimacy from this attribute. Maps have a claim to reality and the power to name; that is all the more the case because they purport to omit all irrelevant and unimportant details with the abstract means of the sketch in order to focus on the essential. They suggest sober-mindedness and objectivity, thus laying claim to the status of virtually ideal evidence. That they produce new contexts and meanings, as it were, by reduction, for example, by leaving out all the contexts that do not play a role in the legal and police discourse, and by graphic rendering, goes without saying and is not ignored in visual inspection reports. It is often stated there that the sketch "illustrates" a specific interpretation of the facts.[80]

Let us summarize. Regardless of the value of the stolen goods or the seriousness of the crime and of whether they had been ordered by the investigating judge, gendarmes, victims, or mayors, house searches and visual inspections (and the associated search for clues and production of sketches, reports, and lists) were performed with increasing frequency and were transcribed in great detail. They did not structure the production of truth primarily because they violated suspects' private sphere and honor, although that was the contemporary view, mainly of jurists. Nor did they serve the main purpose of making evidence collection "objective," although just that was suggested not least of all by the administrative style of the reports, lists, and sketches. Instead, the documents substantially changed the course of investigations because, by omitting all the contexts that played no role in legal and police discourse, they constructed a specific crime course with great truth content that reduced complex facts to simple questions of property. As a result, all the contexts that were perhaps important from the perspective of a Daniel Fischer or an Anton Zimmermann were cut out of the reality of the case; questions regarding emotions, the social framework, and honor had no place in the enumerative accounts about apple cores and fat globules in lentil soup. Indeed, the representations in reports, lists, and sketches that suggested objectivity did not even allow these and similar questions to arise.

Of course, the significance of this construct was not limited just to its influence on the public or on the structuring of criminal trials from the outset; also affected were the actors from the justice and police realms.[81] Producing a lookout description meant at the same time ingraining a specific view of suspects. The logic of the lookout description predetermined the organizational structure according to which the gendarmes and jurists were to train their vision in order to arrive at this "factual view." The organizational structure gave them a ready set of descriptive categories that they could apply more effectively with every lookout description.

While the gendarmes and jurists transformed criminals ever more perfectly into lifeless figures, they could in the same breath assign themselves a new role as practitioners of law who worked with modern scientific methods. They thus participated in a symbolic policy that structured their relationship to the suspect from the beginning. They were the ones who (just as the justice officials in the case of the certificates of character and crime lists) had the power of definition, and they expanded that power with the new techniques. It was an especially important outlook; after all, "the activity of observing, the basis of all police work," constituted "the foremost and critical part of its entire essence and character."[82] This new police logic had already been present in police manuals in this or a similar form for some time. The police were to maintain order first and foremost by concentrating on "observation, prevention, repression, and detection."[83] While low-level policemen should be characterized by "good judgment, some local knowledge, skill in reading and writing, good sensory tools for activity and perception, and impeccable conduct,"[84] especially with regard to morality, and former soldiers especially lent themselves to that role, the "ability to see and hear" was an important requirement for higher service.[85] Those capabilities in particular were drilled in by creation of lookout descriptions, visual inspection reports, and sketches, and were perfected to the point where every splinter of a robbed mail coach could be cleanly collected, described, and interpreted. The "police language and craft"[86] had been so to speak learned in the course of composing reports and sketches. The process of learning and practice had already begun years before the 1868 establishment of the first Electoral Hessian criminal commissioner's office in Kassel.[87]

To the extent that the gendarmes mastered these "techniques," their influence on truth production increased.[88] Thus the sharp observations of the gendarme in the Fischer case led to further evidence collection and that in turn to new suspicious facts. Consequentially, at least in the century's last decade, a shift in the power relationships took place within the preliminary investigation. Now Gustav Zimmermann's dictum regarding the police could find agreement even for Electoral Hesse's rural society: "[The police's] main activity and the actual police role ... consists in tracing and chasing down factual material for the objective and subjective findings in the case, material that it presents not in a relevant evidentiary form but rather as formless factual information (in reports to the state attorney and communications with the court), and [that it] identifies and collects as a supplement to the investigation of the investigating judge. For that reason, it can be said of the police that it conducts research, locates, traces, and brings to light, while the inquisitorial judge ... examines."[89] Indeed, the investigative procedures were now shaped by the intensively tested new forms of preliminary investigation on the part of the police, or in rural areas, the constabulary.[90]

"Tracing" and "investigating," for which house searches and crime scene investigation provided the best options, were methods used at every available opportunity to establish interrelationships and to generate meaning – that is self-evident. Likewise self-evident is the fact that the structure of the rules for capturing things and actions in writing was determined by the legal definition of theft.

Notes

1 1848 Law on Criminal Procedure, Article 176. It is stated there that, if in the preliminary investigation "adequate proof for prosecution" was lacking or "absolute proof for exoneration [was] not present beyond the shadow of a doubt," the accused should not be prosecuted further under criminal law. This statement indicates indirectly that the aim of the preliminary investigation was to collect evidence.

2 Other codes of procedure of the time are similarly silent; see Claudia Töngi, 2004, 51, on Uri.

3 1863 Law on Criminal Procedure, Article 109.

4 1877 Code of Criminal Procedure and Implementation Law, Article 188: "The preliminary investigation should not be prolonged any further than necessary to provide the basis for a decision as to whether the main trial is to be opened or prosecution of the accused is to be suspended."

5 Heinrich A. Zachariae, 1868, 313.

6 In the nineteenth century, the view that the strict rules of evidence originally designed to prevent arbitrariness were less than conducive to finding truth slowly gained acceptance. While complicated systems for classifying evidence were created in the first half of the nineteenth century, this type of classification was completely abandoned for the first time in Saxony in 1838, and at that point so-called free production of evidence was introduced. See Rudolf Stichweh, 1994, 269ff.

7 Rudolf Stichweh, 1994, 295. Stichweh posits the hypothesis that "the significance of subjectifying the process of making legal decisions lies in the fact that it succeeds in individualizing case handling and differentiating the proceeding as a cognitive legal process"; Rudolf Stichweh, 1994, 293.

8 See the study from the field of the anthropology of law by Susan U. Philips, 1998, who treats the current practice of judges in U.S. courts.

9 See Elisabeth Koch, 1994.

10 The legal terminology for taking evidence, evaluating evidence, etc., will not be used here because analysis of legal practices is also involved and cannot be accomplished effectively by simply doubling the specialized legal terminology.

11 In the following pages, the term "interrogation" refers both to interrogation of the accused parties and to questioning of witnesses. Equating them, although not completely proper from a legal standpoint, simplifies matters but is also justified in particular because both forms of statement are to a large extent similar in the basic communicative and functional aspects central to the present study.

12 This was a component as a matter of course in trials of the Early Modern Period; see Andrea Griesebner, 2000, 164–167.

13 On the subject of lookout descriptions in the eighteenth century, see Andreas Blauert and Eva Wiebel, 2001.

14 Central to this was also a further element of modernization that was not evident – introduction of a records office. On everyday administration at the beginning of the nineteenth century still, see Stefan Brakensiek, 1999, and for the eighteenth century, see the insights that Michaela Hohkamp, 1998, provides us in her study, showing that the Triberg provincial governor simply refused to set up an archive.

15 Andreas Roth, 1997, 431.

16 266 Hanau 236.

17 266 Hanau 302.

18 268 Hanau 111. The requested documents were as a rule issued within a week by the responsible court, state councilor, or mayoral office. Only requests which had to be sent outside the borders, for example to Hesse-Nassau, could take longer (see 266 Hanau 203; in this case such a certificate was requested on May 2, 1850 and arrived on May 10).

19 At mid-century, it sometimes happened – although rarely – that complete record files were sent from the home court and the investigating judge first had to create such a crime list; see 266 Hanau 297.

20 266 Hanau 195.

21 Peter Becker, 1999, 361, describes the importance of transforming records offices that collected criminal cases into records offices that collected personal data.

22 Peter Becker, 2002, 64ff.

23 266 Hanau 203, Letter of the mayor of Dorndorf, May 10, 1850.

24 268 Hanau 8, Report of the mayor of Hitzingen, February 28, 1853.

25 268 Marburg 14.

26 To all appearances, people knew the individuals well personally and could therefore also give their nicknames; for example, in the case of the defendant Charlotte Birk, accused of shop theft, it was said that she was "called Listchen"; 268 Hanau 8.

27 266 Hanau 203, Letter of the mayor of Dorndorf, May 10, 1850.

28 268 Marburg 14.

29 On attribution of alcohol consumption to the male sphere in the Early Modern Period, see Lyndal Roper, 1995.

30 This orientation toward middle-class values seems to be reflected even more clearly in the certificates of character after establishment of the *Reich*. At that point, there were so-called character reports that had a clear formal structure used to check central aspects of middle-class life. The following aspects were

to be considered in such character reports: "name, age and marital status, religion, family circumstances, financial circumstances, reputation," and a list of prior convictions; see 274 Marburg, State procurator's office, 17.

31 See Manuel Frey, 1997.

32 On the debate in Electoral Hesse, see Cameron Munter, 1983, and Martin Kukowski, 1995b.

33 On this subject, see the works of Peter Becker, 1992b, 1994, 1999; Peter Becker, 2002, on alcohol, 75ff, and on sexual "excesses," 117ff. Unlike Becker, I would like to emphasize that not only this new police outlook played a role in the construction of new criminal types but also other debates such as the one about the so-called social question and the middle-class discussion of self-understanding.

34 Peter Becker and William Clark, 2001b, 26.

35 Stefan Haas, 2005.

36 In this context, it should be kept in mind that until the beginning of the nineteenth century, clergymen and sometimes teachers usually issued such certificates. They were thus thoroughly experienced in producing this text genre; of course, they viewed it very differently from the representatives of the administrative offices.

37 The suspect's father instructed the clergyman to use the occasion to soundly punish the son; he added that "a similar punishment could also be administered on this occasion to his wife; she had spoiled the boy completely." 266 Hanau 145.

38 Heinrich Zachariae, 1868, 334, created an extensive catalogue of questions that the certificate of character was supposed to answer.

39 266 Hanau 297. With his agreement, he himself legitimized this figure newly created by the administrative language of the nineteenth century.

40 The edition of Andreas Blauert and Eva Wiebel, 2001, which is decidedly worth reading, goes extensively into trickster and thief lists, but also wanted profiles.

41 Andreas Blauert and Eva Wiebel, 2001, 55f.

42 At this time, photographs were already occasionally used for apprehension. See Ludwig Hoerner, 1980, who presents an 1860 book of criminal photos belonging to the Hannover police. See Also Susanne Regener, 1999, 40ff. So it was in the Erich von Lippe case; the announcement in the *Eberhardt Police Gazette*, Vol. LXXXIV, 143, states at the end of the wanted notice on von Lippe, "Photographs can be supplied"; see 269 Marburg 218. In legal journals, there were also already discussions about the pros and cons of "using photography for the proceedings in criminal matters"; see Ludwig Hoemer, 1980, note 1.

43 See Peter Becker, 2001b, 146f, who here, too, makes reference to Robert Heindl, *System and Practice of Dactyloscopy and other Technical Methods of the Criminal Police* (Berlin, 1922).

44 268 Marburg 62.

45 The case of *this* "someone" is particularly interesting because it is one of the rare examples of a property crime in which a lookout description was actually considered necessary to determine the identity of a person, at the same time

making clear how unhelpful lookout descriptions were in determining identity. The case involved a man who was caught at the end of December 1856 on the second floor of someone else's house in the process of opening cupboards and drawers. When asked by the homeowner what he was doing, he could come up with nothing better than the dumb excuse that he was looking for a certain shoemaker, so he was taken to the police station. There he especially stood out because of the unusually coarse manner of speech he used in resisting the filing of a report – "Oh shit, go ahead and make a report; I'll shit on your report" – and because of insults made to Police Sergeant Heil, to whom he said, "You are a dumb boy; you belong on the street, such a dirty pig, such a stinking bastard; you are an ox. Holy hell, you are still much too dumb" (68 Marburg 62). However, the problem was not only this peculiar behavior, but the circumstance, unusual for cases of property crime in Electoral Hesse during this decade, that he had given false personal information. While the young man had said at the beginning that his name was Bernhard and that he came from the Rhineland, the Marburg administrative office found out barely three weeks later that the information was completely contrived. In reality, his name was Georg Quehl, he had already been convicted six times, and he was a draft dodger. In establishing his identification, a lookout description, or rather two lookout descriptions, played a role. The first was produced by the Marburg Justice Office; the second came from the Ziegenhain workhouse from which, as it turned out later, Quehl had escaped a short time before. The two lookout descriptions were issued less than a half year apart; yet it was scarcely evident from them that "this person was identical to someone" – as the Ziegenhain people hoped, although that was the case. If in one description black hair was mentioned, in the other he had brownish-black hair; in one description he had a "low" forehead, in the other, a "broad" one; in one, a small nose, in the other, a large one. His facial coloring was yellowish, or pale, and finally his build had changed within a few months from slender to stocky. In short, the lookout description was not really helpful in recognizing Georg Quehl from Görzhain, Oberaula Office, as the man in question. Overall, there were only four statements in these personal descriptions that did not contradict each other: in both lookout descriptions the man's eyes were brown, his teeth good, his chin round, and his age twenty-two. All other information differed, sometimes considerably. Consequently, it is doubtful that lookout descriptions contributed much to determining the identity of a person. That is, lookout descriptions were not especially helpful in either the eighteenth century, as shown by Blauert and Wiebel, or in the nineteenth century, if a person was to be identified. Although lookout descriptions may have contributed little to identification, that did not prevent their widespread use. To the contrary, from the 1860s on, Electoral Hesse had its own forms for lookout descriptions. Furthermore, it became the usual practice to prepare lookout descriptions for all prisoners in prisons.

46 This was the aim in the 1849 case of theft from the book dealer Elwert, in which considerable sums were likewise stolen; see 266 Marburg 72.

47 In the *Upper Hessian Weekly Newspaper* under the heading "Police News" there were the headings "Announcements," "Offenses and Crimes," "Wanted

Notices," "People whose Situations Are to Be Determined," "Articles Found," and "Articles Lost." Similarly, the "General Intelligencers" usually also had a section of official news, for example, the *General Intelligencer for the Alsfeld District*, which was popularly used for Electoral Hessian property crimes; see 266 Marburg 123.

48 That becomes clear in the case of Erich Rudolph von Lippe. He was suspected of having stolen 940 German Marks and three shirts from the house of his uncle in April 1877. At the time of the crime's discovery, he had already fled. Shortly after his flight became known, a wanted notice was placed in the newspaper. The wanted notice for the sales clerk Erich Rudolph von Lippe appeared in the *Eberhardt General Police Gazette,* and a week later in the *Public Bulletin of the Official Gazette of the Royal Government at Cassel*. The information published there corresponded to what could already be found in the complaint report.

49 269 Marburg 218, 1877.

50 *Public Bulletin of the Official Gazette of the Royal Government at Cassel*, May 12, 1877, 775.

51 *Public Bulletin of the Official Gazette of the Royal Government at Cassel*, May 12, 1877. The source of this additional information is not clear.

52 See Susanne Regener, 1999, 130ff; Peter Becker, 2001b, 148.

53 Wolfgang Bonß, 1982, 59. In the area of German history that is largely unexplored, the development of statistics, Wolfgang Bonß's study is by far the field's most stimulating work, although he is concerned with a broader set of issues and early statistics represent only one focus of interest among many.

54 In the following pages, the different forms are generally subsumed under the term "visual inspection," because here once again the primary focus is supposed to be textualization forms that do not differ, regardless of whether the house of the suspect had been searched or the house of the victim had been inspected.

55 That is the case for a sheep theft allegedly committed by Daniel Fischer in 1852; see 268 Marburg 11.

56 Heinrich A. Zachariae, 1868, 164f; see Ludwig von Jagemann, 1838, Article 68, still quite brief regarding house searches.

57 According to the textbooks, house searches were supposed to be ordered by the investigating judge, as they were discussed in the context of the "inviolability of one's own home." They were also supposed to be performed by the investigating judge, under no circumstances by the low-level police personnel, support staff, police agents, or privates or constables of the constabulary. However, many textbooks allowed house searches by the director or police commissioner; see Gustav Zimmermann, 1852, 105.

58 Even if legal doctrine wanted this to be different, according to the Electoral Hessian Code of Criminal Procedure performance was definitely up to police officers; see 1848 Law on Criminal Procedure, Article 145. Indeed, even simple gendarmes actually carried out searches alone; see 266 Marburg 72, 1848. On June 13, 1848, Police Sergeant Erbe reported that he, together with assistants of the book dealer Elwert, had carried out the search of a suspect's house. This case is also remarkable because it extended over two years; it can

be clearly seen here how the investigating judge gradually gained more power to order house searches. In 1848, house searches were still performed by gendarmes in the presence of the victim without a prior order of the investigating judge; in 1849, house searches were not based any more frequently on an order of the investigating judge. Nor can it be observed that searches already performed were legitimized any more often by such an order after the fact. See also 266 Hanau 236; 268 Marburg 11.

59 268 Marburg 11. See 266 Hanau 302; in this case, Senior Gendarme Claus of the Schwarzenfels Rural Constabulary performed a house search on May 23, 1849, because of a theft from the bleaching meadow.

60 266 Marburg 72, 1849, Letter of the chief mayor of Marburg, April 5, 1849. See also 268 Marburg 14, where a mayor made a house search of his own accord.

61 268 Marburg 91. Sometimes witnesses were also present at house searches; see 266 Hanau 302, Presence of the vice-mayor. See also 266 Hanau 236, Interrogation of Christian Trupp, December 12, 1849. Trupp was the son-in-law of the victim and reported here that he and his father-in-law had performed a house search together with the gendarmes after the crime was discovered. In this case, the owner of the articles seems to have been present or in the immediate vicinity during the house search, because he immediately recognized the articles "as his property." In addition, a member of the local council was also present. The presence of the victim is shown in 266 Marburg 72.

62 268 Marburg 91. In this case, a house search was performed because of "bread obtained by begging."

63 268 Hanau 29.

64 Junior State Procurator Meibom, who was investigating a bread theft, calculated forty-five silver pennies in "travel and food costs" for the one-hour walk on foot from Marburg to Cyriaxweimar and back and for a half-day's stay there; 268 Marburg 91, Instruction, May 29, 1854, 6. The visual inspection and preparation of a sketch in the case of a hat theft that was completely insignificant in material terms were also extremely expensive; they incurred costs of fifty silver pennies. 268 Hanau 29, Visual inspection, December 14, 1859.

65 Heinrich A. Zachariae, 1868, 164f. It is striking that the manuals report in detail about the restrictions on house searches, and that in the legal texts little is said about how those searches are to be performed, the methods used, and especially requisite skills.

66 This is not the place to go into detail about the broad debate on the meaning of private and public in developing middle-class society. Undoubtedly the legal constructions regarding privacy contributed substantially to shaping those concepts.

67 How downright grotesque the level of detail in the search for clues could become during a visual inspection is clear from the investigation of a mail wagon robbery that occurred in July 1866 not far from Kirchhain. The luggage compartment had been forcibly opened and ten letter pouches, some with letters containing money, had been stolen. Evidence preservation had begun immediately, and a "drawing expert" had been ordered to "graphically

represent ... the damage to the mail wagon"; 266 Marburg 123, Complaint, July 7, 1866. While this sketch allowed reconstruction of the way in which the theft was committed, the further efforts focused on determination of the stolen articles' value. On the morning after the crime, the senior gendarme from Neustadt and the gendarme from Kirchhain had already set out to inspect the crime scene. On the country road, they found the following carefully noted articles: "a) a black lacquered wood splinter, about 2' long; b) ... 5 fragments of a destroyed cardboard box; c) 3 paper scraps ...; d) a letter without an address and without a signature dated Brotterode June 3, 1866 and with the heading 'my dear birthday child.'" A little later the search continued. Now the following findings were reported: "1. about five steps from the house of Catharina Nolte, a small, black lacquered wood splinter 2. and in the further course several of the same wood splinters (five of them) 3. and finally a square cardboard cover that fits exactly on the small box consigned to the local mayor 4. and further on some cake crumbs. The latter were located near four large chestnut trees standing by the road."

68 Mayors and low-level gendarmes briefly summarized what they had seen and focused on the particular central question: Is the stolen article in suspect's house, or how can the suspect have come in through this window or that gap? Many low-level officials dispensed with preparation of special reports about house searches and mentioned the results of those searches only in connection with the report filed or other information. Justice officials and better-educated gendarmes cultivated a different style. Although their style did not necessarily fit the set requirements of "collect, extract, sift, order, and build up in layers" set down in the relevant police manuals, either (see Gustav Zimmermann, 1852, 67), special narrative techniques can be seen in such cases.

69 Indeed, a separate genre of "visual inspection reports" emerged. In this case, only house searches or crime scene inspections were recorded; that already becomes clear from the heading, which reads "House search of ..." or "Report regarding a visual inspection"; see 268 Hanau 29, 1859, December 12, 1859. The report on the "Search of Catharina Prinz' house, performed here on April 6, 1849" is also typical; see 266 Marburg 72.

70 266 Hanau 302.

71 See 266 Marburg 98, Report relating to the visual inspection of the Freund residence in Weidenhausen, October 28, 1864.

72 268 Marburg 11, Report relating to the arrest of Daniel Fischer, November 3, 1852.

73 268 Marburg 11, 1852, Fürstenberg, November 2, 1852.

74 268 Marburg 11, December 3, 1852, Junior State Procurator Maiboom to the Frankenau Electoral Justice Office.

75 Of course, there was no fingerprint and photograph department until the end of the nineteenth century, especially in rural areas. Even in Berlin, a criminal photograph collection was not established until 1876. In that year, the Berlin fingerprint and photograph service began to systematically perform police photography (see Miloš Vec, 2002, 27ff), and not until 1896 was the Bertillon System introduced (see Andreas Roth, 1997, 96). And yet, even in provincial Electoral Hesse, new attention was devoted to clues, and new

investigative techniques were developed from the mid-century on. Tracks in the snow were considered (see 266 Hanau 302, Interrogation of Christian Trupp, December 12, 1849). Then tracks in soft ground were safeguarded, already using new resources for that purpose; see 226 Marburg 98. This was also the case for the post coach robbery described; there the gendarme stated, "But in addition I saw some cake crumbs even closer to town in the direction of St...feld only in one furrow of the field. Further along that furrow, I noticed a footprint which appeared to have been made by a man's shod foot and which was rather fresh but had already been rained on. I measured the length of the tracks with a straw that I can still provide. Based on the sole imprint, the track was made by the *right* foot. The heel had a heavy horseshoe attached which was missing a piece on the outer (right) side. The other sole imprint exhibited a metal fitting with round-headed nails that ran around the sole; two nails must have been missing only at the front tip." Not only had these objects been provided but also the "above indicated ... straw ...; according to it, the length of the footprint found extends from "a" to "b," as marked in the margin, the width of the footprint at the ball, from "a" to "d," and the width of the horseshoe at the widest point, from "a" to "c"; 266 Marburg 123, July 12, 1866, Statement of Gendarme Caspar Orth. As that was not enough, these footprints were compared to the suspect's. Then a visual inspection was ordered, which with a sketch that followed known models was immediately added to the case records; 266 Marburg 123, Visual inspection, July 18, 1866. Finally, sketches of other shoe soles were prepared and a "man's shoe" was pulled in. The increased attention to clues of all kinds and the associated meticulousness in their textualization, which employed the technique of reduction to the elements most important to the legal system and the police, contributed to construction of what actually constituted "essential." Thus, what was essential to the legal system and the police only took shape in this search for clues. Indeed, the search for clues, not least of all because of the thoroughness and precision in the description of those clues, was of vital significance for the production of truth and assumed an ever greater role in the preliminary investigation.

76 266 Marburg 98, Visual inspection report, October 28, 1864.

77 These lists increased in size over the course of the nineteenth century, as the search for clues intensified. Multi-page "exhibit lists" were not unusual. In the mail robbery case, a whole series of such lists was prepared, providing information, very neatly divided into four columns, on the following subjects: "1. Article description, 2. Name of the owner or the person robbed, 3. Page number, 4. Remarks about storage or return." See 266 Marburg 123; such a list is located right at the beginning of the file after another record and lists the following in the form of a table: "1. Number of file records, 2. Date of action or receipt, 3. Object or contents, 4. Name of the person interrogated, 5. Indication of whether the oath was administered, 6. Number of pages in the file." This file was thus exceptionally well organized; however, after the 1850s, there was an increasing tendency to provide the files with of tables of contents on this sort of form. The forms had the heading "File Index for the Case against ...." This kind of table of contents indicates the evolution of the

administrative office, which in this way produced organizing systems to improve readability.

78 That is the hypothesis of Christina Karallus, 1998.

79 David Gugerli and Daniel Speich, 2002.

80 268 Hanau 29, Visual inspection report, December 14, 1859.

81 In another context, Jens Jäger, 2003, very rightly points out the performative dimension of police action. He can show not only that criminal types were constructed in police records departments around 1900, but that "fingerprinting and photographing" were a "ritualized action ... whose function is to manage a crisis in the existing order caused by violation of the law" (210). Furthermore, he points out that fingerprinting and photographing belong to the realm of symbolic policy by which the police affirms itself and at the same time establishes a specific manner of dealing with crime.

82 Gustav Zimmermann, 1852, 65.

83 What was expected of the police was clearly stated in manuals, for example, in that of Gustav Zimmermann from 1849; see Gustav Zimmermann, 1849, 1105.

84 Gustav Zimmermann, 1849, 1113.

85 Gustav Zimmermann, 1849, 1126.

86 Gustav Zimmermann, 1849, 1128.

87 Gustav Beck, 1931, 66.

88 Ludwig von Jagemann's textbook, which appeared in 1838, states on the subject of the "Rapid Discovery and Recognition of the Offender," Article 129, that the attempt should first be made to learn "the names of those individuals who, according to local gossip and their reputation, can be considered at all capable of such a crime"; see Ludwig von Jagemann, 1838, 147.

89 Gustav Zimmermann, 1852, 103.

90 Andreas Roth, 1997, 427, proposes the theory that the police gained strength during the last decade of the nineteenth century at the expense of the state procurator's office.

5

Techniques for Finding Truth and Other Types of Knowledge Formation

How Can a New Outlook Be Put into Practice?

How did the jurists and gendarmes know how certificates of character, lookout descriptions, visual inspection reports, and crime scene sketches should be produced? How did they know the techniques that ultimately lent these documents the character of proof? From the codes on criminal procedure issued before or after 1848, nothing can be gleaned on how a crime scene sketch should be prepared to give it the character of evidence. Nor is there a single word about how the significance of a visual inspection report is to be assessed. To learn more about the preparation but also the assessment of these types of evidence and thus about the techniques used in the preliminary investigation to decide what is "true" and "untrue," it is necessary to look beyond regulations and textbooks. The answers are to be found in the new fields of knowledge emerging with increasing clarity at mid-century: statistics, jurisprudence, and criminology. These fields concerned themselves with questions similar to those in the preliminary investigation, that is, how can the truth about criminals and their actions be revealed, and what are especially good, that is to say objective, methods for finding truth? The questions were answered in an already familiar manner; here, too, desubjectification, decontextualization, and quantification procedures played an important role. As was already maintained earlier and is to be shown in the following pages, the way in which evidence is produced in the process of establishing justice calls to mind forms of knowledge production typical for a number of sciences that were emerging in the nineteenth century and that (also) dealt with the question of crime. Statistical logic, legal debates, criminological deduction, and court investigation practice went hand in hand and together created – as will become clear – a new image of the criminal as well as new criteria according to which "true" and "untrue" were distinguished from one another.

5.1 STATISTICS AND PRODUCTION OF THE MASS BEING

Statistics as a science had already become established in the eighteenth century[1] but not until around the middle of the nineteenth century did it begin to spark broad interest on the part of the state and the public, which quickly formed statistical associations. Only at this point was a so-called Statistics Bureau created; its most important function was to examine the new administrative offices statistically.[2] As one critic complained,[3] Electoral Hesse had to wait a long time for such a Statistics Bureau – not until after the *Kaiserreich* was founded was such a bureau also responsible for the former Electoral Hesse established in Berlin. Nevertheless, the volume of statistics increased sharply after mid-century in Electoral Hesse, too.[4] From then on, extensive statistics were produced on all aspects of life.[5] Thus, for example, the state procurator had to furnish Kassel with statistical information on the number of prisoners.[6] At the same time, criminal statistics were standardized for all the federal states.[7] With the introduction of standard tally cards with which the state attorney offices had to count each person charged, the "conquest by numbers," as Michelle Perrot called this growing fascination with statistics,[8] reached its temporary peak.[9] In addition to the new state institutions, many statistical associations emerged which, financed by an interested middle class, likewise eagerly compiled statistics. Even in rural and small-town society, an increasing number of clergymen, teachers, physicians, and other representatives of the middle class became enthusiastic about collecting data, as Ian McNeely has shown in an impressive study on Württemberg. In this case, more than control of the administrative offices was involved; it was a matter of owning and participating, of a fascination with statistics broadly shared in middle-class circles.[10]

The result was that, in addition to the simple mass of statistical material, entirely new publications emerged. Starting in the second half of the century, statistics were found almost everywhere: in "citizens magazines," "yearbooks of national history, geography, statistics, and typography," and in the so-called "state gazettes," as well as in the manuals of the individual states' bureaus.[11] In short, statistics were omnipresent from the mid-century on, even in the public at large, which grew increasingly enthusiastic about this form of capturing the world. This fascination fed on the promise inherent in statistics, which claimed to be able to portray social reality objectively, that is, scientifically. After all, statistics was considered an "exact science" that allowed social laws and regularities to be revealed.[12] The hope was to be able to use statistical methods to penetrate scientifically a social reality perceived as increasingly complex. Furthermore, many believed that they could analyze and thus control the serious social changes of the early nineteenth century associated with the dissolution of estates-based society, instead of being – as was thought – helplessly at the mercy of those changes.[13]

How did statistics select its material, and how did it capture particular elements from a given realm? How did it represent those realms, and above all, what did knowledge production look like for the crime statistics that are important in the present context?[14] Can procedures similar to those for preparing certificates of character, lookout descriptions, and visual inspection reports really be identified in this case, as initially claimed?

We can learn remarkably little from crime statistics on delinquents until about mid-century. As a rule, only gender[15] and age[16] (to separate children from adults) are given, while data on social status[17] as well as religious affiliation[18] are rare.[19] Despite, or perhaps because of, the scant data, a particular image of the criminal was presented in these statistics. The crime statistics during the first half of the century gave rise to the notion of a large, amorphous, threatening mass of criminals. The lookout description had – just a reminder – given rise to a similar impression. This impression was due primarily to the statistical principle which did not account for individual people with individual psychological, moral, and social problems but only considered data in quantities above a certain level significant. In this analytical and representational mode, criminals necessarily became the symbol of a collectivity. And because, according to the irrefutable message of crime statistics, that collectivity was growing continuously, the criminal became an anxiety-inducing being, indeed, even frightening figure. Ultimately, the statistics seemed to repeatedly confirm just one message: The number of criminals was increasing daily. Of course, that represented a threat, not only for the property and lives of individuals but for the basic moral framework of the entire society.[20]

After about mid-century, collection of detailed information about criminals began. Thus, for example, the forms for Electoral Hesse's prisons[21] noted not only gender and age, but what "gainful employment" the person engaged in, and the nature of the person's "financial circumstances" and "earlier conduct," that is, prior convictions.[22] Other statistics also collected now included personal data on gender, age, religion,[23] status, length of sentence, and types of "gainful employment or occupation,"[24] which ranged from day laborers to the categories "spouses and relatives." "Property"[25] and "earlier conduct"[26] were also of interest. Frequently crime statistics also contained additional information on prisons,[27] crimes,[28] the "mortality conditions in the penal institutions," separately for men and women, and the ratio of home-grown and foreign prisoners to the population.

These figures, which had in the meantime become very extensive, gave the impression that all of the aspects of life important for investigating criminals were being illuminated. The sheer volume of what was compiled made it seem that an objective survey precisely researched down to the last detail was being conducted.

If the statistically created criminal before the mid-century was primarily a being who had threatening features because he existed in such numbers, those features now came into sharp focus. The criminal was part of a larger trend, but he was also a person who was primarily characterized by economic deprivation. That is to say, the statistics made a connection between crime and a worsening material position. This connection was reinforced by comparison of crime statistics with statistics intended to shed light on the economic situation.[29] Such procedures were meant to show how close the connection was between the economy and crime, and that crime resulted directly from a worsening economic situation. At the same time, how much a particular criminal was affected by the so-called general economic situation, and whether the particular crime could be attributed to economic conditions were not the subject of any research. Instead, connections between the economy and delinquency were simply postulated and supported "scientifically" with extensive graphics in which the development of property crime and grain prices were compared to each other.[30] Thus, a finding of the 1867 Electoral Hessian statistical study concluded that the "lack of food and income [was] the main motive force for [property] offenses."[31] Even when such correlations were not made, it was always asserted, whether in footnotes, as introductory remarks, or at the end of texts based on crime statistics, that there was a connection between criminals and their economic living conditions. Moreover, the alleged material situation of criminals was declared to be the trigger for their crimes.

As an aside, it should be mentioned once more that (as was shown previously by the example of the Anton Zimmermann case) even statistics as detailed as those of the Electoral Hessian study of the 1860s revealed nothing about the crucial questions regarding the individual economy of rural and small-town society in the second half of the nineteenth century. What rights of use people had, how family resources were distributed, what income sources were available besides day laborer work, for example, employment as shoemakers or cobblers, or in city services – none of that was researched statistically. What trade economies people were involved in, what the social network people operated in looked like, and much more did not interest the Statistical Bureau. In short, it is obvious that this form of measuring economic need would have required greater regional, and class-, gender-, and occupation-specific distinctions to be able to provide even only rudimentary explanations for delinquency.[32]

Such distinctions were not investigated; instead, another connection besides the one between crime and social need was made, the connection between crime and individual morality. Even though data on the morality – whatever that is thought to be – of the individual offenders was not collected at all, a connection was postulated between the level of crime and that of immorality: the higher the crime rate, the lower the population's level of morality.[33] Associated with the correlation to material need, that meant: the higher the material need, the more immorality and the more crime.[34] This rationale has been repeatedly fabricated with statistics since Adolphe Quetelet, the founder of crime statistics, spoke of a "penchant for crime."[35] The upshot: Statistics which did not include any data about offenders' living conditions that corresponded to actual practices in poverty economies were transformed into ostensibly objective measures for the moral state and economic situation of offenders. [36]

As problematic as the connections produced by statistics were, a new figure took on a distinct shape in this context. The being from the criminal mass who, acting from economic adversity and showing signs of moral affliction, thus became the symbol – from the standpoint of contemporaries – for increasing pauperization. The result was a scientifically dignified basis for interpreting the number of delinquents as a gauge for the pauperization increasingly detected by contemporaries.[37] This form of making connections can be linked to the social reporting in the second half of the nineteenth century and to early medical and moral statistics and also topographies that are known from England, France,[38] and Germany, but the observable reduction to questions of morality and financial power is also reminiscent of the certificates of character, which primarily contained information about a person's property status and reputation.

The amorphous mass of figures found in these crime statistics, which was characterized by the factors of poverty, a lack of emotional or family connections, and an inclination to perpetual criminality, was fashioned by a decontextualization process similar to those used for criminals in lookout descriptions and certificates of character. The same decontextualization processes that could be observed in visual inspection reports, created figures which, stripped of their social and emotional relationships, mutated into amorphous robots. In both cases the criminals, detached from any motives beyond purely economic ones, seem to be mechanical marionettes.

5.2 SOULLESS CHIMERAS IN LEGAL CASE HISTORIES

While criminal bodies showed up in newspapers dissected into measurement units and forms, pointing directly to the lookout descriptions prepared among other places in the framework of the preliminary investigation, and statistics produced an amorphous mass characterized primarily by social and moral misery, similarly decontextualized figures also appeared with increasing frequency in legal case histories, journals, and textbooks by legal scholars from mid-century on. There was a growing number of criminals with a striking similarity to the soulless beings from lookout descriptions and statistics, especially in the so-called "case histories," crime descriptions directed at a public with literary interests and in part intended to reach a public exclusively of legal specialists through publication in textbooks or legal journals.

At the beginning of the nineteenth century, a type of legal case history predominated that can be best illustrated with the case collection of Anselm von Feuerbach. One of the most important jurists of the time, Feuerbach placed criminals at the center of his legal cases in his *Documentary Exposition of Remarkable Crimes*, which was also favored reading by non-jurists.[39] The case histories, which took equal delight in the criminals' misery and the brutality of the crimes, placed great emphasis on describing the criminals' motives, with psychological or economic explanations. In that manner Feuerbach reclaimed the right to understanding, if not sympathy, for the offenders. However, this criminal type in particular, as known from numerous literary texts – just recall Schiller's *Robbers* – became increasingly rare after the 1830s, at least in legal discourse, and eventually only still led a kind of rudimentary existence in fiction.[40] In specialized legal journals and textbooks, the number of such emphatically sympathetic case studies that always portrayed the delinquent's life and acts in context dwindled markedly. Furthermore, voices in legal circles, but also in the slowly growing field of "criminal psychology," warned of the "novel-like" contents of the case histories from the beginning of the century and grew ever louder. For example, a review of Feuerbach's 1829 case collection stated in a rather disparaging tone, "Moralizing reflections [and] mere general, superficial observations about the human heart and the hidden depths of its passions, etc., are no longer ... enough, given the state of science today, and especially that of criminal psychology. General, superficial psychological observations such as we find in great numbers in this book cause irreparable damage in court forensic and medical assessment."[41] The traditional representation of the criminal now vilified as superficial (it was of course still tolerated in fiction, a matter to be kept neatly separate) was to be replaced by scientific treatment.[42] And "scientific" in the sense of legal science now meant that the case history was to make do without a search for psychological motives and to be limited to exposition of "simple facts."

With that, the legal field – at about the same time as statistics – underwent a fundamental change in its representation of criminals.[43] What did such a legal case history, which now claimed to be factual and objective and was to contain only legally relevant material, look like at mid-century? How were its plots set up and the criminals characterized? The new case histories were modeled on the relational genre and divided the offense description strictly in two parts. The first consisted in the so-called recounting of the history; in it, the background and course of the offense were reconstructed. The second contained the legal assessment of the offense. This legal assessment, which was as a rule a dryly composed subsumption of a case according to the relevant paragraphs, generally took up a substantial portion of the case description, often almost all of it. In contrast, the recounting of the history, which had included the life story of the offender and had previously been the central focus, shrank to a minimum and merged into the legal assessment. It was only supposed to provide the absolutely necessary material for "making a decision based on standards."[44]

Everything that was significant for the legal assessment of a theft was supposed to be an indispensable element in recounting the history, that is, giving the value of the stolen article and describing the kind of theft. In contrast, all questions about possible relationship structures of the accused and other contexts that could explain an offense were unimportant. Consequently, from the second half of the century on there could be no question of insights into a pitiable soul or of recognizing generalizable human circumstances in the context of case histories. Offenders who had been the focus of "recounting the history" were pushed aside, while the legal foundation for assigning a penalty, "the legal assessment," moved to the center of attention, filling pages with a recitation of countless citations from legal textbooks or regulations.[45] Presentation of standards, their derivation, and their application had become the actual core of the history and the actual reason why jurists published and reviewed case histories.

Of course, this new "scientific" type of case history could not get by completely without an offender, even though the value of the stolen article was perhaps granted considerably more space. What did the offenders look like? They are reminiscent of the lifeless and colorless figures of the lookout descriptions and statistics; robbed of any meaningful inner context, they seem to be thrown into a world to which they are only loosely connected and in any case without causal relationships, thus resembling monadic chimeras rather than flesh-and-blood human beings. How was a generally pitiable human being whose fate readers followed spellbound to the very last page transformed into a faceless figure whose actions were now scarcely comprehensible? Only a few flicks of the wrist were enough. First the information about the offender was reduced to a minimum: name, age, occupation, and prior convictions. Sometimes there was a brief reference to upbringing – this information was generally combined with a remark about the completed communion or confirmation.[46] Parents, and thus the social, cultural, psychological, and mental background, were only commented on if the father had prior convictions, and that could be followed up with conjecture on "how bad the upbringing of the detainee" was.[47] A good or a bad reputation was also mentioned. This type of very brief personal description calls to mind the characteristics of the person interrogated that were recorded at the beginning of every interrogation for the purposes of the preliminary investigation. A further process causing fragmentation of complex life histories recalls crime statistics and lookout descriptions; the offender's life and the event sequence of the offense were put in the form of an enumerative list, so that any form of causal nexus or even any explanation of internal and external interconnections disappeared. The life history, as an event chain that developed dynamics and transformed effects into causes and vice versa, no longer occurred in the second half of the century. Likewise, all questions regarding the inner and external development of the offender remained outside consideration. A thief stole articles without this action being placed in an explanatory context. In this case, too, the process amounted to decontextualization and failure to provide a meaningful background for an action.

Finally, the new being, who could almost only still be detected as a shadow, came into existence because the representation of the crime course[48] itself was limited to a compilation of legally relevant data, for example, to when and where particular clothing articles were taken, what food was pilfered, or what other crimes committed. In the same vein, the height of a wall that had been scaled in a burglary was precisely cited, the exact properties of the articles stolen were described in detail, if necessary, with expert reports, and other aggravating or mitigating evidence, for example, time of crime, thoroughly discussed. The things were given a higher priority than the delinquent.[49] The precision of recording calls to mind the inventory lists, sketches, and crime scene descriptions that were created in the framework of the preliminary investigation. Thus, many case histories were more similar to inventory lists than to a description of the offense and offender. Indeed, decontextualized to such an extent, offenders resembled machines that had almost as little life of their own as the many pairs of trousers and vests, geese, stockings, scarves, peas, silver watches, and boots that were generally described more vividly and in greater detail than the thief him/herself.[50]

In the last part of the legal case description, where mitigating or aggravating circumstances were sought, the offender was completely reduced to a being without meaningful inner circumstances and motives, without social connections and interests. This part examined whether the accused was entitled to sentence mitigation in light of "moral conduct" or because there was "still hope for improvement." Criteria such as "middle class position" were also important. A middle-class position could be so "seriously affected" by a penalty that the effect defeated the actual purpose of the punishment; position thus served as a justification for mitigation.[51] Likewise relevant were questions about remorse – for example, crying was frequently interpreted as a sign of remorse[52] – and whether in the case of theft restitution had been paid for the stolen goods or their value. Finally, youth was judged to be mitigating.[53] But here, too, a search for the previously usual over-the-top accounts of hot, remorseful tears or at least a reference to shamefaced sobbing, for the description of a dramatic past with a difficult childhood, or even for only a mention of the good character of a gentleman who perhaps was seduced by a wicked woman or at least was induced by adverse circumstances to commit his deed, will be in vain. Moreover, the closing passages in particular re-enforced the chimera-like, lifeless image of offenders, because the relevant mitigating and aggravating circumstances were reviewed with extreme brevity, as if the matter were a multiple-choice test on which only the yes or no check box could be marked.[54]

Thus, the offenders in the legal case histories from the second half of the nineteenth century had been transformed into figures without souls or interests who, emptied of inner or external motives, seemed to exist outside all social relationships and were scarcely still recognizable as human beings. Although things and especially the jurist organizing the case, with his potential for legal interpretation, had moved into the spotlight, the criminals had definitely not become meaningless. To the contrary, they had mutated into downright threatening figures because they had been robbed of all human attributes. The criminals did not disappear from the case histories; they were, in their ghost-like form, conspicuously present, just because, as in the lookout description, they had lost their membership in the human race. Just as the criminal was a body dissected there into shape, measure, and color, he had passed into another sphere in case histories, too, a sphere that could not be linked even by rudimentary similarities to the human being, let alone to middle-class society, because the criminal in this context was a figure that appeared to act without motives and without inner logic.[55]

5.3 CRIMINOLOGY AS PERFECTION OF LEGAL AND STATISTICAL DISCOURSE AND IMPROVEMENT OF THE PRACTICES FOR EVIDENCE PRODUCTION

The parallels between the criminal constructs of the preliminary investigation, statistics, and legal case histories on one hand and the procedures for producing them on the other point to another science: criminology.[56] That science also developed in the course of the nineteenth century; with regard to its types of criminals and the methods used to analyze them, it has marked similarities to characteristics that can be observed for the preliminary investigation, statistics, and jurisprudence. What is more, criminology's delinquent, as he took on clearer contours in the last third of the nineteenth century, was no more and no less than the systematic formulation of what had been produced over decades in the framework of the preliminary investigation and in legal and statistical texts. But that also means conversely that the conceptions of criminals and criminality developed in criminology, viewed from the standpoint of contemporaries, were not especially strident or even far-fetched; in fact, they fit right into the broad picture. Criminology's contributions represented only a portion of a wider debate in which similar or even identical interpretations were represented.[57] Thus, the criminal figures from criminological publications that often seem outlandish today arose from a combination of elements that had already been envisioned in legal, statistical, and journalistic texts, had to some extent already been worked out, and had definitely already taken form in the practices of the preliminary investigation

The close connections between the preliminary investigation, statistics, and jurisprudence on one hand and criminology on the other become clear from a quick glance at criminology, which of course encompassed very different currents of its own.[58] A number of nineteenth-century criminologists assumed that criminals did not just embrace a life of crime at a certain point in the course of their lives, like a fall from grace, rather they argued that the potential for criminal behavior was built into the human being from the outset. Consequently, people did not become criminals because of damage to the soul, spirit, or body, but were more or less so inclined from birth – and this "more or less" was fiercely contested. The broad consensus was that criminals were a special group of disabled people who lacked morals and reason, and were thus dangerous.[59] The concept of the individual guided by reason was shaken, as was the notion that people became criminals because of psychological or economic need. Moreover, many criminologists assumed that criminals had poorly developed personalities and therefore minimally developed inhibitions; they were a special group reminiscent of both the popularly conjured-up primitives and the "wild men" ever present in the colonial fantasies of the late nineteenth century. These representatives of the so-called primitive peoples *(Naturvölker)* had stopped at a stage of human development generally considered long past in Europe. However, this special group also especially resembled the species of criminal familiar from lookout descriptions, statistics, and legal case histories: figures that, detached from all social and emotional connections, were like beings to whom all human emotions were foreign. They could be reduced to a hodgepodge of unrelated characteristics existing next to each other, including thick lips, a rigid gaze, poor morals, a lack of family connections or property, male gender, and a high forehead.

Nevertheless, the criminological theories not only made an impression in a series of discussions, but could also draw on already existing practices, namely those of the lookout descriptions. In both contexts, it was believed that important information about the criminal could be obtained by measuring and describing his body. As the theory went, the criminal essence was inherent in the criminal's body from the beginning and was visible in the form of specific physiognomic characteristics; it was thus possible, according to Lombroso, to tell scientifically from bodily appearance who was a criminal. For that purpose, the only requirement was a special measuring procedure that Lombroso and others, for example, the Parisian Police Prefect Bertillon, had developed in order to detect the specific characteristics that could be seen most clearly on the head itself: a crooked nose; a sloping forehead; thick, fleshy lips; and large ears.[60] It is striking that many of the body parts that were already considered significant in the lookout description were now measured again: the face, the nose, the head, the lips, and body stature. To measure the individual body parts anew, the criminals were subjected to a precise measurement procedure using the anthropometric process developed by Bertillon. Then the individual body parts were thoroughly described according to a special schema, and at the end, the criminal was photographed according to a specific schema.[61]

The totality of the thus determined data – according to the criminologists – revealed the criminal. Exactly what he looked like becomes clear from the crime museums that were opened in many larger European cities toward the end of the century.[62] Everything that was regarded as important for categorization of the criminal was collected in these museums. The significant elements were primarily the parts of the criminal's body itself: well-preserved reproductive organs, hands, ears, noses, arms, and more. Included were also precise photographs of criminals' various body parts and photographic studies of criminals' posture and gait. Finally, collections of hair, clothing articles, and weapons used in crimes were laid out. Entirely with nineteenth-century museum logic, these objects were hung, set, and laid next to and above each other, creating a hodgepodge of unrelated evidence on view side by side. This arrangement differed in no way from that of the local history museums established at the same time or the distribution in the new pathological museums such as Virchow's in Berlin.[63] In both places the selection of objects and their arrangement were meant to produce meaning, in one case a new conception of homeland or medical science, in another, a new conception of the criminal. In the latter case, the production of meaning could again draw on the work of preliminary investigations or of gendarmes even in Electoral Hesse. Since about mid-century, the gendarmes had collected individual apple cores, wood splinters, and clothing scraps with great care at crime scenes and entered them precisely into inventory lists. The objects only needed to be accounted for on these inventory lists in well-organized administrative offices and then transported to such a museum, where they were possibly prepared and in any case labeled.[64]

In summary, the criminological perspective, as represented so vividly in crime museums, went hand in hand with legal and statistical discussions and with various types of evidence production within the preliminary investigation.[65] In both contexts, a new image of the criminal gradually emerged through comparable processes of decontextualization, desubjectification, and quantification. Neither criminology nor the case histories of subject experts, even less visual inspection reports from the preliminary investigations, were left out in creating these criminals – the sources were mutually dependent, built on one another, and copied and changed themselves at the same time.

Remarkable is the fact that the legal, criminological, and statistical discussions interlocked so tightly, making clear that the methods for producing truth as seen in the preliminary investigation occurred in a space that was anything but sterile; the procedure practiced there can hardly be described as an act of disciplinization and an increase in objectivity, as many contemporaries maintained. But likewise remarkable is that the criminal type in question was a contradictory figure, despite the fact that it was supposed to produce clarity: clarity in identifying people or even in evaluating things. The figure was a being that was measured and described precisely and yet resembled a conglomeration of body parts placed side by side without context and scarcely connected to each other. As precisely and individually as the separate body parts were supposedly researched and photographed, what resulted was a curiously abstract figure. Despite the masterful meticulousness of the detailed description, a standardized and possibly even stereotypical type of criminal emerged, primarily because of the uniformity of the selection, labeling, and representation categories with which the objects were chosen, described in writing and/or processed, and represented three-dimensionally or one-dimensionally. Furthermore, the ostensibly individual calculations for the particular bodies yielded people who could be carbon copies. This paradox had many faces. In crime statistics, the objective was to track down the criminal by precise categorization, and the never-ending, supposedly exact naming of the individual parts achieved the opposite. In criminology, every body part was measured, and still no criminal was recognized. In the lookout description, every hair was included, and yet, gendarmes produced quite different lookout descriptions for one and the same person.

But what does the fabrication of a new being using the processes of decontextualization, desubjectification, and quantification observable simultaneously in the preliminary investigation, statistics, law, and criminology from the mid-century on have to do with the ways in which justice was established? What new perspectives on the analyses of the preliminary investigation are generated in light of such an interconnected approach? The interconnectedness shown here among law, statistics, and criminology, and the new methods of evidence production in the form of certificates of character, visual inspection reports and lookout descriptions elucidate how closely the process of establishing justice, with its techniques, was associated with a great number of new kinds of knowledge formation and thus was not a phenomenon detached from everything else and, like the allegorical figure of Justitia, blind to its surroundings.

Contemporaries wanted to eliminate this interconnectedness and, indeed, dependence on any other form of knowledge but the legal, because the alleged closed containment of the legal space was precisely what lent it legitimacy and helped convey the impression that the reformed legal system was a new forum for determining the truth.

The interconnectedness was disavowed not only by contemporaries, but also by all the legal and scholarly historical studies that analyzed legal case histories while neatly separating them from criminological and statistical representations of the criminal. Only by making such a separation is it possible to interpret the development evident in the case histories as "disciplinization" (*Verfachlichung*) and, at the same time, to describe criminology as a regrettable scientific dead-end.[66] However, if the connections between the different discourses and practices are kept in mind – as the recent history of science demands for all disciplines – the notion of the disciplinization of jurisprudence and the associated claim that disciplinization has led to a better, more factual, equality-based form of establishing justice become untenable.

What is more, other research theories are rendered questionable by an interconnection-based perspective. One example, among others, is the theory proposed by Peter Becker that criminology constructs "negative mirror images of an idealized middle class life plan,"[67] and that the "*uomo delinquente*" moves the criminal, the figure which is the negative version of the "healthy middle class citizen," to center stage as the model for normalcy in the last third of the nineteenth century.[68] This theory is not deceptive because it is wrong; it is deceptive only because it is incomplete. It ignores the fact that the characteristic in question is not limited to criminology alone. Naturally, *ex negativo* constructs of the middle-class citizen were created in criminology, but alcoholic men, immoral women, and neglected children also populate crime statistics, certificates of character, and case histories, even before the emergence of criminology. These shadowy figures can also be found by the score in entirely different debates which were probably far more effective with the public; discussions about the so-called social question were teeming with these and similar beings for no particular reason. Criminology thus definitely did not furnish new interpretive contexts; rather, it singled out elements that had been developed in many other debates.

A third theory also championed in research circles loses plausibility in view of the background sketched of the criminal figures shared in common and the similar procedural methods. The theory holds that the massive creation of relevant texts – police, legal, and/or criminological – is to be interpreted solely as an expression of the state's effort to expand control.[69] Explanations of this sort assume omnipotent actors who moreover made the motives for and consequences of actions align in a downright enviable manner. Likewise, the many non-state actors are overlooked: members of the statistical associations and literati, but also criminologists who all collaborated in developing this wayward, soulless type of criminal. Finally, this interpretation ignores the explanation that most of the desire for control was doubtless produced by just those statistics, criminological debates, and police photographs.[70]

Of course, such a perspective on interconnectedness not only renders older interpretations obsolete but also opens up new ones. First, it becomes clear that the perhaps subjective efforts to reduce the drama and enhance the scientific basis indirectly produced something new: a very effective legal viewpoint – one performative dimension of the new decontextualization procedures is thereby addressed. The new legal outlook created a criminal who had just as much or as little to do with the reality of social history as the criminal figures portrayed in literature. It was an alien, threatening figure only recognizable in shadowy outlines; a figure which had been reduced to the status of an object and, devoid of any inner or external motives, scarcely seemed to still be human. The figure did not appear to be a person to be protected but instead one to be combatted, no longer the object of compassionate understanding but instead the incarnation of evil.

The criminal figures themselves restructured legal actions – a second performative dimension – in that judges regarded defendants less as pitiful victims reduced to poverty by others' debts, with wrongly understood conceptions of honor, and more as threatening figures whose massive increase in numbers was to be curtailed. Nor was this perception without consequences for the thinking of the thieves themselves – that fact is indicated if nothing else by the in-court statements of the defendants, who quoted very precisely the discourses in question.

A third performative dimension of these procedures should be mentioned. In composing a lookout description, as in preparing statistics, a new outlook is created, an outlook[71] based on new procedures for measurement, quantification, and description. Lookout descriptions, lists, sketches, reports, statistics, legal case histories, and criminological discussions reinforced a new view endowed with the aura of science. Every gendarme who composed a crime scene sketch learned to establish new kinds of connections, and he refined this vision with every lookout description. The new outlook was taught even beyond the narrow sphere of statisticians, criminologists, jurists, and gendarmes. The published lookout description, the police photo, and Zola's novels, which were swarming with habitual criminals and known for their overwhelming success, educated many readers in these perspectives.

Notes

1 The field of statistics, which ultimately became important for crime statistics, began to develop at the end of the eighteenth century at the university in Göttingen. Its goal was to collect as much information as possible "relating to the general welfare of a state," and to record it in tabular and graphical form. Gottfried Achenwall, *Staatsverfassung der heutigen vornehmsten Europäischen Reiche und Völker im Grundriß*, Göttingen, 1781 (6th edition), 6; quoted as in Wolfgang Bonß, 1982, 75.

2 In German-speaking areas, the field of statistics only gradually developed an interest in criminals. After England and France had already started collecting statistics on criminal proceedings in the early eighteenth century, individual German territorial states were given instructions at the end of the eighteenth century to perform statistical surveys on judicial business activities. This practice became established in an increasing number of German federal states at the beginning of the nineteenth century. In 1802, indexes of the criminal trials that took place in the "Electoral courts of justice in Bavaria" were published; "criminal tables" were issued in Baden a short time later. Police tables and prison statistics were added to the court tables. For an overview, see Helmut Graff, 1975, 28ff. It is striking that the federal states which had Napoleon to thank for considerable inspiration regarding their legal and administrative development were also the quickest to act regarding statistics. For that reason, these statistics must also be viewed as part of the emergence of modern administration and the modern type of official. On early French statistics, see Michelle Perrot, 2001a, 257–270. In France, *General Account of the Administration of*

Criminal Justice was published after 1827, and *Annals of Public Health and Medicine*, after 1829; in the same year, "geographical crime maps" also appeared.

3 Review of W. Drobisch, *Beiträge zur Statistik des vormaligen Kurfürstenthums Hessen*, 1867. However, the reviewer also finds fault with the work of the Statistical Commission. In his view, the Commission "neither collected comprehensive statistical material ... nor significantly advanced the field by answering important questions." Still, he continues, "[The commission] should not be reproached for this, because it is impossible to know how great the obstacles placed in the path from 'on high' were."

4 See Herbert Reinke, 1990, 170. In Schleswig-Holstein, an 1802 circular decree provided for recording the name, language, offense, sentence, and personal description of all criminals by the responsible authorities; see Kai D. Sievers, 1975.

5 Statistical overviews were already produced in the 1840s, for example, on questions regarding livestock or for population statistics. In addition, there were statistical bureaus in the individual provinces of Electoral Hesse; they produced at least enough material that Bruno Hildebrand was able to publish an extensive work in 1853 on the economic conditions in Electoral Hesse. Furthermore, there was so much energy and central organizational vitality present that in the middle of the 1850s a comprehensive survey of all Electoral Hessian towns could be conducted; central to the survey was a uniform questionnaire on the social, economic, and climate situation. Meant here are the so-called topographies extensively analyzed by Cameron Munter, 1983, and located in Collection H3 of the Marburg State Archive. A portion of these topographies were examined. They provide material on location, climate, residents, houses, and religion, and resemble the medical topographies of the early nineteenth century. However, clear emphasis is placed on recording the property situation.

6 Electoral Hesse's detained prisoners, in *Beiträge zur Statistik des vormaligen Kurfürstentums Hessen*, 3 (1867). Unfortunately, there are no more detailed studies of Electoral Hesse.

7 A 1880 letter of the *Reich*'s Deputy Chancellor states that, as unity of criminal law and criminal proceedings had been achieved, it was now "desirable" to produce "criminal statistics based on the same foundation"; GStA PK HA I Rep. 77, Ministry of Internal Affairs, Tit 114, No. 277, Ministry of Internal Affairs in Berlin, June 25, 1881, "Federal Council No. 96." Such statistics are of special importance for the "actual business statistics of the criminal court" and furthermore, their "substance" can be useful for "very important guidance and discussions about conditions in a number of areas"; GStA PK HA I Rep. 77, Ministry of Internal Affairs, Tit 114, No. 277, Letter of the Justice Ministry dated December 8, 1880, to the Ministry of Internal Affairs. The statistics were also supposed to be useful for "academic research," as the preface states in the published version of the 1881 crime data, the first that were uniform for the *Reich*; see *Zeitschrift des Königlich-Preussischen Statistischen Bureaus*, Supplement XIV (1883), V.

8 Michelle Perrot, 2001a.

9 Edict of December 22, 1888, "regarding production of statistics on administration of criminal justice."

10 Ian McNeely, 2003, 216, states that "excitement about statistical topography and historical folklore had penetrated even down to the village level, where many people happily contributed to these projects."

11 In Prussia, for example, such a journal was published "by its Director." In 1883, the journal was particularly concerned with the "results of the administration of criminal justice in the Kingdom of Prussia ... edited by W. Starke"; the latter was a senior privy councilor for justice and expert councilor (*Vortragender Rat*) in the Ministry of Justice, and made a name for himself with his own extensive publication – quoted here several times; Wilhelm Starke, 1884.

12 See Hans-Erich Bödeker, 2001; Michelle Perrot, 2001a, 257.

13 On this subject, see the comments in the statistical study by Wilhelm Starke, 1884, 88: "Scarcely ever in the span of a single generation have so many monumental factors of various kinds influenced the life of our people as in the period from 1848 to 1878: complete reorganization of the administration of justice and the police ... increases in the size and density of the population ... phenomenal development of industry ... development of world traffic and world trade ... finally, a deeply penetrating socialist movement."

14 Until the mid-century, not much energy was expended on collecting statistical data for criminals, which did not, of course, prevent anyone from making broad statements about them while referring to statistics. Until the middle of the nineteenth century, the courts' business activities much more than criminals and their living conditions, to say nothing of their mental state, was the central focus of statistics. The issue was the question of how many cases were handled by particular courts in a given time span, how many unfinished cases were backlogged, what penalties were pronounced for which cases, and what average costs were incurred. See Alexander Melchers, 1992, 56ff, and Silviana Galassi, 2004, 89, who emphasizes that business statistics were the primary concern for the first half of the nineteenth century. On that subject, see Georg von Mayr, 1867, whose studies on the police executive functions were especially detailed. See as an example, in particular for the Kingdom of Württemberg: *Criminalstatistik Königreich Württemberg*, in *Hitzigs Annalen*, 5, New Series (1846); Schettler, 1849; and *Criminalstatistik Berlin*, in *Hitzigs Annalen*, 6, New Series (1846); *Criminalstatistik Königreich Bayern*, in *Hitzigs Annalen*, 6, New Series (1846); *Criminalstatistik Königreich Sachsen* in *Hitzigs Annalen*, 24, New Series (1851); and *Criminalstatistik St. Gallen*, in *Hitzigs Annalen*, 25, New Series (1851). All these statistics are generally limited to determining the business activities of the justice system. Furthermore, in the years immediately after introduction of jury courts, questions were asked especially intensively and from all angles about the business activities of individual judges and state procurators, but also about jurists, and surveys were conducted about the costs of *Schwurgericht* proceedings. On this subject, see *Criminalstatistik Königreich Hannover*, in *Hitzigs Annalen*, 42, New Series (1855); Lichtenberg, 1852; *Criminalstatistik Königreich Hannover, Fortsetzung*, in *Hitzigs Annalen*, 43, New Series (1855). It also becomes

clear from these examples that statistical surveys played a great role in everyday political controversies. Thus, the commentary to the latter statistics states, "It has already become evident with some certainty at this point that the widely held view which feared a substantial increase in the cost of criminal proceedings from performance of oral trials in criminal cases was entirely unfounded" (75). In addition, the author maintains that a further charge – that the number of employees had been disproportionately increased by the new organization – "appears to have just as little foundation" (78). Ultimately, those were statistics that – for example, in Prussia – had to be provided by the regional justice authorities to the Ministry of Justice. Then the statistics were published in the gazette of the Justice Ministry; see GStA PK HA I Rep. 77, Ministry of Internal Affairs, Tit 114, No. 277. A letter of the Justice Minister dated July 11, 1870, points out that there had already been an order on December 27, 1854, which provided for mandatory implementation of such statistics for the *Schwurgerichte*. Recall here the "record books on the files" prepared by the courts, primarily giving brief information about who was criminally prosecuted in which matter at what time. More exact details about the persons charged are lacking.

15 See the following statistics: *Criminalstatistik Berlin*, in *Hitzigs Annalen*, 6, New Series (1846), 101; Mühry, 1847; *Criminalstatistik St. Gallen*, in *Hitzigs Annalen*, 25, New Series (1851); *Civil-Strafgerichte des Großherzogtums Hessen*, in *Hitzigs Annalen*, 35, New Series (1853); *Übersicht Herzogtums Braunschweig Strafsachen*, in *Hitzigs Annalen*, 38, New Series (1854), 173; Georg von Mayr, 1867, 134 and 156. In these cases, the method of calculation is such that women appear as a subset of generally defined male crime, while men are taken as the norm. On criminal statistics of the Kingdom of Hannover in 1852 and 1853, see *Criminalstatistik Königreich Hannover, Fortsetzung*, in *Hitzigs Annalen*, 43, New Series (1855), 73; *Civil-Strafgerichte des Großherzogtums Hessen*, in *Hitzigs Annalen*, 35, New Series (1853), 207, where the female percentage of the most important crimes is listed. Excepted are those crimes "which according to the factual findings can only have been committed with women as their initiators." The commentary to the *Übersicht Herzogtums Braunschweig Strafsachen*, in *Hitzigs Annalen*, 38, New Series (1854), 175, states for some crimes, "includes women." The structure is reversed in the *Criminalstatistik Königreich Hannover*, in *Hitzigs Annalen*, 42, New Series (1855), 80, where the following statement is made regarding the ratio between convicted men and women: "With a 1:4 ratio of women to men, 294." For this aspect, see Georg con Mayr, 1867, 22f.

16 See *Criminalstatistik St. Gallen*, in *Hitzigs Annalen*, 25, New Series (1851), 179; *Übersicht Herzogtums Braunschweig Strafsachen*, in *Hitzigs Annalen*, 38, New Series (1854), 175, where only children and adolescents were differentiated from adults, but age cohorts were also established.

17 There is a breakdown by occupation in only one of the sets of criminal statistics that I examined. For the female offenders, "unmarried women" is listed as the occupation; see *Übersicht Herzogtums Braunschweig Strafsachen*, in *Hitzigs Annalen*, 38, New Series (1854), 175f. There is seldom any differentiation between urban and rural.

18 See Aurelio Buddeus, 1846, 224; *Criminalstatistik Berlin*, in *Hitzigs Annalen*, 6, New Series (1846), 101; *Criminalstatistik St. Gallen*, in *Hitzigs Annalen*, 25, New Series (1851), 178.

19 See Aurelio Buddeus, 1846, 224, who only asks about family status, but leaves out widows and widowers.

20 Furthermore, the fact that this statistical discourse on crime became involved in various debates in the first half of the century is only mentioned as an aside. Statistics played a role especially within the framework of the so-called social question. Downright paradigmatic in this context is an article which appeared in the *Illustrierte Zeitung* (1847, No. 200, VIII) and reported on a speech of "Freiherr von Reden, who is known for his statistical endeavors." The article describes poverty and its causes; "Proposed as a remedy is exact, particular knowledge about the relevant conditions, measures for collecting mental and moral data." Friedrich Wilhelm von Reden was a member of the Central Society for the Wellbeing of the Working Classes and was deeply committed to statistical penetration of the environment of the lower classes in particular. One of the debates concerned the question of the effectiveness of punishment (see Alexander Melchers, 1992, 7ff). Another one dealt with the question of whether solitary confinement prisons were more effective than prisons that permitted prisoners, at least to some extent, to be together with other prisoners (see Thomas Nutz, 2001). There was talk on all sides of the "decline of culture" and of the "retreat of morality." Statistics seemed to provide every proof imaginable for the propositions; Wilhelm Starke, 1884, 2. See the *Illustrierte Zeitung*, which often dealt with such problems in the 1840s and repeatedly argued with statistical results. For example, see the article of August 11, 1849, but also the series of articles on social poverty begun that year; in the series, any given argument was buttressed with statistical evidence. Unfortunately, there is no in-depth study that examines the importance of statistics for such debates.

21 See Wilhelm Starke, 1884, 13f. For Electoral Hesse, see also "*Kurhessens detinirte Gefangene*," in *Beiträge zur Statistik des vormaligen Kurfürstentums Hessen*, 3 (1867).

22 "*Kurhessens detinirte Gefangene*," in *Beiträge zur Statistik des vormaligen Kurfürstentums Hessen*, 3 (1867), 2. Other categories that had already existed previously were expanded. Overall, the practice from the 1860s on was to collect a whole batch of data about criminals.

23 Georg von Mayr, 1867, 28, used the following categories: Catholics, Protestants and Reformed Church members, Mennonites, Anabaptists, Greeks, German Catholics, Friends of the Light, and non-Christians. Georg von Mayr, 1867, 129, writes, "It is most remarkable that the relevant information on religion" shows that religion has no effect of delinquency. As a rule, no distinction was made between Catholic and Protestant offenders, but only between Christians and Jews; see *Criminalstatistik Berlin*, in *Hitzigs Annalen*, 6, New Series (1846), 101; Aurelio Buddeus, 1846, 224.

24 In *Reich* statistics, the occupation category was subdivided into a total of twenty-nine subcategories – thus, in this case the organization was very granular. Furthermore, with regard to offenders, the question of legitimate

versus illegitimate birth was added; in contrast, economic circumstances were not determined; see Wilhelm Starke, 1883. Under the heading "Status," the heading "Divorced" and the category "Unknown" could also be found.

25 See Georg von Mayr, 1867, 24f. Also interesting in this context is the statement made in Georg Mayr, 1867, 30, about the relationship between criminal status and "parceling of land holdings." However, his statistics correlate the average size of holdings to the rate of men "capable of crime" without distinguishing how great overall the proportion of agrarian population was and how succession was regulated, or what the replacement regulations looked like in law and in fact. These statistics are downright paradigmatic for the statistical construct content.

26 In Electoral Hesse, there were eight subcategories for occupation: "day laborers, servants, factory workers and assistants, tradesmen, business owners and industrialists, literati and artists, officials, wives and family members of the people named in column 24" (that is, of the officials).

27 That applies to Electoral Hesse (see *Beiträge zur Statistik des vormaligen Kurfürstentums Hessen*), Prussia (see Wilhelm Starke, 1883, but also the *Zeitschrift des Königlich-Preussischen statistischen Bureaus*, supplementary volume XIV, 1883) and also Bavaria (see Georg von Mayr, 1867). That means for Electoral Hesse that the new Electoral Hessian statistics sorted prisoners according to the six different prisons and the provinces.

28 In Electoral Hesse there were fifty-six different crime types in all; in Bavarian statistics there were fewer. The *Reich* statistics of the 1880s included seventy-six crime types. See Wilhelm Starke, 1883.

29 In addition, the impression was reinforced by the simple fact that, next to criminal statistics, social statistics were the most widely disseminated; the latter were intensively used for argumentation in the context of debates about the so-called social question.

30 Georg von Mayr, 1867, 33ff.

31 "*Kurhessens detinirte Gefangene*," in *Beiträge zur Statistik des vormaligen Kurfürstentums Hessen*, 3 (1867) 47.

32 See the information on the social and economic living conditions in Electoral Hesse in Chapter 1.

33 Paradigmatically, see Aurelio Buddeus, 1846, 219.

34 See Wilhelm Starke, 1884, 88; Georg von Mayr, 1867, 41f: "In contrast, if the motives for property injury, in most cases theft, are considered, the desire to obtain goods for immediate satisfaction of needs or as barter for luxury items ... stands out; ... food items of all kinds are most intensively sought. But the urge to satisfy food requirements in an illegal manner must be all the stronger, the more difficult it is to obtain food in a legal manner by economic activity. It is therefore obvious to extrapolate from food access disruption to an increase in all kinds of property injuries. Food access disruption can be subjective, when obtaining food becomes difficult because of income reduction but without price increases. However, food access disruption can also be objective, if food prices rise substantially."

35 On the debates in this regard also carried on in the field of criminal law, see Alexander Melchers, 1992.

36 See *Criminalstatistik Berlin*, in *Hitzigs Annalen*, 6, New Series (1846), 102.

37 See Herbert Reinke, 1987; Jürgen Reulecke, 1981, 365, on the statistical surveys and the inquiries of the *Verein für deutsche Statistik* (Association for German Statistics) and the *Centralverein für das Wohl der arbeitende Klasse* (Central Association for the Wellbeing of the Working Class).

38 Adolphe Quetelet is generally viewed as the founder of moral and criminal statistics. In 1836, he published his *Sur l'homme et le développement de ses facultés ou Essai de physique sociale*. In this work, the statistics compiled established a connection between poverty and diseases (for example, cholera) which were dangerous because infectious, and then immediately mapped the diseases on city maps. Especially the English "statistical societies" but also the German Central Association for the Wellbeing of the Working Class devoted much time and energy to creating such ethnographic studies of cities with statistical means and to breathing life into the new genre of social statistics. What developed as a side effect were dark continents, "no-go areas," and the notion of an unclean, poor, and sick sub-proletariat that existed on a mass scale, indeed, only as a mass phenomenon. See Rolf Lindner, 2004, 19–97; in this work, he portrays these new forms of city ethnography very impressively.

39 Paul J. A. Ritter von Feuerbach, 1849.

40 At about the same time as public executions were abolished and the "theater of horrors" was only presented within the walls before the eyes of a small, distinguished group of middle-class men, the criminal in search of, if not sympathy, then at least attention and affirmation, disappeared from the legal case collections. When the move was made to the prison yards inside, it was often argued that the masses looking on up to that point had followed the spectacle of the execution with inappropriate feelings – with pity or a craving for sensationalism. On this subject, see the study of Richard Evans, 2001.

41 The review appeared in the *Jenaische Allgemeine Literatur-Zeitung*, No. 2 (1829); quoted in Joachim Rückert, 1991a, 302. Sylvia Kesper-Biermann generously pointed out to me that this development must be viewed in the context of the emergence of criminal psychology as a science. See also Joachim Rückert, 1991b. Now a clear boundary was drawn between texts which were considered fiction and those designated as fact; reference only to authentic sources in criminal biographies or stories from the criminal milieu was not adequate. On this subject, see also Jörg Schönert, 1992, 153, who points out that with this newly drawn boundary, for example, novels of terror and banditry disappeared from the lending libraries because they were no longer considered suitable reading material for middle-class circles. See Eckardt Meyer-Krentler, 1991.

42 See Jörg Schönert, 1983b, who here for the first time traces in detail the process of refining the discourse on criminals; and Jörg Schönert, 1991a. See also Jörg Schönert, 1987 and 1983a.

43 The history of jurisprudence for German-speaking areas during the nineteenth century has not been viewed differently, i.e., not in terms of disciplinization and thus also of professionalization, and has not to date been researched from the perspectives of more recent historical studies. There are first attempts for France; see Frédéric Chauvaud and Jean-Jacques Yvorel, 1994. Just as in

statistics, the emergence of new publication forms such as professional journals was part of this professionalization process. In these new professional journals in particular, "scientific" treatment of case histories played a great role, when the autonomy of an episteme such as scientificity that was equated with objectivity and endowed with particular dignity was to be signaled. (The first studies on nineteenth-century legal journals have been available since the collected volume of Michael Stolleis, 1999.) It was only logical that these journals became the privileged place for publication of the new type of case histories, while the old "Pitaval" genre was increasingly avoided by professional jurists and attributed to the belletristic sphere. Of course, there was a "New Pitaval" and also other comparable collections on the book market – but they were no longer considered scholarly texts. On the "New Pitaval," which was published between 1842 and 1890, and on Ludwig Demmes' *Das Buch der Verbrechen*, which appeared after 1852, see Joachim Linder, 1991.

44 In addition, text conglomerates were now published more frequently in the relevant legal journals, which no longer concealed their origin, that is, it was a simple matter of publishing a verdict and its justification, with any dissent as well. Thus, in 1850 the verdict from the court of first instance and the reasoning behind it were published in *Hitzigs Annalen* under the title "The Incorrigible Thief," followed by the appeal pleading and the verdict of the court of second instance. See Dr. Giesecke, 1850.

45 Frequently more than three dozen quotations were listed to answer the question of how high the obstacle to be overcome had to be to possibly reach the threshold for a qualified theft. In a few rare instances, the case description also served the purpose – as earlier – of providing information about social phenomena regarded as especially important. Thus, for example, the theft case was meant to throw "a few rays of light" on the vagabond life of released prisoners. Of course, that case was neither described in detail nor precisely analyzed, as, for example, criminologists did a short time later. See habitual thief, in *Hitzigs Annalen*, 26, New Series (1851), 95.

46 See Bopp, 1850b, 167, who says that, "... [A]ccording to his statements, [he] diligently stuck with the church and school in his youth but did not learn to write or to read handwritten material, and he is even inexperienced in reading printed text and is unable to advance."

47 Bopp, 1847, 146.

48 Wolfgang Naucke, 1983, 62, classifies concentration on the crime as part of the process of "disciplinization."

49 This apparent disappearance of the person becomes especially evident in the few exceptional cases in which texts after 1840 still examined crime motives or conceptualize images from inside the offender's head. For instance, that is the case in passages where defense attorneys had the word. Their narratives still continued to follow patterns of representation that we know from the end of the eighteenth and beginning of the nineteenth centuries. For example, the simple circumstance that a maid stole money from a guest's room would not have been reported in those narratives, as that act would have satisfied the aggravating factual finding for qualified theft because it would have constituted servant theft. Instead, we hear something about the thoughts and inner

motivations of the maid – which are of course surprisingly reminiscent of the set pieces known from literature and conventional case histories. In particular, the maid, upon seeing a box that appeared to hold money, was struck by the "unfortunate idea" of stealing it, because she was engaged "to the shoemaker's apprentice Röhre ... and was now thinking of poverty," "which gave her no prospects of [being able] to marry him." In this situation the well-known economic motive, and indirectly also that of marriage, comes up; she wanted to steal in order to lead an honorable life as a housewife; see Jannasch, 1848, 147.

50 For an example of this , see Anton Bauer, 1839a.

51 See Bopp, 1848, Case XV, 76.

52 See Bopp, 1850b, 177.

53 See Bopp, 1848, Case IV, 71.

54 Furthermore, the narrative perspective contributed to reinforcing the image of the shadowy being devoid of any human elements. As a rule, an author-narrator controlled the portrayal. In contrast to the case histories at the end of the eighteenth and beginning of the nineteenth centuries, the perspective of the criminal was seldom taken up. That only happened when that perspective could be overridden, called into question, or exposed to be false by addition of further perspectives. Thus, regarding the strikingly detailed description of the life history of Johann Friedrich Mohr the statement is made that he complained in his childhood about bad treatment and "inadequate nourishment" from his foster parents. Bad care – that was legally relevant – could indicate neglect and a mitigating circumstance. Or the bad treatment could provide an almost classic motive, well-known from numerous literary models, for the subsequent crimes. Instead of this reference to "inadequate nourishment" being made the point of departure for an analysis of the inner and external motives of the offender, it was, in this case history from the second third of the nineteenth century, exposed as a spurious and false assertion that showed the offender to be a liar. It was by no means – the statement went on – bad food that drove Mohr away from his foster parents; instead, he had had to leave his foster parents because he could not become "accustomed to order." See Anton Bauer, 1839c.

Appraising comments that did not contain any legally based arguments but instead took the form of personal opinions rarely appear, sometimes only in the concluding sentence. Even in a case that definitely meets all the criteria for "bizarre" because it has to do with a man who had lived almost his entire life from theft and after all was convicted of 155 thefts, the description contains only one judgmental concluding comment. Furthermore, the final comment is weakened still further because it is passed off as a quotation from another work: "Even common criminals frequently stand out for their mental capabilities, and those capabilities must be given credit for turning stealing, in its own way, into an art." That is the closing line of the work by Bopp, 1847, 184.

55 Contemporary criminal law reformers such as Franz von Liszt and Gustav Radbruch himself referred to the literary representation of criminals in a positive way, for they believed that they should admonish jurists to read literary texts because especially valuable practical knowledge was revealed

there and the subject of the action could be studied well; see Jörg Schönert, 1991b, 500ff.

56 The concept "criminology" is defined in broad terms here; it would be more correct to speak of criminological discourse, as the concept did not appear until 1885. Miloš Vec pointed that out at a conference sponsored by Gerd Schwerhoff and me in Göttingen in 2006; Miloš Vec, *Entstehung und Scheitern von Kriminologie und Kriminalistik als semiotische Disziplinen*, in Rebekka Habermas and Gerd Schwerhoff (Eds.), *Verbrechen im Blick. Perspektiven einer neuzeitlichen Kriminalitätsforschung* (Frankfurt and New York, 2009), 383–414.

57 That contradicts the view, seldom expressed explicitly but evident from the general direction of the study, which holds that Lombroso marked a break, or stood at the beginning of criminology. Most studies on criminology subscribe to such a perspective; for example, see Richard Wetzell, 2000.

58 Research on criminology, especially in German-speaking areas, has grown substantially in recent years. Because the present book has gone through a long research and writing process, not all of the more recent publications could be considered.

Naturally, a precise analysis of the very diverse trends within criminology might be in order here. However, as the objective is not to examine criminological discourse in detail but to situate criminological discourse within the context of other types of discourse, such an analysis can be dispensed with. See the very detailed study of Silviana Galassi, 2004, who very rightly warns of equating Lombroso to all of criminology. In this context, attention should be paid to the school of thought within criminology that sought the causes for criminal behavior in social conditions.

59 See the studies of Peter Becker, 2002, 1999, 1992a, and 1992b. He describes the transformation of criminal discourse in the nineteenth century. In the first half of the nineteenth century, the criminal was conceived of "as a fallen angel" who had deviated from the right path because of alcohol, prostitution, poverty, etc. In the last third, this image had changed: In the new view, the criminal was born to crime and consequently could no longer be saved.

60 See Susanne Regener, 1999, 212.

61 On bertillonage, see Miloš Vec, 2002, 31–47; on the practice of bertillonage, see Andreas Roth, 1997, 101ff. Of course, other knowledge streams entered in at the end of the nineteenth century, among others, emerging forensic psychiatry, which will not be discussed here.

62 There is a dearth of research literature on criminal museums; see the informative commentary of Susanne Regener, 1999, 177ff.

63 On this subject, see the very instructive contribution of Angela Matyssek, 2001. Here, too, the wooden vessels of a particular region or the skulls with a specific type of abnormality or disease were placed in glass cabinets next to and above one another without connection, or perhaps at most arranged by size. See also Alon Confino, 1997, on the logic of the organization in local museums.

64 While these museums lived from criminology, just as criminology continued to develop in these museums, another type of representation developing at the same time also played an important role. I am speaking of police photography, whose entirely unique form of aesthetics was closely connected to Bertillon. In her outstanding study, Susanne Regener established that there were efforts from the 1860s on to photograph criminals so that they could be apprehended more easily (see Susanne Regener, 1999). Instead of photographing people in their social frame of reference, thus so to speak making their class clear – as did middle class portrait photography, which tended to portray ladies and gentlemen of the middle class with little pillars or in front of bookcases – police photography was supposed to be as objective and neutral as possible, with no kind of indication of the social status of the photographed subject. That means that no other object, no meaningful background, no gestures, and no special clothing were to be in the picture; instead, a gaze straight ahead, an upright posture, and head held straight, were a must. In addition, a side view had to be taken to provide information about the "entire person." After all, it was believed that police photography had supplied the "perfect" tool for lookout purposes that would make lookout description efforts superfluous. So that these photos could be made, criminals were forced into apparatuses specially designed for that purpose; they produced exactly the right posture. See Miloš Vec, 2002; on police photography and its police function, Jens Jäger, 2001. What resulted from these premises were photographs that, because of the strictly regimented arrangement of all the subjects, all looked alike, and had little to do with the person photographed. Thus, this form of photography displayed clear parallels to the photography that developed almost simultaneously in mental institutions and in the emerging field of ethnology. Obliteration of the individual was furthered by adoption of visualization strategies – for example, the side portrait – that had little to do either with everyday habits of viewing or any precursor within the history of visualization. The photographs were so unusual that viewers judged the photographs' similarities very severely. Everyone realized at once that it was a police photograph and consequently that the person portrayed must be a criminal.

65 Against this background, it is understandable why Lombroso caused a furor so quickly: not so much because he developed new ideas, but because much of what turned up in his works had already been discussed for a very long time and only now was especially concisely formulated. Lombroso did not launch any new discussion but his theory intensified the existing debate, inducing both his opponents and supporters to write new essays, hold new conferences, and even found new journals. Lombroso succeeded above all in decisively accelerating development of the new science of criminology. Marie-Christine Leps, 1992, 36ff, pointed out that Lombroso's work furthermore became a "discursive event" because he was involved in institutionalizing a new kind of knowledge formation. Silviana Galassi, 2004, 245ff, views Lombroso's function as a polarizer of debates to be the essence of his stimulating effect. Because the debates assumed a polarizing character and many people became involved (for example, court physicians such as Lombroso's probably best known

adversary, the Frenchman Alexandre Lacassagne, who in 1886 founded the journal *Archives de l'Anthropologie Criminelle des Sciences Pénales* – on Lacassagne, see Philippe Artières, 2000), the debate widened. Jurists like Franz von Liszt, who held an intermediate position between Lombroso and Lacassagne, took part. On these debates, see Silviana Galassi, 2004, 190. Silviana Galassi, 2004, lodges the criticism that Lombroso is often equated in scholarship with the field of criminology in the nineteenth century. She emphasizes that the debate was broader and that even after the refutation of his atavism theory, many of Lombroso's assessments did not lose importance for the interdisciplinary debates. When prison reformers became involved in these debates, some very different debates came into play; as an example, take Benjamin Appert, called an outsider by Thomas Nutz, 2001, 258. He was very active in publishing, including in the *Illustrierte Zeitung*, and provided physiological descriptions of prisoners there that he attributed explicitly to Lavater's influence. Appert also composed descriptions that worked with categories subsequently popularized by Lombroso; see, for example, his article in the *Illustrierte Zeitung*, No. 493 (1852), 371.

66 This process was interpreted for jurisprudence as "disciplinization" (*Verfachlichung*), the term of Wolfgang Naucke, 1983. The term applied exclusively to the change in representation within jurisprudence and differentiated the representation at the middle of the nineteenth century from that at the beginning of the century, as demonstrated, for example, by the Pitaval stories. "Disciplinization" is understood to be the development of an independent legal discourse characterized by "separation of the scholarly, specialized legal world (of the science examining criminal law's contribution to preserving the state and society) from the myriad effects that a crime can have on mind and spirit." Disciplinization thus means representation of the criminal that was "de-dramatized, bureaucratized, and banalized" (Wolfgang Naucke, 1983, 64), and what is more, pledged a greater demand for truth, that is, representation that had clearly separated fact from fiction. This interpretation reiterates the contemporary view that jurists tirelessly promoted themselves when they talked about themselves and their work. Another argument speaks against the disciplinization hypothesis. Although the new legal procedures for recording and describing criminals resemble those in criminology and statistics, no one would describe the development of those disciplines in terms of "disciplinization." It is too obvious that measuring noses and underarms was hardly conducive to bringing anything to light about different criminals. A positive view of this approach would also be inappropriate because the racist implications of such procedures are by now clearly apparent. Consequently, the legal outlook can neither be considered part of the disciplinization process nor viewed in the context of professionalization at all. It is instead part of a comprehensive process in which a whole series of academic disciplines concerned with the criminal developed new measures for objectivity and new methods of description and representation.

67 Peter Becker, 2002, 62.

68 Peter Becker, 2002, 370. In this context, see also the work of Silviana Galassi, 2004, 29, who sees the context similarly, i.e., that at the same time as the criminal, "his antithesis," the middle-class citizen, is constructed.

69 This criticism follows the same line as that of Jens Jäger, 2001.
70 Herbert Reinke, 1987, shows that statistics first produced this need. See also Andreas Roth, 1997, 429: "Numeric documentation first made crime a mass phenomenon . . .; but at the same time, it also revealed the deficits of the police efforts . . .."
71 Peter Becker, 2002, also speaks of this in connection with the development of criminology.

6

Techniques for Finding Truth

How Do People Become Jurists and How Does Property Come into Being?

As important as complaint records, visual inspection reports, and sketches were for structuring investigations, the interrogation of suspects and witnesses, together with the evidence produced by new techniques, stood at the center of the preliminary investigation. The hope was to obtain a confession, or at least crucial clues pointing to the perpetrators, from such interrogations. What were the procedures in this part of the investigation? Were there similar techniques for bringing the truth to light or separating true from untrue? Who actually performed these interrogations?

6.1 JURISTS

The people who directed or performed the interrogations were generally legally trained, whether the investigating judge, who conducted the interrogations,[1] or the investigating procurator, who did not conduct interrogations himself. However, in cases that were to be tried later in high courts, the investigating procurator named the investigating judge and gave him instructions about what was to be asked.[2] Substitutes not explicitly provided for in the code of criminal procedure might also be used[3] – all, almost without exception,[4] were jurists.[5]

What did the role of these jurists in the preliminary investigation involve? This question is most likely to arise if the assumption is not made, as many contemporaries did and many more recent legal studies have,[6] that jurists were simply "appliers of law"; in reality, they collaborated actively in the process of establishing justice. Did they exert primarily political influence, as more than a few contemporaries and many current research works believed and believe? And if so, were the Electoral Hessian jurists actually liberal, as asserted on the basis of the conflicts surrounding Ludwig Hassenpflug,[7] or moderately conservative, as appears to be the case for Prussia?[8] Or was their influence perhaps on a completely different level?

Actually, some facts seem to suggest that the jurists' basic position on how justice was established and what verdicts were ultimately handed down was important. At least there are indications that political attitude was viewed as meaningful by contemporaries; for example, a conspicuous number of new appointments to important positions in the Electoral Hessian judicial system during the years 1848–1849, when the radical demands of the March Revolution that basically changed the judicial system seemed, at least for the short term, to result in a complete restructuring of the political and judicial systems.[9] In fact, it can be observed that, aside from the high court president, who remained the same despite the events of 1848 and 1849, significant personnel changes came about on almost all levels of the judicial system. Of the six 1847 high court councilors, only one was still on the bench in 1850.[10] Although the personnel changes on this level of the judicial system were less pronounced between 1850 and 1854, that is, between the revolutionary and restorative years, they still remained noticeably common even then. In 1854, only half the high courts created in Kassel retained the high court councilors already in that same position in 1850.[11]

Yet aside from this turbulent phase and despite the assertions of many contemporaries and parts of the research community to the contrary, I maintain that political attitudes played a secondary role in the judicial system, or at least were classified by contemporaries as less significant.[12] Disregarding the short phase 1848/49 to 1854, the state made no serious interventions in the structure of the judicial system. To the contrary, the continuity in the judicial system in the long term is in fact striking; the same people, frequently also relatives and close friends, are encountered repeatedly at different levels. That is true both for the period before 1848 and for the phase after 1852. Until 1848 not even the massive political tremors of the 1830s caused the personnel to be replaced. Personnel continuity predominated at all levels of the hierarchy, whether among the senior jurists[13] or at the level of the justice offices.[14] The effect of political influence on appointments to the bench[15] thus seems to have been less extreme than much of the reform rhetoric suggests, at least with regard to the judgeships within the court of appeals.[16]

Nor is there evidence of any significant personnel changes for the period after 1853. Even in the turbulent period of minister impeachment in the wake of the disputes about the Marburg law professor Sylvester Jordan, who could not but expect considerable difficulties at the Marburg university because of his oppositional views, politically unpopular jurists were not replaced to any extent worth mentioning. Likewise, personnel changes remained within bounds in 1866, when Electoral Hesse was incorporated into Prussia – consider, for example, the situation in the former Marburg High Court.[17] Only at the higher level of high court of appeals councilors and the regional court were there significant personnel changes.[18] This personnel continuity – aside from the short phase between 1848 and 1854 – is surprising because many contemporary statements give exactly the opposite impression.[19] The authorities, at least, did not seem to regard the political attitudes of jurists to be particularly relevant.

In fact, a great deal suggests that other factors were perhaps more important for the practice of establishing justice than explicitly stated political positions. More important – as I will show in the following pages – were above all a command of legal knowledge, mastery of a specific moral code, and a certain habitus. What was the nature of the legal knowledge, code, and habitus, and how did they structure the process of establishing justice? What did it mean to be a jurist in Electoral Hesse at mid-century?[20] How did a person become a jurist, what techniques did a person learn, and what kind of specific cultural and social practices were involved?

In Electoral Hesse, just as in Prussia, legal training at mid-century was for the most part standardized and professionalized because the university course of study and several examinations were predefined and compulsory. After secondary school (*Gymnasium*) and award of a leaving certificate, a three-year course of study in jurisprudence had to be completed. One year of this course of study had to be spent at the Marburg regional university.[21] At the end of the course of study, a rather theoretical examination was administered by the law college.[22] The individual who wanted to enter state service had to pass a further examination. The examination was administered by the Kassel legal examination commission, which consisted of two high court of appeals councilors and one appeals court councilor, and took the form of a written examination on civil law and an oral examination on all the subjects tested at the university. The grade on the examination determined the course of the individual's career. With a grade of "good," the individual became eligible for a law clerkship at a high court. With any mark lower than "good," the individual became only an intern or was trained to be a court recorder at a lower court.[23] Only clerks admitted to the high courts had the opportunity to become judges, state procurators, investigating judges, or attorneys. Thus, at this stage of education, the two examinations set an important switch for the future career; after mid-century, it was as good as impossible for an intern trained at a lower court to ever obtain a position as a judge at a high court.[24]

On the examinations, the objective was always to check whether the candidate had mastered the well-defined canon of knowledge regarding civil and church law – and also criminal law on the side – and could reduce complex facts and circumstances to their legal essence. For various reasons, criminal law did not play a great role, representing only one part among many in the university course of study: the Pandects; Roman legal history; German private law; German legal history; civil procedural law; and state, international, church, and criminal procedural law were taught.[25] The law school and "examination commission" examinations emphasized civil law. For example, the criminal law section of Victor von Meibom's law college examination consisted of exactly two questions: "*Quod est furtum simplex*? (What is simple theft?)" and "*Quod non est qualificatum*? (What is not qualified?)"[26] The rest of the examination covered other areas of jurisprudence. The examination in Kassel was similar; an entire day was devoted to the written test, which did not relate to criminal law but instead involved "working out a relationship report (*Relation*) from civil procedural records with expert reports and a draft of known facts ... without permission to use literature aids."[27] Nor was criminal law the highest priority in the oral examination: Candidates had to translate parts of the Roman *corpus iuris*, and were tested on church law, German private law, Roman law, feudal law and state law, and then, too, on "criminal law."

As criminal law was assigned rather marginal importance on the examinations, it was the subject for which prospective jurists were least prepared by their training. The Kassel jurist Wilhelm Koch stated very much to the point, "... [A]nyone who enters practice in our criminal courts will find himself completely bereft of any clues from which he could gain understanding of sentencing, particularly as, when inquiring about the principles of sentencing, he will receive from most of the practitioners the less-than-comforting answer, at least for the moment, that the juristic rhythm will impart this knowledge only with time."[28] In a way, necessity was made into a virtue when the relevant works made a point of emphasizing that judges instilled special "respect for practical experience,"[29] and when judges were praised for having "little desire to theorize but instead a strict focus on the concrete case." Of course, as was asserted, behind that lay not arbitrariness, but the art of limiting oneself to the concise and necessary. Learning that particular art was "one of the main tasks of the trainee."[30]

Jurists were also poorly prepared for criminal law because it was not one of the areas that was held in high esteem, and what is more, neither recognition nor fame was to be won there. Criminal law was thought to pose few challenges intellectually, to be rather insignificant for society as a whole, and to be largely irrelevant in terms of the important questions of law or even as part of the history of law, which was highly regarded in the nineteenth century. In academia, there was little interest in criminal law. It lacked the aura of antiquity that many other areas of jurisprudence so deeply revered, especially in an educated middle class still seriously infected with neohumanism. Criminal law was not a path to advancement either in scholarship or legal practice. It brought jurists into direct contact with the *Volk,* the "common" people held to be uneducated, and was disdained for that very reason. [31] Victor von Meibom, later a junior state procurator in Marburg and in charge for many of the property crimes examined there, made a statement in his memoirs to the effect that criminal law was among the matters that interested him least; that was paradigmatic for many, if not most jurists.[32] Until well into the last third of the century, activities related to criminal law were among those entrusted to law clerks. Accordingly, Victor von Meibom declared regarding his tenure as a junior state procurator that he was lucky to have had "very capable law clerks come to work in the junior procurator's office, [staff] to whom I could safely entrust, under my general supervision, most of the business of my office, both written work and appearances in public court sessions, except for *Schwurgericht* cases and other important cases that I handled personally."[33]

How was the knowledge of the prospective jurists checked after the examinations? During the law clerk and intern period, evaluations were prepared, so-called competency credentials. They were composed by the lower or high court judges who supervised the law clerks or interns.[34] High court judges thus had the right to rate the next generation of jurists. Furthermore, in addition to making entries in the competency tables, the high court staff had to decide about the career course of the future judges and procurators based on a certificate issued at the end of the law clerks' tenure. The decision was made at this point whether a person was qualified to be a judge. A contemporary commented regarding this selection process that the denial of competency to be a judge "essentially [precluded] the prospect of a career anywhere but in the recording or administrative office."[35] The individual's professional future was determined here once and for all: either a judge or a procurator (those two positions were interchangeable), or an attorney or court recorder.[36] The training track was thus on one hand decidedly formalized, but on the other highly dependent on the judgment of jurists already in office. No great imagination is required to see the resulting dependency relationships and tendencies toward self-recruitment.

In addition to knowledge of jurisprudence, other factors were decisive for one's career. To obtain an interesting position in the judicial system, it was advantageous – if not in fact necessary – to have family or other connections and to cultivate them.[37] Just how important the family of origin was, is evident from the high rate of self-recruitment among jurists.[38] On the down side, this high rate also demonstrates just how difficult it was for individuals who lacked the requisite family background to pursue a legal career. Almost all judges, state procurators, or even appeals councilors came from jurist families. In any case, it was imperative to be of middle class, or in Hesse, even of noble origin.[39] The highest-ranking positions, for example, at the Kassel High Court of Appeals, were often filled by men of knightly lineage. They included, for example, the High Court of Appeals Councilor Carl Moritz von Baumbach,[40] who came to prominence at mid-century in a series of Electoral Hessian property crimes before the Marburg court. As the example of Edwin von Bischoffshausen illustrates, high court councilors were also often from knightly families, although those positions were usually only stepping stones.[41] As the Electoral Hessian knightly families were variously related to each other by blood and marriage, there were many connections that could be exploited for professional advancement.[42] Positions below the Kassel Court of Appeals and above the justice offices were given preferentially to old middle-class jurist families. In middle-class circles as well, the family networks within the judicial system were close-knit: Sons of jurists likewise became jurists.[43] As a result, real jurist genealogies developed, usually in a line of automatic promotions up the stages of the hierarchy.[44] Sometimes entire clans, wives, uncles, in-laws, and nephews, came from jurist families. The circles for marriage and socializing were intimately connected.[45]

Family connections were not only of importance because of the obvious protectionism practiced in all professions during the nineteenth century. Noble and middle-class backgrounds ensured that future jurists possessed not only legal knowledge[46] – as shown by Christina von Hodenberg in her study of Prussian knights[47] – but also the other qualifications indispensable for their profession. After all, it was not possible to practice the profession of jurist without a whole set of other skills, which are commonly referred to as "middle class habitus." The person had to possess a "true, unrestricted education" that included musical performance and reading but also long walks and "cultivated socializing." Likewise important were the values of "thrift," "self-discipline," and "diligence."[48] That is quite evident from a look at the qualification tables that every law clerk had to fill out annually. In addition to the column containing information about grades, the tables contained the following columns: "b) exegesis, judgment, c) accuracy, thoroughness, d) business competence, e) diligence, f) orderliness, g) attentiveness … h) law-abidingness and morality."[49] The more laudatory the comments noted here, the faster the person was advanced.

Furthermore, command of specialized legal language and Latin also played a role in official and unofficial education. Latin held a prominent position in the secondary school education shaped by neohumanism, and this orientation continued at the university level; the examination at the law college was conducted completely, that of the high court of appeals partly, in Latin.[50] In addition, candidates wrote their dissertations in Latin. Latin was not only the language of scholarship, but also the code for gender-specific, social, and cultural distinction. Thus, people in educated middle-class circles came together to recite Latin or Greek texts to each other – of course, this was a practice not limited to jurists.[51]

Essentially, the scientific "objectivity" and "truthfulness" associated with Latin fundamentally belonged to this habitus. Furthermore, the emphasis on Latin reinforced participants' conviction that they were serving only the one ineluctable truth. Indeed, a specific professional ethos was involved, the readily professed "impartiality dogma."[52] It is thus not in the least surprising that so many jurists, especially judges, cast themselves in the role of the just paterfamilias, of the figure discharging almost sacred duties; they were consequently not reluctant to compare their own activities with those of a priest.[53] This self-sacralization was in keeping with a further trait of the jurist asserted in the same breath, that is, that of being a friendly leader and "guidepost for the *Volk* in political matters." In this context, jurists claimed a "thorough knowledge of the state's and the people's needs."[54] This self-fashioning was well served by their belief that they were familiar with all the people's concerns, particularly those of the lower classes. Thus, for example, they could say definitely that the causes for crime lay in a lack of education and overindulgence in spirits.[55] Of course, the self-assessment that they were servants of the simple folk, outright celebrated in numerous works, could scarcely hide the fact that they in no way valued the close contact with the lower classes associated with criminal justice service, and in fact complained about it.

Jurists were thus not just trained in a specific logic of deduction and in procedures of decontextualization – think only of the case histories that were supposed to be repeatedly studied and analyzed during their studies. They had little experience with questions of criminal law, came predominantly from jurist families of the upper middle class and nobility, and were men with a habitus of objectivity and impartiality, combined with a self-image of themselves as servants of the people. That, and mastery of the usual self-fashioned canon of the educated middle class distinguished them as virtuous men of moderation and reason more than political convictions of one color or another, at least aside from the turbulent years of the mid-century.

6.2 INTERROGATIONS, OR HOW DOES PROPERTY OWNERSHIP COME ABOUT?

What did this habitus, the strikingly meager knowledge of criminal law, the surprising insignificance of political attitudes, and the high self-recruitment rate have to do with establishing justice? Did all of that play any role, for example, in the interrogations that were to be conducted exclusively by jurists in the framework of the preliminary investigation?

The interrogations very clearly exhibit, as I will assert in the following pages, a ductus of reduction, objectivization, and objectivity that once again was entirely in keeping with the juristic habitus. The kind of questions and the form of recording answers were structured by this habitus, and the recorded answers of the witnesses and defendants had thus gone through a legal acid bath. The acid bath did not regard as important those aspects of the statements that were still considered especially significant at the beginning of the nineteenth century: anything that could help reveal individual motives, background relationship networks, and complex connections, thereby providing insight into actions and their logic. No, it was no longer a matter of "discovering guilt ... and the motive force for the deed," of unlocking a complex character. No longer did anyone want "to recommend" other "auxiliary sciences such as psychology and anthropology," at least according to the textbooks.[56]

The concerned warnings about too much sympathy with the suspects did not need to be repeated, nor did the contention that it was in general still about character assessment. Approaches of the kind suggested by Jagemann even in his textbook from the 1830s will be sought in vain in the interrogations after the mid-century; he had written, "Only the interrogator who proceeds psychologically in interrogations may boast of success; for everyone else, success can only be considered a matter of chance."[57]

Now it was exclusively about questions that could be answered with seemingly ineluctable clarity, by means of the procedures of deduction and decontextualization. Was this the suspect who had stolen a particular thing with a specific value from a given person? In hundreds of interviews the same questions were hammered on: What belongs to whom and what is its value? It was stated repeatedly what property was and what theft was. Why particular actions were taken and whether they could also be interpreted in terms other than property crime was not a concern.

This process, which exactly fits the juristic habitus, is especially clearly illustrated by the so-called recognition procedure (*Recognition*), a specific form of interrogation.[58] In the "recognition procedure," a witness or a suspect was shown an object or a person that was then supposed to be identified. In the records, people were confronted for pages with things and asked to identify the things – of course, only regarding the question as to how the thing was related to the person in terms of ownership. Any other answer but that the thing belonged to some person or another was not an option. The structure of the interrogation rendered articulation of any other potential relationships between things and people impossible; it was not provided for that an object could belong to multiple people, that it was only being used by a person, or that it had perhaps been loaned or had been made available for a limited time by a third person in exchange for another object or might be used only for certain activities.[59] What did such a "recognition procedure" actually look like, for example, in the Zimmermann case? By means of what techniques was an energetic attempt made – for a decidedly worthless object – to pin down the precise value of the object and to clarify ownership unambiguously in accordance with the modern property concept?

Two questions were central: first, whether Zimmermann had stolen a head covering, and if so, exactly what kind of a cap it was; and secondly, whether he had stolen pieces of bread from the two beggar boys, and if so, how many. To settle the cap question it had to be determined whether the cap found on the accused belonged to him. First, his brother was asked, after being shown said cap, whether he recognized it.[60] He stated that it was his brother's cap, which he had obtained from a farm laborer friend in exchange for a fur cap. To check his statement, the Marburg Electoral Court conducted intensive research, followed up on various clues, and finally found a female stocking maker by the name of Clötz. She was asked when the cap was shown again whether she had knitted it.[61] She answered in the affirmative.

The questions about a head covering that was almost worthless and furthermore – as had been determined in the meantime – had not been stolen by Zimmermann could have stopped at that point at the very latest. Instead, with relentless, increasingly grotesque meticulousness, additional "recognition procedures" were set in motion. A third person, the farm laborer named by Zimmermann's brother, was shown the cap. He confirmed that he had exchanged that cap with Zimmermann for a fur cap. However, he could not conceal slight doubt about the identity of the cap, as "at the time of the exchange there was a bell on the exchanged stocking cap."[62] Finally, Mother Scherrer was shown the cap and asked whether it was her son's.[63] Thus, a total of four people were asked just to confirm a statement made right at the beginning of the interrogation. That brought matters not a step closer to the cap of the Scherrer boy, which had also allegedly been stolen.

The second, and in this case actually more important, set of stolen items, the pieces of bread which the boys had obtained by begging and which Anton Zimmermann had ultimately stolen from them was subjected to a no less intensive "recognition procedure." Once again, the first step was about determining the material value. To that end it was crucial to ascertain the precise quantity of the begged bread. For that purpose, a total of exactly twenty-three men and women were interrogated. The question was asked twenty-three times whether the particular person had given the two boys bread on the day of the crime, and if so, how much.[64] Twenty-three people had to go to Marburg to make their statements and justify themselves to the assessor Mackeldey and the court recorder; twenty-three men and women made an almost two-hour journey to state whether they had given two beggar boys a half loaf or one piece of bread or none at all. Each of those twenty-three times the boys had to be identified as the persons who had received the bread, and the exact amount of bread given had to be stated.

In other property crime cases, too, questions were asked about the material value of things and ownership using costly recognition procedures. Very detailed descriptions of hundreds of just such worthless objects were often generated, mostly because of intensive questioning by the court.[65] According to legal logic, the interrogations may have had the objective of determining precise value and the ownership situation, but the dynamics quietly emerging in these recognition procedures, conducted at such great expense, at times took the form of an outright obsession with the comprehensive recording of things, and the consequences were momentous. This obsession did not focus on precise recording of every conceivable level of the things' meaning, that is, which persons attributed what emotional or symbolic meaning to the things. To the contrary, as already known from statistics, criminology, and the case histories, the procedure forced the things to be removed even further from any social context and made all other meanings of the things, for example symbolic or emotional, disappear. Similarly all forms of connection between things and people that did not add up according to the modern property concept were eliminated. Thus, just as the visual inspection reports blocked out all other contexts and logical connections outside legal perspectives, the interrogations eliminated any evidence irrelevant to the allegedly objective consideration of value and ownership – simply by inquiring again and again, in countless repetitions, about material value alone.

This approach gave rise to the impression that things only had a single, material meaning. Other relationships between persons and an action and between things and persons were simply denied. Everything that had been celebrated at the end of the eighteenth century as the revolutionary new insights of "criminal psychology," for example, that it was important to consider the relationship of "the damaging party to the damaged party,"[66] had lost any meaning. That the theft of an object could itself have many forms, that relationships to objects could not be reduced to the question of ownership, that property itself was a designation for forms of connection and entitlement, that the people in question were caught up in life contexts that made it possible to interpret their actions as something other than theft got left out. That is surprising, considering that in nineteenth-century rural society since the so-called peasant liberation at the latest a central concern had been the difficult transformation of ownership forms. Indeed, the fact that completely different scenarios for property possession continued to exist at mid-century – loans, mortgages, leases, rentals, use, to mention just a few – was omitted.

That was the way it worked – not intentionally, of course. In interrogations of this kind, not a great deal about motives can be brought to light; the chance of arresting anyone but the person already suspected was slight, and ultimately scarcely any new information was discovered about the possible background. Yet the interrogations were very effective. A new property concept developed as an indirect effect, because the recognition procedures repeatedly hammered in that a particular thing had a specific value and was the property of a given person. In other words, in criminal proceedings that involved property theft, and especially in the preliminary investigation, the modern property concept took on a more concrete form. Jurists thus not only played a significant role in the theoretical formulation of the new, absolute property concept, but they also contributed decisively to structuring property practices through naming acts, practices based on the general process of decontextualization on one hand and the specific process of reduction to the legal definition of theft on the other – a definition that went hand in hand with a specific habitus of objectivization.[67] Clear is that other possible aspects associated with the offense, for example, questions of honor or recognition, had no place at least in this part of the process of establishing justice.

6.3 INTERROGATION RECORDS

The words "verify that [it] is the same"[68] were constantly recorded in interrogation records. A correct statement would be that interrogation records "represented" interrogations. As the term "representation" already suggests, the above words should indicate that meaning was created, and not only reproduced, in the interrogation records. As is to be shown in the following pages, the interrogation record, too, was not uninvolved in the techniques of truth production that took form in the preliminary investigation.

What is an interrogation record?[69] An interrogation record is a certain text genre that was particularly important because it was the basis for the main trial. Ultimately, the investigating judge composed the so-called organized summary (*Übersichtliche Zusammenstellung*) based on these records; the records, in turn, were the basis for the decision on whether a case was to be pursued or not, and they decided what the charging document would look like. Furthermore, the interrogation record was important because it contributed substantially to the process in the interrogation by which the new property concept assumed a new form invested with great authority. Not only the wide-spread decontextualization process, the juristic habitus, and the specific recognition procedure, but also the record genre participated in turning the initially harmless claim that someone had stolen a piece of bread into a trial whose course lent form to the new legal system and the new property concept. Ultimately, an interrogation record was nothing less than the transformation of a complex reality into a specific interpretive schema that purported to reproduce that complex reality – the record is seen and discussed as such in more recent research, which takes into account the textual dimension of records.[70] But contemporaries also already viewed and discussed interrogation records in that manner – as will become clear in the following pages. Contemporaries did not in the least believe that the records were complete and exact reproductions of reality; to the contrary, they were very much aware of the constructed content – if the claim was to be upheld that the texts reflected truth, it was all the more important that the constructed content become invisible.

The contemporary debate held that an important task of the interrogation record was "to retain to the extent possible the speaking (questioning, answering, or relating) person's own words."[71] The goal was supposed to be a description which fostered in the reader the impression "that he himself had been present."[72] The sense of such a record was "that a third party who reads it in the future can envision the essential aspects of what happened."[73] To that end, many codes of criminal procedure provided that the interrogations had to be recorded stenographically.[74] In locations – Electoral Hesse, for example – where stenographic recording did not occur, the question arose as to what was "essential."[75] There was only one answer to this question: "To follow the rule" that "everything essential" should be recorded and "everything inessential" be left out, "legal mastery of the relevant material" was indispensable – according to contemporaries.[76] And indeed, the essential was what was significant legally. That central rule for writing up the record[77] applied for both visual inspection reports and interrogation records and was understood by contemporaries to mean that only what was legally significant should be put in writing. Of course, because it did not become immediately evident in every interrogation what would be legally relevant and what would not, it was sometimes recommended that the record should not be written until "the person being interrogated has been completely questioned and all the details have become clear. It is best, before writing begins, to recapitulate once more orally what the person who appeared said and to ask him whether his statements have been correctly interpreted."[78] Others emphasized the necessity of precisely dictating the records, "which last[ed] for hours,"[79] to the recorder. A case was thus being made for a textualization process that was anything but a verbatim reproduction.[80] More than a few jurists viewed this particular procedure as very dangerous and therefore advocated immediate, stenographic record writing. The jurist Jäger asks in 1855, "Does anyone who has the slightest life experience believe that a record is the literal expression of the interrogated person's statements and is not instead more or less colored in its wording by the style of the interrogator?"[81] There was thus a contradiction inherent in interrogation records already reflected upon by contemporaries. On one hand, it was clear that every "record ... could only be an excerpt composed by the inquirer from the description of what happened" – indeed, that "hardly anyone would maintain in complete seriousness that the written presentation of the investigation in the record is a certain and convincing means for learning the truth."[82] On the other hand, if the aim was "to obtain a true and complete account," the record should not be only a "sketch instead of a veritable painting."[83] For that reason, it should be clear, appropriate, explicit, concise, and simple.[84]

The fact that the record was supposed to simultaneously be an exact mirror and a filtered reproduction of what had been experienced was not new. What was new was that it was seen as contradictory, indeed, as a problem. Michael Niehaus has pointed out that until well into the eighteenth century it was unproblematic, even taken for granted, that a "verbatim record" was not a verbatim record.[85] Only at the turn of the century, in the wake of much discourse about authenticity, did this become a problem and was it finally declared a contradiction. The more openly this contradiction became the subject of some discussion, the greater was the necessity to make the contradiction disappear, if the records were to have any authority at all in the process of establishing justice. Records had to be true texts; ultimately, they were the basis on which decisions about justice and injustice were to be made.

If this contradiction is taken as the starting point of analysis, the question arises as to which interrogation record techniques succeeded in representing as objective and true fact a complex reality transferred into an interpretive schema consistent with the new property concept and the modified theft definition. Getting right to the issues up front – a variety of procedures were available that, as it were, lent the new property concept set forth in the records enhanced authority. What did those records actually look like? The header of the interrogation record was to a large extent standardized. It contained information about the person who had conducted the interrogation and sometimes also about the recorder, the place, and the time of the interrogation. Standardized data about the person interrogated were also present.[86] A range of possibilities existed, especially with regard to recording the questions of the interrogator. A first interrogation model took the following form: The questions were not clearly formulated but only implied. In this case, the questions were phrased in the passive voice, causing the questioner to disappear and creating the impression that the questions were literally generated of their own accord and that they emanated from an urgent abstract necessity, imparting to them the authority of objectivity.

Thus, for example, in a 1850 case that related to "inciting the theft" of three shirts, the following rudimentary questions were recorded in the interrogation of the suspect Conrad Raab: "Conrad Raab was brought out and interrogated without fetters; admonished to speak the truth, he sticks with his previous [his previous statement is meant] when shown the shirts and questioned." The second rudimentary question then appears: "Asked to state where, if the shirt D was his, the two remaining and still missing shirts of the widow Wörner had gone." The record continued in that style, with the answers recorded in complete sentences and the first person singular.[87] Rudimentary, abrupt questions, ostensibly concentrating on what was most important, suggest true content and give the impression so typical for the nineteenth-century administrative culture that the questions were based on ineluctable facts and on objective, factual circumstances. The latter were checked in the interrogation, but in the final analysis their existence appears to have already been certain. The person interrogated thus only had the option to affirm or deny – at least that is the impression that emerges. Perhaps the suspect actually recounted complicated stories for hours, but only "yes" or "no" was recorded.

A second, far more common interrogation model also gives the impression of objectivity and likewise contributed substantially to the structure of the answers. It is a record type that contains neither implied nor fully formulated questions. There are only answers that fall under one of four headings: "Upon questioning," "Upon special questioning," "Upon confrontation," and "Upon special confrontation."[88] "Upon questioning" indicates the intensity or pressure that was developed in the interrogation; it does not refer to the content. The content of the question was not included in the record.[89] Thus, the record contains nothing but answers to questions that are not obvious. The questions for this procedure had probably already been formulated in advance, that is, there was already a fixed but not evident underlying model that the investigating judge had contrived and submitted to the interrogator. The witness or suspect could thus only react to this model but in no way influence the schema itself. In such a procedure, the statement possibilities, as if in a corset, were tightly structured according to the rules for the particular legal information of interest – without the information of interest being evident, because the questions never appeared in the interrogation record itself. The result is the appearance that the persons interrogated organized their narrative according to the information of interest to the justice system, in fact, that only what was legally significant happened at all. This impression is reinforced by the fact that the answers are often in the first person singular.[90] The use of the first person singular, together with embedded segments of direct speech in the answers, suggests that the record is the verbatim play-back of an account by the person interrogated. In reality, the record is an account constructed by the gendarme or official, transformed by the questions into a completely distinct narrative; the narrative usually seems arbitrarily disjointed because only the statements considered legally relevant were strung together. The effect of such a narrative, produced for the first time in the record, was to almost necessarily confirm in the interrogations an allegation initially encoded in the formulation of the question by the investigating judge.[91]

A third record variant consisted in consolidating the oral statements of the individual suspects or witnesses made in the interrogation to create a cohesive narrative. Neither questions nor answers come up. Instead, a complete account is presented that – at times enhanced by verbatim speech – is very plausible. For example, in the case involving the theft of a hat, it read, "The day laborer Johann Friedrich Brandeis, ... married, ... [personal data follow here], from Häuserbach, confirms the content of the charges and notes further that he set the hat aside when he was chopping wood, and when he was done with the work, he forgot to take it home with him."[92] The complete account presented here only contains the legally relevant elements, thus eliminating connections and interpretations that might indicate anything more.

Regardless of what record type was used with its own particular authentication strategies, every one of them implied that it was an exact reproduction of what was said and not the reduction of various frames of reference to the one legally relevant question, that is, who stole what.[93] At the same time, the modern property concept took shape in all the interrogation records, while questions of honor and recognition, debates about the emotional and symbolic meaning of things and relationships, and other conceptions of property were pushed aside.

However, interrogation records were even more. Just like the lookout descriptions, they were powerful staging efforts by jurists, who clearly showed themselves off to their advantage, while they transformed witnesses and suspects into colorless, thoroughly difficult to comprehend figures[94] instead of using the older methods of "criminal psychology" to construct the "uniqueness" – of course standardized – of the individuals interrogated, as Ludwig Jagemann required before the turn of the century in his study on investigation. Here again, the subjects of the procedure in particular, that is, the investigating judges, the assessors, the gendarmes, and the law clerks, were moved to center stage.[95] They were the ones who, acting as subsuming acrobats, made reality "objectively" describable and thus assessable. To that extent, the interrogation records attest to "professionalization." For that purpose the standardized training of jurists that concentrated on formalization and the jurists' middle-class habitus were more than helpful. However, the quality of the information produced was not improved. Although record writing was a procedure that generated an increasing volume of information – in the end, investigative records for property crimes around mid-century often swelled to one, even two hundred pages – the quality of the information in the interrogation records actually deteriorated.

Other interpretations that pursued different relevance categories for the framework of relationships between people, and between people and things, were very difficult to introduce into the preliminary investigation even after the 1848 reforms because of the authentication strategies and reduction procedures cited,[96] but there was still a back door that allowed the unexpected to enter the proceedings. Furthermore, changes in the interrogation records of the kind seen after the mid-century also opened up options conducive to annoyance. According to the authentication strategies, the interrogation records were supposed to be characterized as true by the persons interrogated themselves. The records were to be read aloud to the persons interrogated – that was written in every relevant textbook and was emphasized repeatedly – and to then be signed as confirmation of their accuracy. The process of reading the records aloud and then signing them may at the mid-nineteenth century still have been a practice that for many people signified dominance, underlining the unequal positions in the investigative procedure, as those people could only confirm what had been read with their mark, an "X," not by their signatures; they thus had to so to speak publicly proclaim their illiteracy.[97] On the other hand, this situation also provided the person interrogated with an opportunity. Thus, in Electoral Hesse, "read aloud, approved, and released"[98] could be written at the bottom of the record, or "after reading had taken place,"[99] an addendum was added in which the person interrogated could make further statements.

Precisely that opportunity was seized upon by the sales clerk and suspect Hartenstein. He was accused of having stolen goods from his employer Guckemus and having hidden some of the items in his bureau. After his interrogation was over, he stated in his addendum that "Mrs. Guckemus knew exactly what I had in my bureau; therefore, either she must have been in the bureau herself. Or someone else who reported about it to her; either she or the other person must therefore ... have put the things in the bureau." In this manner, he made it necessary for the investigating judge to deal with a relational framework that had not been considered before. The investigating judge asked, "What interest might Mrs. Guckemus have had in that?" Hartenstein answered, "She did not like me from the very beginning and always treated me like a dog."[100] Hartenstein thus succeeded in steering the investigation in a different direction, and possibly influencing the structure of the later verdict, because "bad treatment by the employer" could be claimed as a mitigating factor.[101] Questions about the conduct of Guckemus were subsequently asked in other interrogations, and finally, in the main trial itself the request for mitigation of punishment by the defense was substantiated with precisely the argument in question. Anyone, witnesses and suspects, could make use of the opportunity presented by the obligation to affix one's signature – anyone who was familiar with these provisions of the code of criminal procedure.

6.4 THE PRELIMINARY INVESTIGATION AND MAKING LAW

The preliminary investigation, that part of the process of establishing justice which was scarcely considered, not to mention spelled out in any detail, in the codes of procedure after 1848, represented – in a nutshell – a central site of truth production. Toward the end of the century, this circumstance became the subject of a heated debate in which the decidedly excessive share that the preliminary investigation had in the legal process was sharply criticized. Indeed, many people went so far as to advocate the complete elimination of the preliminary investigation; others wanted to admit the public or at least to strengthen the position of the defense attorney.[102] At mid-century and then until well into the last decades of the century, only a few scattered voices were raised and no attempts made to actually modify anything about the conduct of the procedure.

Until then, the many procedures before the public proceeding understood to be the main trial went on as usual. In the initial complaint, a strict interpretation of a complex set of circumstances had already been made by the gendarme – this interpretation had reduced the information provided by the person filing charges to what was considered legally significant. The principle of decontextualization, which could already be seen in the report, played a central role in the preliminary investigation at the point where the evidence that had become so important – lookout descriptions, certificates of character, and visual inspection reports – was supposed to be produced; that principle was applied in techniques that attempted to separate true from untrue evidence. Decontextualization techniques not only reduced the crime course to the few legally significant aspects of the event but at the same time eliminated – whether in the lookout descriptions, recognition procedures, or interrogation records – any other issues possibly also relevant in these proceedings, for example, honor, relationships, and symbolic and emotional structures.

Moreover, in the course of the preliminary investigation the decontextualization, desubjectification, and quantification techniques generated a new image of the criminal, just like the one that also simultaneously took shape in statistics, case histories, and criminological studies: the being of the masses, without motivation or relationships, lacking any memory of human emotions. That being not enough, in property trials these new techniques produced something further – as especially the recognition procedures and the interrogation records, with their highly objective content, made clear. The new property concept was taking on increasingly sharp contours, and with every trial it became a bit closer to common practice.

All these truly central innovations that decisively influenced the process of establishing justice cannot be attributed to newly set-down legal regulations, which, once issued, revolutionized the preliminary investigation. The innovations were changes associated with the enhanced significance of evidence (owing of course to legal reforms) that went hand in hand with the emergence of the modern sciences of statistics and criminology, which in turn developed all sorts of dynamics of their own. That also explains why most of the changes did not take the same course as the guidelines for the new modern state of law explicitly established and loudly demanded by the legal reformers. Indeed, it cannot be asserted that the new techniques cited led to greater equality and uniformity of law.

Yet there were innovations that were in keeping with the aims of many supporters of the March Revolution demands. The innovations regarding the structure of the interrogation records, for example, the requirement that the records now be signed, had the effect of strengthening the rights of individuals participating in the process. In addition, suspects could, within the framework of the preliminary investigation, demand a hearing and in that way play a role in shaping the proceedings. I must add the qualification that such an event seldom occurred and even less frequently achieved the intended goal. A person who took advantage of this right was Balthasar Mengel, who was arrested in Marburg and accused of having stolen articles worth more than 200 thaler in a robbery. In investigative detention, Mengel repeatedly expressed his wish to be brought before the court to object because he wanted to be interrogated "about the false charges made against [him]."[103] He was not only brought before the court but was also able to object: "I consider my arrest to be unjustified and consequently ask that the records be presented to the Electoral High Court with the request that my release from detention be ordered."[104] In response, the review chamber of the Marburg High Court met one day later and dealt with the objection by finding that it was "unfounded" in view of "the present state of the investigation and the magnitude of the crime in question."[105] As the crime was a case of serious theft, the court did indeed remain adamant and insisted on detention and continuation of the investigation against Mengel.

Notes

1 With the reforms of 1863 (see the 1863 Law on Criminal Procedure, Article 107), this investigating judge was often called the "second investigating judge."

2 The junior state procurator generally gave this kind of direct instructions when he, as opposed to the investigating judge, considered the interrogations not yet concluded and the evidence situation as yet unsatisfactory.

3 It could sometimes be observed that people conducted interrogations not covered in the codes of criminal procedure. Thus, in the case of the break-in at the printer Elwert's – in whose publishing house, by the way, such weighty legal works as those of the Marburg Junior State Procurator Meibom had appeared (the first in 1856, the second on Electoral Hessian private law, with Roith; see Jürgen Vortmann, 1992, 81) – which had occurred in 1848 (266 Marburg 72), the investigation was conducted by a investigating judge, Carl Wilhelm Ferdinand Harbordt, who was the regional court assessor in Marburg. In other cases, justice officials conducted the interrogations under the direction of an investigating judge who was a high court assessor (266 Hanau 145, 1850). At that time, the person in question was a former high court clerk, thus an individual who had studied law but had bad marks in his first and second closing examinations and was serving as an "interrogation judge" (*Vernehmungsrichter*). That is the case for a certain Schlarbaum, who turned up once as a high court clerk and is named as such in an 1850 trial (266 Hanau 195), then in the same year conducted the investigation in another case (266 Hanau 203).

A senior official and his intern also performed interrogations at a lower court (266 Hanau 297, 1850). A certain criminal court assessor Laudenbach, from the Frankenau Justice Office, led the investigation in the case of a sheep theft; however, the case was very clearly directed by Junior State Procurator Meibom (268 Marburg 11, 1852), which frequently occurred (268 Marburg 14, 1855; 268 Marburg 91).

4 Much as already seen for evidence collection in house searches and forensics, even gendarmes sometimes participated in interrogations from the 1860s on. Especially in the rare cases of property crimes involving large amounts, an entire army of interrogators was activated. In the Elwert case, the investigating judge repeatedly assigned new investigations to the Marburg constabulary; they were carried out by various police sergeants. In one case, a rather vague search for suspects was to be conducted, causing a policeman named Schmidt to nab a formerly manacled ex-convict for allegedly suspicious behavior and to march him off to be interrogated; then a likewise appropriately ill-reputed person was interrogated by another police sergeant, which once again came to nothing.

5 The investigating judges were often still in law clerkships at the high court or were assessors at the beginning of a very promising career. For example, Victor von Meibom (see Jürgen Vortmann, 1992, 68) worked as a second investigating judge during his law clerkship tenure as an assessor at the Rotenburg High Court. Carl Schmidt, who as a investigating judge dealt with a theft in Wächterbach in 1859, was at the time an law clerk at the Hanau High Court (see 266 Hanau 236 and 266 Hanau 195; see *Kurfürstlich-Hessisches Hof- und Staatshandbuch*, 1850, 124ff). Cöster was also such an assessor; he later turned up in documents as the senior lower court judge in Hanau (Wilhelm Rabe, 1955, 362). The practices changed after 1863: The office of assessor was now located at the lower court; it consequently lost its status as a way station and increasingly became a final destination for jurists who had poor marks and lacked social networks. Until 1863, assessor was a way-station position that usually followed the law clerkship. Until mid-century, a third examination was necessary to qualify. Assessors were consequently still quite young jurists who were at the beginning of their careers. If a person was an assessor at a high court, as was usually the case for investigating judges, he in most cases had a promising career ahead, that is, he had good marks and a solid family network. Investigating judges were thus young, hopeful jurists of the next generation. From that perspective, the 1863 reorganization appears to have led to a worsening of the investigative conditions, as the jurists were now more poorly educated, less motivated, and endowed with less social and cultural capital. On the other hand, the 1863 reorganization made possible – in terms of increased control by the state of law – an entirely welcome increased distance between the junior state procurator and the investigating judge. Before, both had worked at a high court and the assessor had necessarily been in a certain dependency relationship because of his youth, but now the investigative process could proceed more independently, far from the high court.

In any case, from the perspective of justice, the criminal proceeding was seen as less valuable when the personnel involved were thought to be less qualified.

This reduced worth or reduced significance, attributed by the jurists themselves to the criminal jurisdiction in the judicial system, had already been evident in the education and even the personal testimonials of the jurists. Despite all assurances about the dignity of office and all references to commitment as leaders of the *Volk* through Justitia's convoluted paths, the perception of reduced worth seems to have gotten worse rather than better.

6 Frank Theisen, 1997, 483, seeks in his work "to demonstrate the extent to which societal/social problems and political conflicts are reflected in the case facts, the trials, and the judgments" and reaches the following conclusion: "Criminal law consists of ... law based on statute in the face of a determinedly operating justice machine and what possibilities resulted from it for the state. Legal positivism admitted no interpretation in this area. *Nulla poena sine lege* [no penalty without a law] ... Electoral Hessian justice could only be as good or bad as the laws that it had to apply and to which it was bound."

7 See also Stefan Brakensiek, 1999, 368ff, speaks of the liberal Hessian judges, as distinct from the conservative administrative officials.

8 Christina von Hodenberg, 1996.

9 The following comparison of personnel structure changes within the Electoral Hessian judicial system is based on analysis of the *Kurfürstlich-Hessischen Hof-und Staatshandbuch*, editions of 1847, 1850, and 1854.

10 A second high court councilor had in the meantime become director of the criminal court, having thus also remained in government service in a high-level position. His name was Philipp Heinrich Becker.

11 Staff continuity was created by the High Court Councilors Bode, Süs, Schuppius, and Neuber; Ferdinand von Schutzbar also rose from his position of high court assessor to become a high court councilor. Between 1847 and 1850 only twelve lower court districts of the Marburg High Court District could be compared to each other because the remaining three were unoccupied at one point or another. In any case eight of these twelve lower courts kept the same regional court judge. Thus, on this level considerable continuity is evident, which extended to the level of the lower personnel. Of the thirteen comparable regional court offices, seven were occupied by the same person from 1850 to 1855. Of the eleven lower court districts of the Marburg High Court District that could be compared between 1847 and 1854, only a single one was occupied in 1854 by the same regional court judge as in 1847. One step down in the hierarchy, on the level of the lower courts, the situation looked just the opposite. As is well known, during upheavals in Hesse in 1830 the territorial estates, among others, were called in, and a long-promised constitution was passed. Furthermore, the political climate had changed in the 1830s. After the upheavals, Friedrich Wilhelm became coregent; in reality, he assumed all rights of rule. See the overview description of the period in the history of the Hessian region by Hellmut Seier, 1995.

12 Benjamin C. Hett, 2001, made very similar observations about the German *Kaiserreich*.

13 This question is difficult to answer on the province level because there a single court, namely the high court, had replaced a number of courts – just recall the

College of Trustees (*Pupillen-kollegium*), the Consistory Court (*Konsistorium*), and the criminal court – and the so-called government, which also had judicial functions. In this context, the newly created Forest Reproval Commission should undoubtedly also be mentioned. Despite these difficulties, great continuity can be ascertained at the level of the leading jurists. Thus, for example, in the first criminal senate of the Marburg High Court, created after 1821, both high court councilors were former government councilors (they were Heinrich C. Scheffer and Ludwig A. Hein). All three chancery clerks had been carried over from the previous government. Even the chancery messenger had served previously in the government. In the "civil senate" of the high court the continuity was similar.

14 In this case the question of continuity and discontinuity is almost more difficult to answer because the boundaries of the particular offices had changed considerably. The former senior town official at the Marburg Office, a certain Hille, became the Marburg District Councilor. The Marburg Regional Court Assessor became Marburg Regional Court Councilor Friedrich Hille, who was still working in the Caldern Office as the senior official in 1821. On the other hand, the new Marburg Regional Court Judge, a certain Carl Wachs, had previously been the senior official in Gemünden. There were new faces in only four of the twelve justice offices. In Frankenberg, a certain Georg Theiß, unknown until then in Electoral Hessian administrative and justice service, became the senior justice official. A Ludwig Theiß can be found as office clerk in Gemünden in 1821. In the Neukirchen, Rosenthal, and Treysa Justice Office, justice official positions were likewise filled by people who had not before that time served in comparable positions in the Province of Upper Hesse. At all levels from director to chancery messenger, the newly established high court was composed primarily of former members of the Marburg government. The new administrative positions of district councilor were filled by former officials. Even the new justice officials were predominantly former senior officials. Only one-fourth of the new justice officials had not worked in Upper Hesse before either as senior officials or court recorders; they came from outside the Province of Upper Hesse or from other professional groups. This extremely high continuity went hand in hand with the close family connections evident in many places between the judicial and administrative officials; the same family names turn up repeatedly, and often the justice officials and their recorders at one and the same court were father and son; see Stefan Brakensiek, 1999, on Lower Hesse.

15 1831 Constitutional Charter, Article 60. That is evident from the fact that appointments to the relevant offices between 1830 and 1833 did not lead to any changes in the composition of the high court. The question becomes more complicated at the level of the justice offices, because the lower court districts had been reorganized at the same time, on December 21, 1831, with the result that the previous twelve justice offices were now fifteen. Of these fifteen justice offices, four had been staffed with new justice officials; in six justice offices nothing had changed, while in the remaining offices small shifts had taken place. The changes in personnel between 1831 and 1833 cannot be characterized as serious.

16 This is not the place to go into the situation of the appeals court of justice *(Appellationsgerichtshof)* in its role as the State Court of Justice. The 1831 constitution had assigned the high court of appeals (*Oberappellationsgerichtshof*) this function by codifying the ministerial responsibility for justice. After 1831, a whole series of trials were brought by the territorial estates concerning constitutional court decisions in the modern sense. A number of trials were initiated during the two Hassenpflug governments in particular. At that time, political appointments to high court of appeals councilor positions were clearly evident. See Wolf E. Kellner, 1964, and the detailed study of Hansjochen Kochheim, 1966.

17 The members of the Marburg High Court swore allegiance to the Prussian king on February 14, 1867 (see Otfried Keller, 1982, 27). For the judges and the state procurators, that was the most important change for quite a long time. The staff had changed little since the great rebuilding phase between 1848 and 1852–1854. The appointments to the justice offices were likewise made without any changes worth mentioning. Great continuity can be seen between 1852–1854 and 1864. Of the twelve justice offices that existed both before and after the reform, eight remained occupied by exactly the same justice officials. They are the justice offices in Wetter, Treis, Kirchhain, Amöneburg, Neustadt, Rauschenberg, Frankenberg, and Rosenthal. Changes occurred again in 1869. See Otfried Keller, 1982, 32ff. On the district court level, only a few new appointments occurred; see Otfried Keller, 1982, 30.

18 Otfried Keller, 1982, 32. A senior tribunal councilor already employed up to then in Electoral Hesse became the regional court president; a man from the Rhineland became the regional court director, while the regional court councilors were appointed from the ranks of former Electoral Hessian judges. The state procurator came from Berlin. Thus, two of the three highest positions at the Marburg Regional Court were occupied by former Prussian officials – which can be described as a marked change in personnel, compared to the previous seventy years. However, that only affected the upper echelon of the justice system; in the local courts, there were no changes. All twenty local courts retained the same staffing. In Marburg, the local court changed to the extent that it moved in 1894 from the so-called old *Probstei* to a newly constructed courthouse on University Street; Otfried Keller, 1982, 40ff. See in this context the detailed study of Thomas Ormond, 1994, who deals with certain charges leveled at the Prussian justice system. In the *Kaiserreich*, Prussian judges were repeatedly accused of "class justice" and special loyalty to the government, or rather, of strict regimentation of the judiciary imposed by the Ministry of Justice. Ormond shows how insubstantial these accusations were.

Of course the elector was also explicitly prohibited from dismissing unpopular officials. There had already been regulations of this kind at the end of the eighteenth century to protect against arbitrary dismissals. In the 1831 constitution this provision was affirmed; the following statement was made in Article 56: "No state servant may be removed without a judgment and law, or dismissed against his will …." Furthermore, officials had to swear an oath of office in which they pledged to uphold the constitution of the land. This passage was followed by a further statement: "No instruction may contain anything that is contrary to law"; see 1831 Constitutional Charter, Article 60. These unambiguous regulations made the civil service laws of Electoral Hesse almost as modern as those in Baden and Bavaria; however, it goes without saying, given the circumstances of the Jordan case, that they did not render obsolete the question of practices which subverted the regulations.

19 More than a few contemporaries maintained that the judges at the high court of appeals (*Oberappellationsgerichtshof*) in particular were exposed "to all the tricks and dangers of the court cabal"; see Jordan and Murhard, quoted in Hansjochen Kochheim, 1966, 69.

20 Unlike the situation for Prussia, no description exists for jurist education in Electoral Hesse. On Prussia in detail, see Wilhelm Bleek, 1972.

21 In Electoral Hesse education for the justice and the administrative systems was not separate; in both cases, a course of study at the university in Marburg was expected, and this course of study was structured similarly for both; see Wilhelm Bleek, 1972, 274. I owe thanks to Alexandra Ortmann for the preliminary prosopographic work for this part of the study.

22 Regarding the first law examination, Marburg, April 18, 1861, the Law College, reprinted in Hermann Ortloff, 1863, 204f.

23 F. Oelzen, 1867, 18.

24 Exceptions are to be found for the most part for the period before 1848. Worth mentioning here, for example, is Johann Adam Baumgard, who, after he had passed the law college examination in 1821, spent almost ten years as a high court attorney in Marburg, and then after working at the Eschwege Justice Office, became a high court councilor; see Karl-Heinz Nickel, Harald Schmidt, Florian Tennstedt, and Heide Wunder, 1990, 379. A further exception was Otto Gleim, who turned up as a court recorder in 1845 and then successfully passed an "examination . . .to [become] judge"; see 250 Electoral Hessian Ministry of Justice 806. In 1863, he was named the high court councilor in Rinteln.

25 Wilhelm Endemann, 1867a, 31.

26 Jürgen Vortmann, 1992, 46.

27 Regarding the second law examination, Kassel, May 21, 1851, Electoral Hessian Legal Examination Commission, reprinted in Hermann Ortloff, 1863, 205.

28 Wilhelm Koch, 1855, 2f.

29 Wilhelm Endemann, 1867a, 41.

30 Wilhelm Endemann, 1867a, 44.

31 Christina von Hodenberg, 1996, 145.

32 Jürgen Vortmann, 1992, 34: "... [C]riminal law has never interested me." That may have changed toward the end of the century because a few large criminal trials excited great public attention; see Benjamin C. Hett, 2003.

33 Jürgen Vortmann, 1992, 80f.

34 Until the 1840s, the practice in Electoral Hesse was to add an extraordinarily difficult examination at the end of the law clerkship.

35 Wilhelm Endemann, 1867a, 34.

36 In the Electoral Hessian qualification tables listing the accomplishments of the interns and law clerks, a heading at the end read "[H]ow well suited to individual positions as assessors, lower court judges . . . ." The high court staff then entered a recommendation in that column which often decided more than just the first steps of a career.

37 Interesting in this regard is a place in Meibom's memoirs where he does not hide the fact that his father campaigned for such a position. That practice for obtaining appointments does not seem to have been looked upon negatively. See Jürgen Vortmann, 1992, 67: "To realize my always cherished wish to return to justice service, my father took action in Kassel, speaking . . . to the executive committee of the ministry . . . and . . . receiving the promise that on a fitting occasion my wish would be granted." Also interesting here are Meibom's numerous references to his social practices, which led him repeatedly into jurist circles; see Jürgen Vortmann, 1992, 79ff, where Meibom reports, for example, that, during his tenure as a junior state procurator in Marburg, he had contact with the retired High Court President von Baumbach. He had already had a close circle of legal friends during his law clerk tenure.

38 Christina von Hodenberg, 1996, 33ff.

39 On this subject, see the studies of Konrad Jarausch, 1990; Christina von Hodenberg, 1996; and Hannes Siegrist, 1996.

40 Karl von Baumbach-Nassenerfurth, 1932, leaf 2.

41 He was a high court councilor in Hanau from 1840 to 1851, then became a government councilor and regional director in Kassel; see Karl von Baumbach-Nassenerfurth, 1832, leaf 9. He belongs to the group of public servants who resigned to protest Hassenpflug's policies; see Philipp Losch, 1909, 15.

42 Only one example here should be enough: A brother of Edwin von Bischoffshausen, Christian James Oliver Terenz, was married to Natalie, the daughter of the High Court Councilor Theodor von Carlshausen.

43 For example, not only did Hanau Senior Local Court Judge Cöster come from a jurist family, three of his brothers likewise found positions at the same place; see Wilhelm Rabe, 1955, 362.

44 For example, the son of the Marburg High Court Councilor Röttger Ganslandt became the general state procurator in Kassel; see Karl-Heinz Nickel, Harald Schmidt, Florian Tennstedt, and Heide Wunder, 1990, 411ff.

45 See Christina von Hodenberg, 1996, 33ff; she states that "relationships by marriage of the first to the fourth degree were the order of the day among court employees" (34).

46 A file for a civil case had to be processed in the written examination. A report had to be written on it, with a draft decision; see Jürgen Vortmann, 1992, 44.

47 Christina von Hodenberg, 1996.

48 Christina von Hodenberg, 1996, 84.

49 266 Marburg High Court 67 Table, Reports on qualification of the law clerks and law interns.

50 Jürgen Vortmann, 1992, 45.

51 Meibom speaks of such a circle in Tübingen; Jürgen Vortmann, 1992, 97.

52 Christina von Hodenberg, 1996, 14. In the relevant textbooks, too, impartiality is always the first thing emphasized, and partiality is always given as the main reason for excluding a judge; see Johann J. W. von Planck, 1857, 8.
53 Ludwig von Jagemann, 1850, 70.
54 Christina von Hodenberg, 1996, 70.
55 Peter Becker, 1992a, 293.
56 Ludwig von Jagemann, 1838, 295.
57 Ludwig von Jagemann, 1838, 314. At this time, long tables were still created to differentiate the various personalities of suspects. "Stubborn people," "chatterboxes," "unscrupulous people," "passionate people," and many other types were neatly differentiated; see Ludwig von Jagemann, 1838, 555ff. On this subject, also see especially the "Grundsätze des Criminalverhörs," in Ludwig von Jagemann, 1841, 497ff. This work provides numerous examples of approaches for dealing with various "types of people" in interrogations.
58 The "recognition procedure" illustrates this tendency most clearly, but public questioning abstained from shedding light on the individual's background, from clarifying inner motives, and from chasing down other contexts in which the crime could possibly be seen.
59 See Heinrich A. Zachariae, 1868, 225ff.
60 268 Marburg 91, Interrogation, May 29, 1854.
61 268 Marburg 91, Interrogation of Clötz, May 29, 1854.
62 268 Marburg 91, Interrogation of Ludwig Schenk, June 2, 1854.
63 268 Marburg 91, Interrogation of Maria Scherrer, June 8, 1854.
64 268 Marburg 91, Relationship report ... regarding the people who ... gave Heinrich Scherrer and Louis Engelberg bread at their request.
65 In the case of the high-worth servant theft that the Peter Hartenstein was suspected of, a whole series of interviews were conducted with the sole intent of enumerating the articles. They were not shown individually in this case; instead, the witnesses and the theft victims were confronted with lists itemizing the particular articles exactly – there was a total of five such lists. The pages-long exhibit list was produced because the court wanted to examine every single article that was in Hartenstein's possession to establish whether it belonged to the accused or was a stolen article; see 266 Hanau 203. The wagon shafts and tongue and the shaft sleeve stolen in November 1849 and valued at 24 silver pennies were recorded so precisely that even traces of wear were noted; see 266 Hanau 236.
66 This is still different in the textbook of Ludwig von Jagemann, 1838, 413.
67 Or as Sally E. Merry, 2000, 261, states more generally, "Law as texts embodies cultural conceptions of persons and specifies relationships and actions as legitimate or criminal."
68 Heinrich A. Zachariae, 1868, 226.
69 On this subject in detail, see Peter Becker, 2005. His observations are based on an analysis of textbooks from the nineteenth century on law and administrative theory. Many analyses overlap; I generally do not point that out explicitly in the following pages. In contrast to Becker, I attempt to also tie in interrogation records from the actual criminal trial.

70 On this subject, see also the collected volume of Michael Niehaus and Hans-Walter Schmidt-Hannisa, 2005.
71 Heinrich A. Zachariae, 1868, 13.
72 Heinrich A. Zachariae, 1868, 6.
73 H. Bernhardi, 1887, 18.
74 Heinrich A. Zachariae, 1868, 10, note 2. In 1879, shorthand was explicitly ruled out in the commentary to the code of criminal procedure.
75 Friedrich Noellner, 1843b, 317.
76 H. Bernhardi, 1887, 19.
77 Friedrich Noellner, 1843b, 317, states critically that this rule was not actually a rule, and that the arbitrariness of the jurists determined what a record contained: "[n]othing more than what the judge or the court recorder consider significant."
78 H. Bernhardi, 1887, 21.
79 Friedrich Noellner, 1843b, 317.
80 Ludwig von Jagemann, 1838, 603, also assumes that records are dictated and develops extensive rules for that case.
81 Jäger, 1855, 2–5.
82 Jäger, 1855, 1: "For in general everyone will know and concede that a number of matters and circumstances come up in the interrogation which are very influential in deciding the case but cannot, to the best of my belief, be reproduced in writing . . .."
83 Friedrich Noellner, 1843b, 319.
84 Ludwig von Jagemann, 1838, 604ff.
85 Michael Niehaus, 2003, 260ff.
86 Usually included were first and last name, age, and place of residence, sometimes status, sometimes religion. A statement was also made about the person's economic circumstances and prior convictions. Occupational information was rare. Sometimes it was noted whether the person interrogated was related to the accused. The foregoing is the information that according to the older theory of proof determined the credibility of the witness. In the "free taking of evidence" that concern was no longer supposed to play a compelling role, but these data were still requested anyway.
87 266 Hanau 297, Interrogation of Conrad Raab, August 24, 1850.
88 The first interrogations in the 266 Marburg 72 case were structured in this manner.
89 Of course, the information could also be abbreviated so that only A.B. or Z.S. could be found between the records of witness statements. See 266 Marburg 72.
90 Another form of recording that was common in the Early Modern Period and could be encountered even in the nineteenth century – although rarely – involves recording the testimony in indirect speech. That is the case, for example, for the records in 268 Hanau 111. However, the investigations in question were apparently conducted by the administrative district office, indicating that different recording procedures were still customary in the administrative service.

91 Especially for a series of interrogations involving a sometimes impressive number of witnesses who were asked exactly the same questions, individual observations were condensed down to one ineluctable fact – ineluctable because of the kind of recording, which suggested authenticity. That very phenomenon can be seen in the case of the break-in at the printer Elwert's. The investigating judge Harbordt gave the order to determine through interrogations whether the suspect, Balthasar Mengel, a twenty-four-year-old cloth-maker's apprentice who already had a prior conviction, had "spent an unusual amount of money" shortly after the break-in; 266 Marburg 72, April 14, 1849, Letter of Investigating Judge Harbordt. Allegedly unambiguous facts came to light: Mengel's mother had had five thaler changed during the period in question; "the accused repeatedly acquired new articles of clothing and lived very well with his mother and sister for the whole winter, even though they earned nothing," as was stated in another interrogation, without the female witness being able to provide concrete information when questioned. The "accused ... had many articles of clothing made, namely, a sporting jacket, breeches, two vests, and a pair of striped trousers"; 266 Marburg 72, Interrogation of Daniel Götting, April 30, 1849. Then he purchased a "paletot" and a "jacket" from a rag-seller – according to the statements of a plowman, as could be read in the next record. Another record contained the statement that Mengel had all of ten thaler on his person; 266 Marburg 72, Interrogation of Justus Krähling, April 21, 1849. Reading these records quickly gives rise to the impression that the suspect was almost convicted just because so many interrogation records reported his heavy spending.

92 268 Hanau 29, Interrogation, November 18, 1859.

93 Authentication strategies included swearing in witnesses, or indicating that a later swearing-in would occur, and representing the record as official documentation. For example, it was customary to confirm in the margins of the page where sentences had been stricken that they were actual strike-outs. Thus, in the case of the sales clerk Hartenstein, a record had the following annotation written in the margin next to a strike-out: "one line and three words stricken out, as certified by Schlarbaum"; 266 Hanau 203, Interrogation of Friedrich Guckemus, May 6, 1850. In this case, Schlarbaum was the "high court clerk's assistant" Wilhelm Schlarbaum, who had written the record. This fastidious confirmation that no unlawful change had been made to the interrogation record signaled that these were texts which had the character of official records, because they contained statements with a claim to truth. The 1848 Law on Criminal Procedure, Article 162, states that "Persons providing information shall only be sworn in if it is suspected that, although obligated to provide evidence, they are holding back from full disclosure of their knowledge, or if it is to be feared that interrogation and administration of the oath cannot occur during the trial. In the latter case, the statements of the person providing information are to be recorded in as much detail as possible." In many interrogation records, and even more frequently after the 1860s, the following statement appears before every interrogation: "[A]fter indicating that the oath will be administered soon after questioning"; see 266 Marburg 98. Of course the oath had a variety of other functions.

It socialized the witnesses and suspects and lent the testimony a certain aura; ultimately, the oath was a central performative act that also had religious meaning. The oath was thus considered a further guarantee for the authenticity of what had been set down in writing.

94 There are hardly any analyses of nineteenth-century interrogation records that could have been used for comparison, except for that of Claudia Töngi, 2004. However, in his article on records from the Early Modern Period, David W. Sabean, 1996, suggests, using the example of marking expressions perceived as offensive with "*cum bona venia* [with your kind permission]" or simply with "c.v.," that this gesture is to be understood as the exercise of hegemony (*Herrschaftspraxis*).

95 See Claudia Töngi, 2004, 67ff.

96 And that had nothing to do with the fact that no defense attorney was admitted to the preliminary investigation, as many reformers maintained.

97 On the subject of writing as the exercise of hegemony (*Herrschaftspraxis*) in the course of eighteenth-century proceedings, see Silke Göttsch, 1991, 450.

98 266 Marburg 72.

99 See H. Bernhardi, 1887, 17; Heinrich A. Zachariae, 1868, 11.

100 266 Hanau 203.

101 Hartenstein also sought to accomplish just that in an appeal proceeding where he tried to use the same argument as a mitigating circumstance – however, in vain.

102 For example, see the articles of Alois Zucker, 1902 and 1904, who would like to replace the preliminary investigation with a reformed preliminary inquiry by the state procurator's office. I owe thanks to Alexandra Ortmann for the references to this debate.

103 266 Marburg 72, Interrogation of Balthasar Mengel, April 25, 1849.

104 266 Marburg 72, Marburg, April 25, 1849.

105 266 Marburg 72, Review chamber, Marburg High Court, April 25, 1849.

PART III

IN THE COURTROOM, OR WHAT IS LAW?

Filing a complaint, involving the court, and producing evidence are one thing. What form the trial takes is another thing altogether. According to what criteria were violations of the norms judged there? According to what principles was justice administered in a particular instance, who participated, and what instruments were used?

These questions were answered clearly and decisively by contemporaries and by large portions of the current research community. Events in court have been characterized since the 1848 legal reforms at the latest by legal equality, legal uniformity and scrutiny of the proceedings guaranteed by public involvement – that was the predominant view expressed in the nineteenth century and that is still to some extent the view in current assessments. Precisely that appraisal is to be put to the test in the following pages, as it – I maintain – idealizes more than it illuminates. According to my first thesis, the appraisal says more about the strong politicization of the legal debates and middle-class discussions of self-understanding at the middle of the nineteenth century than about events in court.

7

Reforms for More Legal Equality, Justice, and Public Openness?

7.1 THE REFORM OF CRIMINAL PROCEDURE: THE PALLADIUM OF FREEDOM

The reforms introduced in Electoral Hesse and many other states of the confederation in 1848 introduced major changes to the code of criminal procedure. The inquisitorial trial, conducted secretly and in writing, had managed to get along without distribution of tasks among judges, state procurators, and defenders. In its place, the proposed code of criminal procedure provided for a public trial with functional separation of the court's tasks. The legal reforms were a political issue of the first order – or in the words of contemporaries, they seduced hotheads into engaging in "passionate combat"[1] – and were regarded as a genuine political act, which explains the prominence assumed by the demand for public, oral courts, for example, within the demands of the March Revolution as well as in many individual petitions of the sort addressed by the Frankfurt National Assembly of 1848 in St. Paul's Church. The reason for this politically charged atmosphere was simple: The trial reforms were considered the embodiment of everything associated with a new, more just society based on the principles of equality and uniformity. They became the symbol of a better society that was established in the microcosm of the court and was to hold true in the macrocosm of the entire society. In these new procedural codes – according to contemporaries – far more was at stake than simply remedying "the main evil of our ... criminal justice practices, their arbitrariness, their lack of protective forms, of personal freedom"[2] and promoting a legal system based on the principles of equality. It was not only a matter of arousing in offenders "the resolve to improve" without at the same time wounding their "honor and human dignity."[3] There was also more to it than – as the officials affected repeatedly brought up[4] – "cutting the court's business expenses"[5] or reducing costs.[6] It was about the whole thing, society and the state included. In these debates, a quasi-natural connection was unobtrusively established between a certain legal system and a certain social system.[7] In real terms, this construct meant that the public, oral *Schwurgericht* trial, the political concepts of the liberals,[8] and a middle-class society still to be built became identified with each other. The new *Schwurgerichte*, that is, "jury courts," were equated – according to one contemporary – with "liberal political institutions."[9] The institutions were especially characterized by the new significance of the public, which one jurist expressed with the following words in his description of a *Schwurgericht* session: "The entire public in attendance is so to speak also serving as judge, and not only of the accused, but also of his judges"[10] – that is, the *Schwurgericht* itself became the symbol for a model state in which control by the people, that is, an active concept of participation, played a central role.[11] This form of trial was a symbol for the "palladium of freedom"[12] and thus the declaration that "the people" had "come of age."[13] The jurors and the new principles of oral presentation and public openness – three elements that by no means necessarily had to belong together – stood *pars pro toto* for a new, middle-class social system that promised more freedom, equality, and justice – according to the liberal perspective.[14] In short, as much as the introduction of the public, modern penal goals, and the equality postulates of the new legal system were emphasized, in the final analysis the debate was not only about a new legal system. It was about a new society.[15]

However, the trial reforms were not only the symbol for a new middle-class society; in the course of the debates, they became something primevally German and consequently underwent a further expansion of meaning. The "jury court" was stylized into the symbol for a genuinely German form of establishing justice.[16] The legal system and both the national and federal identities – for example, as Electoral Hesse[17] – merged more and more completely; as a primeval German institution that had arisen directly from the *Volk*, the "jury court" took center stage. Indeed, it became the incarnation of the "people's sense of justice."[18] The construction of a genuinely German legal system identified with the jury court gave rise to the almost inevitable need for liberation from foreign law[19] under which people felt they had lived for long enough. The fact that the only jury court existing on German soil was indisputably of

French origin appeared to be of as little interest as the fact that there were numerous foreign examples of the jury court.[20] These institutions became "German" because historical studies were written which purportedly proved that courts of lay assessors had already been common practice in the Middle Ages, if not already among the early Germanic tribes. According to this view, the *Volk* had already been able to decide about right and wrong, and this ancient German practice in particular was to be reinstituted in Germany's laws,[21] especially as this trial form "had been slumbering for so many years in the consciousness of the *Volk*."[22] Through this "invention of tradition,"[23] legal history itself furnished the arguments for introducing jury courts.[24] The relevant works on the history of law were considered so momentous that they were intensively discussed in the so-called motives (*Motive*) – explanations included with the draft laws – or cited as authoritative sources.[25]

The description of the new code of criminal procedure as a genuinely German code that furthermore emanated from the *Volk* (however that was to be understood) and as the quintessence of freedom and equality was accompanied by a re-interpretation of the inquisitorial trial in use until then and regarded for centuries as the guaranteed means for legitimately establishing justice. The inquisitorial trial, usual in all the states of the confederation until the mid-nineteenth century, was now interpreted first, as un-German, second, as cruel, and third, as arbitrary.[26] Consequently, the inquisitorial trial was labeled an "artificial Roman-Gothic construct of the legal field"[27] which should be eliminated for that reason alone. That the un-German argument had special meaning in the era of burgeoning nation states is perfectly clear.

Moreover, the inquisitorial approach to establishing justice was considered cruel because torture was supposedly the order of the day in the inquisitorial trial. Of course, it was unstintingly ignored that the rack was not a necessary part of such trials. Furthermore, the fact that torture had never been used much and even less so long before the nineteenth century, and that it had already been abolished to some extent in the eighteenth century – in Electoral Hesse already in 1786[28] – was not mentioned. For instance, Welcker,[29] in his encyclopedia of statecraft, illustrates his statement that it was deplorable to extract truths – on top of that, false ones – with torture, using the example of an accused person who was first given "a terrible flogging to elicit the truth." Then, when that did not do any good, "two long, deep wounds were burned into his back with a white-hot piece of iron, and finally, as a result of the hellish agonies of a thirst brought on by salty food and denial of drink, causing the tortured man to seek to quench it with his own urine, he was forced to confess."[30] Indeed, people went so far as to equip ancient torture devices with new, vicious technical additions to demonstrate the especially despicable nature of that legal system; a notorious torture instrument, the "Nuremberg Iron Maiden," had knives added in the nineteenth century before it was put on display.[31] As a result, everyone could plainly see how cruel the inquisitorial trial was.

In the end, the inquisitorial trial was – according to Jagemann – regarded as the expression of "domestic tyranny and slavery."[32] This imputation derived from a kind of justice criticism that had been frequently put forward since the mid-eighteenth century. Passages equating barbarism, tyranny, and despotism with the inquisitorial trial could already be read in Voltaire and Beccaria and were popularly quoted.[33] The fact that the pre-modern legal system was by no means arbitrary but instead functioned according to a catalogue of very carefully thought-out criteria was ignored. According to the logic of the earlier system, identical crimes could be judged differently, but the variation was anything but arbitrary.

Opposed to those who welcomed the legal reforms as a new palladium of freedom and as the embodiment of the basic principles for a just society and who viewed the reforms as something primevally German and the end of arbitrariness, was a small group of critics which grew larger toward the end of the nineteenth century. Those critics definitely did not want the old inquisitorial trial back; they were also prepared to declare themselves in agreement with the primevally German interpretation, and they were absolutely advocates of the reforms, but they believed that the reforms did not go far enough, as the latter did not adequately provide for equality and justice. The number of voices increased, especially in the wake of the Socialist Laws, uttering critical statements that now as before celebrated the abolition of the inquisitorial trial as the dawning of freedom, but with regard to the independence of the jury courts, were more skeptical.[34] Aside from the numerous critics who considered the juror's power fundamentally too great and wanted to impose limitations in this area, there was another type of critic who in the long run became quite important. I am talking about Karl Marx's criticism of the contemporary legal system. He believed that he was able to recognize forms of "class justice" and therefore saw no equality before the law and no independence of the courts. In the first volume of *Das Kapital*, Marx cited cases from the English system of the 1860s which – as he asserted – proved that the "English jurisdiction" was the "servant of capital."[35] Friedrich

Engels, in his influential work *Die Lage der arbeitende Klasse in England*, had already denounced the "partisanship of the justices of the peace," which ostensibly exceeded "anything conceivable."[36] The interpretations developed by Marx, Engels, and others were modified in one way or another by a number of Social Democrats in the *Kaiserreich*, presented, and finally expanded in such a manner as to place the entire justice system under suspicion of repression.

Whether of a positive or critical nature, many of the contemporary commentaries that strongly politicized both the image of a pre-modern legal system based on cruelty and arbitrariness and the image of a modern legal system monitored for equality and public openness (which was of course to some extent viewed from the critical perspective of class justice toward the end of the century) still find expression today in relevant studies. Of course, scarcely any historians today would characterize the legal reforms as "primevally German," and in the meantime there have also been crucial corrections in the all too atavistic conceptions of the pre-modern era. Thus, Early Modern Period researchers have exposed the theory of a pre-modern legal system based on arbitrariness and cruelty for what it is: a fairy tale from the end of the eighteenth and the nineteenth centuries that says more about the liberal legal reformers than about justice in the Early Modern Period.[37] Instead of further elaborating on this fairy tale, many individual studies have been able to show in minute detail that the pre-modern era was characterized by a carefully thought-out system of "judgment according to circumstances" which was associated for the most part with waiving punishment[38] and with a pronounced tendency toward pre-trial conflict resolution;[39] arbitrariness will be sought in vain.

Yet central contemporary views stubbornly persist, especially with regard to the nineteenth century. Most of the research on the legal system of the nineteenth century perpetuates as before the rather simple contemporary rhetoric which views the 1848 reforms primarily from the perspective of the – of course variously assessed – growth of equality and thus of justice.[40] This interpretation is simple because it is limited to reconstructing the intentions of reform and then without hesitation identifying them with the institutions' practices and the outcomes[41] instead of separating intentions, practices, and outcomes from each other, thus also taking into account the dynamics among those very different levels. Some studies share the viewpoint of the liberal law reformers and for that reason pursue the goal of proving that the reforms attained exactly the increase in equality that the reformers so vehemently claimed. That is, the assumption is made that the reforms of criminal procedure around 1850 advanced[42] middle-class emancipation, humanization of the penal system, and equality before the law.[43] Other studies take the side of the contemporary advocates of the class justice theory. For example, the social historian Dirk Blasius, in his now classic study of criminality in the nineteenth century, attempted to show that justice was administered in accordance with class justice. With this theory, Blasius primarily wanted to take issue with the research that for its part only perpetuated the liberal rhetoric of the nineteenth century and in the process ignored – according to social historians – that the nineteenth-century judicial system could be regarded "to be not only a history of emancipation . . ., but also a history of blocked emancipation."[44] Christina von Hodenberg avoids the term "class justice," but argues along the same lines. She emphasizes that the judges, because of their specifically middle-class property, equality, and gender ideas, administered justice according to class-specific criteria.

Although a fundamental revision of contemporary interpretations as seen in research on the Early Modern Period has still to be undertaken, first signs are evident, even in works on the nineteenth century, of updates to the meanwhile all-too-familiar story that portrays the rise of the modern state of law as the beginning of a system based on equality and uniformity, like the phoenix from the ashes. In more recent times, efforts have been made to develop analyses which do not lose their way in the contemporary "either-or" and would rather analyze than perpetuate the dichotomization of the modern and the pre-modern that the nineteenth-century liberals sent forth into the world.[45] However, contemporary debates, their figures of thought and interpretation schemata that sharply separate intentions, practices, and outcomes from each other must still be radically historicized. As I touched upon under the concept "doing law," the first attempts have recently begun to appear in various studies.[46] For example, the work of Benjamin Carter Hett criticizes the theory of class and repressive justice when he points out that "judges could display resistance to manipulation."[47] He argues further that courts were not places which could be reduced to intentions or functions but were places where "many issues of law and legal politics were contested."[48] This argumentation leaves behind the logic of contemporary rhetoric and attempts to understand the positions of liberals and social democrats for what they were: contributions to a debate about law that must be analyzed, not perpetuated. Hett takes pains to present more than one "counter-narrative."[49] The study by Willibald Steinmetz also pursues that goal.[50] He understands the events in court not in the functional sense but as an act of communication in which negotiations over justice and injustice took place according to certain rules that must be deciphered. In this, he draws on considerations from the "anthropology of law," whose analyses also focus on events in court and less on investigation of programmatic plans or interpretations of possible intentions.

With the need to historicize contemporary debates as my point of departure, I will in the following pages concentrate on analysis of the practices in court, and while coming to grips with the intentions of the reforms of criminal procedure, will inquire about the methods that were believed to find or produce truth.[51] The central focus is the jury court and its public, oral trials; they are to be examined step by step from introduction through opening to structuring of the trial's course and the role played by the defense attorney, witnesses, defendant, state procurators, and jurors. This detailed inspection from up-close will quickly make clear – that much can be anticipated – that the purely quantitative significance of the jury court for the administration of justice was overrated; ultimately, the majority of all criminal cases were still, as before, decided without any involvement of jurors. At the same time, it will become evident that the jury court, with regard to its public effects, was of great importance for the legal negotiation process in theft cases – and not only there. However, the court was of central importance not so much because of its role in a legal system structured according to equality principles and under the scrutiny of the public, a system that put into practice in the microcosm what the new middle-class society was supposed to achieve in the macrocosm, that is, justice through participation of as many people as possible. Instead, the court, which now held public sessions, was of great significance because on one hand it legitimized the new legal system, and because on the other, the public did actually gain a vital new function – but in a sense different from what many contemporaries believed.

Notes

1 Lucius, 1843, 259.
2 Friedrich Noellner, 1843a, 58f, quotes here from a report of the Electoral Hessian estates assembly.
3 Friedrich Noellner, 1843a, 73.
4 Petra Overath, 2001, 127, emphasizes that workload reduction was a central motive for reforms by Bavarian officials.
5 Friedrich Noellner, 1843a, 64.
6 Lucius, 1843, 282, disputes the argument that the jury court is cheaper.

7 It was asserted on all sides "that a nation's criminal trial attests most accurately to the state of its public life"; Friedrich Noellner, 1843a, 58.
8 Claudia Schöler, 2004, 183, shows this close connection to be the codification that became the "symbol for German national unity." The connection between criminal trial reforms and political institutions became similarly close; see Peter Landau, 1987.
9 Wächter, quoted in Peter Landau, 1987, 265.
10 Bopp, 1851a, 181.
11 These legal reforms and the nation that was constructed in accordance with the early liberal social system were popularly treated as synonymous; see Ludwig von Jagemann, 1849.
12 As described by the representative and Palatinate notary Köster in a petition dated March 21, 1819; quoted in Peter Landau, 1987, 255.
13 Lucius, 1843, 262.
14 An example of this can be read in the article of Lucius, 1843, 260ff, where he expresses his amazement that the Saxon state could not decide at that point in favor of reforms. It had "always kept sight of constitutional principles with constancy and integrity," principles that had "proven ... to be truly liberal" compared to Prussia, "the neighboring absolute monarchy," which did not see itself in a position to introduce the jury trial. That the equality and freedom of the middle class – that is, the male part thereof – was perhaps the main issue is another subject entirely and will not be further explored here. (For an assessment of these claims that views the advancement of the rising middle class as the central focus, see Günter Haber, 1976b. See also Dirk Blasius, 1974, 150.) Given the colonial system developing simultaneously in the background, it must also be emphasized that this legal system only meant to imply equality for middle-class European men; see Nils O. Oermann, 2003.
15 The speed with which the reforms followed each other in 1848 should not hide the fact that decades had been required to work out, change, expand, try out, publicly discuss, and implement these reforms. Contemporaries already made that clear; see Hepp, 1851, who points out in detail the changes especially in the codes of criminal procedure before 1848 in Württemberg, Saxony, Electoral Hesse, Prussia, and other German states. Of course, that does not mean to imply that 1848 was the moment when the discursive forms were put into practice in one fell swoop. The forms also changed too persistently in practice for that to happen, that is, such a figure of thought is based on an all too dichotomous construct of norm and practice. The impression that the 1848 reforms were simply taken back in 1850, 1851, and 1852 is equally specious.
16 Peter Landau, 1987, 265.
17 Wilhelm Endemann, 1867a, 39, writes "The administration of justice in Electoral Hesse is thoroughly home-grown, nothing foreign. Fostered by a solid, consistently maintained organization, the profession of judge in particular had a good foundation there." The article relates to the annexation by Prussia, and it must be emphasized at this point that even before the resulting debates, no distinction was made in the discussion between national and federal attributes. In fact, in a smooth-flowing transition both appear to have derived their meaning equally from the contrast to "foreign." That would be

further evidence for Langewiesch's federal nationalism thesis; see Dieter Langewiesch, 2000.

18 See Offenbrüggen, 1851, who deals critically with the contemporary figure of thought, "Law is one side of the *Volk*'s life."

19 Ludwig von Jagemann, 1849, 7, believed that he could now clearly understand "how foreign [systems of] law, the Roman, the Canonical, the Langobardian, and the French . . . pushed their way in because of presumption on the part of the jurist clique, the aristocracy, or the conquerors."

20 See Helmut Klaere, 2003, here in detail on the prehistory of the *Schwurgerichte* in the nineteenth century.

21 The historical school of law also offered proof that there had been an ancient Germanic court public; see Marie T. Fögen, 1974, 55f.

22 Ludwig von Jagemann, 1849, 8. In his journal prospectus, Jagemann posits a really new theory on the emergence of law: People should "observe with [their] own eyes and ears" and look to the *Volk* to find the views "rooted" there; in that way, law will develop "on its own."

23 The term can be traced back to Eric J. Hobsbawm and Terence Ranger, 1994.

24 That went so far, that some jurists, for example, the Tübingen professor Dr. Hepp, 1851, 271, believed that they had to prevent "resort back to the medieval course of German criminal trials by introduction of jury courts, so to speak reversing the wheel of legal history."

25 On May 10, 1842, the draft of a code of criminal procedure that had "*Motive*" appended was presented to the first and second chambers of the Kingdom of Saxony's assembly of the estates; see Lucius, 1843, 279ff. Lucius disputes the draft's reasons for a new Saxon Code of Criminal Procedure that refers to the "Old *Völker*" who, "especially in Germany, had originally and over many centuries known accusatorial trials, people's courts, orality, and public openness" to be the central characteristic of justice institutions. Furthermore, it is the same Lucius, 1843, 280, who comments dryly that "no reason [could] be learned" from "the early existence of the *Schöppengerichte* [courts of lay assessors]" to "want to reintroduce them."

26 This construct in the article of Friedrich Noellner, 1846, is downright typical.

27 Ludwig von Jagemann, 1849, 1, opens his prospectus on the new journal *Der Gerichtssaal* [The Courtroom] by contrasting the old form of the justice system with a new one that had arisen "amidst the freshly awakened and enlivened *Volk*."

28 Fritz Amrhein, 1955, 86.

29 This article was vigorously discussed. See the critical opinion of Lucius, 1843, 264.

30 Carl T. Welcker, 1847, 57.

31 See Klaus Graf, 2000, 285.

32 Ludwig von Jagemann, 1849, 4.

33 See the exemplary reworking of this criticism of justice in Regula M. Ludi, 1999, 72–124.

34 Regarding the critical voices, see Peter Collin, 2001.

35 I took this reference from Willibald Steinmetz, 2002, 8. Karl Marx does not use the term "class justice" here, but describes cases in labor law that were

clearly decided in court within the meaning of "class justice." See Karl Marx, 1962, note 190, 447–449.

36 Friedrich Engels, [1845], 1969, 491.

37 See the summary assessments of more recent research in Andrea Griesebner, 2000, 297ff; Joachim Eibach, 2003, 286ff; and Karl Härter, 2003, 458ff.

38 The insightful opinions of Karl Härter, 2003, 464, are critical regarding the concept of waiving punishment; instead of waiving punishment, he speaks of flexibility based on "circumstances" and "*poena extraordinaria* [unusual punishment]."

39 For an overview of the Early Modern Period's penal system, see the introductory volume on the history of crime by Gerd Schwerhoff, 1999; Schwerhoff focuses for the most part on the Early Modern Period.

40 Research is limited for the most part to positivistic descriptions of the legal and administrative reforms. These works exist for Hesse and are most helpful.

41 This also has the effect that contemporary jurists' representation of themselves as omnipotent regulators is adopted unquestioningly and therefore is not analyzed as "self-fashioning." This reduction ignores the implementation process, or set of practices, emphasized in more recent works on administrative history (Stefan Haas, 2004), a process that plays a role in constructing the truth. But these practices determine the process of negotiating truth and law; the "anthropology of law" and the most recent cultural history of administration agree with older works by Foucault and the studies on hegemony in the Early Modern Period. (Exemplary here is Michaela Hohlkamp, 1998. In this context, the debate about implementing norms is especially important. See Achim Landwehr, 2000a and 2000b; André Holenstein, 2000; and Jürgen Schlumbohm, 1997).

42 Christina Hodenberg, 1996, 183, asks "to what extent social recruiting and the professional influence of judges were reflected in the administration of justice," a question that – she maintains – she cannot answer with substantiation because of "the still persisting lack of research on nineteenth century court practice," even though her study definitely does just that.

43 Uwe Wesel's complete overview of the history of law, published in 1997, is a recent example of such a phenomenon.

44 Dirk Blasius, 1975, 125.

45 As important as Weber's and Foucault's basic assumptions still are, the criticism of their approaches (regarding the criticism of Weber, see Wolfgang Knöbel, 1998; Joachim Eibach, 1994; and Michaela Hohkamp, 1998) has in the meantime led to re-orientation in the history of law and administration. More recent studies of the cultural history of administration have to a large extent taken leave of Weber's questions and work more intensively with the methods of the more recent history of science; see Peter Becker, 2001a. Indeed, Weber's and Foucault's interpretations are today characterized quite rightly as master narratives that should be deconstructed rather than adopted, that being the case for a number of reasons. On this subject, see also Rebekka Habermas, 2003. Such a deconstruction of a master narratives on the history of law was accomplished by Willibald Steinmetz in an exemplary fashion for the master narrative on class justice authoritatively co-formulated by Karl Marx; see

Willibald Steinmetz, 2002. Eckard Formella already developed a number of arguments against the theory of class justice in 1985: First, it is questionable if the new criminal law was implemented, and if it was, with what rigor; see Eckard Formella, 1985, 105. In his work, Formella mostly argues without source material, asserting that no trial material has survived, which in the meantime can no longer be supported. Second, the assertion that the poor had more difficulty pressing their claims in the court is simply wrong; to the contrary, they could count on mitigation of their sentences by pleading social hardship; see Eckard Formella, 1985, 106: "Taking into consideration the social hardship situation of criminals often even resulted in mitigation of their punishments." Third, the right to grant pardons was still actively used, and low-income groups in particular profited from that practice.

46 Not until very recently did historical research deal with the process itself as a location of truth production. This research gap is all the more surprising because Michel Foucault already called attention to this central location of truth production in his articles of the 1960s. Of course, Foucault limited himself to reconstructing the discursive level. In his wake, a series of works appeared that took discursive production of interrogation records as the starting point of their analysis, for example, the work of Ulrike Gleixner, 1994; see also Ulrike Gleixner, 1995a, 70, who emphasizes the following aspect: "For the person interrogated, the construct has become an inescapable truth – a fact. The construct and its realization in social, mental, and legal connections to society are one and the same. Its self-evidence comes from its permanence." In the following pages, this approach will be linked to one that allows more room to agency and as a result makes a case for a connection that holds discursive interactions and agency to be interactive. The preliminary considerations for such an analysis are to be found in Rebekka Habermas, 2003. Such an analysis was performed in an exemplary manner in Claudia Töngi, 2004, 39ff. She described the "separate phases of the trial ... from the perspective of the actors (39) and in the process linked the logic of the trial and the logic of the actions to each other. Other works, such as that of Petra Overath, 2001, 121–155, focus on reconstruction of court events.

47 Benjamin C. Hett, 2001, 35.

48 Benjamin C. Hett, 2001, 477.

49 Benjamin C. Hett, 2001, 13, explicitly opposes intentionalist and functionalist research perspectives, aiming in his study "to follow judges and lawyers, prosecutors and public officers, criminals and journalists into places where they worked and where they interacted."

50 Willibald Steinmetz, 2002. This work is not concerned with German criminal law, but with English civil law, more precisely nineteenth century labor law. However, the work is important in our context because the methodological considerations developed there have likewise moved beyond the great master narratives of the nineteenth century, whether of liberal or Marxist provenance.

51 My intention here is to look at as many of the factors and forces as possible that participated in producing truth: codes of procedure, substantive criminal law, techniques of questioning and presentation of evidence generated in the preliminary investigation, but also the accused, judges, defense attorneys,

gendarmes, crime victims, the public, witnesses, and others. Thus, the law set in court is not a matter of simply applying laws – contemporaries already saw that exactly the same way when they, for example, Oskar von Bülow, emphasized that judges were not simply subsuming robots, to the contrary, that the legal creativity of judges should be taken into consideration. However, the contemporary debate focused on the judge and his "interpretation of the law." That is the term still used today, setting off loud criticism of the justice system because this "interpretation of the law" has been branded arbitrary. Such a point of view, however, denies the significance of other actors and the character of truth production as a collective and constructive act. Furthermore, since the end of the eighteenth century the question of the "judge's obligation to apply the law" has been at the center of important debates. Analysis of the trial form as interaction has been attempted in occasional more recent studies on criminal history; for the eighteenth century, see Rebekka Habermas and Tanja Hommen, 1999; Harriet Rudolph, 2001; and Andrea Griesebner, 2000, 56ff and 105ff; for the nineteenth century, see Claudia Töngi, 2004; and Petra Overath, 2001.

8

The Meaningfulness of Jury Courts for Justice

8.1 IN WHICH COURT?

Let's begin the close-up view of the trial at the point where the decision was made as to the place, more specifically, the court in which the trial was actually supposed to take place. Since 1848, there had basically been two options: the newly instituted jury court, or a court in which only the state procurator and one or two judges, sometimes with the addition of an attorney, had final say. But how was the important decision made about the court in which a case was to be tried?

For this question – as was already indicated in connection with court density – the kind of crime and the anticipated severity of the penalty were decisive. Which cases were brought before a *Schwurgericht* and which were adjudicated without jurors? Since 1851,[1] *Schwurgerichte* had generally had jurisdiction[2] for high treason, offenses against the sovereign, certain "press offenses," and cases that were punishable with at least a five-year sentence of detention, forced labor, or prison, or a sentence of at least four years in irons.[3] What did that mean in concrete terms for handling property crimes? The answer leaves nothing to be desired in the way of clarity; the overwhelming majority of thefts, that is, the so-called simple thefts, did not end up in *Schwurgerichte* but instead in lower courts.[4] Only a tiny number of thefts, so-called qualified and repeated thefts, were actually tried before a *Schwurgericht*. They were either thefts in which extremely valuable items had been stolen – which did not happen very often – or the accused had prior convictions.[5] As a rule, the latter had to expect at least the high court, even for theft of almost worthless articles.[6] For example, a case of the theft of a sheep in 1852 was brought before a

Schwurgericht because the accused already had four prior convictions for theft.[7] A similarly hard line was taken with Anton Zimmermann, whose bread theft was tried before a *Schwurgericht* for the simple reason that he already had six small thefts on the record books.[8] In short, decisive for where a theft case was tried was the value of the article stolen, the kind of theft, and the number of prior convictions – without any of these criteria outweighing the others.

Consequently, the place where justice was established in questions of property was not – as was suggested in public debates at mid-century – the *Schwurgericht*, which was called the palladium of freedom. In fact, it was the lower courts where law clerks or jurists with poor career prospects suffered under the burden of countless legal tasks that had become the central locations for negotiating law after 1848. The overwhelming majority of all criminal offenses – even over and above property crimes – were tried in very short trials before lower courts.[9] The findings are crystal clear. In terms of sheer numbers, *Schwurgerichte* did not play the same role as suggested in public debates; justice was not generally established where the numerous articles on the "Experiences of an Assize President," the many contributions on "A Juror regarding the *Schwurgericht*," or the reports entitled "A Word to Correct the View on the Defense Attorney's Job before the *Schwurgericht* " reported.[10] Justice was as a rule established in a *Schwurgericht* only in exceptional cases.[11] Stated differently, the majority of criminals did not come into contact at all with the legal institution that was represented as the virtual embodiment of the modern legal system.

8.2 "FINAL SUMMARIES," "CHARGING DOCUMENTS," "SUMMARY DESCRIPTIONS," AND MUCH MORE – THE MAIN TRIAL AS A CONTINUATION OF THE PRELIMINARY INVESTIGATION WITH OTHER MEANS?

After the decision about which court a case was to be tried in, preparations for a public trial could begin. However, even before the ceremonious opening of the public trial two documents began to play a role that likewise do not really fit the image of the trial projected by contemporaries; they are the "final summary" and the "charging document." The two documents, which had to be prepared before the beginning of every trial, do not fit the image – as will be shown in the following pages – because they tied the preliminary investigation and the main trial so closely together that there can be no thought of the main trial being the exclusive location for establishing justice, as sought by the reforms.[12] While careful examination of the preliminary investigation already raised questions about the main trial alone being decisive for establishing justice, these documents strengthen the suspicion that the main trial was definitely not the only place where justice was established, under the scrutiny of the public, which had now become so important.[13]

What is the "final summary?" It is a document which was created by the judge presiding over the preliminary investigation[14] – or after 1863 by the junior state procurator – at the end of that investigation; the document was entitled "Short, organized summary of the results."[15]

What did these "summaries" look like and to what extent do they provide further evidence that the production of truth did not take place exclusively in the main trial? The first remaining "organized summary" among the property crimes analyzed for the Marburg region is for the 1853 trial against a certain Burghard Dohl.[16] Its structure is paradigmatic. It is a summary that dispenses in part with complete sentences, contains numerous references in parentheses to interrogations which had occurred, and more closely resembles a collection of catch words than a cohesive text. The document contains exactly four blocks of information. First, information about the suspect is provided: name, age, occupation, and class are noted, as well as possible prior convictions and financial circumstances. Second, the "subject of the complaint" is described, that is, the course of the crime is portrayed, generally as presented in the original complaint. The value of the stolen objects is usually indicated here. Third, the evidence status is laid out. Information is provided on whether a confession is present or how the other interrogations fit into the picture, and on what other insights have been gained. It is noted whether confessions contradict each other and what visual inspections have revealed. Fourth, assessments of the case are included.

Such "summaries" were the critical basis for the decision to be made by the review chamber at the end of the preliminary investigation as to whether a trial was to be initiated, and if so, in which court – a lower court or a *Schwurgericht*. Furthermore (and that is important for our context) the summary served as the model for the "charging document" to be composed by the state procurator. The charging document could be (and often probably was) written exclusively on the basis of this summary. As a rule, exactly the same information was found in the charging document, of course in a somewhat different linguistic form – a form that established causalities instead of working with strung-together information and lists. For example, the charging document in the Anton Zimmermann case was subdivided into exactly the points that the "summary" had already used for its organization, but was written as continuous text with precisely formulated sentences.[17]

The charging document, condensed from the "summary," was one of the most important documents in the entire process; the course of the crime was defined there, and that definition carried so much weight that during the public trial a divergent interpretation was rarely put forward in any case. In the charging document the possible offender was described exactly, and an inherently convincing narrative was presented that more or less suggested a verdict to the court. Of course, the charging document not only determined the interpretation of the crime course, which actually was not supposed to be researched exactly until the case was in the court, it was also important because it contained a "witness list" that likewise was taken from the "organized summary." How important it could be in cases of doubt that one particular witness and no other testified is obvious, and this decision, too, was not made in the trial but at an earlier point. To be sure, the court could name further witnesses, but as can be observed, the court generally followed the original list.

Thus, the "organized summary" had central importance for the entire process. That document laid the foundation for the charging document and the choice of witnesses. It was the link between the preliminary investigation and the trial – a document that summarized the results of the preliminary investigation, presented them to the trial court, and essentially pre-structured the trial.[18] It was the connecting element that made the preliminary investigation the point of departure for the main trial. Precisely this important function of the preliminary investigation was strictly disavowed by the reformers; emphasis was very energetically placed on ensuring that no significant connection existed between the non-public and the public parts of the process. Criticism at the end of the nineteenth century seized upon this very point; in 1904, a certain Alois Zucker leveled the criticism that the main trial had deteriorated to nothing more than a "final decoration" of the preliminary investigation.[19]

Aside from the organized summary and the charging document, further evidence also indicates that justice was not established exclusively and uninfluenced in public court but that important decisions had already been made in the preliminary investigation. At least a few examples should be mentioned. Even the first appearance of the accused, the moment in which the court public got a first impression of this person, was shaped by information that had been gleaned in the preliminary investigation. After the accused had been brought in "without fetters,"[20] the certificate of character prepared for the purposes of the preliminary investigation was read aloud – thus immediately confronting the public present with stereotypical interpretations from the repertoire of the discourse on criminals. Then the accused was asked whether he could confirm the information contained in the complaint report on his name, age, occupation, and place of residence and/or birth. As inconsequential as this procedure may appear at first glance, it was crucial. The accused, in his/her first appearance, was reduced to just this information, thus stripped of all protective middle-class identity markers, and shrunk down to the characteristics that cast him as a public object seen from a bureaucratic viewpoint. In this position, the man or woman accused only had the opportunity to confirm the view of his/her own person constructed in the preliminary investigation. As a rule, there was no opportunity for further explanations. The records thus stated tersely, for example, with regard to prior convictions: "The accused was confronted with the prior conviction from the appended document . . .; [he] acknowledged it as correct and executed upon him."[21] The accused thus described him-/herself in categories that gendarmes and jurists had determined in the preliminary investigation and quietly transformed himself into the person whom the writers of the preliminary investigation had created in the records. The potentially open question of who a person might be was not answered here publicly; instead, the labeling of the man or woman as a potential offender established in another context was proclaimed to the public. At the very beginning of the trial, the accused thus once again became the decontextualized and segmented being into which he had already been transformed once before in the preliminary investigation.

Following the presentation of the offender, the charging document was then read aloud; as it was directly "based on the summary," it also pointed quite directly to the preliminary investigation. Likewise, questioning regarding the "matter" confirmed the close ties between the preliminary investigation and the main trial, but "questioning regarding the matter" only meant that the accused was asked whether he/she could affirm the facts of the case, which the state procurator had taken from the "summary" of the investigative records and condensed in the charging document. Questions structured in such a manner meant that the accused could only address his/her own offense in one of two ways: affirm or deny the narrative determined in the preliminary investigation. For example, the record of the Peter Hartenstein trial states at this point that the accused made "the same admissions as in the preliminary proceeding," "but [he continued] his denial otherwise."[22] Relativizing matters, including other circumstances, referring to other background situations, assuming a new perspective on the events surrounding the crime, or accentuating the circumstances differently were rendered more difficult by such a procedure.

The last example for how the main trial was structured by the results of the preliminary investigation will only be touched on briefly. I'm speaking of the "summary description," which was provided by the judge at the conclusion of the oral main trial and which was the basis for the jury instructions. Although the description was, according to the code of criminal procedure, supposed to summarize "objectively" the events of the oral trial, that is, the testimony heard there and the evidence considered, it appears that in practice – at least conceivably – the summary actually had already been written before the trial on the basis of the records. That in such a case the preliminary investigation had to be of inordinate importance for the verdict goes without saying.[23]

Despite the many examples of the structural interconnections between the preliminary investigation and the main trial that could have been cited, not a word was spoken in the public debate until the end of the century about this close linkage. Nor was it even mentioned that essential information regarding the crime had already been established at the beginning of the trial and that now it was only a matter of making that information public. To the contrary, the main trial was considered a self-contained phase of the criminal proceeding.

But how could the impression of self-containment arise when the self-containment and exclusivity of the public trial as the location for establishing justice did not actually exist? What gave rise to this impression when it was not really the case? It arose – as will be argued in the following pages – because this exclusivity in particular was crucial to the legitimacy of the new process. Only if the trial could be made plausible as the exclusive location for establishing justice under the scrutiny of the public could the new judicial institutions appear to be locations of justice and equality and thus achieve legitimacy. To create this impression, no costs or efforts were spared. Using rhetoric, rituals, and symbolism, every attempt was made to obscure the connection between the preliminary investigation and the main trial and to stage the court as a self-contained location where a previously entirely unknown truth was found under the watchful eyes of the public. For the staging to be effective, the presence of the public, the "scrutiny" of the court by the public and the jurors was indispensable. This function in particular, that is, support for the staging, constitutes a previously often underestimated factor, though not the only one, contributing to the importance of the public in the court of law.

Notes

1 The jurisdiction of the *Schwurgerichte* was limited in the 1851 reforms. Before that, they were supposed to deal with offenses for which a penalty of three years in prison, two years of penal servitude, or a year and one-half in irons was expected. Many jurists had the impression, not only in Electoral Hesse, that administration of justice by *Schwurgerichte* was too time-consuming and not always entirely correct. In the case of political crimes, the verdict was too quickly not guilty, while for property crimes the judgments were very harsh; see Peter Collin, 2001. Hence, limits were placed on one of the institutions that a few months before has been considered an incarnation of the rule of law.

2 1851 Law on Administration of Justice, Article 12: "The jurisdiction of the *Schwurgericht* is not precluded if a lesser sentence than appropriate results from the trial."

3 However, if a complete confession was present in these cases, they could also be assigned to a criminal court.

4 After 1848, there were lower courts that had jurisdiction for simple thefts; criminal courts that dealt with offenses against the sovereign, incitement offenses, press offenses, thefts repeated for the first and second time, and dangerous thefts; and in addition, *Schwurgerichte*. Thus, a significant portion of the trials that had been handled before by the high courts were moved to the criminal courts and *Schwurgerichte*.

5 Of course, there were definitely also cases that were not tried before the *Schwurgerichte* even though many prior convictions were present and the thefts tried were qualified. Such a case was that of the prisoner in irons, Schade (266 Marburg 98), who fled from the local jail where he was serving a sentence and stole tools from there, then broke into a church and stole a large sum of money, and finally entered a clothing dealer's to steal clothing. Schade was sentenced to five years in irons, but by a high court.

6 Thus, the theft of a used hat ended up before a high court only because the accused already had prior convictions; see 268 Hanau 29.

7 268 Marburg 11.

8 268 Marburg 91. The theft of six sausages, two cakes, and eight loaves of bread also only ended up before the *Schwurgericht* because the accused had four prior convictions; see 268 Marburg 14.

9 The 1848 Law on Criminal Procedure, Article 203, provided that the lower court trials were to be collected and periodically dispatched. As Articles 206–222 show, the proceedings were much abbreviated. See also the change made by the 1863 Law on the Constitution of Courts, Article 5. There it was stated that lower courts judge "with the assistance of lay assessors." On the situation in Electoral Hessian courts at the beginning of the nineteenth century, see Stefan Brakensiek, 1999, 128ff.

10 These titles are taken from the two professional journals that were especially concerned with events in *Schwurgerichte, Die Allgemeine Schwurgerichtszeitung* [The General *Schwurgericht* Newspaper] and *Der Gerichtsaal* [The Courtroom]. Especially at the end of the 1840s and the beginning of the 1850s, the *Schwurgericht* was a hot topic in these professional journals.

Regarding the two journals, see Andreas Roth, 1999. In this context, it must be emphasized that the lack of contemporary regard for the role of the lower courts steered the attention of historical scholars to the *Schwurgericht* in another way. The lack of press reporting on the trials and the destruction of the court records left behind an empty spot that can hardly be filled in. The enormous prominence of the *Schwurgericht* trials, as further enhanced in the new genre of court and criminal novels so popular that they were often published as serials in daily newspapers, cannot hide the fact that the majority of the trials were on a different track.

11 There are no records on lower court proceedings in the Marburg Main State Archives. That is in fact one reason why there has been no analysis of those trials; however, such an analysis could be conducted on the basis of normative sources and textbooks alone. Regarding the situation at the Electoral Hessian lower courts at the beginning of the nineteenth century, see Stefan Brakensiek, 1999, 128ff. Not only are most of the hand-written lists about the proceedings in tabular form generally missing, but most notably even printed texts about lower court trials are absent. Apparently, neither newspapers nor professional journals dealt with these trials. Furthermore, the proceedings were so completely obscured for the long term that to this day no research literature exists.

12 Thus, commentaries state, for example, that "...only the content of the immediate judgment proceeding may decide the verdict, but certainly not the preparatory stage of the trial. An essential goal of the latter is preparation of the charges, which predetermine the theme and terrain for the main trial, as well as for the process of reaching a verdict itself, which cannot be carried out successfully without material that has be collected, analyzed, and obtained"; see Paul Sundelin, 1860, 100.

13 Many other indicators of this linkage could also be mentioned. Particularly noteworthy are the records of the main trial itself. What exactly is shown by the main trial records that give rise to this suspicion? At first glance, the records make hardly any sense because they contain an immense number of abbreviations, numbered lists, and number series that cannot be decoded initially. Only when the records of the preliminary investigation are at hand does it become apparent that the initially incomprehensible shorthand and number series all refer to precisely those preliminary investigation files. The mere circumstance that the records of the public session can only be decoded by consulting the preliminary session clearly indicates how closely the main trial and the preliminary investigation are linked; however, the abbreviations, number series, and numbering in the main trial records prove that the statements of witnesses, defendants, or experts made before the court public are not reproduced in this document at all. Instead, incomplete sentences were noted down, and usually the page given on which the statement in question could be found in the preliminary investigation record – just as if the statements of the preliminary investigation and the main trial were *eo ipso* identical. An important reason for this unconventional recording technique is that the main trial record (see Hartwig Reichling, 2003, 26–38) ultimately only had the function of documenting conformity to all the official provisions of the code of criminal procedure. Thus, contemporary professional literature

stated that the court recorder had the task of "accounting for the routing and content of trial files, and of collecting and organizing the documents of the individual trial" (see Karl Binding, 1893, 79. On the court recorder, see also Johann J. W. von Planck, 1857, 10ff). The recipients of the records were after all just possible appellate bodies that were only interested in compliance with the code of criminal procedure and therefore did not have to receive a cohesive narrative.

Although the background reason for this unconventional recording technique may have been official, these main trial records, composed with constant references to the preliminary investigation, also show that the preliminary investigation files must have been at hand in the main trial – they must have lain open before the court recorder of the presiding judge. Furthermore, the fact that the main trial records only seldom note additions to the content indicates that the evidence already presented apparently proved satisfactory in the public court session. Doubts, reinterpretations, challenges, or even just additions appear to have been scarcely ever sought or found by the actors involved.

14 Otherwise, nothing basic changed in the 1863 revisions to the code of criminal procedure. See 1863 Law on Criminal Procedure, Article 115.

15 1848 Law on Criminal Procedure, Article 172; the 1863 Law on Criminal Procedure, Article 115, provides that the state procurator decides when the preliminary investigation ends and then submits the files.

16 268 Marburg 11, 1852ff.

17 The language ductus does not necessarily conform to legal terminology. In the closing part, which is located in the summary under the heading "Comments," an appraisal of Zimmermann's character is given: "The accused is a person who can probably be considered capable of the crime of which he is accused, as he [is] generally bad, especially as he has already ... been convicted of theft several times"; see 268 Marburg 91, September 11, 1854, Charging document.

18 See Claudia Töngi, 2004, 70ff, who likewise elaborates on the closing report.

19 Alois Zucker, 1904, 20ff.

20 The code of criminal procedure contains the provision that the accused shall always be brought to the court "free of manacles" (1848 Law on Criminal Procedure, Article 64). The purpose was to prevent him or her from being robbed of his/her dignity by the manacles. However, dignity was already dispensed very unequally by the court because of the dress code alone. While one group dressed in simple black, signifying objectivity and middle-class power, the others, the accused and witnesses, were the only ones who appeared in "civilian clothing." The perception of the accused described in the following pages also tarnished his/her dignity for a very long time.

21 On this topic, see the record of the Hanau Criminal Chamber session of August 10, 1849, in the case of Johannes Richter, 266 Hanau 302.

22 266 Hanau 203.

23 On this subject, see the comment of the Hanau High Court Councilor who, recalling that this "concise description" was to be composed from an "objective standpoint," pointed out that the summary was not supposed to be written

already before the oral trial. That was "because [it] would too greatly restrain free movement in the trial itself and too readily provoke efforts to force statements of the witnesses and the accused into the form that they had already been given in the summary" (Victor von Haynau, 1852, 29). This comment is revealing first of all because it calls attention to the possibility of writing summaries before the trial, which was actually supposed to be the first place where the critical points of the crime were illuminated. Secondly, Haynau speaks of the possibility of forcing statements into a pre-existing schema. In short, the "schema" of the *Schwurgericht* president, which he created in his "concise summary," was of considerable importance for reaching a judgment and probably reflected the legal logic that the president invoked in his instructions to the jury.

9

Legitimation through Procedure

9.1 THE COURTROOM AS THE PLACE OF TRUTH: THE ROLE OF THE PUBLIC

How was the illusion of a self-contained sphere of legal action produced? First, a special room was chosen, where, second, special rules of behavior applied, which, third, the public scrutinized. That means that even the relatively inexpensive public staging of trials at the small high courts required separate, specially equipped rooms, as also familiar from churches, coronation rooms, and council chambers. These unique rooms emphasized the special nature of the activities that occurred there, a character that transcended the everyday, and detachment from all other, far too mundane spheres. Framing was built, indicating that self-contained events were involved. In Electoral Hesse, as in most of the federal states outside the Rhineland, rooms of this sort were not created until the last third of the century. In Marburg, too, an entirely distinct, monumental style of court architecture developed, conspicuously signaling to everyone that the court was a self-contained sphere. A separate court building was opened for occupancy there in 1871,[1] and after that "cathedrals of law," in many respects "state buildings of the castle variety," were erected in other parts of Hesse.[2] Only with the newly constructed court buildings, which represented their own form of architectural dominance, was the framework gradually perfected.[3] Then came courtrooms characterized by barriers between the public and the court, elevation of the judge's bench, and placement of the judge's bench and the accused opposite each other, an arrangement in itself intended to make the importance of the public visible and tangible to all.

At mid-century, there could be no question of such spacious facilities or the generally dark paneling of the courtrooms, which were meant to convey dignity, solemnity, and a character beyond the mundane, and which also made clear that the rooms were not private but official. Without these architectural means of shaping space and dominance, without dedicated buildings, the framing of the court sessions must have still been relatively incomplete. However, in Marburg, at least, the topography of the place even before the construction of a dedicated building signaled that the court holding public sessions was to be viewed as a special location. In the beginning, the high court was housed in the Marburg landgraviate chancery[4] – in a Renaissance building below the castle. The government of Upper Hesse Province also resided there. The court was thus situated within the area in which the Electoral government building was located. This placement in the immediate proximity of the castle produced a certain closeness to the state and consequently signaled that the location was an official and formal.

While the special, self-contained character of the location was for a long time only indicated incompletely with architectural means, there were other possibilities to which ever greater importance was attached after the 1848 reforms, for example, the rules of conduct and dress codes that were no less significant than the rules governing the chamber's arrangement. They were supposed to underline that the court represented a different, dignified world where secular matters were alien. As a consequence, the court president and the presiding judge, when opening the *Schwurgericht* trial, had to take care that the trial opening and the further steps, for example, the swearing-in of the jurors and witnesses, proceeded with particular "dignity and solemnity."[5] The solemnity of the opening was emphasized by the collective act of all the people present in court rising to their feet. The ritual of standing up and sitting down, also usual in a religious context, produced a distinctive sphere at once solemn, official, and special in a manner evident to all. Likewise, the jurists' black clothing emphasized the ceremonial character of the trial.[6] The official clothing of the court officers and court recorders, as well as a specific grooming code, including a prohibition on beards for justice officials,[7] ensured that the special nature of the following events was marked as such. The clothing made amply clear that official acts were being performed there, as familiar from ecclesiastical contexts.

Besides the specific arrangement of the chamber and the special rules governing habitus and clothing, it was primarily the presence of the public that ensured distinctive framing for the events in court. The public's very presence made the trial – if we try to interpret the events from the public's world of experience – a special event that was regularly compared in court reports and legal debates to a theatrical performance.[8] People talked about "brilliant dramas"[9] in which "defense attorneys" played "certain roles,"[10] and about defendants who were actually "literary figures."[11] The public alone made the court theater on one hand and on the other a place where, as in the church service, a ritual was performed that came to life through re-enactment by the public.[12] Only because the public rose together for each swearing-in, whether of the accused, the witnesses, or the jurors, did the act of rising and the court as a whole achieve dignity and significance. Great importance was attached to that particular result. In that context, a legal article about public trials stated, "But in any case, the swearing-in of witnesses in *Schwurgerichte* should be more solemn. When in the course of a few hours, six-eight-ten witness oaths are – I would like to say – reeled off one after another, with everyone present in the courtroom rising for each swearing-in, all the whooshing up and down and the many noises often make it a really ridiculous, degrading comedy; all the witnesses to be interrogated in a trial should at least be sworn in all at once not more than once or twice a day."[13]

The public had an important role in imparting meaning to individual ritual acts and thus in underlining the solemnity, exclusivity, special nature, and self-containment of the court (and at the same time in obscuring the strong interconnection with the preliminary investigation), but the public was also significant in a second way. It lent the court legitimacy because – at least according to legal reformers – it had a single central task; the public, as the representative of the "*Volk*," scrutinized whether the court followed the letter of the law.[14] This meant that as long as the public was in the courtroom nothing unjust could happen – at least that was the hope. Consequently, the public did in fact have a prominent role. That is apparent on one hand from the remarkably large number of articles regarding the public in court, and on the other, from the manner in which the so-very-important public is described.

What were the public's attributes? First of all, the public was described as a protective shield. It was supposed to prevent arbitrary, unequal application of the law by the "cabinet justice" system, feared in the liberal public especially because of the prosecution of political crimes.[15] The public then appeared in the role of a multiplier for the message that justice was established according to just standards. Publications proclaimed everywhere that the public functioned as the state's megaphone, as it had been convinced of the legitimacy of the process by the experience of the proceeding and was conveying just that message to the outside world. Finally, the public was portrayed as a collection of people who had been cleansed by the experience of a trial, because they had seen with their own eyes that crime did not pay. Thus, a description of *Schwurgericht* practice in Baden emphasized that the public, "just from trials of cunning and crafty criminals, took away the sincere conviction that even the greatest subtlety and cunning does not hold up before jurors when truth departs, and [that] all lies and crimes remain in vain."[16] According to this view, for the part of the public that already had a strongly developed sense of justice, the openness at the trial served the purpose of reinforcing that feeling and of giving the public the "satisfaction"[17] of experiencing in the trial how a criminal it often knew was punished.

However, the public was also a fragile entity that was itself endangered by the trial; in particular, its "morality" was seemingly threatened. What the public saw and heard in court could, it was believed, endanger morals and decency, sometimes assuming such alarming forms in the judges' eyes that the public was barred from the trial – the situation was covered in the Electoral Hessian Code of Criminal Procedure by a peculiar paragraph which stated that an "outrage to the moral order" suspended the principle of openness to the public.[18]

In some cases, the imputations were so overwhelmingly negative that people came to outright fear the "public." In many articles, it threatened to mutate into an amorphous mass that used the court as "a source of vice and [as] a school for shrewd behavior" instead of a "teacher of justice."[19] Clearly stated, "For rogues and thieves, the public presence in the court process, especially in criminal matters, provides an advanced school where they can learn their dealings with care and carry them on in a like manner ...."[20] With that, the public had been transformed into a real source of danger, threatening to twist the task of the court to its opposite. Instead of justice being established, possibilities for violating the law were being disseminated and even learned for the first time. This danger could escalate and become a threat to "public order," then requiring special means that might again extend to prescribing exclusion of the public in the procedural code. The background for this provision is obvious: It was feared that information would become known that could entice others to commit crimes.[21]

A further source of danger from the public lie in its actual conduct in court; that conduct could be unseemly and disturb the special ceremonial order of the institution and thus the ritual framing of the trial, which was important in many ways – among other things, in making the continuity with the preliminary investigation disappear. Finally, "sometimes a woman's scream" could emanate from the public; an "indecent attack" could come from it, or it could even happen that "a pickpocket plied his trade" during the trial.[22] Many believed that they had to speak of the conduct of the public in terms of "running wild."[23] In those cases as well, the Electoral Hessian Code of Criminal Procedure provided for the possibility of removing "individual members of the audience, or the entire audience, from the session for a certain period."[24] It is striking that two of only three paragraphs in the 1848 Code of Criminal Procedure having to do with the audience have thereby already been cited: The members of the audience were presented as troublemakers and as people possibly to be expelled from the courtroom.[25]

A further dimension in how the special order in court could be undermined was seen in the danger of contamination by the public. That was in fact what was going on when complaints were raised about the "exhalations" of so many people contributing to very "impure air" in the courtroom. In the context of the discourse on hygiene, which was also always a commentary on the social situation of society – as Alain Corbin's study has shown[26] – the presence of a public which to all appearances did not come only from the middle class could so entirely call into question the order of the court that contamination metaphors were used; the purity and seclusion of the search for truth was likewise threatened. A public classified as dangerous seems to have been such a feared phenomenon that the Cologne Appeals Court Councilor Schlink advised that it would be best to hold sessions in the morning, because at that time "people" attended to their "business dealings," and consequently the courtroom would usually be empty.[27]

A final danger that could derive from the public was its "impulsiveness." The public was viewed by many contemporaries as barely guided by reason, indeed, as downright irrational. That was dangerous because defense attorneys and jurors could be tempted by the public reaction to allow their assessment of a crime to be guided more by feelings than by reason. The truthfulness of the process for negotiating justice would thus be undermined. The emotionality attributed to the public had a threatening character – this aspect also played a considerable role in the deliberations at about the same time regarding barring the public from executions.[28] Likewise, parallels can be found to the debates about the danger emanating from the presence of women in the galleries of the state parliament. There, too, the public, in this case consisting of women, was represented as potentially dangerous; that kind of public was emotional, and its very presence tempted speakers to give "brilliant, overly effusive speeches."[29]

The public thus appeared on one hand to be the guarantor for the state of law as well as the communicator and object of the legal awareness that was supposed to be bolstered. On the other hand, it was the negative image for everything that should not occur in the courtroom. That is, in speaking about justice, the public promoted injustice (by simply watching the tricks and deceits of the accused), and it undermined the secluded, exclusive location – whether through squalor or impulsiveness – thus making apparent the interconnection with the preliminary investigation and with all the dimensions of reality outside the court. The conceptions sketched of an ideal positive and vice versa negative public once again make clear the one and only role the presence of the public was supposed to have: the task of scrutinizing the proceedings. The public's role was supposed to be limited to monitoring whether the court was following or violating its legally defined rules. The public was not supposed to form its own opinion, merely gather information, or even entertain itself, let alone use the court as a school for crime.

In short, the rules for architecture, habitus, and dress, as well as the presence of the public, were not just decorative props but were indispensable; they were supposed to serve the purpose of producing a self-contained, exclusive location for negotiating justice, thereby obscuring the strong link between the preliminary investigation and the main trial. The public was indispensable, too, because, as the representative of the *Volk*, it was to see that the legal rules were upheld in court. At the same time, or rather to the extent that the desired impression could be convincingly conveyed, it lent legitimacy to the new justice institutions.

Of course, how the public really handled itself, and whether it in fact limited itself to its intended task or was even in a position to see that the rules were upheld, is another story and will be examined in more detail later.[30] Although any adult could attend trials after the 1848 reforms, we know scarcely anything about who actually made use of that opportunity. Nothing is noted about the public in the court records; it is simply not addressed – unless the public was barred. Especially in the case of less sensational trials, and most of the property crimes must be regarded as such, there is some question as to whether there were spectators at all.

9.2 JURORS – SCRUTINY BY THEM, AND NOT ONLY SCRUTINY OF THE TRIAL

Next to the public presence in court, the introduction of jurors was the most important element of the 1848 reforms of criminal procedure – at least from the contemporary perspective. This part of reform was discussed from various points of view. There was wide consensus that the introduction of jury courts was necessary because the jurors would represent the *Volk* in court; they would consequently ensure greater justice because they were the "freest and best judges regarding the question of guilt,"[31] and at the same time the judicial system could gain ever greater trust within the populace. Thus, the jury court could arouse "the interest of the *Volk* in legislation ... and in that way assure its adherence to the existing legal order ...."[32] Not until the last decades of the nineteenth century were critical voices raised, accusing the jurors of promoting class justice.

A question immediately comes to mind here: How convincing is the notion that jurors were representatives of the *Volk* who provided for greater justice? Even if they were far more than representatives of the people (which a great deal suggests), asking further, did they necessarily have to be simple dispensers of class justice? To follow up on these questions, the jurors and their duties in court must be examined in more detail.

Who were the jurors? The jurors were representatives of the "judging community."[33] For Electoral Hesse, that means that there was one juror for every four hundred souls.[34] However, not everyone was eligible for jury service. In Electoral Hesse in 1848, only men over thirty years old with state and local citizenship could be jurors, provided they had no prior convictions, did not belong to the clergy, were not employed by the court, and had no relationship to the accused.[35] These provisions (which were relatively generous compared to other states) excluded the overwhelming majority of the population. Moreover, crucial for admission to jury service after a change in 1851 were other factors: a certain income, possession of particular civil rights, "physical and mental health,"[36] and a certain educational level, which generally implied more than the simple ability to read and write. In many federal states, education was measured by a "certain income level," or having taken "university examinations" or state examinations.[37] As can be seen, Electoral Hesse was not the only place where reform revisions were made with the aim,[38] among others, of narrowing admission to jury service so that only men who earned a good deal could become jurors.[39] As a consequence, until the renewed reforms in 1863 jury service was the privilege of middle-class men, a few large-scale farmers, and male members of the nobility.[40] The constituent elements in this definition of juror, that is, gender, age, property, and education,[41] were similar in all the federal states, and the rationale for their use can be reduced to a handful of arguments. The characteristics typically attributed to the female sex by the nineteenth-century middle class and cited as the reason for women's exclusion from service – lack of reason, emotionality, excessive impulsiveness, and susceptibility to corruption – require not further explanation. Furthermore, the definition of what was meant by education and its relative importance for the nineteenth century are known; education was viewed as indispensable because anyone who had a "low level of education" would have needed to have the legal facts too "broadly and exhaustively ... presented."[42] Not least of all, the rationale was that "the further down a person goes into the lower classes, the greater the ignorance" encountered and thus "the more uncertain and lacking in substance the votes" taken among such jurors "will reveal themselves to be."[43] In other words, as stated by the Appeals Court Councilor Schlink, "[A]ccording to my deepest conviction, the aristocratic element [is] with regard to mental ability and wealth ... the basis for the *Schwurgericht*."[44] Despite a good deal of criticism,[45] the restriction of jury service to male representatives of the educated, economic middle class was widespread,[46] and that was the case even though jurists such as Anselm von Feuerbach had already pointed out in the pre-March era the problems of narrow social limits for the pools from which jurors were selected.[47]

Before this backdrop, Dirk Blasius advanced the theory that limiting access to jury service primarily served the purpose of securing important advantageous positions for the middle class in administering justice. According to this theory, the upper middle class, which was particularly worried about property loss, wanted to use such limitations on access to ensure its exclusive influence in court.[48] Blasius underscored this assessment by pointing out the fact that the punitive sentences for property crimes in *Schwurgerichte* were particularly high.[49] He thus carried forward the contemporary interpretation, developed for example by the Prussian Ministry of Justice and shared by many liberals; they, too, maintained that especially severe penalties for property crimes could be observed in *Schwurgerichte*. Indeed, according to contemporary statistics acquittals in theft cases tried by *Schwurgerichte* appear to have been rare.[50] Jurors apparently judged property crimes harshly. Still, that does not have to speak in favor of the theory that the middle class especially feared for its property. After all, jurors inclined to severity for many other crimes. In a study on death sentences in nineteenth-century Bavaria, Petra Overrath shows that upon introduction of jury courts the number of death sentences for a whole series of crimes – including those that do not imply specific middle-class interests – tended upward rather than downward.[51]

A further objection to Blasius, voiced by Peter Collin, asserts that *Schwurgerichte* – as already indicated – were responsible for a minute portion of property crimes because of their limited jurisdiction, which was reduced further in 1850.[52] The majority of thefts were not tried by *Schwurgerichte* and consequently could not be judged according to the interests claimed by Blasius. At the same time, however, the middle class also did not make any effort to expand the jurisdiction of the *Schwurgerichte* for these crimes, to the contrary.

Furthermore – the third objection – Blasius' theory is at odds with an observation that many contemporaries made, that is, that jurors tried whenever possible to avoid their duties.[53] Thus, there can be no absolute assumption that influence was being intentionally secured.

Added to this is a fourth objection, that is, that most of the thefts did not affect the middle class at all, but were rather crimes committed within the lower class. Why would a Marburg citizen have feared Anton Zimmermann, if he only stole from beggar boys who instilled anything but trust? At last, it seems to me, central to criticism of Blasius' all too intentionalistic interpretation is the fact that members of the middle class, but only men, were very much present in court even without jurors. The middle class had already been able to secure influential positions at all other levels of the justice system – judges, state attorneys, and defense attorneys likewise generally came from the middle class. Blasius' theory reproduced the image already created in nineteenth-century debates of an *eo ipso* objective court whose objectivity was only hampered by jurors.

Even though the connection between property, education, gender, and jury service thus cannot be interpreted primarily as expressing the intent to safeguard middle-class influence, a certain social isolation process, characteristic for the entire legal field, was reinforced as the result of this limitation on jury service. In the case of the property crimes (and not only in such cases) male representatives of the middle class, and less often of the nobility, usually met male representatives of the lower class in court (in about a fifth of the cases, its female representatives as well); people, who by virtue of position were certified to possess "mental capability, a sense of honor, and fortitude,"[54] encountered there defendants whose bad reputations and poverty had already been confirmed in writing during the preliminary investigation. Furthermore, the court was one of the few places where those two classes met and had to communicate according to established rules – and that in public. When jurors were introduced, the situation in the legal system did not change such that the "*Volk*" now had the opportunity to scrutinize the establishment of justice; instead, middle-class men increased their presence and transformed the place to a public location of the middle class. The narrow selection criteria for jurors produced "representatives of the *Volk*" less in the modern sociological sense than in the contemporary liberal sense, and yet, as the argument goes, the case cannot be made that the administration of justice exclusively served middle-class interests. The question thus remains whether jurors were able to perform the monitoring functions assigned to them by contemporaries. How could people who were subject to such exclusive selection criteria in any way oversee an objective form of truth production?

All of that leads to the question as to what tasks jurors had to perform in the course of a trial. When did they appear in court and with what function? Their first appearance was very ritualized and elevated above the rest of the events. It drew attention from the very opening of the trial to the elevated position that the jurors were supposed to assume in the symbolic order of the court. Still within the framework of the trial opening, twelve people were selected with the help of the two trial parties from the group of thirty-six jurors of the current *Schwurgericht* rotation,[55] were officially appointed, and sworn in.[56] During this procedure, the court and the spectators stood as usual for swearing-in ceremonies. After the reading of the oath,[57] which obligated them to judge the case independently and without bias, the jurors, separately and with "a raised right hand," spoke the words, "I so swear, so help me God,"[58] thus calling on a still higher power than Justitia. Only after all twelve jurors had taken this oath could the court and the spectators be reseated and the trial begin.[59]

While these time-consuming rituals assured the jurors a special position in the symbolic order of the court right at the beginning, comparable importance on the level of the jurors' actual options for exerting influence will be sought in vain. To the contrary, their great symbolic significance on one hand was correlated to limited opportunities to really help shape the process of establishing justice on the other. The discrepancy between the jurors' great symbolic and very limited practical importance is especially evident in the trial against Ludwig Loos, alias Hofmann. There, as in most of the other trials examined, the jurors almost never intervened in court events despite the possibilities for intervention reserved to them. After their ceremonious installation, the president had the charging information and "charging document" read aloud by the court recorder.

Thirty-six-year-old, previously convicted Ludwig Loos was accused of having committed within one month one attempted robbery and a total of seven in part qualified thefts in the surrounding villages and having stolen butter and children's vests – in addition to used shirts, chickens, bread, and sausage. The jurors were familiarized with the theft type, the victims, and the stolen objects in each instance. The junior state procurator explained the offenses from his perspective and began the hearing of evidence by questioning witnesses. At this point in the proceeding, it was possible for jurors to address questions to the witnesses[60] – according to a new regulation in 1863, jurors even had the right to ask the president to take actions "which they considered relevant to illuminating the truth."[61]

The new regulation opened up one of the first possibilities for the jurors to actively participate in truth production. However, a reading of the main trial records gives the impression that jurors seldom if ever made use of the right to question witnesses. For example, in the Loos case, which was unusually long, lasting for two mornings and an afternoon, not a single question from a juror is reported.[62] So why didn't the jurors use the opportunity to learn more details about the Loos case? Why did they remain silent in that case, as in almost all other trials?

One reason for their silence may have been that it was not easy during such a tedious and monotonous process "to hold the jurors' interest"[63] – as the Electoral Hessian high court councilor in Haynau stated. After all, in the Loos case the jurors had to endure the testimony of eighteen witnesses and the reading of a number of records on the first morning. On the next morning, another twenty-one witnesses were added.[64] Perhaps it was ignorance or simple unwillingness to make the trial still more complicated. Possibly the remarks of the state procurator, defendant, defense attorney and witnesses were so convincing that no inquiries were required; perhaps the jurors were too unfamiliar with the process. Perhaps the jurors simply had no "great experience" in "understanding and assessing such legal actions," or they lacked the "requisite mental capabilities" – as numerous commentators alleged.[65] Or was it that the well-educated middle-class jurors could not comprehend the language, content, or social context of the statements from the lower class, while they for other reasons did not adequately understand the legal jargon?

Whatever the reasons for this striking silence, it contradicted the prominent place of the jurors in the symbolic order of the court. Furthermore, the jurors through their inaction implicitly endorsed the form of the trial as shaped in the preliminary investigation by procedures, questioning methods, and presentation of the circumstances, from the visual inspection report to the sketch. Furthermore, the jurors' presence and failure to exercise their right to pose questions reinforced the authority of the court and enhanced its importance and position as an institution that advocated scrutiny by jurors but did not need that scrutiny because it functioned perfectly of its own accord so that no further questions were required.

Besides the right to pose questions during witness examination, the jurors naturally had other possibilities for influencing the course of the trial. Furthermore, there was a central point in the trial process where, in accordance with the code of procedure, they had to take action: the point at which they were supposed to decide about the so-called questions of fact. Answering the questions of fact provided the basis for reaching a verdict and was therefore of decisive importance. Questions of fact were presented by the president after he had outlined the "concise summary" in "simple sentences, without the slightest mention of his personal view and the results of the evidence included for and against the defendant."[66] This summary was supposed to aid the jurors, who as a rule were untrained legally, in recognizing what was crucial in the testimony and evidence – guidance which, in the contemporary view, they urgently needed.[67] Whether intentionally or unintentionally, the president thus at the same time decisively swayed the case history on which the verdict was based in the direction of the legal rationale.

In contrast to English criminal law, jurors in Germany did not have the task of arguing for "guilty or not guilty"; instead, they had to answer a series of questions to the best of their knowledge and conscience with "yes" or "no" – that is, the so-called questions of fact. At this central point, too – putting it right up front – the jurors proved to be passive participants in the process, and once again a striking discrepancy is evident between their great symbolic importance and the lack of both interest and opportunity to help shape the legal negotiation process. In connection with the questions of fact, the lack of involvement was not due to jurors avoiding active participation in the process – if they had done so, they would not have performed their critical task, that is, to pass judgment on the crime. Instead, the noticeable passivity of the jurors at this point can be explained in terms of the criminal code, which made it structurally impossible for them to actively influence the finding of truth.

What was the nature of these structural difficulties? First, the jurors had no control over the type of questions presented to them for answers. The various codes of criminal procedure differed as to who was allowed to formulate the questions; often it was stated that the court as a whole had the right to work out the questions.[68] That was the case for Electoral Hesse[69] and it meant in practice that the *Schwurgericht* president and the two other judges developed the questions. Then they were read aloud to the court, and only the state procurator and the defense attorney could suggest changes or additions to the questions.[70] How important it was to be able to formulate or change the questions themselves is illustrated by a close look at the question list in the Loos case because it becomes clear there how decidedly the questions likewise supplied the answers. In the Loos case, there were three or four so-called questions of fact for each theft. First the question was asked whether Loos had stolen an article from a certain person on a certain day; second, whether he had done it in such and such a manner; third, whether he had done so with the intention of acquisition; and fourth, whether Loos was the defendant in court.[71] In this process, it becomes apparent that questions of fact – according to the code of criminal procedure – were questions that focused on whether the defendant had committed a crime, and if so, how, taking into consideration certain circumstances which might be legally significant for the sentence.[72] The jurors were supposed to judge whether a crime had occurred, which circumstances might be relevant according to legal criteria, and whether the accused was the offender. Assessment questions were to be left out, as were questions about the meaning of the act in the particular context of the actors. Jurors were only supposed to be "judges of the facts" – according to the ostensibly wide-spread conviction among "men of the law in Germany."[73]

Separating establishment of a crime and assessment of that crime is obviously impossible because establishment of such always involves assessment.[74] Yet this purported separation was the basis for the division of labor between the jurors and the judge, and determined the trial process decisively; first the jurors were supposed to answer the questions of fact; then the judge fixed the level of the sentence on the basis of that definition of the crime. However, not only did the separation between the so-called questions of fact and questions of law represent an arbitrary legal construct, but it was also a powerful act of staging. It produced the impression that events were objective and could be proved in an almost scientific procedure that divided labor and was ostensibly deductive[75] – precisely that procedure was carried out in court. The procedure itself thus produced its own legitimacy.[76]

The structuring of the questions helped produce an aura of objectivity and veracity, but there was also a second effect in criminal property trials:

a disambiguation of the relationship between things and people. In other words, the question raster reshaped the idea of absolute property. As already in the preliminary investigation and particularly in the "recognition procedures," a central effect of the question procedure was transformation of a complex set of circumstances into a property crime that could be simply and unambiguously defined according to legal criteria. All other possible legal interpretations of the events were taken out of the picture here, too, because no questions were asked about relationships, motives, thoughts, considerations, prior histories, or the symbolic and emotional dimensions of things, to say nothing of alternative meanings of actions. That effect can be observed in the Loos case. The first question was, "On April 30 … around noon at the Marburg-Frankenberg Street location, did the defendant, Ludwig Hofmann, called Loos, from Triesbach, 1) say, after looking all around, 'Don't you have anything on you' and violently reach into the skirt pocket of Catharina Bosshammer … whom he did not know and who was on her way from Sarnau to Oberasphe, and 2) when she replied 'No,' grab her arm with his left hand, while with his right hand tearing open the ties that closed her coat over her chest?"[77] This detailed question presents a complete narrative and suggests the unambiguousness of the defendant's act, yet that still had to be proven. Reaching into the woman's skirt pocket may undeniably have indicated an attempted theft but can also have been a sexual assault, physical violence, intimacy, or teasing.[78] The offender himself appears to have been known for a long time, and the assumption was made that he was only pursuing one goal with the act attributed to him. The possibility of other motives was ruled out. In this same manner, a total of twenty questions were asked relating to the numerous thefts with which Loos had been charged. The articles themselves once again played a prominent role in the process.[79] The defendant was repeatedly asked whether he had taken a black chicken, a hammer, tongs, a drill, an ax, a piece of fabric, or a vest jacket from a widow, an assistant mayor, a miller, or a day laborer by entering at night through an unlocked cow stall, with a ladder, or by breaking in. The questions were consequently only checking which legal criteria for a qualified or simple theft were met.

The question list always ended with the same stereotypical question: "Is the defendant the same person who incurred and served the sentences listed in the charging document?"[80] That was usually the case because the *Schwurgericht* cases very often involved repeat offenders. Last not least, this question, which was a reminder of the defendant's criminal past, reinforced the impression that the jurors had already formed from the previous questions; they must almost necessarily have concluded that they were dealing on one hand with an offender and on the other with a question of property ownership.[81]

Let's summarize: The questions for the jurors were loaded in the truest sense. They constructed a difference between offense and guilt questions on one hand, and among main, secondary, and "possible" questions on the other, thereby suggesting objectivity and truthfulness. The particular formulations and the arrangement of the questions carried over the perspective already adopted in the preliminary investigation; relational structures, motives, and interconnections not subsumed under the legal definition of theft were denied. The possibility that an accusation of theft could have been part of a dispute, for example, about honor and social positioning, could therefore not enter the picture. Furthermore, the questions likewise carried forward the preliminary investigation's definition holding that possession under certain circumstances constituted ownership and excluded other types of relationships between objects and persons that were entirely usual according to the ownership concepts predominant in rural society.

Nevertheless, it could be argued that the jurors were not simply victims of structured questions. Perhaps – it could be objected – the jurors had their own logic and applied it to circumvent the implied inevitability of the question raster.[82] Naturally, individual logic of this kind can be assumed in principle, but not much of it is evident yet in court at mid-century. In the case of Ludwig Loos, who was charged with no less than nine property crimes, the jurors satisfied the expectations of the court almost completely. The foreman of the jury was able to answer all but one of the questions of fact with "twelve yes votes."[83] The jurors had thereby made the preliminary decision critical for the judge to render his verdict and in it had supported the charges. In other trials this important phase took a similar course; the questions of fact formulated by the court were basically answered by the jurors in the positive. The attributions, judgments, and interpretations made in formulating the questions were thus acknowledged as true, and at the same time, this procedure for truth production was legitimized. Perhaps – but we know little about this – the positions of the jurors actually did change in the course of the following decades; they may have gradually learned to exercise their options.

Up to the end of the century, the behavior of jurors as seen in the Loos trial was not at all unusual; their most important task was neither to establish class justice nor to act as the guarantors of justice.

The accusation of class justice directed against the jurors ignores the overall composition of the judicial system (which because of its class homogeneity may perhaps have to own up to this accusation – more about that later). At the same time, the considerable importance attributed in the contemporary debate to jurors as guarantors safeguarding justice only proves to be correct on the symbolic level – for example, in swearing-in procedures. In the trial itself, especially during the important phase of hearing evidence, the jurors had scarcely any opportunity to intervene. Their most important task according to the code of criminal procedure, resolving questions of fact, proves upon closer analysis to be a complicated process that in many, but of course not all, parts was predetermined and provided few options for controlling the proceeding. At the points where jurors could have actively intervened in the course of the trial, they rarely or never seized the opportunity. Nevertheless, the jurors were important for this phase of the process; they were indispensable as central actors for symbolic policy, legitimized the procedure, and finally represented *pars pro toto* the entire "*Volk*." Furthermore, in the case of property crimes this part of the trial in particular contributed to public formulation of the new property concept. Consequently, the jurors were of considerable importance, although not in the sense which contemporary debates and the symbolic order within the trial wanted us to believe.

9.3 DEFENSE ATTORNEYS

Although contemporary debates, and some current researchers, suggested that structural reorganization of the methods for establishing justice went hand in hand with the *Schwurgerichte*, that change was not attributed solely to the new functions of the public and jurors. Considered crucial was also the new position of defense attorneys in the trial process;[84] they were able to decisively improve the position of the defendant – that is the assumption – because a defense attorney was not just possible in *Schwurgericht* trials but mandatory.[85] In the case of "verified poverty," it was even possible to request free legal representation.[86] In the following pages, the above assumption in particular will be examined. Is it true that the guaranteed presence of a defense attorney radically strengthened the position of the defendant in the *Schwurgericht*? Did the presence of a defense attorney facilitate loosening the rigid corset that constrained defendants in court? Could attorneys help defendants out of their usually passive role in the courtroom, a role that defined them primarily as objects subject to negotiation, testimony, description, and repeated identification?[87] To explore these questions, the rights available to defense attorneys in court and the degree to which they exercised those rights must be illuminated. In the process, it will become clear that defense attorneys, because of their specific educational situation, could not take full advantage of the latitude available to them and consequently acted as mentally absent as the jurors.

What possibilities for actively shaping the proceeding did the code of criminal procedure provide for defense attorneys? Their position within the proceeding as defined in the procedural code was not by any means as strong as might be thought, given the nature of contemporary debates. The position of the defense attorney had clearly improved, at least at first glance, because of his new rights as provided for in the 1848 Code of Criminal Procedure. The defense attorney was appointed officially and confirmed by the defendant in the first hearing, immediately after the detainee had been brought before the court without fetters; he now had about a week before the beginning of the trial to familiarize himself with the case.[88] The attorney had access to the files; could name additional witnesses; had the right to question the witnesses, request evidence collection, and present a closing argument; and he could submit and argue an appeal. Yet the defense attorney rarely appeared in court. Indeed, the defense attorneys in *Schwurgericht* trials, at least when property crimes were involved, were for the most part conspicuous before the Marburg and Hanau courts by their verbal absence. For example, the possibility of "naming further witnesses"[89] was not used a single time in the existing *Schwurgericht* cases. As witness testimony before the court was of particular evidentiary importance and apparently as a rule only repeated the statements made in the preliminary investigation, the defense attorney, through his conduct, abstained from correcting the interpretative setting constructed in the preliminary investigation. It remains unclear why defense attorneys did not make use of this option. Perhaps the attorneys made little or insufficient effort to read preliminary investigation materials and consequently did not stumble across inconsistencies or alternative meanings. Perhaps a contributing factor was the fact that, until the accusatory trial was introduced, no good method existed for expanding the preliminary investigation by taking new evidence. This option was therefore not familiar; there was no established practice, neither for the defense attorney nor the state procurator, who would have had to agree to such an expansion of the witness list. Perhaps the long drawn-out – as noted – preliminary investigation had already produced all the potential witnesses. Perhaps all the attempts to expand the list simply failed – after all, the court could also deny the request to interrogate new witnesses.[90] The attorney Bopp gives accounts of such matters in his reports on his experiences as a defense attorney in a jury court.[91] Whether because of neglect or simple continuation of old practices, defense attorneys, by not exercising the option of naming new witnesses, accepted the interpretation established in the preliminary investigation.

The second right of the attorney was the right to question. It directly involved the part of every trial that was in many regards most exciting, witness questioning and the taking of evidence. After the defendant and his defense attorney had been presented, jurors selected and sworn in, the charging document read, and the defendant interrogated concerning the matter at hand, the witnesses were called and the defense attorney could question them. Furthermore, it was possible to make "objections to the credibility" of the witnesses.[92] However, neither the right to question witnesses nor the possibility of casting doubt on their credibility seem to have been used by defense attorneys in Marburg theft trials. As in the case of the jurors, references to such additional questions and comments can only be found rarely. The legally trained attorneys, much more so than the jurors, would have had to elicit additional information by their questions to be able to supplement, or even cast doubt on, the narrative constructed by the gendarmes and judges in the preliminary investigation. However, the attorneys used this option just as infrequently as the right to add witnesses.

One reason for this may have been the unattractive procedure associated with the right to question. Defense attorneys could only question witnesses indirectly, through the president: "The defendant and his defense attorney can in the same manner address questions to the witnesses, but only by mediation of the president."[93] This regulation meant – as the contemporary jurist Zachariae put it – "unequal treatment of the state attorney and the defendant or his defense attorney."[94] The regulation prevented intense questioning of witnesses by the defense attorney. Cross-examination as typical in English trial law was barred.[95] As a result of this regulation, one of the most effective means of inducing witnesses and defendants to reveal a new interpretation of events was blocked.[96]

However, at the point of the closing argument at the latest, the silence was broken – at least that was suggested by the accounts in the contemporary press. If the defense attorney had a rather marginal role with only limited opportunities to speak up until the closing argument, that point would have been his chance to present his own interpretation of events.

There for the first time he could have thoroughly developed the perspective of the defendant without intervention of a president recasting his words. What was the situation with the closing argument? If contemporary descriptions are to be believed, that was the place where the attorney had to make a "fluent and carefully chosen"[97] presentation with "skill and geniality" to appeal to the "emotions or reason" of the public, or in *Schwurgericht* trials, of the jurors.[98] Here, reports claimed, the appeal was to "feelings" not reason, instead of being limited to the "factual question ... of the extent to which the allegation has been proven."[99] A "brilliant drama" was performed.[100] However, press articles that reported about such fiery closing arguments only covered property crimes in exceptional cases. Particularly the articles that went into individual trials in more depth and described the closing arguments in detail were only concerned with property crime when a spectacular robbery-murder or an especially slick sleight-of-hand crook was involved. We have found practically nothing in the relevant press about closing arguments for property crimes in provincial towns like Marburg, where often a day laborer confronted another person and the article stolen was bread obtained by begging, an old hat, or used shirts.[101]

Nor do the court records reveal much information about closing arguments. The record of Anton Zimmermann's trial states tersely that after the state procurator had presented his request for the defendant to be found guilty in accordance with the charging document, "the High Court Clerk Dr. Wolff presented the defense of the defendant and asked for an acquittal."[102] In the proceeding against Ludwig Loos in Marburg during the same year, the record is similarly vague about the closing argument of the High Court Attorney Schantz, stating that he "presented the defense of the defendant and requested that the latter only be found guilty of the thefts to which he had confessed; beyond that, the defense attorney left the determination of the defendant's guilt to the judgment of the jury."[103] In short, the records only reflect the content of the defense attorney's request. The description in the record may be the result of the record's relevance criteria and perhaps says little about the length, polish, and complexity of the argumentation in the closing argument actually presented in court. Yet, much suggests that the closing arguments for property crimes were more likely than not "excessively short or even suspiciously silent" – as a contemporary commented.[104] Last not least – as will be demonstrated in more detail in the following pages – collegial dependencies, lack of acceptance of the field of criminal law, and low pay may have kept attorneys from devoting a great deal of energy to the closing argument and thereby possibly clashing with the state procurator and the president on a fundamental level.

Most of all, the verdicts suggest that participation of defense attorneys did not improve the defendant's position to the extent which a superficial glance at the press would have us believe. The judgments in property trials seldom involved sentences less than what the state procurator had requested. Anton Zimmermann had been released only a few weeks before from prison where, on account of several thefts, he had served "a sentence of two months forced labor" for "the first time he was apprehended"[105] and had already committed a "nocturnal field theft," a "potato theft," and "theft of a found article" before he stole the bread from the two beggar boys; still, the sentence was five years in irons.

There were many reasons why the defense attorneys rarely used the options definitely available for structuring and intervention. One reason – as I already indicated – was the attorneys' specific social and educational situation. What was the nature of that situation? Who were the defense attorneys? Where did they come from? How did they position themselves socially and economically? Attorneys,[106] like all jurists, had to go through a course of education and a legal clerkship. In Electoral Hesse, the individuals who had not received a recommendation for a career as judge after their legal clerkship could request admission to practice as attorneys.[107] As it was indispensable to have both decent examination grades and social, financial, or intellectual capital to receive such a recommendation, only the legal clerks without those particular requisites became defense attorneys. Or as contemporaries put it, "The position of attorney was a lesser one, in fact, frequently a make-do position compared to that of the judge."[108] At the same time, a distinction must be made between lower court and high court attorneys.[109] Lower court attorneys had a bad reputation, had little financial power, and were often decried as "shysters."[110] A certain High Appeals Court Councilor Endemann wrote in 1867, "[I]ndeed, it was and is a less than enviable fate for an ambitious jurist to become grey as a lower court attorney."[111] High court attorneys had better prospects to carve out a comfortable existence; they lived in larger cities and were sometimes among the dignitaries. But a gap in income, influence, and prestige opened up even between better situated attorneys on one hand and judges, later to be state procurators or even legal councilors, on the other, at least in the rural and small-town society of Electoral Hesse. Even high court attorneys were in a difficult situation within the legal community.

The attorneys' less than enviable lot had many facets. One facet becomes clear when the long, unsuccessful efforts to produce a separate code for attorneys are considered. Such a code was intended to make attorneys independent of the courts because, as unaffiliated advocates, they would no longer have to wait for the state to assign them a position but could freely take up residence where they wished.[112] In a letter to the Electoral Hessian Ministry of Justice they had already demanded a code for attorneys – a first attempt to organize themselves independently from the state. The petition was denied, exactly like the other demands for independent law offices.[113] Not until 1863 was the regulation requiring that attorneys be appointed by the territorial lord rescinded.[114] Until then, attorneys had to seek admission to legal practice in a particular justice office,[115] had to swear an oath to the sovereign, and lived on extremely low fees[116] set by the court in question – which explains why the attorneys frequently attempted to obtain a judgeship at the local court or one of the attorney positions at the high courts, desirable for their better pay and prestige.[117] Until 1863, the attorneys were thus tightly held in a web of dependencies. They were dependent on the Electoral government because of the need to be appointed. They were economically dependent on the court in question because the particular fee regulations determined their income[118] and because the court could also evaluate attorneys negatively, which could have consequences as extreme as disbarment.[119] In addition, they were part of a "class of professional brethren living cheek by jowl," where "no member . . ., whether he wants to or not, can escape their influence."[120]

Not until free legal offices were established did attorneys' social and to some extent economic position improve, whereupon their number increased markedly.[121] In addition, introduction of the public main trial provided attorneys with a new stage; finally, their work options expanded and then their incomes in the wake of industrialization, especially in the area of civil law.

Of course, the attorneys' position remained precarious until far into the last third of the century. This situation is also evident from the attributes ascribed by contemporaries. Despite the impression often given by some researchers, the attributes were definitely not limited only to the self-stylization worked out by Hannes Siegrist, that is, that defense attorneys were "protectors of citizens from the police state" and "indispensable advisors who helped the citizen find his way in the thicket of laws."[122] Instead, the notion was widespread that attorneys – in particular defense attorneys – were primarily truth-twisters. This aspect becomes clearly apparent from the numerous articles in legal journals stressing that attorneys had above all to possess the ability to persuade, and to that end, to affect "the emotions and reason of the jurors."[123] The emphasis on speaking ability, including good rhetorical skills, humanistic education, and solid knowledge of history and literature, can be found among the attributes mentioned by the attorneys themselves. But the attempt to award an educated middle-class seal of approval to this sort to speaking ability did not hide the fact that the real or supposed rhetorical prowess of attorneys was not a neutral attribute that only represented a kind of supplementary competence for the public trial. In fact, other legal actors, who were forced to demonstrate their speaking ability more frequently only because they had more occasion to do so according to the procedural code, were not viewed in these articles from the same perspective. In connection with state procurators and judges, the issue was not rhetorical capabilities. In their case, such attributes as a sense of justice, knowledge of the material, and goodness were emphasized – attributes which were not acknowledged in attorneys. This suggests that the speech of state procurators and judges did not have persuasion as its goal but rather determination of facts, while attorneys very basically sought to persuade without always taking into account "justice and truth" in the process.[124] This assumption implies that attorneys were inclined to twist the truth rather than find it – that they "allow themselves to be led astray, to set aside their consciences (if they have one) and better judgment to gain a reputation for having the talent to outwit other people and drive their reason to arbitrariness, with the intention of drumming up business."[125] A certain Court Assessor Sundelin summarized this perspective as follows: "Thus, the jurors, the judge, and the state procurator pursue the goal of the entire proceeding, that is, truth and justice; the defense attorney is only there to prevent punishment of the defendant by any means."[126]

Added to this, a series of provisions outright discriminated against attorneys. The regulation which provided that the court president should explicitly remind the defense attorney "to put forward nothing contrary to his conscience or the deference due the laws, and to express himself with decency and moderation"[127] was criticized by the Darmstadt attorney Bopp, who was literarily very active. Why, Bopp asked, was the attorney of the complaint – he meant the state procurator – not admonished to conduct himself properly? In any case, he, Bopp, was "reminded vividly of the time in my youth when my French dancing teacher put my feet in place to show me how one performs '*avec décence*.'"[128] Not only

Bopp, but many attorneys felt pressured to point out their "morality and honor,"[129] their "education in history and philosophy," and their "knowledge of human character" and "the school of life," which had taught the attorneys that they could undertake the important task of "inspiring the nation's sense of justice."[130] At the same time, they also opposed the one-sided disciplinary right of the judge (that no longer applied to the state procurator) and declared that they were entirely capable of ensuring the worthiness of the profession on their own.[131]

Attorneys were thus considered by jurists who had found a place in government service to be in a kind of "hostile relationship" with the courts and the latter's task of finding truth.[132] This supposed antagonism was reinforced by the attorneys themselves, who never tired of emphasizing certain moral values, such as protection of the socially weak, the motive of justice, or even more melodramatically, the "struggle for a more just society,"[133] thereby tacitly implying that those values played much less of a role for judges and state procurators. The emphasis on the zeal of attorneys[134] and the metaphors of the "courtroom as a stage" and the "trial as a drama" supported the notion that the defense was less concerned with truth than with gripping and therefore perhaps fabricated stories. The theater metaphor moved the defense's activities away from truth and justice in the direction of show business and entertainment, thus undermining the standing of the attorneys.[135]

Taking on a criminal defense was therefore neither financially nor socially attractive for established attorneys, and it is consequently not surprising that specialization in criminal law did not occur. But this also meant that the defense was as a rule conducted by jurists who did not compensate for their scant training in criminal law with energetic practice[136] and were thus anything but professionally qualified experts with regard to the matters negotiated in court.

If the poorly trained defense attorneys, who were scarcely able to eke out a living from their clients, were in a difficult position because of their many dependency relationships and ambiguous attributes in court, the same was also true of the public defender. Court-appointed attorneys were appointed for any given case from the pool of legal clerks at the high court, if the accused could not freely choose or afford an attorney himself. That these assigned defense attorneys were far from happy about such obligations[137] goes without saying, given the fact that official attorney services were unpaid.[138] Furthermore, appointment as a public defender was also uncomfortable because the future legal elite – only those individuals who made it to legal clerkships at high courts – worked as defense attorneys in trials for which their direct supervisors and later evaluators acted on the side of the judges and state procurators.[139] As jurists in training who as a rule had careers as judges or state procurators at high courts ahead, who came from so-called good, that is, middle class or noble, families, and who had already been members of the appropriate social circles during their training, those defense attorneys were undoubtedly in a different situation from the ones who had to make a living as attorneys in the long run. Nevertheless, common to both was a strong dependence – in that event, undoubtedly emotionally and in habitus – on the other jurists acting before the high court.

The difficult situation of the defense attorneys economically, socially, and in habitus contradicts the image presented in many contemporary publications, that is, the attorney as an eloquent and dedicated representative of the new liberal order who left nothing untried to very forcefully help his client obtain his due. The reality was far from the image repeatedly conjured up primarily in the middle-class press of an untiring champion for the rights of all the down-trodden and persecuted, a champion who as an elegant and rhetorically brilliant jurist won over the jurors with impassioned closing arguments.[140] In Electoral Hesse, at least, the defense attorney's actions before the court were less heroic than awkward; ultimately, it can probably be assumed that the adverse situation cited was not without consequences for the élan of the defense attorneys. Such involvement could scarcely have had positive effects financially, socially, and professionally – on the contrary, a negative character assessment was an entirely realistic expectation. Attorneys had definitely not been "part of the elite of modern society and civilization" since the middle of the century, as is sometimes claimed by researchers – that image arose because the numerous attorneys active on the liberal side especially after 1848 created the impression that attorneys were by definition politically active and strident liberal representatives of the developing middle class.[141] Instead, attorneys were – as Hannes Siegrist says – "marginalized . . . in the system of production, reproduction, and control of knowledge."[142]

Notes

1 Otfried Keller, 1982, 78.
2 See Klemens Klemmer/ Rudolf Wassermann/ Thomas M. Wessel, 1993.
3 On courtrooms, see Monika Wienfort, 2001, 300.
4 See Reinhard König, 1999.
5 Victor von Haynau, 1852, 16.

6 See the description in Claudia Töngi, 2004, 73, on the ritual aspects of the court session. See Benjamin C. Hett, 2001, 158ff, for a description of the trial and its symbolic aspects since the founding of the *Reich*. In that work, Hett also emphasizes the increasing uniformity in symbolism and clothing that characterized the court after the founding of the *Reich*.

7 250 Electoral Hessian Ministry of Justice 349, Prohibition on justice employees wearing beards and petition for regulations governing exceptions, 1857–1858.

8 Next to church services, the trial was the most established event with public character in the mid-century world of experience. In addition, with the advent of the first parliaments, a third form of state or church public event from the 1810s on was the federal parliaments whose sessions could be followed from the galleries. Of course, parliaments were only present in the royal capitals. In his 1784 lecture, "*Was kann eine gute stehende Schaubühne eigentlich wirken?* (What can a good permanent theater actually accomplish?)," Friedrich Schiller was concerned with the same comparison. Of course, for him the court was corrupt and acted arbitrarily (it was, after all, still the old inquisitorial trial – and Schiller consequently subscribed to exactly the same tradition of attribution as the liberal reformers of 1848); theater, on the other hand, had the positively described power of the "jurisdiction of the stage." On this subject, see the presentation given by Thomas Weitin at the conference on the history of crime organized by Gerd Schwerhoff and me in Göttingen; Thomas Weitin, *Literaturen des Kriminellen*, in Rebekka Habermas and Gerd Schwerhoff (Eds.), *Verbrechen im Blick. Perspektiven einer neuzeitlichen Kriminalitätsforschung* (Frankfurt and New York, 2009), 367–380.

9 Wilhelm Endemann, 1867b, 270.

10 Bopp, 1850a, 336.

11 Bopp, 1851b, 95. Such attributions are found mainly in the case of trials that attracted considerable attention because the stories dealt with were inherently dramatic, for example, in trials about murder, passion, and deception. Likewise, trials involving prominent or interesting people and thus quickly categorized as "*causes célèbres*" undoubtedly drew an audience and appear, at least in their staging in the media, to have had much in common with plays; see the 1868 media staging of the murder by poisoning of Chorinsky and Ebergenyi in Konstantin Imm, 1991, and also the work of Inge Weiler, 1998. See, especially for the meaning of the public in the *Kaiserreich*, Benjamin C. Hett, 2001, 341; he describes a new debate regarding the danger posed by the masses to the process of establishing justice, because it is assumed that the masses, stirred up by the press, could negatively influence the court. Hett is thus just concerned with trials that attracted great attention. See Petra Overath, 2001, 135–137, on the behavior of the public. She shows (170) that, in records where strong public reactions were mentioned, the Minister referred to the "people's sense of justice" that was being expressed regarding clemency appeals. However, she, too, is referring to capital crimes.

12 Claudia Töngi, 2004, 74, describes the opening of a trial in Uri as follows: "... the court session was formally opened by invocation of the Holy Ghost

and recitation of five Our Fathers." We know nothing of comparable religious framing in Electoral Hesse.

13 Jäger, 1855, 10.

14 Regarding the following pages, see Willibald Steinmetz, 2002, 512; Alexander Ignor, 2002, 243ff; and Marie T. Fögen, 1974, 56ff.

15 See Günter Haber, 1979a, 609.

16 *Schwurgerichte des Großherzogtums Baden*, in *Hitzigs Annalen*, 40, New Series (1855), 191. It is further stated there, "But it is mainly the feared presence of the public in the trial that helps with the results and is much more of a deterrent to the criminal than an enticement, undoubtedly giving rise to moral feelings" (192).

17 Bopp. 1851b, 101, calls attention to this aspect. In this work, he describes four cases in which the public was excluded because of the danger of doing harm to the public's morality, and he criticizes that action. In particular in the case of a father and daughter convicted of "incest," Bopp found the following, "The crime involved had, as noted, already for years been causing serious public outrage, which would have been entirely redressed if the proceeding had been completely open to the public.

18 1848 Law of Criminal Procedure, Article 35. In Uri, regulation was considerably stricter; there the public was only admitted at certain points in the proceeding, only when it was a question of "facts and results, but not discourse and negotiations"; see Claudia Töngi, 2004, 78.

19 The author of this article emphatically opposed this assumption and writes that "... experience proved the opposite." See *Schwurgerichte des Großherzogtums Baden*, in *Hitzigs Annalen*, 40, New Series (1855), 191.

20 Bopp, 1851a, 178.

21 See Eduard Brauer, 1856, 138. In Electoral Hesse, this applied according to the 1848 Law on Criminal Procedure, Article 35, "to forging coins and paper money, at the discretion of the judge."

22 Schlink, 1851, 31.

23 Of course, this referred to negotiating the political facts; see Schlink, 1851, 31.

24 1848 Law on Criminal Procedure, Article 41.

25 See also the 1863 Law on the Constitution of the Courts, Article 31.

26 Alain Corbin, 1984.

27 Just how important a particular form of behavior defined as "decent," that is, conforming to middle-class behavior patterns, was considered in court, and the extent to which the public was discussed from the perspective of rule violations, is shown by the Braunschweig Code of Criminal Procedure, which places great emphasis on the public attending the session "with their hats off, unarmed, and observing the proper decency"; Eduard Brauer, 1856, 140.

28 See Richard J. Evans, 2001, 318ff. He very convincingly describes the debate about executions. It becomes clear in the process that the public's attendance at executions was regarded as a main problem. Complaints about the "rabble" that delighted in executions or inclined to emotional outbreaks and then ultimately interfered with the regular course of the execution were numerous. The execution was actually supposed to produce "effects of terror and revulsion" (321). Executions were finally moved within the walls, and there only

men who were immune to such displays of emotion and uncontrolled, impassioned intensity because of their middle-class origins were supposed to be granted entry.

29 On this subject, see the example of the debate that took place in the 1819 Bavarian *Landtag* (Parliament) sessions, as described in the *Baierische Landtagszeitung* in the months of April and May 1819.

30 Although we know a great deal about the public, on one hand ideal and on the other feared, as it was constructed in numerous contemporary articles, we know very little about the people who actually followed the trials. In any case, practically everyone was allowed entry. Thus, for example, it was said in Prussia that only people who were "not adults or who did not fully possess the rights of citizenship" were to be excluded (Eduard Brauer, 1856, 138). The regulations were similar in other federal states, including Electoral Hesse. See 1848 Law on Criminal Procedure, Article 34: "The oral trial is open to the public, but only adults are granted entry." That means that all grown men and women had access to the courtroom. None of the codes of criminal procedure created in the wake of 1848 made any distinction by class or gender in their access provisions. Yet a few years previously, there had still been a "sizable minority," as Günter Haber called it, which called for a "census" to limit the court public; see Günter Haber, 1979a, 618. Anselm von Feuerbach, for example, still believed at the beginning of the century that only those people who, based on "property, office, or business [were] respected citizens and had already taken the oath of citizenship," should be allowed entry. Otherwise, he feared that trials would become "entertainments for the common folk and rabble"; Paul J. A. Ritter von Feuerbach, Vol. 2, 1825, 24.

31 Paul Sundelin, 1858, 5.

32 *Schwurgerichte des Großherzogtums Baden*, in *Hitzigs Annalen*, 40, New Series (1855), 186.

33 Johann J. W. von Planck, 1857, 14.

34 1848 Law on Criminal Procedure, Article 247.

35 1848 Law on Criminal Procedure, Articles 232ff.

36 Johann J. W. von Planck, 1857, 15.

37 Johann J. W. von Planck, 1857, 16.

38 The purpose of these revisions was also to restrict the jurisdiction of the jury courts for political offenses; see Peter Collin, 2001, 211ff.

39 1851 Law on Administration of Justice, Article 42. In other federal states, for example, in Prussia, the restrictions were considerably more severe; see Peter Collin, 2001, 195.

40 Now a person had to pay twelve thaler in class tax, nine thaler in property tax, or six thaler in commercial tax to be admitted to the jury bench. Other federal states often had special regulations for the educated middle class, which was not always financially well-fixed; for example, Prussia granted that class an equal right to entry; see Peter Collin, 2001, 18. Otherwise, Electoral Hesse was typical regarding the tax regulation.

41 These categories correspond exactly to the categories that were decisive for granting the right to vote; indeed, one of the basic liberal principles was that the ability to act politically was tied to these qualities; see Dieter

Langewiesche, 1988. Ultimately – according to the prominent liberal Welcker – the objective was to preclude the "despotism of the masses" as much as possible, by ensuring that "the most insightful and best people" possessed control of the state. (See the declaration of Representative Welcker about the most recent essay of A. Boden, in the *Mannheimer Abendzeitung*, No. 11 (1844), quoted in Günter Haber, 1979a, 611. Jury service was to be organized like the right to vote.)

42 Schlink, 1851, 36.

43 Schlink, 1851, 38.

44 Schlink, 1851, 39.

45 Peter Collin, 2001, 205ff.

46 See also Günter Haber, 1979a, 611ff.

47 Dirk Blasius, 1974, 152, cites Anselm von Feuerbach and the Prussian Minister of Justice von Kircheisen as critics of the jury courts usual in the Rhineland since the French occupation. Kircheisen was especially critical of the fact that there was in no way class equality between the jury and the accused because the latter generally came from the lower classes. See also Peter Landau, 1987, 270ff. Others, for example von Gneist, pointed out that "[i]t is difficult to make many of our fellow citizens understand that a jury court of twelve rich men selected by an administrative official is the same jury that was admired for so long along the Rhine and wished for here." See R. von Gneist, *Die Bildung der Geschworenengerichte in Deutschland*, 1849, 151; quoted in Peter Collin, 2001, 206.

48 Dirk Blasius, 1974.

49 Günter Haber also advocated this theory and consequently makes the following generalization, "The great significance that the middle class liberals attributed to trial reform could instead be explained by the fact that they regarded not the '*Volk*' to be directly threatened but instead the position of the rising middle class, of which they themselves were the majority." See Günter Haber, 1979a, 600.

50 See Dirk Blasius, 1974, but also the numerous "criminal statistics," as published, for example, in *Hitzigs Annalen*.

51 Thus, the theory that Petra Overath, 2001, developed for Bavaria.

52 Peter Collin, 2001, 203ff.

53 The potential jurors ostensibly sought to hastily "leave the city or their homes ... on the opening day of the court of assizes so as not to be found during the ... selection by lot and by hiding thus to escape from their civic duty"; Schlink, 1851, 29.

54 1848 Law on Criminal Procedure, Article 248.

55 In addition, in Electoral Hesse the provisions regarding selection were changed to the effect that the thirty-six jurors and eight supplementary jurors provided for each *Schwurgericht* were no longer taken from a list created by the district council or provincial government, as still prescribed in 1848 (1848 Law on Criminal Procedure, Articles 246–252; 1851 Law on Administration of Justice, Article 42). Instead, after 1851 they were selected by the high court director "at his discretion"; 1851 Law on Administration of Justice, Article 42.

56 Thirty-six jurors had been called; they had to expect severe penalties for an unexcused absence; see 1848 Law on Criminal Procedure, Article 272. The penalties started at twenty-five thaler and could extend to seventy-five thaler and implied the loss of state and local rights for a period of two to four years. The names of the jurors were written separately on pieces of paper and read off. Then the accused and the junior state procurator were officially informed that they had the right to reject up to nine jurors each without giving any reasons. They had been asked in advance if any reasons for the rejections as listed in Article 236 were present: relationship by blood or bias toward one of the parties. Then the remaining slips of paper with the juror names were placed in an urn, and the *Schwurgericht* president pulled twelve out, which he read aloud; they were ultimately the jurors responsible for the trial. The right to reject jurors was definitely used by the state procurators but also by the accused.

57 The following statement was made in the trial of a certain Loos that took place in the mid-1850s: "It shall be sworn and pledged before God and Man that in the matter charged against Ludwig Loos for attempted robbery and multiple instances of petty and qualified theft you will follow the trial with studious attention, conscientiously examine the incriminating and exculpating evidence presented, not consult about the verdict to be issued with anyone but your fellow jurors, and deliver that, your verdict, only on the basis of the existing evidence and according to your free and complete conviction, taking responsibility for it before God and your conscience, without the hatred, favor, or respect of any person. So help you God!"; see 268 Marburg 50. See also the regulation in the 1848 Law on Criminal Procedure, Article 295.

58 1848 Law on Criminal Procedure, Article 295.

59 Solemnity was achieved, among other things, by the formal oath being spoken slowly and with "raised voice," and of course by having everyone in the courtroom stand each time. Victor von Haynau, 1852, 16, emphasizes that as particularly desirable.

60 1848 Law on Criminal Procedure, Article 310.

61 1863 Law on the Constitution of the Courts, Article 155.

62 That such questions did not actually exist can be seen from the fact that, in the view of the courts, the witness statements appear to have been identical to those from the preliminary investigation – thus, there are abbreviations that refer to the interrogation record from the preliminary investigation, but scarcely any supplementary information, qualifications, or corrections that go beyond that. The very fact that the identity of the statements was shown indicates that, from the perspective of the court, additional informational content was extremely rarely revealed by witness testimony; otherwise there would have had to be additional information recorded (similarly, Hartwig Reichling, 2003, 33). However, had jurors regarded their own questions as necessary, it would have to be assumed that supplementary information would have had to be added to some statement or other – if the jurors had exercised their right to ask questions thoroughly and adeptly. It can therefore be assumed that the jurors' questions had not simply been eliminated by recording techniques.

63 Victor von Haynau, 1852, 21.
64 268 Marburg 50. To this was added reading the visual inspection report aloud and showing "layout sketches." The pedantry and excessive attention to detail in argumentation already familiar from the preliminary investigation were conspicuously repeated here; indeed, all of the evidence had to be immediately put on view.
65 Victor von Haynau, 1852, 9.
66 1848 Law on Criminal Procedure, Article 315. The formulations in the preprinted forms are also similar; see 268 Marburg 50.
67 Whether such an appeal was even necessary, given the social composition of the jury, is questionable. In any case, there were many who believed that the jurors decidedly needed guidance, indeed, "instruction" – which they were supposed to get from the *Schwurgericht* president; Paul Sundelin, 1858, 6. In addition, the difficulty of communicating with jurors was often noted, because they were in some cases "without the means ... to express their thoughts cohesively, logically, and exhaustively"; Schlink, 1851, 32. It was feared that jurors might be led by other forms of logic, for example, by simple "emotional impressions"; Carl J. A. Mittermaier, 1858, 20. For that reason, Appeals Court Councilor Schlink believed that "the personality of the accused, which judges take into consideration at most during sentencing, is for jurors always the main thing, and if the accused has to that point been above reproach and only stole a trifle out of necessity, ... there is the justified hope" that he will only be given a light sentence. The fear of losing control is also a factor here, as was already made clear in the comments on the court public.
68 See Heinrich Zachariae, 1868, 484ff.
69 1848 Law on Criminal Procedure, Article 317.
70 In 1863 a change was made in that this right was now explicitly emphasized; see 1863 Law on the Constitution of the Courts, Article 317.
71 In this case, a total of twenty questions relating to over a half-dozen thefts were asked each time according to the same pattern; see 268 Marburg 50.
72 1848 Law on Criminal Procedure, Article 318.
73 Eduard Brauer, 1856, 189f.
74 However, this construct was at the same time the subject of contemporary legal debates, that is, it was by no means uncontroversial. That was already pointed out by Eduard Brauer, 1856, 189; see also Peter Landau, 1987, 278ff.
75 On legitimation through procedure, see Niklas Luhmann, 1969.
76 The division of the questions about the crime into main and secondary questions that concerned either the crime or the circumstances of the crime suggests that courts were places where objective and true determination of the facts was only possible on the basis of precise distinctions in the questions. The main questions were supposed to relate to the crime itself. The secondary questions were supposed to relate to how the crime had been committed in order to establish mitigating or aggravating circumstances. In addition, there was the category of possible questions.

Furthermore, the reduction of the answer options to an absolute "yes" or "no" also contributed significantly to this picture; the reduction on one hand severely limited the possibilities for formulating the questions and at the same time implied that alternatives for posing the questions were inconceivable. The questions, depending on whether they were positively or negatively structured, already necessitated a considerable construction effort; the enormous limitations imposed by the yes-no options for answers only added to the difficulty.

77 268 Marburg 50.

78 The second question puts the course of the crime in concrete terms: "Did the accused not desist from this act ... when a man showed up in response to Bosshammer's cries for help?" The third question already implies a positive answer to question one and only asks about the intent of the offender: "Did the accused have ... the intention of appropriating Bosshammer's money or things otherwise in her possession against her will?" See 268 Marburg 50.

79 They were already listed separately in the fourth question, as in an exhibit list, in connection with the question of whether he had stolen the articles. A dozen other questions relating to the kind of theft and the objects taken then followed.

80 See 268 Marburg 50.

81 This question series, whether short or as extensive as in the Loos case, had to be answered one question at a time with "yes" or "no" by jurors who had been sequestered for that reason in a jury room; the results were noted for each question on the margin of the report. In Electoral Hesse, fewer votes needed to be cast for innocence of the accused, and more for guilty, to achieve clarity. See 1848 Law on Criminal Procedure, Article 324: "A decision on each of the questions submitted to the jurors is reached for the accused if five of the twelve jurors in their declarations agree with each other in his favor, or against the accused if eight of the jurors agree to his disadvantage." The voting was conducted by a foreman elected by all of the jurors (see 1848 Law on Criminal Procedure, Article 323); the foreman was supposed to submit each question separately and take a vote on it.

In most of the federal states, a regulation was introduced stating that a two-thirds majority was necessary for a guilty verdict; see Peter Landau, 1987, 283; for the individual regulations, see Heinrich Zachariae, 1868, 516ff.

82 The jurors were supposed to let themselves be guided by what the president in his jury instructions called the "conscience of the honest man" and the "common sense of the educated person." The jurors were to decide without consideration of the person, "without hatred or favor," and "without regard for the consequences of their verdict." See the 1863 Law on the Constitution of the Courts, Article152; the instructions that the president gave when handing over the questions to be answered stated similarly in 1863 that "the jurors [have] to deliver their pronouncement without regard for the consequences of the verdict." See 1863 Law on the Constitution of the Courts, Article 161.

Everything that could "prejudice the jurors" is to be avoided (1863 Law on the Constitution of the Courts, Article 153). The fundamental thought is clear: Not legal nitpicking was sought, but a concept of justice similar to that ostensibly rooted in the *Volk* as a whole and based individually on an "intimate conviction" (see Peter Landau, 1987, 281; for critical remarks, see Carl J. A. Mittermaier, 1858), whereby the "available evidence" – according to the code of criminal procedure (1848 Law on Criminal Procedure, Article 295) – was naturally of central importance.

The criteria that the jurors were to use for orientation thus conformed on one hand to the expectations of neutrality characteristic for the figure of the judge, and on the other, to what was popularly called the "consciousness of justice in the *Volk*." Such "consciousness of justice in the *Volk*" was understood to be "the spirit and character [of a people] formed by climate, composition of the soil, relationships among neighbors, fates, religious belief . . .."; see Jodocus D. H. Temme, 1851, 592. However, this "consciousness of justice in the *Volk*" was not a fixed entity but to the contrary a very controversial matter. The more references were made to it, the more variously it was interpreted. Despite considerable differences in definition – as for example in a debate of the 1850s in the *Archiv des Criminalrechts* – some attributes were broadly shared; Jodocus D. H. Temme, 1851, 595. Equating of the consciousness of justice in the *Volk* in this way with the middle-class legal perspective can also be very clearly deduced from the terminology used for the guidelines to the jurors in the judge's instructions speech: The terms, the "honest man" and the "common sense of an educated person," clearly indicate a middle-class canon of values and thus the group from which the jurors were for the most part recruited.

83 268 Marburg 50. The one exception relates to a theft from the schoolteacher Jean Vial that was allegedly committed on the upper floor of his house. In this case, two jurors did not believe that Loos had stolen "twelve to fifteen shirt-like vests, two duvets, and a pillow case."

84 There are no detailed works on the function of the defense attorney in trials of the Early Modern Period. Harriet Rudolf, 2001, 131, summarizes the situation to the effect that "[t]he function of the defenders in the criminal trials of the Early Modern Period appears ... rather to be of a representative nature: Their involvement in the trial legitimized the decision as lawful and reasonable without their actions having in practice had any significant influence on the decision." See also Andrea Griesebner, 2000, 62ff.

85 An exception was made for "press crimes," which were punished less severely with a one-year sentence. See 1848 Law on Criminal Procedure, Article 52. That was the rule in almost every federal state after 1848; see Klaus Armbrüster, 1980, 112ff; see Johann F. Henschel, 1972, 103ff; see Eduard Brauer, 1856, 70ff; Karl Binding, 1893, 90ff. In contrast, the basic possibility of procuring a defense attorney now existed in high courts, but it was not mandatory; see 1848 Law on Criminal Procedure, Article 195; see also 1863 Law on Criminal Procedure, Articles 35ff.

86 1848 Law on Criminal Procedure, Articles 50ff.

87 But defendants were laced into a corset of rules at many points where completely open questions were involved, at least at first glance open, for example, during witness interrogations. Witness interrogations were anything but open because the position of the accused as a suspect was repeatedly reinforced. The code of criminal procedure stated first of all, "After every statement, the president asks the witness whether the present accused is the person he had spoken about"; 1848 Law on Criminal Procedure, Article 308.

This formulation was repeated verbatim on the forms for *Schwurgericht* sessions, but was supplemented there by a notation to show confirmation or modification, "... affirmed ... that" (as on the form in 268 Marburg 62). In reality, that meant that for perhaps twenty witnesses interrogated on one morning in a *Schwurgericht* session, the same stereotypical words were repeated twenty times, confirming that the "accused appeared to the witness to be the person in question" or that "he [the witness] was able to definitely recognize the accused again as the person in question." (Those were the formulations in the record from the trial of Ludwig Loos, 268 Marburg 50.) As absurd as the meticulously precise identification appears at first to have been, this enquiry proved momentous. The result was necessarily reinforcement of the impression that the accused was the guilty party – only because it was emphasized that the accused was the object of questioning and was only acting as such in the court room. As all the statements were repeatedly connected to the accused, his position was gradually transformed into that of an offender – a process that had begun with the preliminary investigation.

88 In this week and during the trial he could "look at the files and confer with the accused without the presence of a court person."

89 That is what is written on the form provided for that purpose; see 268 Marburg 50.

90 1848 Law on Criminal Procedure, Articles 73 and 304.

91 The issue here was that he wanted to name an expert who was supposed to exonerate the accused; see Bopp, 1850a.

92 1848 Law on Criminal Procedure, Article 305.

93 1848 Law on Criminal Procedure, Article 91.

94 Heinrich Zachariae, 1868, 205. The regulation was definitely not to be found in every federal state; Heinrich Zachariae, 1868, 205, note 25; he speaks here of Electoral Hesse, Hesse-Darmstadt, and Prussia as exceptions; see Eduard Brauer, 1856, 169ff.

95 On the subject of cross-examination, see the outstanding analysis of Willibald Steinmetz, 2002, 505ff.

96 Furthermore, this regulation strengthened the position of the president. All threads came together in him because of the way in which the right to speak was structured; only he could grant the right to speak, and he could transform all of the other participants into "extras."

97 Schlink, 1851, 36.

98 Ibid.

99 Paul Sundelin, 1858, 14.

100 Wilhelm Endemann, 1867b, 270.

101 Regula Ludi, 1999, 455, says about the press, "[B]anal property crime was left out."

102 268 Marburg 91.

103 268 Marburg 50. See also the terse recording in cases in which the defense attorney departed considerably in his summation from the motion of the state procurator and for example demanded acquittal; see 268 Marburg 14.

104 Wilhelm Endemann, 1867b, 270.

105 268 Marburg 91, Charging document.
106 On attorneys, see Konrad H. Jarausch, 1990, and Hannes Siegrist, 1996. See also the informative analysis of Ulrike Döcker, 1996, who of course focuses chiefly on the last third of the nineteenth century. See also the local study of Peter Wettmann-Jungblut, 2004.
107 In the nineteenth century, attorney status was a way station for almost every jurist, who of course whenever possible passed through this beginning period of his career quickly to get to another position right away.
108 Wilhelm Endemann, 1867a, 35.
109 In criminal matters, the possibility of having separate representation had been abolished; Wilhelm Endemann, 1867b, 267ff.
110 Wilhelm Endemann, 1867a, 35.
111 Wilhelm Endemann, 1867b, 269.
112 On this subject, see also Hannes Siegrist, 1996, 389ff.
113 Thomas Platner, 1990, 160.
114 Oelzen, 1867, 20.
115 Frank Thiesen, 1997, 159.
116 Frank Thiesen, 1997, 162, contains an extensive quotation of F. Oetker, with figures.
117 Frank Thiesen, 1997, 160.
118 Wilhelm Endemann, 1867b, 280, emphasizes that.
119 Klaus Armbrüster, 1980, 123.
120 Wilhelm Endemann, 1867b, 272.
121 Benjamin C. Hett, 2001, 76, speaks of a 400 percent increase in Berlin. On the other hand, researchers emphasize that the increase in the number of attorneys led to a glut of attorneys and thus led to falling incomes; see Kenneth Ledford, 2000. Nuanced local studies on this subject are needed. None exist for Electoral Hesse, with the consequence that the exact development of the economic situation must remain speculation.
122 Hannes Siegrist, 1996, 385f.
123 Schlink, 1851; Paul Sundelin, 1858, 7, even speaks of "declamatory art and skill."
124 Bopp, 1851a, 178.
125 Ibid.
126 Paul Sundelin, 1858, 7.
127 Bopp, 1851a, 340.
128 Bopp, 1851a, 341.
129 Paul Sundelin, 1858, 10.
130 The quotations all come from speeches that were given at the 1847 assembly of German attorneys in Hamburg; quoted from *Die Versammlung deutscher Anwälte in Hamburg 1847*," in *Illustrierte Zeitung*, No. 165 (1847), 130f.
131 On the subject of the court of honor for attorneys established in this context, see Günter Holly, 1989; Kenneth Ledford, 1996; Benjamin C. Hett, 2004, 123–144.
132 Wilhelm Endemann, 1867b, 284.
133 Ulrike Döcker, 1996, 102.
134 Paul Sundelin, 1858, 13.

135 Unfortunately, there is no study just on this very striking aspect of the discussion regarding trials; see, among others, the contemporary descriptions in Jäger, 1855, 8, for example.

136 On this subject, see the description in Benjamin C. Hett, 2004, 123–134.

137 See 268 Marburg 50. There the defense attorney mentioned tries to get rid of a case – but without success.

138 Wilhelm Endemann, 1867b, 272. See there the case of the attorney Dr. Löbell, who repeatedly attempted in vain to claim fees from the court for an appeal matter he defended. But as the defendant had no assets and Löbell acted as the public defender, he was told emphatically by the court that he had "no fees to receive"; see 266 Marburg 98, Petition of the High Court Attorney Dr. Löbell in Marburg for a cost determination in the criminal matter against the prisoner in irons, Wilhelm Schade.

139 For example, Dr. Wolff had to act as the public defender more than once, and other young jurists in training, such as the legal court clerk Bezzenberger, went before the court as public defenders; see 268 Marburg 62.

140 On the situation in Bavaria, see Petra Overath, 2001, 138ff.

141 This assessment appears to have been accurate for Electoral Hesse as well, because many attorneys there were also active in parliament on the side of the liberals. However, the reverse, that attorneys were by definition politically active citizens, is not supported, at least as far as the majority of attorneys is concerned. See Frank Theisen, 1997, 169, on the proportion of attorneys at the Electoral Hessian assembly of estates in the first half of the nineteenth century.

142 Hannes Siegrist, 1996, 938. By strictly pursuing a professionalization theory, Siegrist is able to give this ambivalence a name, but he does not analyze it.

10

Irritations, Dissonances, and Various Other Matters

More Than Just Theater

Let's summarize: The introduction of public, oral trials and especially *Schwurgericht* trials cannot be described simply as a linear increase in legal equality, certainty, and justice. The simple interpretation of legal reforms as a history of modernization proves to be the continuation of a deeply politicized legal debate of the nineteenth century. Many reforms which initially gave the impression that more control and thus less arbitrariness had come to the process of establishing justice and that the defendant's position had been strengthened, prove on closer examination to be less unambiguous changes. The *Schwurgerichte* thus played a much smaller role quantitatively than the attention generally paid them would suggest. The overwhelming majority of trials took place in overloaded lower courts that had to manage without jurors. The qualitative significance of *Schwurgerichte* – as well as of the public main trial overall – must be viewed in a more nuanced manner. Contemporary rhetoric and rituals endeavored successfully to present the public trial as the exclusive and above all, self-contained space for finding legal truth, which took place outside all spheres of influence. This impression was reinforced even more by the introduction of the public, jurors, and in a limited manner, the defense attorney. Yet the importance of the preliminary investigation was great, as many interpretations and narratives originated specifically in this non-public segment of the process. In addition, it was evidently not really possible to introduce an alternative interpretation, another set of relationships, a different history with any success in the public, oral main trial. Did the staging of allegedly neutral spaces monitored by the public thus only lead to enhanced legitimacy of the state process for establishing justice? Was the preliminary investigation only "re-enacted" in the main trial, as Jäger maintained in 1855 about jury courts?[1] He remained for the most part alone in his criticism of the new court proceedings – not until some years later was that question discussed by broader jurist circles in the course of creating the *Kaiserreich*'s code of criminal procedure. Was the main trial just rehashing truths that had already been produced previously?[2]

As much evidence as I was able to collect for just such a "counter-narrative," the public trial was anything but a farce whose sole purpose was to stage publicly interpretations that had been established earlier. In this trial, things happened that had neither been decided already in the preliminary investigation nor provided for in the code of criminal procedure, much less discussed in contemporary debates. In an analysis consistent with "doing law," dynamics arising in public trials should not be interpreted as deviations from predefined procedures, deviations that are unimportant and can therefore be disregarded; instead, those dynamics must be made the point of departure for intensive consideration. As a matter of fact, far more is involved than small discrepancies, random dissonances, and ordinary exceptions to the rule; rather, these are the dynamics that made any event in court more than just a drama foreseeable since the preliminary investigation, a drama with the sole purpose of legitimizing the procedure. The dynamics and dissonant aspects can be deduced from the behavior of the witnesses, from the verdicts, and from what the public and especially the press made of the trial.

10.1 FEMALE WITNESSES, MALE WITNESSES, AND OTHER COMMUNICATION PROBLEMS

Nothing surprising should actually have been expected from the witnesses in the main trial. As shown, they themselves and their testimony were already known from the preliminary investigation. Only rarely were any further witnesses added, and their testimony generally provided little that was unanticipated. Yet more was involved than a mere repetition of the preliminary investigation, to be staged here publicly. As it happens, the witnesses, together with the public, were the factors that could most markedly disrupt – from the perspective of the court president or the presiding judge – trials which were very clearly already pre-structured. With those factors, an irritating element entered the courtroom. But the irritations were neither loud nor especially conspicuous, nor did they have the character of intentional actions. In fact, to all appearances the witnesses were likely upset because they did not know the rules of behavior in effect since the introduction of public trials.

The disturbances consisted in minor carelessness, perhaps in misunderstandings, or, for example, in witnesses not appearing in court, appearing late, or only showing up after being summoned repeatedly. Thus, in the case of a long theft trial for which twenty-one witnesses were summoned for the first day of trial, five did not appear. One had in the meantime immigrated to America, but others had less plausible explanations for staying away. A married couple was not at home, according to the testimony of a daughter who was likewise summoned and did appear in court; she claimed not to know where they were – an excuse both simple and unconvincing. Another female witness who was also summoned and did not appear had supposedly been "unavailable because of a very small child at home." The next day, the trial was supposed to continue with twenty witnesses. At the trial opening, exactly half that number was absent. Only four of the witnesses ultimately appeared for witness questioning. However, they had to endure warnings because they came late.

In the trial of Anton Zimmermann, the two mothers of the minor beggar boys who were robbed were immediately sentenced during the trial to a fine of two thaler or alternatively to two days of detention because they had not appeared.[3] Ironically, one of the two had been unable to appear because at the time of the trial she was in jail, serving a sentence "for willful failure to appear."[4] She had received the sentence because she had not complied with a summons in connection with the preliminary investigation. At that time, she argued in vain that she had "not been at home" for the summons, "and [that] it was incorrectly delivered to her."[5]

Failure to appear, as can be observed in a series of proceedings, is surprising in light of the severity of the penalties not only threatened but also enforced for not appearing. The absences are also surprising, if the substantial expenditures by the court for summonses are taken into account. All witnesses received an official summons from the state procurator.[6] According to the code of criminal procedure, this printed summons – representing one of the first forms used in the legal system – was supposed to give the exact location, the date, and the time of the requested appearance.[7] Especially if the summons was going to a person who did not live at the location of the court – which was almost the rule in rural Electoral Hesse – the expense for the summons was considerable. Sometimes a correspondence developed between umpteen court employees and the main court, and each time it was precisely noted which person had been located, or not located, and where the person in question could possibly be. Then, for the preliminary investigation or in preparation for the main trial, several witness lists were even drawn up with name and place, and a further note was added in the column "Comments on summons sent."[8]

Despite this meticulousness, witnesses stayed away. There were at least two reasons for this. As most of the witnesses came out of the defendant's immediate environment, they perhaps did not want to testify in court – either they found themselves in a conflict of loyalties, or they were afraid of the possible consequences.[9] For example, in the proceedings against the day laborer Loos, one witness regretted the statement he had made in the preliminary investigation and in court stated for the record that "he had perhaps said too much back then."[10] A statement made right out in public could have consequences: All the neighbors – of that you could be sure – would hear about such a statement immediately. The impression that people did not want to say anything, because for better or for worse they did not view this as the place to talk about conflicts, fairly jumps to mind, given the silences sometimes louder than words, or frequently, the very stereotypical, almost say-nothing replies in court.

A further reason for the failure to appear possibly indicates communication difficulties between the witnesses and the justice system. Maria Scherrer, the mother of the beggar boy who was robbed, was not necessarily lying when she stated that she received the summons but it was incorrectly delivered. Often the situation might have been even more banal: Perhaps many of the summoned witnesses simply could not read. Perhaps they did not understand the meaning and purpose of a "summons" or did not know how to handle this term and the paper that was supposed to be signed for the court officer. The large number of witnesses who arrived late for the sessions speaks for such communication difficulties; their idea of the meaning of such precise dates and times does not appear to have necessarily been the same as that of the court.

In any case, witnesses were not, or were only inadequately, up to the new role that they were supposed to play in the public trial. They appear not to have known exactly, and perhaps did not want to know exactly, what it meant to testify publicly as a witness, without being asked forcefully to pay or having to make statements, which they perhaps did not want to do. The witnesses of the 1850s, 60s, and 70s had apparently not established any routine in their dealings with the new institution and could not, or did not want to, simply meet the demands made of them.

This circumstance also explains why the 1848 Code of Criminal Procedure required almost twenty paragraphs to establish all of the contingencies regarding witnesses.[11]

Of course, even greater misunderstandings and irritations could arise in the course of witness testimony, if communication between the court and the witnesses did not function properly. Indeed, contemporary legal journals spoke of real communication problems. What was meant? It was claimed that judges, defendants, and witnesses could not communicate with each other because they came from different social contexts. Or as Chancery Counselor Jäger from Tübingen stated, "The peasant's unpracticed train of thought is much more circuitous and rambling than that of the educated man, and before his account comes to the point where his testimony starts to have a connection to the subject of inquiry and thus has any value for the investigation, he must unload a heap of information."[12] The most frequent assessment heard was that "such people" were "without means" "of expressing their thoughts coherently, logically, and exhaustively."[13] Communication problems were repeatedly reported and instructions for overcoming them provided. For example, Ludwig Jagemann urgently advised judges "to stay in constant contact with all the better elements of the "*Volk* " so as to become familiar with the "language of the *Volk*." He emphasized at the same time that it was a difficult proposition "to penetrate the lower classes," as they were very distrustful.[14]

Not only contemporaries but also current researchers have devoted attention to communication and the associated problems related to "such people." Since the Bernstein theory of a restricted lower class code and the elaborate code of the middle class,[15] which was well received during the early 1970s in various disciplines, a debate has simmered about the question of how the command of language by the different classes helped shape the situation in court. In the course of the debate, the deficit theory implicitly inherent in Bernstein and to all appearances already long since formulated among jurists in the nineteenth century was replaced by a difference theory which holds that no socially conditioned inferiority of certain speakers exists but only otherness.[16] More recent works, which are less concerned with formal language codes than with argumentation structures and thought patterns, not only call into question the deficit theory established by nineteenth-century contemporaries and by Bernstein but stand it on its head. Instead of unconsciousness and speechlessness being attributed to "such people," this "speechlessness,"[17] whether actual or possibly only feigned in court, could also be powerful, as the works of Arlette Farge and Michel Foucault suggested.[18] Martin Dinges introduced the concept "use of justice" (*Justiznutzung*) in this context for the eighteenth century.[19] But Arlette Farge, Michel Foucault, and a number of others not only provided new answers to Bernstein's unambiguously answered question of who possessed more power, they also pointed out that the two supposed codes cannot be clearly separated from one another. In addition, they were able to show that the two codes were connected, actually interwoven. Regina Schulte has also called attention to that fact. She speaks of "semantic conflict lines,"[20] meaning two different interpretive and moral worlds that collided with each other in the nineteenth century, especially in rural regions; a "peasant-village culture," having assimilated the "interpretations offered by middle class culture," was also confronted with middle-class justice when prompted by the judge to speak.[21] Schulte focuses attention on the interference between styles of speech and makes clear that absolute separation is not possible.[22]

For the situation in Electoral Hessian courts, the upshot is that the construct of two opposed worlds and languages developed by contemporaries is as implausible as the construct of elaborate and restricted codes. What remains is a linguistic difference between the juristic and non-juristic actors in court, which was magnified by the conditions imposed on speaking as established in the code of criminal procedure.[23] What remains is a striking number of witnesses who could or would not follow the instructions of the court. What likewise remains is the fact that the two sides had an exchange relationship with each other; the speaking and silence of one side depended on the speaking and silence of the other side. Of course some communication problems arose from this difference, but they do not necessarily imply any structural inferiority of one to the other.

The communication problems or simple dissonances in Electoral Hessian courts in the second half of the nineteenth century were of scarcely any consequence for the defendants, because they had few opportunities to take the floor. That was because – compared, for example, with the situation in English courts – the rules about speaking and remaining silent were structured such that the defendants' options for speaking were quite limited.[24] Other than denying the charges, defendants could only have an irritating effect on the course of the proceedings by intimidating or positively influencing the witnesses so that the latter then did not repeat accusations made in the preliminary investigation.[25] Indeed, in the case of witnesses, the communication differences led to some extent to substantial dissonances and irritations that obstructed the course of the proceeding. The obstruction had various consequences: Some witnesses responded with payback of the same kind; others were able to keep quiet about things that possibly had been a burden to others beside themselves.

In any case, the dissonances by no means always ensured less severe penalties, nor were they perceived as criticism of the proceeding itself. However, there were definitely points at which it became apparent in court that despite carefully thought-out rituals and codes for clothing and habitus, despite the authority of the preliminary investigation and the clear rules governing what could and could not be said, as specified in the codes of criminal procedure, events in court were, perhaps especially after the reforms, open to dynamics that were beyond the control of the court. Witnesses, less often the defendants themselves, and even the public (that I will go into later) were able with their behavior to set limits on the drama and in that way to undermine the public main trial in its function as the provider of legitimacy for the new legal system.

10.2 VERDICTS, OR INCONSISTENCY IN THE ADMINISTRATION OF JUSTICE

Dynamics and dissonances were also indirectly apparent at another point in the proceedings: in the verdicts. Jury court verdicts for property crimes – getting right to it – were neither conspicuously lenient nor inordinately severe. More than anything, the verdicts seesawed markedly. They attested to the inconsistency in the administration of justice and thus to another source of irritation. That was the case even though many contemporary statistics seem to indicate that the number of acquittals after the introduction of the *Schwurgerichte* fell rather than rose.[26] Indeed, many jurists, for example, Appeals Court Councilor Schlink, believed that "jurors are much stricter in cases of offenses against property than [in those] against people."[27]

The inconsistency of the verdicts was not due to a lack of rules, even though Electoral Hesse was one of the few federal states without codified criminal laws. There were evaluation standards that, until introduction of the 1867 Prussian criminal code, could be gleaned from a whole series of regulations and decisions of the high court of appeals. Moreover, never before had theft and the penalties fixed for it been more precisely defined. Basically, the logic for assessing penalties was such that the penalty level for simple theft was the starting point, and the "aggravating factors" compounded it. Until mid-century, the sentence for simple theft was fourteen to twenty-one days in jail.[28] With the introduction of the 1867 Prussian criminal code, the penalty for simple theft was "not less than a month." Aggravating factors were stolen articles of great value, repeated offenses, or certain kinds of theft, that is, "qualified or grand theft," use of force, nighttime offenses, or use of tools. If any of these applied, the sentence had to be increased for each factor by a certain time increment. For example, until the 1860s, "grand theft" carried a sentence of one-half year up to five years.

As unambiguous as the regulations were, the verdicts varied widely. The verdict in the case of Anton Zimmermann, who had prior convictions but had only taken left-over bread, was considerably more severe than the appropriate regulations called for.[29] The previously convicted Zimmermann got five years for stealing bread, while a likewise twice-convicted person found guilty of defaming an official was sentenced to less than two years for multiple thefts of articles with a significantly greater value.[30] Another young man, who already had four previous convictions for theft and in 1855 again stood before the court for stealing six sausages, two cakes, and eight loaves of bread, received a sentence of three years in irons.[31] Contemporary statistics indicate that the fourth "instance of apprehension" for an ordinary theft carried a sentence with the very broad range of nine months in jail to twelve years in irons.[32] Not only in the *Schwurgerichte*, but in the high and criminal courts as well, the sentences varied in an inexplicable relationship to the type and frequency of crimes.[33] For two small thefts from the bleaching green, the sentence was six weeks in the workhouse.[34] The theft of a relatively worthless article was punished with only a month in jail, even though it was a planned theft at night. However, the court believed that it could apply the mitigating circumstance of family theft because distant family relationships were involved.[35] A day laborer was sentenced to nine months even though he supposedly had only stolen a worthless hat; of course, he had already had to serve time for two previous convictions.[36]

Not particular severity or leniency but decided inconsistency is typical of the Electoral Hessian legal institutions in the second half of the nineteenth century.[37] This pronounced uncertainty – or stated positively, individual variability – in verdicts was the reason for Wilhelm Koch's publication of a comprehensive essay on "Sentencing Practice ... in theft cases," augmented with a great deal of statistical material. The introduction states the following about the situation in Electoral Hesse: "To the person who seeks to become familiar with criminal law practices in our land, the chief subject ... that comes up when deciding any sentence will appear to be a secret for a very long time, namely, the question of how the sentence is to be determined in individual cases – the doctrine of sentencing."[38] This inconsistency in the administration of justice is surprising in light of the fact that one of the main demands of the reformers had been to push through equal treatment in court. Indeed, the legal reformers had specifically justified their new ideas by referring to the allegedly very great arbitrariness of the legal system in the Early Modern Period.[39] It is interesting that the cause of the too stiff or too light sentences in *Schwurgerichte* is explicitly traced back both by contemporaries and by some modern researchers to the participation of jurors. However, the jurors' participation in the administration of justice extended only to decisions about the questions of fact, and the jurors therefore had only indirect influence on the penalty level, because the critical decisions for assessment has already been predetermined by the structure of the proceeding and consequently bore the stamp of the jurists involved rather than that of the jurors.[40]

The variability in adjudication could become even greater because the court verdict – no matter how it turned out – was not the last word. After all, in addition to the possibility of appeal, the sovereign's right to grant pardons was firmly embedded in the constitutions of almost all the federal states. Moreover, in Electoral Hesse jurors had the option of recommending the sovereign's mercy for defendants. After the verdict was announced, the defendant was advised of the possibility to appeal and the jurors were told "that they had the right to recommend that the defendant receive the mercy of the local ruler."[41] Reference to the possibility of appeal could be found almost verbatim in criminal trials, but mention of the pardon option was a practice specific to the *Schwurgericht*. The right to request a pardon for the defendant indicates a dimension of the jurors' position that seems anachronistic, because research on the nineteenth century has long viewed the pardon as an Early Modern Period relic of arbitrariness that had no business in a modern institution such as the jury court.[42] However, use was made of the right of jurors to ask the ruler for a pardon, at least in property crimes, as the exception rather than the rule. More relevant was another form of mercy; every year a certain number of the inmates in Electoral Hessian penal institutions and houses of corrections were pardoned on the occasion of the "All-Highest Birthday Celebration of the Regent."[43] The institutions were invited to submit petitions for pardon, which the high courts were then supposed to address "in reports," whereupon some of the petitions were granted by the ministry of justice.[44]

As little as the inconsistency in verdicts met the goals envisioned by the reformers and as little as the inconsistency contributed to system function – it neither created legitimacy nor promoted class-specific interests – it was characteristic of the new methods of searching for truth. Still, inconsistency was an irritant to the system of truth production and called attention to dissonances; it shows how incompletely court practice after the mid-century resulted in the simple drama intended to enhance the legitimacy of the new justice system. Inconsistent sentences were, in fact, dysfunctional as a means of legitimizing the new procedure.

10.3 THE COURT AND THE PROVINCIAL PRESS – THE DRAMAS OF EVERYDAY LIFE

A last aspect of dissonance to be presented here goes beyond the failure to fulfill the hopes for reform and to increase the reform's legitimacy; it is closely connected to the introduction of the principle of public inclusion by the 1848 criminal procedure reforms. What is meant here is the public outside the courtroom, that is, the representation of court events in the press, which only became possible at the point where journalists, along with many others, were able to follow those events. From them, readers learned a great deal about how the new state of law worked. Apart from the doubtless more important everyday talk of the people who already had to do with the court, reading the court reports was the means that first established the justice system's presence and brought it into the everyday life of the small towns and villages – if only through reading newspaper reports. In such reports the state of law, with its new institutions, took on clear outlines. There the presiding judges, who made "pithy, humane speeches ... with heart-warming words,"[45] took on human shape. There it could be learned that jurors were people discharging special duties, distinguishing themselves by "willingness to sacrifice" for "the state and all of humanity," and "performing good offices."[46] There the state procurator came into being, often remarkably delivering "well thought-out speeches," marked by "highly astute combinations."[47] There people learned how the new institutions worked: that there were rules for the search for truth and rituals for speaking, that several levels existed in the court hierarchy, and that appeals could be submitted.

It was precisely this central element of the court's openness to the public that gave rise to considerable irritation and dynamics within the court itself. The way trials were represented in the press followed a logic that did not necessarily contribute to enhanced legitimacy of the new legal institutions, promote greater equality in legal proceedings, or lead to establishment of class justice – that, at least, can be proven for the province of Electoral Hesse. There the most important medium for communicating about court proceedings, the newspaper, projected an image of court events brimming with dissonance. At least at first glance, the image contradicted all the reform efforts and hardly contributed to strengthening the legitimacy of the state of law. Instead, court reporting in the province calls to mind perspectives that were mainly significant outside jurisprudence. Stories reported there concerned disputes about honor and recognition, and questions focusing on relationship problems and individuals positioning themselves in everyday life. But the result was that the court was transformed in provincial newspapers into a place – as will also be asserted – that had very little to do with the space created by the rituals of the code of criminal procedure. In the provincial press the courtroom did not appear to be a place for ceremonious, and as it were, removed truth-finding at the highest level of legal refinement, supported by the solemnly staged belief that a new concept of equality and justice was being advanced. Instead, it was portrayed as a place where everyday problems could be negotiated.

Although there are no detailed studies of the provincial press in general and in Electoral Hesse in particular,[48] it can be assumed, as has been shown for the national sector,[49] that the newspaper market and thus the readers in Marburg and the vicinity were revolutionized. At the same time, it should be noted that the changes in the province apparently took effect later; an increase in the number of newspapers, and thus also in the number of court reports, cannot be observed until the last third of the century.[50] Certain is that the illiteracy rate in Electoral Hesse in the 1870s had fallen to 10 percent and general mandatory school attendance had for all intents and purposes been established.[51] Thus, a basic precondition for reading the paper had been met. The numerous new papers – for example, the *Marburger Tageblatt*, not published, however, until 1874, or the *Hessische Morgenzeitung* – attest to a second precondition; a great deal of reading material was available, and that was not only the case in metropolitan Berlin but also in the province. Of course, the papers were not equally affordable. The *Marburger Tageblatt*, for example, cost all of twenty silver pennies. But it was enough if a few people read the reports and passed on what was read.[52] News relating to important local events was especially suited to being disseminated in this manner. The question of who had been charged with what crimes was undoubtedly among the more interesting questions in rural or small-town society.[53] What did these reports look like? How were the court, judges, jurors, defendants, defense attorneys, and witnesses portrayed in the Electoral Hessian newspapers?

Courts and criminals were addressed in the *Marburger Tageblatt* – aside from the new genre of "miscellaneous news items," which will be discussed later – either under the heading "Provincial and Local" or in the new genre of court reports. In the "Provincial and Local" column, brief reference was generally made only to a court session:[54] "The first session of this year's *Schwurgericht* term is set for the April 27 and the days following. Initially, only three crimes, that is, [cases of] grievous bodily harm, often repeated theft, and attempted infanticide, will be tried"[55] – according to the report on April 6, 1874. In the course of the 1870s, the reports became more detailed, the exact time was given, and it was noted when a *Schwurgericht* session started and which case would be tried. The name of the defendant, his place of origin, and the charges were mentioned. The report on April 13, 1977, stated, "The upcoming *Schwurgericht* here starts on April 16, and the following cases will be tried: 1) Monday, April 16, at 9:00 a.m., against Heinrich Priester from Wahlhausen, for attempted arson; 2) Tuesday, April 17, at 9:00 a.m., against Christoph Manz from Wetter, for crimes against morality; 3) Wednesday, April 18, at 9:00 a.m., against Bernhard Prinz from Kirchhain, for crimes against morality ...."[56] A few issues later, reports about these defendants once again appeared in the "Provincial and Local" column: "... Heinrich Priester from Wahlshausen,[57] after having been found guilty by the jurors, was sentenced by today's *Schwurgericht* to nine months in prison for attempted arson in accordance with Articles 306, 43 and 44 of the Criminal Code; three months of the sentence are to be considered time served."[58]

On one hand, these reports were informative about personal data and charges, but on the other, with regard to the exact circumstances of the crime, the criminal, or even the course of the court session, they remained silent.[59] The motives of the defendant remained unclear, as did the crime course. What kind of immorality was involved, who the victim was, and how and why the fire was set were not disclosed. The exact course of the proceedings, the judges, the jurors, and the defense attorneys were not reported. Only the crime, sometimes with information about the criminal code paragraphs, was occasionally given. For that reason, the reports do not appear initially to be particularly informative, let alone entertaining.

However, considering the place where these news items were printed and read, the brief reports could actually be surprisingly informative.

After all, in the context of small-town and rural society little more than the mention of a name was needed to call to mind all sorts of connections with regard to familial, economic, and social relationships. Thus, if the full names of the defendant and the female witness were given in the press, their status as public figures was confirmed by that mention – as had long since been rumored.[60] That means that the defendants cited here, who at first glance seemed just as faceless as in the legal case descriptions in which offenders appeared to act outside all social and familial frames of reference, were transformed in the context of the provincial newspaper into people of flesh and blood with pasts and social and economic networks that were very familiar territory.

Of course, to really get into the particular story in detail, further information was needed beyond the reports in the "Provincial and Local" column. Precisely that was provided by the second genre that reported about court events in provincial newspapers: the court report. The court report, which became increasingly popular in provincial newspapers from the 1870s on,[61] resembled a display window – however, one not so much presenting the depths of the soul as was the case in crime novels, or the ruinous effect of bad heredity in a criminological context. Nor was there a great deal to be learned about the legal rules for establishing justice, much less the portrayal of a sacred, protected place for the high art of objective truth production. In court reports, the focus was elsewhere: themes from everyday life and its morals, questions dealing with honor, recognition, and self-positioning, and discussions of problems such as what right and wrong might look like in the workaday world of a less-than-simple life in the country. Even the figures in the spotlight pointed to the everyday and were anything but unusual. The extensive reports there concerned students who were accused of a substantial theft[62] and discussed why an ill-reputed carpenter had to answer for premeditated arson.[63] A case of attempted murder by a day laborer merited[64] an extensive court report just as much as a father with six children who stood before the court for a morality crime.[65] In their selections, the reports of the local press differed from those of the supra-regional papers.[66] The latter focused on cases which could cause a sensation because the crimes were of an unusual nature or because the offenders or witnesses were prominent or especially interesting, or were juicy configurations worth watching. Especially popular were women who committed murder with poison,[67] crimes of passion,[68] and so-called *beaux crimes* (beautiful crimes), understood to be cases involving people from moneyed circles. "*Drames de folie*" (crimes involving madness) likewise attracted notice in the supra-regional press.[69] Thus, the greatest attention was given in national papers to violent crimes, crimes by prominent people, and crimes that plumbed the spiritual depths, although the latter appeared quite rarely. Property crimes, which actually constituted the greatest percentage of crimes, received scarcely any attention in the crime reporting of the supra-regional press, in contrast to the situation in the regional press.

The figures in provincial court reporting came from everyday life, and in their portrayal they remained strikingly ordinary. In contrast to the figures in the supra-regional press, they were not transformed into different, more significant, more exotic figures; just as little effort was devoted to making their environment, milieu, and crimes more exciting by subtly spinning the narrative. In the big newspapers and journals, on the other hand, the individual crime stories were embellished with numerous suspense elements and written in a sensational tone. The more exotic and adventurous the hero of such crime histories and the contexts in which he moved were, and the more often he lived in foreign settings, the more fascinating. Rarely was there any attempt to spare the cliché or leave out an empty phrase. Consequently, the supra-regional press was teeming with "dissolute harlots who had early-on degenerated into debauchery, deceit, and deception," modern "Robin Hoods,"[70] or big, handsome, noble men with blond beards and blue eyes, who were "clever, bold, proud, commanding, and often elegantly dressed" while engaged in "daring escapades." The criminals of the supra-regional press were provided with the stereotypical attributes known from statistics and criminological discourse.[71]

Provincial reporting abstained from such excursions into the exotic and did not boost the stories to the level of the sensational with foreign touches and hyperbolic narration techniques. Yet the provincial reports were no less interesting, neither boring nor focused just on simply listing bits of information. For example, the student "Friedrich A.,"[72] charged with theft, was described in detail using the data that had been collected in the preliminary investigation and read aloud in the main trial. In addition to his name, age, occupation, and the occupation of his father, the report revealed that the accused "had played the role of a son of well-to-do and generous parents."[73] Furthermore, it was mentioned that he became quite pale when he heard about the theft. Then he was described as having "behaved with obviously affected ingenuousness" and voiced denial "with absolute certainty."[74]

Thus, in the province, too, the court reports were narratives which with more or less hackneyed literary stylistic devices were able to dramatize a story so effectively that readers followed eagerly. The vividness of the actions and offenders placed greater emphasis on re-enactment by the readers and thus translation into the readers' own realm of experience than on transporting the public off into foreign worlds or prominent circles. Furthermore, the point was to portray emotional states and situations that were not exactly foreign to readers, and to tell stories in which subjects like honor, old scores that had to be settled, affronts, illnesses, envy, and jealousy were raised. It was precisely the familiarity and everyday character that lent stories such as those found in the *Marburger Tageblatt* their special character; people knew what it meant to set a stable on fire, or where the pharmacy student who was robbed, Welp, was living when they read that he was staying at the restaurant owner Quentin's. Often the defendant or his victims were personal acquaintances, or prior to the trial – on the basis of gossip or a preceding report – people had long since formed an image of the story. In any event, the complete names of the witnesses and likewise the victims were given, which is remarkable for rape but for other crimes as well.[75]

After the end of the 1870s, the readers of the provincial press learned an increasing amount about court personnel and the logic of their actions. It was noted which judges had jurisdiction, what the names of the jurors were, who the defense attorney was, and how the actions in court of those persons, as well as of the defendant and the witnesses were to be assessed.[76] In contrast to the national press, the individuals were usually known in the local context. People knew who the juror Hirt was and what to make of the defense attorney Loebell. People knew the ropes and could follow the sessions either in person or through the press, frequently over the course of many days, like a soap opera. Not least of all because of this familiarity with the individuals and the focus on everyday crimes close to individuals' own world, the court did not seem primarily to be the place where experts shined light on tangled, alien, yet fascinating worlds in which they sought to meticulously track down the truth by following precisely defined rules. Instead, it appeared above all to be the place where existential questions of everyday life were dealt with by people frequently known at least by reputation. Little was said in these reports about the rituals of objectivity and exclusivity; neither the authority of the space nor the dress code was the main focus. In short, the staging that was supposed to lend legitimacy to the legal proceeding was scarcely of interest in the provincial press.

Why – the question arises here at the latest – did people bother to read stories that derived their material from the everyday world, the known, the ordinary? Researchers provide no answer to this question, as they have concentrated almost exclusively on the national press. According to Dominique Kalifa in his study of the Parisian media landscape, the answer to the question about interest in the media representation of criminals will necessarily turn out differently for the national press, because the criminals there were transformed into exotic creatures.[77] These exotics, indeed, to some extent even the heroes, were in any case alien and threatening figures, "radical transgressors of morals and order," and the purpose of their representation was for "the criminal [to] speak to the reader about the duplicity of existence and the world."[78] At the same time, this form of representing the criminal resulted in a kind of "counter-memoir" to which the semiliterate population also contributed.[79] Kalifa's theory builds on an interpretation by Michel Foucault, who wrote in another context, that is, regarding a memoir written by a murderer himself, that this testimonial, despite all the moralizing, instruction, and conformity, had an undertone: "And for all that, these reports glorify murder in one way or another by their very existence; their general popularity reveals the desire to know and to retell how human beings were able to rise up against authority, overcome the law, and expose themselves to death through death."[80]

But Electoral Hesse was not Paris. In the Electoral Hessian provincial newspapers, the carpenters, day laborers, and pharmacy students were not suited for heroic roles in a "counter-memoir" story. Why did the provincial court reports nevertheless capture the interest of such a large readership? The reasons were the exact opposite of those given by Dominique Kalifa for Paris; people sought and found in the reports the trusted, the familiar, the known, and used the stories in exactly the same way as gossip. Indeed, the stories were printed gossip. They afforded an opportunity to mull over questions that affected everyone: questions of honor, illness, jealousy, love, hate, adversity, and envy. In reading and speaking about the stories, people attempted to find their own positions and those of others, and to think things over – here was a background for reflection and strengthening identity. People could talk about why the carpenter Amrhein had set the fire, a student had hidden his money so badly, and a maid-servant blushed in court. Subjects for discussion were also whether the attorney Loebell had argued insightfully, why the juror Hirt had remained silent, whether the sentence had been too severe, and whether the witness had been too chatty.

But this reflecting, gossiping, and repositioning was more than only a form of thinking over one's own position on one hand and the social order on the other. It was likewise more than sharing in the power of speech, which could also exercise social control – as Regina Schulte has emphatically pointed out.[81] In the case of court reporting, the "right to know and judge"[82] – as Arlette Farge called it – associated with gossip meant that people claimed the right to pass judgment on the kind of truth production. By reading the reports, which implied not just passive receiving but also active interpreting, people became familiar with various facets of legal truth-finding, while at the same time having the opportunity to comment on the matter.[83]

How did the court sessions fare in commentaries? What remarks were made about the manner in which justice was established? Did it meet with approval? Was it better than before the law reforms? Was the implementation of the principles of equality praised, or was the lack of meaning criticized? Were there comments on the special "Germanness," or was the new critical role of the public emphasized? Was the legitimacy of the proceeding discussed? Were thoughts expressed about whether the trial rules and the judgment criteria were observed? In reports on events in court, no commentary, none at all, neither positive nor negative, can be found in the Electoral Hessian papers. The commentaries that can be located are on another level. They concern the life stories recounted, the defendant's problems, the hardships of the victims, and the perspectives of the witnesses.[84]

In the spotlight were the carpenter, the student, or the day laborer, and questions of honor, perhaps hardship, social positioning, jealousy, and other emotions.

In short, provincial court reports were not simply publicizing an institution that was after all being used on an increasingly massive scale. They were also showing that this institution was anything but a distant, foreign state contrivance, and that it was instead amazingly relevant to the everyday life of day laborers, maids, and peasants. In the process, the reports portrayed the court in a manner which had little to do with the legal understanding of finding truth because the focus was not legal or criminological logic, or stage-management of exclusive places for finding truth. Instead, courts appeared to be places for dealing with existential problems. At the same time, the court reports in the provincial papers seized the opportunity to assess the processes for negotiating law; through the simple description of events, people laid claim to the "right to know and to judge."[85] This "right to know and to judge" was not limited to judging the conformity of the proceeding to the prescribed legal formalities, the role foreseen for the public. Instead of limiting itself to this role and thus helping the public assume the prominent role assigned to it in the relevant debates, the press and consequently the public did something completely different. It transformed the court into a place where the central questions of everyday life were dealt with and claimed the right to judge these trials by criteria that had but little to do with legal criteria for right and wrong or true and untrue. Considerably more interesting than the legal criteria themselves or even the possibility to check whether they were observed was the opportunity to judge the stories recounted in court according to personal criteria for a good and proper life. Thus, the reports contributed to making the new courts known but not to endowing them with greater legitimacy – the result expected in the contemporary debate about the great importance of public openness.

10.4 FAITS DIVERS

Crimes and court proceedings were the subject of detailed commentaries not only in the court reporting genre but also in another kind of press text toward the end of the nineteenth century. What is meant here is the "*faits divers*," the so-called miscellaneous news items.

In Electoral Hesse, an entire smorgasbord of topics was treated in the "*faits divers*."[86] The subjects included the poor relief expenditures in Cologne and a church outrage that was committed by "ruffians"; then a robbery and murder in the vicinity of Aachen was reported, and finally, a cat that was fifty-two years old and lived in the North American state of Maine.[87] The offerings included a report jammed with statistics on the "subway in London," followed by the report that the newspaper *Gazetta*, which was published in America, would not appear between Christmas and New Year's because the editor wanted to use the time "to get appropriately plastered." Finally, a "new robbery technique of London thieves" was detailed.[88] The next subject was a well-dressed gentleman who entered a shop in Cologne and asked the employee to fill his hat with syrup because he wanted to play a joke. No sooner had the employee complied than he had the hat on his own head and the gentleman had left the shop with the cash drawer.[89]

On another day, subjects under this heading were a "funny story" and discovery of the "oldest direct evidence of the existence of the human race."[90] The new column "*Faits divers*" thus indicated a heterogeneous assortment of news types. Not limited by either geography or topic, the reports covered cats and thieves as well as storms and subways, and came from Marburg and Hanau as well as Cologne, New York, or even India. The reports resembled each other only in their structural form: They were seldom longer than five to fifteen lines.[91]

If crime in general was only one topic among many in these provincial "*faits divers*,"[92] barely 5 percent of all the news items printed under the heading "Miscellaneous" related to property crimes.[93] The few thieves who turned up in the Electoral Hessian "*faits divers*" were by no means typical representatives of their species. They were neither day laborers who had pilfered the hat, bread, or selectively a farm implement from another less prosperous farm laborer, nor a shop clerk who stole from his boss and was not especially careful or crafty in doing so. The person in question was not a thief with a disassembled body, as typical for lookout descriptions. Nor was he the thief figure that showed up in statistics, that is, a being who stole out of economic necessity, indicated moral distress, and only appeared as one of the masses. The thief of the *faits divers* had just as little resemblance to the literary construct of an individual figure who, forced into crime by many emotional and social situations, became the object of attention because of extraordinarily tragic entanglements or other remarkable circumstances. Instead, the male thief and the much rarer female thief of the *faits divers* were a particular type of phenomenon; he or she came from the big cities of the *Kaiserreich* or from European or even American metropolises.[94] With regard to their accomplishments and/or social origins, they were unusual and frequently prominent. Prominence for a thief means, for example, that the thief came from the house of the czars,[95] or that the delinquent worked for the local crown prince.[96] Finally, the methods of the delinquents were often unusual. Instead of compelling adolescents to hand over bread by their boisterous demeanor or simply taking home an apparently ownerless hat, London thieves in the relevant newspaper reports usually cut the fur trim off coats.[97] In addition to particularly crafty methods,[98] very unique stolen articles were often involved. For example, instead of beat-up pots, used shirts, or old bread, an entire bridge was stolen by so-called stone thieves.[99]

However, more often because of their singular geographic origins, prominence, or outlandish methods, the thieves of the *faits divers* stood out because of their hilarity. Many criminal descriptions in the "Miscellaneous news items" were "funny"[100] or "comical stories."[101] The criminals, or their stories, were constructed for the comic effect, which was produced by certain forms of incongruity – for example, by incongruity of place and action. This was the case when, for example, criminals were placed in contexts that disappointed the expectations associated with thieves – whether the expectations came from literary texts, criminological discourse, or a statistical viewpoint. That is the case in the portrayal of a female thief, a worker's wife with multiple prior convictions, who was visited at the police station by her husband and four children. The children threw their arms around their mother's neck and fell on their knees before the judge, but not, as might be expected, to declare remorse with many words and tears or to plead innocence and beg for mercy. Instead, the husband proved to be remarkably pragmatic, only wishing to be relieved of the unwanted burden of child care. He refused to take the children home with him. With the words, "If they have my wife, they can keep my children, too," he left the room of the investigating judge.[102] The female thief was neither a brutal or pitiable figure, as known from other texts, nor did she appear to have exhibited a proper understanding of the judiciary as an institution of a venerable state of law. Instead, the judiciary was used as a better child care facility.

Another thief gave back all the stolen articles after he learned that the victim wanted to ask a Catholic priest to "talk to" the thief.[103] "Superstition achieved better results in this case than thorough police searches," was the commentary, calling attention to the incongruity between the crime and the prosecution method. The case of a thief who claimed to have stolen to prevent thefts also belongs in this context. He developed a complex line of argumentation that suspended the logic of right and wrong: "Bad people" had tried to persuade him to commit thefts. "For that reason, I took their jackets and pants so that they would get a taste of how it feels when someone takes away other people's rightful property."[104]

Then there was the report about New York thieves who asked that people put pieces of paper with their addresses in their wallets so that fellow thieves would not always be forced to throw away the wallets – that would be a shame, especially if the wallet contained mementos to which the owner was justifiably attached.[105] This was a case of a thief who sympathized with his victims, but did not to give up his line of work – he, too, completely upended the conventional perspective.

In other *faits divers*, not the thief but the victim was the central focus and was exposed to ridicule. For example, in one story the man of the house had supposedly been robbed. He ran out onto the balcony, shouting "Thief! Thief! Help," was thought by the neighbors to be the burglar, and was immediately taken to the nearest police station by a patrol that fortuitously happened by.[106]

In reality, the *faits divers* thieves had nothing in common with the home-grown day laborers who stole old hats and bread obtained by begging, or with the pitiable social cases in literature, or even with the creatures in criminology created by complicated decontextualization procedures. In part, they resembled rogues who mocked the victims, but also the justice institutions and the concept of a higher level of justice in general. The male thieves, and the few female thieves, appeared to be more comical than threatening or even alienating figures. They brought up property and property crime for discussion in front of a comical backdrop. The legal and the real-world notions of right and wrong were made ridiculous. The "Miscellaneous news items" column itself contributed to the hilarity, because jokes and other stories about the unusual and the special were printed there next to reports about criminals.

In short, the *faits divers* aroused no compassion, no sympathetic empathy, no fright, no fascinating delimitation, but instead laughter. What kind of laughter? Was it derisive or relieving, the expression of amusement, laughter at the situation, or even subversive laughter? The system created in practice in the numerous legal debates, criminological discussions, massive statistics, and trials was not called into question. "Occasional release from its authority" was nevertheless provided – to quote Hans Robert Jauß, who applied this term to the function of ironic identification.[107] Furthermore, the criminals in the *faits divers* provided – according to Michelle Perrot – a "crime show."[108] The disorder in things and people brought about by incongruity was entertaining.

However, more was involved than laughter or even just a chuckle. Roland Barthes described the *faits divers* as a kind of text that is "disrupted in its causality,"[109] because the expected consequences did not occur: The syrup, as the fine gentleman had said, was actually supposed to help prepare for a practical joke on a friend. Instead, it landed on the head of the shop clerk and the gentleman disappeared with the cash drawer. A thief stole to show others how reprehensible stealing was and furthermore used the situation in court to present his motives to the jurors in elaborate detail and vividly portray his own thefts. A man took his children to the police station to have them put in jail with his arrested wife, not, as a truly caring father, to allow the children a visit with their mother.

Barthes wrote further, "in *faits divers*, any causality is suspected of being a matter of coincidence."[110] Such a suspension of causality was especially remarkable, given the legal deductive method that was presented in a nutshell in the case descriptions and in court, where it was also practiced; the statistical methods that by analogy created long causal chains; and the criminological techniques that used physical clues to establish causal relationships on completely different levels. The literary practice of finding explanations for criminal actions in social and psychological defects, so typical in portraying criminals, was also turned on its head in the *faits divers*. Likewise, all methods of evidence production from the preliminary investigation – whether the lookout description, the crime scene sketch, or the visual inspection report – appeared to be completely ridiculous causality fetishism in light of the *faits divers*. None of the causality chains so central for production of truth applied in the *faits divers*. No thief had bad genes or a damaged soul; no recognition procedure proved the ultimately single objective and most relevant truth that a stocking cap had such and such a value and belonged to so and so; no lookout description professed that this person was identical to that one.

Furthermore, the impossibility of such links was shown, and all the procedures for establishing causality were exposed to ridicule. The thief was not the *ex negativo* construct based on middle-class notions of order; his actions eluded all notions of order. In the *faits divers*, he acted in a world that was topsy-turvy, of course not in the sense of a programmatic counter-proposal à la Bachtin, but much more basically, in a world characterized by unpredictability, ambiguities, chance, and incongruities. Nothing threatening was inherent to this world, but instead that which is easy-going, even pleasurable.[111] This criminal figure thus clearly also differed from all the literary criminals, whether they were continuations of Schiller's robbers, or victims of social conditions or unequal justice dominated by the old nobility and worse, as were popular during the late nineteenth century in crime novels.

In Electoral Hessian *faits divers*, questions about proper trials, equality of law, or even uniformity of law did not play a role. No problems of morality, everyday decency, or sensible handling of everyday problems – as could be observed at times in the court reports of the provincial press – were discussed. Nor were assessment of criminological characteristics, statistical perspectives, and legal refinements of subsumption touched upon. Deductive procedures and decontextualization techniques will be sought in vain. All these procedures and techniques, which possessed so much authority and scientific awareness and were considered significant for truth production in the legal system during the second half of the century, were not in the foreground here; in fact, not a single report that even remotely takes up these and similar subjects can be found.

To the contrary, all the forms of subsumption or deduction, these approaches to explanation, were subverted; the *faits divers* were in fact about representing "all causality"[112] as suspect and purely coincidental. Indeed, the judicial system was thus robbed of all its legitimacy; its very essence was called into question, and crime itself seemed to be what was actually fascinating.

10.5 REFORMS IN THE COURTROOM: THE COURT AS A PARADOXICAL PLACE

Was the reformed court a place of equality, justice, uniformity, and public scrutiny, or merely a stage to gain greater legitimacy for the new legal system? In any case it was a place with irritated witnesses and disparate sentences, a place where the dramas of everyday life were recounted and where, thanks to the press, many people participated in judging these dramas. Some people could also laugh about them. Were the legal subsumption acrobatics as a whole exposed to ridicule as a consequence? Was the jury court unimportant because the majority of the crimes, especially property crimes, were handled by lower courts? Was the public trial an insignificant place for establishing justice after the 1848 reforms because the actual search for truth had long since taken place in the preliminary investigation and was only put on the stage publicly there? Did the introduction of the oral, and most notably, the public trial thus not represent any serious progress?

Certainly the significance of the preliminary investigation was vastly underestimated by contemporaries and research. Nor did the jury court at all play the role in establishing justice that contemporaries attributed to it. Without a doubt, it is also clear that the talk of "Germandom" and the function of the public and the juror as an all-controlling force must be qualified because it was the expression of a debate about self-understanding within the middle class. The debate repeatedly sought reassurance about the requirements for a society not based on estates, even if that meant transforming the society of the Early Modern Period into a horrific picture of arbitrariness, inequality, and torture.

Yet despite all these qualifications, what happened in the courtroom was decisive. The mid-century reforms transformed the courtroom – and the "performances in the courtroom," as Sally E. Merry says in her study on the Hawaiian legal system in the nineteenth century[113] – into more than a place where the decision of the preliminary investigation was endowed with greater legitimacy and where the suggestion of objectivity, separateness, and scrutiny was created. To a great degree, the reforms made the court into a downright paradoxical place, and that definitely had its effect.

The court was paradoxical after the middle of the century because, after it had formally for the most part [114] left the inequalities of the estates behind and was explicitly supposed to be a place of equality, it had become anything but a class- or even only gender-neutral place, even though great efforts were made to give just that impression. In fact, the court has been transformed into a location dominated exclusively by middle-class manliness. It was a genuinely middle-class place because all the significant actors playing ex officio roles there and the jurors in general came from the middle class; on the basis of their education, especially with regard to their language behavior, they had a middle-class habitus geared to distinction and also to belittling the "lower classes"[115] in a gesture of paternalism. Moreover, this habitus was gender-specific, having been shaped by the middle-class manliness construct, that is, the man of reason and moderation,[116] which manifested itself especially clearly in the self-image of the judge as the just father.

Just how exclusively middle class the court was, became clear in the case of property crimes; in them, both the defendant and the witnesses as a rule came from classes other than the middle class, and sometimes women turned up. The contrast in habitus, language, and carriage could not have been greater. Thus, two different worlds encountered each other in court; the differences in their appearance, linguistic skills, and claim to power and influence could not be overlooked by anybody. That there was an accompanying imbalance of power and thus inequality (of course not in the sense suggested by the contemporary concept of "class justice") requires no further explanation – on one hand. On the other, no effort was spared to make the court appear to be a place where precisely these class- and gender-specific differences and the associated unequal distribution of power were suspended. Moreover, the entire public staging of the jury court sought to portray the court as a neutral place for truth, as a place removed from class and gender, and as a place that was in no way connected to a world outside the court – even the preliminary investigation. Nevertheless, the entire trial was based on just that preliminary investigation, and the contemporary class society in miniature was probably seldom more evident than in court.

However, the contradiction between a place of genuinely middle-class manliness and the staging of equality generated demands for change, depending on whether and how acutely the contradiction was perceived –

and the consequences of this new form of trial are thus addressed. The contradiction itself had the potential to serve as the motor for dynamics and transformation, and did just that, because the accusation of class justice voiced by contemporaries definitely did not remain without effect.

Second, the court was a paradoxical place because on one hand the new methods conducive to finding truth, equality, and uniformity that were called for on all sides and were supposed to be scrutinized by the public were not realized, and yet, on the other hand, the effect produced gave some individuals better chances than before to assert their rights. The grandiosely publicized rules were not realized because the public and the jurors in fact exercised little scrutiny, the defense attorney could hardly guarantee the defendant equality of treatment, and last not least the sentences showed anything but uniformity. Still, for those who knew the rules for questioning and the trial techniques, the trials represented a real increase in the number of options, compared to the old estates legal system – ultimately, many possibilities for defense were now much facilitated.

However, for the people who had not mastered the rules as well, the court was a place they sought out to present their conflicts, even if they had difficulty finding a sympathetic ear for their own interpretations. Although the terms for dealing with these conflicts frequently had to be learned, sometimes they even got their due there – of course, in a form that may have differed from the jurists' notion of law. In any case, the defendants were sufficiently mistreated that the victims and thus as a rule the people who had been called upon by the court definitely obtained justice. They could be present at a well-staged ritual in the course of which the defendant forfeited his honor and became what the victim had already stated in his complaint: a thief, a rogue, a person with lesser social clout.

The other people who had taken part in the proceeding as witnesses or the public did not leave the courtroom without gain, either. They learned how justice was established according to the new rules and what new notions of equality supposedly underlay the search for truth. Sometimes the rules of this judicial system had to be learned with effort, for example, when a witness did not understand what a summons was; sometimes, with fear, when it necessarily became clear how little room there was for other interpretations; but perhaps also at times, with amusement. In these trials, the new justice system also took shape.

Third, the court was paradoxical because rules for establishing justice were presented there with all the meticulousness conceivable, rules based on a clearly defined legal doctrine for argumentation. What constituted simple and qualified theft was unambiguously defined. What was significant or not for judging a criminal, was no less plain. That contexts, morals, relationships, symbolic arrangements in everyday life, and questions of honor and identity had no place there could be found written more than clearly in the relevant legal texts. Yet the court appeared, at least in the provincial media, to be a place where the problems of everyday life were dealt with, on the basis – that is far more important – of completely different criteria. There questions were actually asked about relationships, contexts, morals, social places, and individual motives, questions that went beyond determination of material value and the height of the wall that had to be climbed to commit the burglary. Furthermore, the public claimed the right to take part in how the problems were judged, even if it was only in talking about the descriptions of the problems in the court reports. Mediated by the press and thus by the public, the *Volk* invoked so frequently in the debates of the mid-century really did pass judgments – if only in talking about the courts.

Probably the most important characteristic of the judicial system after the middle of the century resulted from this new right to speak, which had to do with the new function of the public. The public was supposed to be present in court – that was the basic idea – to monitor whether the legal rules were observed. As important as the function of scrutiny was for compliance with the rules of truth production, it should not be overestimated. That is because on one hand the preliminary investigation, which took place outside the public realm, was critically important for the process of negotiating law, and on the other, because it was very easy to overlook that the public could do things in the courtroom which had not been considered in this form during the legal reform debates or even written up in legal texts. Among the public functions that were not explicitly defined was the legitimation of the procedure as has been described here. Perhaps even more momentous is a further performative dimension of the public; it claimed the right to judge the court and its proceeding according to criteria that did not have to be in any way the same as those established legally. The public could judge a trial to be unjust even though all the rules of decontextualization had been followed down to the smallest detail. The public could regard questions of morals or honor to be more important than observance of the relevant deductive procedures.

As significant as the commentaries on negotiating law already were in the Early Modern Period – there in the form of rumor, but also in the written word, for example, on flyers composed about a criminal's life and death on the occasion of his execution – the public judgment of legal proceedings took on a new meaning from the middle of the nineteenth century on. Based on the important new function assigned to it, the public could actually voice demands regarding the structure of the process for establishing justice – even if only as indirectly as in the provincial newspapers. These demands could have as their goal simple compliance with the legal procedures, but could also bring social and moral questions into play and level the criticism that the latter were scarcely taken into account in the particular form of truth production.

Finally, the *faits divers* make clear why the public was perhaps the most important factor in the new legal system. The public did not allow itself to be limited to the clearly outlined task of monitoring compliance with the fundamental trial procedures, but instead expanded its options to such an extent that it called the basic legal logic into question by using humor. The thus understood public made possible dynamics that effected change in the legal system by making the rules of law themselves the subject – and in the *faits divers*, a mostly humorous subject at that.

The public trial really was more than – as was written in 1904 – "just theatrical costuming for the administration of justice."[117]

Notes

1 Jäger, 1855, 8, refers to the theater metaphors described previously, explaining that the jury court proceeding only "re-enacted" what had already come to light in the preliminary investigation. From his perspective, the artificial character results from this double enactment.

2 In the course of developing the *Reich*'s code of criminal procedure, a vigorous debate arose among jurists about whether the preliminary investigation, as an anachronistic vestige of the inquisitorial criminal proceeding, should be abolished. This debate continued far into the twentieth century and did not come to an end until a late date – not least of all because of the repeated failure of reforms of the code of criminal procedure. The points criticized included the written nature of the proceeding, and above all, the strong structuring effect of the preliminary investigation, which could too markedly anticipate the actual trial. On the course of the reform debate, its central arguments, and the proponents of those arguments, see the retrospective accounts of Helmut Haug, 1930; Otto Meiners, 1922; and Kajetan Schwaiger, 1928. It is amazing that the debate about the code of criminal procedure and the preliminary investigation appears to have been completely forgotten by scholarship since these accounts.

3 268 Marburg 91.

4 Ibid.

5 268 Marburg 91, Interrogation of Maria Scherrer, June 8, 1854.

6 It was noted in the files how and by whom the summons had been received, because if the witness in the case did not appear, he had to expect a penalty if the summons had been correctly delivered.

7 The code of criminal procedure was quoted verbatim – 1848 Code of Criminal Procedure, Article 82: "The penalty is to be increased to fifty thaler and six weeks in jail for repeated failure to obey." That a penalty of up to twenty thaler or fourteen days in jail was to be expected for failure to appear was noted on the forms. On the other hand, the persons summoned received, upon appearing, a so-called witness fee that varied between five (see 266 Hanau 195) and thirty silver pennies (see 268 Marburg 50, Witness fee list). The bailiff, who personally delivered these summonses to the summoned witnesses, noted directly on the summons if someone had not been found. For example, it was written there that the summoned plasterer Heinrich Keller of Dreihausen had "already been absent from Dreihausen for a long time and [had] until now not returned ... and therefore [could not be] summoned"; 268 Marburg 50, Keller summons. Or it was noted, "in his absence, made known to his wife," "in his absence, made known to his mother." Summoning witnesses was thus performed by the justice system precisely and with application of considerable administrative effort.

8 How much work was expended on summoning witnesses becomes clear from the amount of space summons provisions took up in the pertinent laws and textbooks.

9 Claudia Töngi, 2004, 53.

10 268 Marburg 91.

11 1848 Law on Criminal Procedure, Articles 77ff; 1863 Law on Criminal Procedure, Articles 38ff.

12 Jäger, 1855, 2, states further, "... which in his view serve as the necessary introduction to the matter itself, while the more intelligent person knows all too well that this entire introduction, which often goes back to the grandparents or great-grandparents, is not at all pertinent. However, these people are so caught up in and accustomed to such a circuitous way of thinking that it is, as is known, an extraordinarily awkward matter to call out to them 'come to the point, attorney' .... It has happened that they fall silent upon any demonstration of impatience by their interrogating judge, and to questions about the reason for their silence, they respond, 'the gentleman there told me to be quiet.'"

13 Schlink, 1851, 33.

14 Ludwig von Jagemann, 1850, 55.

15 Basil Bernstein, 1972.

16 What that can mean applied to the court situation was shown by Hermann Bausinger, 1976, with his study on *Sprachschranken vor Gericht* – in it he still assumes deficits in that he understands "language barriers in court" to mean class-specific codes, groups, and everyday languages which were used in court and limited the ability of speakers to express themselves in that specific place.

17 Michel Foucault and Arlette Farge examined the "*letters de cachets* [officially sealed letters]" from this perspective – they were letters used by the population of Paris in the eighteenth century to appeal to the justice system as a means of

getting disagreeable relatives and other vexations out of their hair, see Arlette Farge and Michel Foucault, 1982. Studies such as that of Ruth Harris, 1988, on the late nineteenth century also speak for such an interpretation. Harris investigates the self-dramatization of "*criminelles passionelles* [female perpetrators of crimes of passion]," who represented themselves to the Paris courts as literary heroines and thus confirmed the interpretation the court psychiatrists had of mental illness. That confirmation opened the women's way to an insanity defense because, as mentally ill persons, they had diminished or no criminal liability. However, many of the defendants were in this case from the middle class.

18 Arlette Farge and Michel Foucault, 1982.

19 Martin Dinges, 1992. In this way he made clear that certain notions of justice were again circulating within the population, for example, justice as caritas, as the authority that protects the weak, and that people tried to assert these "justice fantasies" in the court with very distinctive means, including language.

20 Regina Schulte, 1993.

21 Regina Schulte, 1993, 425.

22 Silke Göttsch still sees an unbridgeable "discrepancy between language styles" in court during the eighteenth century; the discrepancy left the defendant only with "retreat to his failure to understand his own behavior"; Silke Göttsch, 1991, 447.

23 There is one further important difference not discussed here, i.e., the gender difference, that structured the situation in court. On this subject, see Ulrike Gleixner, 1995a and 1995b; Rebekka Habermas and Tanja Hommen, 1999.

24 On this subject, see the analyses of Willibald Steinmetz, 2002, 493ff, who shows with the example of cross-examination that plaintiffs had considerable difficulties less because of the bias of the judges than because of the "predefined forensic communication forms" (510).

25 In contrast to the difference between the legally trained actors (also including the defense attorneys) and those without training, the similarities between the defendants and the witnesses were great, because both as a rule came from the same social group, indeed, even from the same village. Their differences in speech and gestures must have been minimal and communication between them consequently less difficult. They spoke one and the same language, and with it they could make themselves understood in court, even if they remained silent there or did not even appear. The intimidation of witnesses by the defendants revealed by Petra Overath, 2001, 230, could thus take place in court for the most part unnoticed.

26 Peter Landau, 1987, 288ff; see Peter Collin, 2001, 2006.

27 Schlink, 1851, 34.

28 Hermann Kersting, 1853, 664.

29 In this case – in 1854 – reference was to the *Constitutio Criminalis Carolina*, Article 126.

30 268 Marburg 62.

31 268 Marburg 14.

32 Wilhelm Koch, 1855, 85ff.

33 Basically, the penalties for property crimes tried by high courts, criminal courts, and *Schwurgerichte* ranged from six weeks to three or four years in prison, which was considered severe for penalties above a year, or in the workhouse, which was always considered a severe punishment; see Otto L. Heuser, 1853, 32ff.

34 266 Hanau 302.

35 266 Hanau 236. In this case, no Early Modern Period judgment logic that sanctioned foreigners and natives with differing degrees of severity can be demonstrated; for verdicts according to the circumstances of the Early Modern Period, see Karl Härter, 2003, 456ff.

36 268 Hanau 29, 1859. Here, too, it becomes apparent that the regulations governing which courts were to adjudicate crimes were not applied consistently. Although the jurisdiction of the courts had been regulated since 1851 such that *Schwurgerichte* only had jurisdiction if a crime was to be punished with at least a five-year term of imprisonment in a fortress, workhouse detention, or prison, or at least four years in irons, and – until 1863 (1863 Law on the Constitution of the Courts, Article 23) – always had jurisdiction if the defendant had already committed a property crime at least twice already, quite a few cases were tried in high courts, even though the defendant had already been apprehended three or four times; see Wilhelm Koch, 1855, 85ff.

37 That contradicts the theory of Dirk Blasius; see Dirk Blasius, 1974.

38 Wilhelm Koch, 1855, 1. This circumstance was not undetected by the Electoral Hessian Ministry of Justice. But the inconsistency practices with regard to court jurisdiction and sentencing were interpreted by the ministry as excessive leniency, which was the reason that more severe penalties were demanded. That is evident from the reports of the Ministry of Justice in which the general state procurator was urged in February 1852 to strictly implement the new court jurisdictions that had gone into effect in 1851. At the same time, precise minimum sentences were also set. See 268 Marburg 103, Files regarding administration of justice, No. 1327. The letter states further that in trials in which the penalty fell below this minimum sentence, the state procurators were to file appeals. In Prussia, on the other hand, there were influential voices in the Ministry of Justice which in contrast even regarded the sentences for property crime cases to be questionably high; they demanded a greater degree of moderation from jurors. Both debates indicate above all that the prosecution of property crimes drew much attention from the state and that theft was punished very disparately.

39 On punishment practices in the Early Modern Period, which in the meantime are interpreted as judging according to the circumstances, see Andrea Griesebner, 2000, 296. In this work, she takes up the debate on standards and practices and shows that the variation in sentences imposed was considerable, of course not because of differences in standards and practices, but because the normative codes were only a framework and not mandatory for sentencing. See Joachim Eibach, 2003, 388, on the variation in sentences for property crimes during the eighteenth century. See Karl Härter, 2003, 456, who refers to "circumstances" as a category. Circumstances in the positive sense of

exonerating the defendant were primarily social capital and home location, which was also evident in the petitions.

40 The dominant involvement of jurists receives too little attention in research. For example, Petra Overath, 2001, traced the increase in death sentences mainly to a voluntaristic act of the jurors that had its roots in their middle-class origins. She sketches a structural conflict between strictly judging jurors and jurists who were less inclined to the death penalty. The third judicial authority was the king, with his right to pardon, with which he pushed the rising number of death sentences downward again. To this was added the press, which, through its emotional reporting about executions, worked against the government attempt to streamline executions. See Richard J. Evans, 2001, on the complex of "streamlining" executions and pardons in the nineteenth century. Also completely omitted is the question of the attitude of the population toward the sentences and what influence, however indirect, the population had on the verdict. Regarding verdicts for capital crimes, we at least know that large segments even of the lower classes were not averse to stiff penalties, which could also mean the death penalty. See Petra Overath, 2001, 195ff; Richard J. Evans, 2001, 353ff.

41 268 Marburg 50.

42 On a new assessment also of Early Modern Period practice, see the exemplary study of Natalie Zemon Davis, 1988. Harriet Rudolph, 2001, also thoroughly examines pardon practices in the eighteenth century and can prove that what is involved is less an arbitrary act than a complicated communication process which was determined by many factors, but which very basically must be thought of as a means allowing defendants and their families to formulate their interests. At the same time, the act of pardon represented "an important moment of self-dramatizing hegemony in the Early Modern Period"; Harriet Rudolph, 2001, 324.

43 On this subject, see Hubert Kolling, 1994, 523–533.

44 1831 Constitutional Charter, Article 126: "The sovereign is authorized to impose or mitigate penalties, and to strike down trial results."

A prerequisite for a issuing a general pardon was that the offender had "behaved properly" in the penal institution, had been "diligent and very reasonable," or "displayed a great deal of remorse for the crimes committed" – as was said about a forty-five-year-old offender who had already spent seven years in the Marburg jail. Furthermore, if the chaplain was able to say something positive about his "religious conduct" and – very important – if the high court had no basic objections, there would be an act of mercy. Of course, in years such as 1850, in which the Marburg jurists believed that it was "in the public interest" for "the already too light penalties" to preclude such a pardon, mercy was not an option. See 250 Electoral Hessian Ministry of Justice 563 (1850–1859), Pardons, Letters of the Marburg High Court, July 27, 1850.

As a rule, offenders were recommended who had been sentenced for life or to a stiff sentence of at least six or seven years in prison and had already served two-thirds of that sentence. Property criminals and offenders could thus only hope for a pardon if they had used force, stolen especially large sums, or were serious repeat offenders. Consequently, most of the property criminals, the small thieves, did not receive pardons. See 250 Electoral Hessian Ministry of Justice 563 (1850–1859), Pardons.

45 *Marburger Tageblatt*, No. 87 (1880).

46 Ibid.

47 *Marburger Tageblatt*, No. 92 (1880).

48 The existing works on the so-called provincial press generally focus on a content analysis of political opinions. See Siegfried Löffler, 1964–1965. Basically, the objective here is not to make a case for comparability of the local and national press. French works show (see Anne-Claude Ambroise-Rendu, 1998) that there were fundamental differences in reporting but also in reading behavior and in reception. On the Hessian press, see Heinz-Otto Hitzeroth, 1935.

49 On this subject and on the role that criminal reporting in general played in newspapers: Philipp Müller, 2005; Benjamin C. Hett, 2004; Gregory Shaya, 2004; Eric A. Johnson, 1995, 55–95; Klaus Marxen, 1991; and Jörg Hennig, 1991. In these cases, only the big city or national press is examined.

50 For this reason, the following analysis of newspaper reports also focuses on the end of the actual period of examination.

51 See Sylvia Kesper-Biermann, 2001, 88, for alphabetization in Electoral Hesse.

52 Richard Evans, 1989, 182–186, and 205–223, and Frank Bösch, 2003, demonstrated such information being passed in the *Reich* within the context of "pub talk"; but in the big city of Hamburg, sensational trials were instead the topic of conversation.

53 In her analysis of provincial newspapers, Anne-Claude Ambroise-Rendu, 1998, 94, says that, compared to the national newspapers, the provincial newspapers reported less about serious crime and that as a result "the geography of discussing threat" remained "primarily urban." That cannot be said of Electoral Hesse.

54 The items in the column were almost exclusively news reports from Marburg that maintained an objective tone, whether the report was about a meeting of political groups, beautification, or an agricultural organization. Articles could also be read there about the *Reichstag* delegate from Marburg, about a "top female singer" and her performance (*Marburger Tageblatt*, No. 35, 1874), or the number of new enrollees. Between these reports appeared from time to time short notices about court sessions.

55 *Marburger Tageblatt*, No. 7, 1874.

56 *Marburger Tageblatt*, No. 86, 1877.

57 Note the different spelling, which contradicts the report's claim of objectivity and truth.

58 *Marburger Tageblatt*, No. 88, 1877. The other defendant had it better; the next edition said about him, "... the teacher Christoph Manz from Wetter today stood before the jury box for a sexual offense, but was found not guilty by the jurors, acquitted of the charges, and immediately released from detention"; *Marburger Tageblatt*, No. 88, 1877.

59 Announcements or reports about *Schwurgericht* sessions in Marburg can be found in almost every edition of the newspaper. As only *Schwurgericht*

sessions were announced in this column, scarcely any thefts appeared but primarily crimes punishable by many years of imprisonment, such as homicide, sexual offenses, embezzlement of large sums of money, arson, and perjury.

60 Anne-Claude Ambroise-Rendu, 1998, 103, also views these reports in the provincial newspaper against the background that "the newspaper wants above all to be close to its readers." That certainly explains one aspect of this report whose content had probably long since been spread further by rumor.

61 Jörg Hennig, 449, wrote already in 1991: "The history of court reporting has not yet been written"; this statement holds true even today for German-speaking countries. There are only references around the edges in Jörg Hennig, 1991; Eric A. Johnson, 1995, 60f; Konstantin Imm, 1991.

62 *Marburger Tageblatt*, No. 36, 1874.

63 *Marburger Tageblatt*, No. 87, 1880.

64 *Marburger Tageblatt*, No. 89, 1880.

65 Ibid.

66 On the national level, this genre took shape with the advent of the 1848 court reforms. Indeed, the *Schwurgerichtszeitung* that appeared from the 1850s on was a newspaper consisting almost exclusively of court reports. Other papers, such as the *Vossische Zeitung* or the *Frankfurter Zeitung*, took longer and did not begin printing thorough, regular court reports until the 1870s. On the representation of crime in the German language press, see the works of Philipp Müller, 2002 and 2005; he goes into the performative dimension of the press in detail and furthermore is able to impressively trace the participation of the Berlin population in criminal activities. I owe the stimulus for this chapter to a whole series of conversations with Phillip Müller (London); I would like to thank him for that. See also the study of Maria Heidegger, 2002, on Tirol.

67 See the study of a murderess adept in poisoning by Joachim Linder and Jörg Schönert, 1983a and 1983b, which is especially instructive because extensive text material is published there. See the single thorough study on the subject by Inge Weiler, 1998, who uses the example of murder by poisoning to trace the literary, legal, and psychiatric portrayals of crime.

68 See the important work of Joelle Guillais, 1990, for France, and the work of Ruth Harris, 1991. Both very convincingly prove the overlap of various discourses. In this context, the study by Judith R. Walkowitz, 1992, should be mentioned; it is in the meantime a classic.

69 See the work of Dominique Kalifa, 1995; it is the first detailed study on the representation of crime in the Paris press.

70 This is another example of how hazy the line between fiction and fact was in the representation of the criminal. On this subject, see also the references of Dominique Kalifa, 1995, 224, to the "Apaches," who so captured the intense interest of the French public and signed the names of literary criminals to mark their crimes.

71 There was no lack of theatrics – exclamations supposedly uttered during confrontations in court, such as "My God, that is just how he looked!" are found in great numbers in these articles. All of the quotations have been taken from the article *Der Raubmordprozess gegen den Handelsmann Schall* in the *Illustrierte Zeitung* 18 (1851), 230f.

72 *Marburger Tageblatt*, No. 36, 1874.

73 *Marburger Tageblatt*, No. 36, 1874; see the records in 269 Marburg 171.

74 *Marburger Tageblatt*, No. 36, 1874; on this subject, see also the descriptions in the court records themselves. Such statements are not to be found in the records. The case in question involved the theft charge against Friedrich Arnold, 269 Marburg 171.

In the case of the report about the ill-reputed carpenter Amrhein as well, the information provided sheds more light on the accused and his character, and attempts graphically to help readers understand him. The report states that he "enjoyed a close acquaintance with prison." See *Marburger Tageblatt*, No. 87, 1880. The affable, even casual tone set also puts the carpenter in a bad light. In addition to implicit opinions of the court reporter – for example, when he writes with ostensible neutrality, "I am withholding further comments on the subject" (*Marburger Tageblatt*, No. 91, 1880) – there are also very clear opinions undoubtedly taken from the trial. In this way, the character of Amrheim, who stood accused of arson, was once again taken apart with all the means of the criminological art, because it was "of particular importance to clearly explain the character and the moral values of the accused, as well as his social position within the community, because simple peasant circumstances are involved" (*Marburger Tageblatt*, No. 87, 1880). The report explained that the accused had "completely renounced . . . religious and moral principles" and that he was "rebellious against the moral order" (*Marburger Tageblatt*, No. 87, 1880). No less clear were the words describing the state procurator, who "elucidated the guilt of the accused . . . in a uniquely apt, simple, and completely convincing manner." It was then like confirmation when the report ended with the alleged remark of the carpenter, who had been sentenced to six years in jail: "Yeah, he responded, then they might as well make it life, or just take off my head." To that, the journalist remarked in his commentary, "Certainly an illustration indicative of the crime committed."

75 Thus, the rape victim of the fifty-three-year-old paterfamilias Kappauf, a certain Marie Hohmeier from Treysa, was named by name; see *Marburger Tageblatt*, No. 89, 1880.

76 A precise listing of people can be seen in the *Marburger Tageblatt* after the end of the 1870s. Although the articles appeared as before in the "Provincial and Local" column, no longer just the name of the accused, the charges, and the court date were given, but within the framework of the longer court reports, all the court personnel, including the jurors, are now listed exactly for each case.

77 Dominique Kalifa, 1995, maintained in his study, which is of course based on analysis of the Paris big city press, that figures from the belletristic past were repeatedly conjured up not only in literary texts but also in newspaper reports (just think of the reference to Robin Hood). What is more, a traditional line of great criminals had been compiled and had become very familiar to readers. The evaluation of the Hamburg watch report by Evans and now by Frank Bösch, 2003, likewise emphasizes the significance of scandals.

78 "It is the people's memory of vice that is invoked, the great motifs of their culture that are celebrated"; Dominique Kalifa, 1995, 272.

79 Dominique Kalifa, 1995, 275.
80 Michel Foucault, 1975, 237. Dominique Kalifa, 1995, also emphasizes that such an interpretation should not lead in the wrong direction toward the social romanticism already very popular among contemporaries; instead care must be taken that the representation of criminal behavior communicated by journalists always has a moralizing content, and furthermore, that the classic attributes cited by criminology are seldom missing. As is known, those attributes transformed criminal figures into inhuman, unmotivated monsters.
81 Regina Schulte, 1992.
82 Arlette Farge, 1992, 290.
83 In evaluating the watch reports, Frank Bösch, 2003, does not directly connect the watch reports to the newspaper reports or analyze the newspaper, but he emphasizes that the newspaper reports were actively absorbed and that they were even "dealt with playfully"; Frank Bösch, 2003, 333.
84 Naturally, the content of the newspaper articles cannot be equated to the talk of the readers resulting from them. Yet the structure of the court reports allows inferences about what was said regarding the new forms of trial. Possibilities for historical research on media reception have not advanced past infancy and cannot be used in the framework of this study. However, on the basis of existing research it can be assumed that readers read newspaper articles critically – but the basis for the discussions generated by them was the contents and proposed interpretations of the articles. See the description of pub talk about crime in Frank Bösch, 2003. Furthermore, indications of media co-orientation can be found – that is, articles being slanted toward the opinions ascribed to the reader and his interests; on that topic, see Gerlinda Smaus, 1999.
85 Arlette Farge, 1992, 290.
86 In the *Marburger Tageblatt*, there were two categories, "Provincial and Local" and "Miscellaneous," where criminal activities appeared. In "Provincial and Local," mostly short news items about crime from the immediate vicinity were noted in dry language rather than reported. In "Miscellaneous," events, some of a criminal nature, that had taken place in the German *Reich* and abroad were described in more detail, sometimes three lines long; they claimed to have the character of "curiosities." The "Miscellaneous" category also appeared in the *Kreisblatt*; it was replaced in the 1870s by the category "Various." Then the *faits divers* turned into the column entitled "Diverse"; they were in the *Unterhaltungsblatt*, for example.
87 *Kreisblatt*, No. 4 (1869).
88 *Kreisblatt*, No. 11 (1875).
89 *Unterhaltungsblatt*, No 52 (1871).
90 *Kreisblatt*, No. 34 (1875).
91 The locations were always given at the beginning of the news report – in a different typeface – usually followed by the date and then the report. Thus, the reports listed in the *faits divers* column followed the same pattern as other reports from the field of politics, economics, and society. The structure suggested objectivity and a claim to truth. The objectivity and claim to truth were subverted to some extent by the style chosen and the content treated, which often had comic features. Sometimes even the procedure of claiming

objectivity and truth by citing place and date at the beginning was played with; in this spirit, a genre would be ironically quoted for the sole purpose of contradicting it. For example, the following news report appeared in the *Kreisblatt* for August 1878 in the "Miscellaneous" column: "Ravenna (an Italian robber story)" was the introductory lead-in here, ironically following the usual procedure of giving the place, and date and then so to speak changing it (see *Kreisblatt*, No. 100 [1878]). What came next was the story of the kidnapping of an Italian mayor by robbers who successfully extorted a ransom from the family. The story was not without a certain exotic flavor that was hinted at by the term "robber story," as that term indicated a literary genre which had already become part of children's literature in the second half of the nineteenth century and for that reason alone could not claim to be serious. The structure of an article which appeared in the *Marburger Tageblatt* in the "Miscellaneous" column was similar; it was introduced with "Marburg. (mistaken identity)," and then a grotesque story of a theft was related; see *Marburger Tageblatt*, No. 1 (1874).

92 The marginal existence of thieves in the *faits divers* can be attributed to the circumstance that only about 10 to 15 percent of the reports appearing in the "Miscellaneous" columns of the local papers referred to crime in the Marburg area. The calculations were only performed for samples from randomly selected time periods. In the *Unterhaltungsblatt*, crime was the subject in 11.4 percent of the reports that appeared in the "Diverse" column between May 1877 and August 1877; and in the *Marburger Tageblatt* from April to May 1877 and in April 1879, in 16.3 percent and 8.7 percent, respectively, of all the articles in the "Local" and "Miscellaneous" categories.
That means that about half of all criminals who appeared there were property offenders – which corresponded approximately to their actual significance, but compared to the pre-1850 situation in the "Police Reports" column represented a decrease.

93 Analysis of the *Marburger Tageblatt* from April to May 1875 showed that in the "Local" and "Miscellaneous" columns together, 8.7 percent of all notices related to thefts. Analysis of the reports that appeared in the "Diverse" column of the *Unterhaltungsblatt* showed that to be the case for 4.9 percent of the reports between May 1877 and August 1877 and for 5.2 percent of the reports in April 1879.

94 They often made their mischief in Berlin. This analysis is based on evaluation of samples from the *Kreisblatt*, the *Unterhaltungsblatt*, the *Wochenblatt*, and the *Marburger Tageblatt*. No second German big city shows up as frequently in the "Miscellaneous News Reports" of the 1860s and 1870s. Among the European capitals, Paris, together with London, is most often represented.

95 *Kreisblatt*, No. 1 (1874).

96 *Marburger Tageblatt*, No. 17 (1874).

97 *Kreisblatt*, No. 11 (1875).

98 *Unterhaltungsblatt*, No. 88 (1973), describes such a case. See *Unterhaltungsblatt*, No. 115 (1873); the report there relates to a monkey that steals. See *Unterhaltungsblatt*, No. 123 (1873); the report there tells about a boy who became a thief to finance his planned robinsonade.

99 *Marburger Tageblatt*, No. 78 (1877).
100 *Kreisblatt*, No. 34 (1875).
101 *Kreisblatt*, No. 95 (1878).
102 *Unterhaltungsblatt*, No. 77 (1871).
103 *Unterhaltungsblatt*, No. 33 (1872).
104 *Unterhaltungsblatt*, No. 57 (1873).
105 *Unterhaltungsblatt*, No. 112 (1873).
106 *Kreisblatt*, No. 95 (1878).
107 Hans R. Jauß, 1982, 284.
108 Michelle Perrot, 2001b, 279. See also Marine M'Sili, 1998. In his article in the French *Gazette des Tribuneaux*, Frédéric Chauvaud, 1998, makes the statement regarding the representation of petty crime – the focus of analysis in his study – that it was kept in the tone of a "farce"; its representation evoked laughter and prompted moralizing in equal measure. In the provincial newspapers of Electoral Hesse, this form of representation is not limited to petty crime – in the legal sense; there major robbery is also portrayed in the same manner. Of course, capital crimes remain exceptions to such representation.
109 Roland Barthes, 1964, 191.
110 Roland Barthes, 1964, 194.
111 On the basis of this process, Roland Barthes, 1964, 197, moved the *faits divers* into the proximity of literature: "... [Its] status is probably that of literature, a formal order in which meaning is at once posited and frustrated; and it is true that the *fait divers* is literature, even if this literature is reputed to be bad." In the context of his story *Die beiden Freundinnen und ihr Giftmord*, which was published in 1924 and was based on a real case, Alfred Döblin spoke of similar breaks in causal chains: "Psychological connection or even causality, how to look at it? You fiddle with the causality principle. At first you know, then you apply psychology. Knowledge of disorder is better there than knowledge of order"; quoted as in Joachim Linder and Jörg Schönert, 1983a, 357; see also Joachim Linder and Jörg Schönert, 1983b.
112 Roland Barthes, 1964, 194.
113 Sally E. Merry, 2000, 261.
114 However, in contrast to patrimonial and other estates jurisdictions, the special courts for nobles and also for universities in Electoral Hesse were not eliminated until the 1870s.
115 Ludwig von Jagemann, 1850, 55.
116 On the middle-class manliness construct, see Rebekka Habermas, 2000.
117 Alois Zucker, 1904, 26. It continues, "... which is in reality only based on the results of the preliminary investigation."

Conclusion

The Making of the Modern Legal System – Thieves and Property

> "A philosopher produces ideas; a poet, poems; a clergyman, sermons; a professor, compendia, and so on. A criminal produces crimes .... The criminal produces not only crimes, but also criminal law and thus also the professor who gives lectures on criminal law.... The criminal likewise produces the entire police and criminal justice system, thugs, judges, executioners, jurors, and so on ...."
>
> Karl Marx[1]

That theft, property, and law are connected is obvious – and yet, the connections are complicated, as is apparent in the descriptions just presented under the heading "*faits divers.*" I have sought to show some facets of the interrelationship of property, theft, and law. In the following pages, I will attempt to link these facets to each other, starting from Michel Foucault's deliberations, which were in part formulated almost simultaneously by Dirk Blasius. The purpose is to take another look at the question posed at the beginning of this study and still not yet conclusively answered: What are the characteristics of this new legal system, and what methods were used to "establish" justice anew with every theft trial in the nineteenth century? The objective is not, as in the previous chapters, to bring together further puzzle pieces in order to answer questions about what the individual steps of the process for establishing justice were and how they were related to contemporary and current interpretations. Instead, an attempt will be made to fit the individual pieces together more closely to form a complete picture, a picture that accents many factors differently from previous research but still, like that research, emphasizes the importance of openness to the public in the new legal system. Indeed, for the manner in which justice was established in the nineteenth century, the public played a central role. However, the public role did not function as the legal reformers had intended and as traditional legal historians have long believed.

THE DYNAMICS OF THE THEFT TRIALS

The German criminal historian Dirk Blasius was there from the start and dealt intensively, and not just tangentially as the French philosopher Michel Foucault did, with the question of the connection between property and theft. Still, both Foucault and Blasius came to strikingly similar interpretations of the connection between property and theft at approximately the same time, 1975.[2] Both started from the premise that a change in the property system in the late eighteenth century had led to existential poverty in the lower classes, which had in turn resulted in the growth of property crime. Increasing property crime then led to fixation on the new property concept within the middle class. This fixation – there is consensus on this point – led in turn to imposition of more severe sanctions. The "industrial class" – as Foucault alone maintains – learned about these sanctions by watching the practices of the "*Volk*."[3] Foucault and Blasius no longer agreed in their assessment of these sanctions. Blasius emphasized that the middle class thus betrayed its own basic notions of criminal law – criminal law as the "lever for middle class emancipation."[4] As a result, he continued, the limits of middle-class emancipation concept became clear. Foucault, as is well known, did not relate middle-class society to an emancipation concept; instead, he viewed it as a disciplinary society, which made the intensification of criminal prosecution entirely logical.

That these three premises regarding the connection between property and theft as postulated by both Foucault and Blasius (change in the property system produces adversity, adversity produces thefts, and thefts call forth a sanctioning reaction from the state) are problematic, is ultimately demonstrated by the example of Anton Zimmermann and his neighbors. In Electoral Hesse, in any case, neither he nor other thieves reacted according to this behavioral stimulus-response formula. There – according to the theory developed in the first chapter – the interaction of other forces could be observed. In the second half of the nineteenth century, agrarian reforms and legal and economic changes placed the lower classes in a difficult position that drove many to emigration or commuting to distant jobs. Those who remained lived in a complex poverty economy, although generally without suffering from hunger.

Furthermore, their situation was precarious because the village system had changed so much that people who lived "on the margins of subsistence" had to repeatedly redefine their social position. They did precisely that when, in conflicts usually with other young men in comparable situations, they at times believed that they also had to fight for their honor, or when they perhaps thought that, in a social system that had become fragile, they had to assert – or could only assert – their positions by accusing someone of theft. That consequently also means that the cause of the rising number of theft trials should not be sought primarily in a state of economic hardship. Instead, social uncertainty was equally crucial, or even causative, for people's attempt to define their exact position in the village, even in terms of a theft accusation that ultimately had to be tried in court. Of course, this circumstance does not negate the fact that the poverty of the parties involved may have been one reason for one person appropriating an object that another person could complain belonged to him. However, it is of central importance that such an action could only become a criminal offense as the result of lodging a public complaint regarding the original claim of ownership – and what is more, before state institutions.

Of course, the fact that the complaint about a theft was associated with these struggles for social recognition was of no interest in court. In the court the conflicts were considered theft, not discussions about social position. The theft interpretation surfaced officially in situations in which on one hand debates about property were the predominant theme and on the other decontextualization procedures came into play, lending support to such an interpretation. In other words, in such contexts it was only logical for jurists and gendarmes not to interpret the account of a day laborer about the theft of a used hat as part of a broad conflict but to view it as a report about a property crime. Theft thus came about not only, and not even primarily, because of need; instead, theft was the result of dynamics in which thieves, alleged and real victims, gendarmes, and jurists participated.

Thus, although the causality relationships between the property system and property crime constructed by Foucault and Blasius are less than convincing for a variety of reasons, their ideas are a step forward because they focus attention on the dynamics arising from theft. I have attempted to sketch two aspects of these dynamics: The first was related to the property concept, the second, to the legal system.

I do not maintain as did Foucault that a disciplinary state arose from theft, but it can be said that a new concept of property took shape in the theft trial. Numerous question and record forms from the preliminary investigation and the public trial with its rules of what could and could not be said were contributing factors. That fact is clearly evident in both phases of the court proceeding. Methods of questioning and recording were structured such that all options for relationships between people, and between things and people, with emotional, symbolic, or social implications and not associated with determining material value were negated. Whether in the so-called exhibit lists, in the recognition procedures, or in the questions of fact that were placed before the jurors, it was always a matter of creating and asserting an absolute property concept and thus of excluding any relationship structures not associated with that concept. That was all the easier to accomplish because at the same time a type of decontextualized, desubjectified, and quantified criminal was developed in criminology, jurisprudence, and statistics; such a criminal could not be thought at all capable of relationships, much less motives. Thus in chronically new negotiations about the question of what belonged to whom the modern conception of absolute property took shape.

In addition to a precise property concept a second type of dynamics evolved; the manner in which justice was established, or in Foucault's words truth was produced, began to change. This change resulted – as I attempted to trace in many individual steps – from the interaction among the codes of criminal procedure issued in the wake of the 1848 revolutions, from new criminological, statistical, and legal discourse, and from changed requirements for the production of evidence that gradually led to new kinds of evidence. These changes took place less frequently in the main trial than during the preliminary investigation. Neither contemporaries nor current scholarship have paid particular attention to the preliminary investigation or found it worthy of any detailed analysis because it was, and is, assumed that it only made preparations for the actual location of establishing justice – the public court. But in that early part of the legal process decisive events occurred: There the central techniques were developed for sorting out "true" from "untrue" in the modern state of law.

In this restructuring of the manner in which justice was established, one particular change played an important role. Since the abolition of the inquisitorial trial, the actual task of the preliminary investigation had no longer been to extract a confession but instead to gather evidence. The new meaning of evidence as the basis for judgment resulted in an entirely new arsenal of evidence types being produced in the framework of the preliminary investigation. Furthermore, the central focus of the preliminary investigation was just that production of evidence, which developed real dynamics of its own there – regardless of how important the crime was.

Gradually an ever-wider variety of forms and instruments for truth production evolved – whether as a result of visual inspection reports, crime scene sketches, or recognition procedures. As diverse as these types of evidence were, they closely resembled each other; they were all based on the same process of radically reducing complex facts down to what was considered most essential legally. Common to this process of reduction to the legally logical were the methods of decontextualization, desubjectification, and quantification, which as the result of various authentication strategies laid great claim to truth and objectivity.

The decontextualization procedures did not derive from the relevant criminal codes. To the contrary, the codes consistently said nothing about how evidence was to be collected and facts were to be generated. However, important instructions on exactly what procedures were to be followed and what techniques were to be used to evaluate the evidence were developed in a whole series of fields from jurisprudence to statistics and criminology. Ultimately, the new fields, which could claim almost scientific validity and thus greater authority for their theories and methods, also changed the notion of the criminal. Every series of statistics or criminological study was believed to furnish information on the criminal's characteristics. At the same time, every preliminary investigation that made use of such scientific procedures shaped the professional identity of those who employed those methods in the preliminary investigation: the gendarmes and the jurists. Just as the criminologists and statisticians who presented their knowledge with such authority that they were given the right to pass moral judgment on complex social situations, gendarmes and jurists also established a new professional identity that gained clearer contours with the writing of each visual inspection report. Gendarmes acquired a new police outlook, and jurists exercised their specific logic to reduce complexity.

THE LEGITIMACY OF THE PROCESS FOR ESTABLISHING JUSTICE

Neither contemporaries nor current researchers registered that the techniques for truth production took shape in the preliminary investigation, changing the professional identity of the gendarmes and jurists and simultaneously generating a new image of the criminal. That was because the public trial rather than the secret preliminary investigation was already the focus of interest among contemporaries and claimed to be the sole place where justice was established. Starting in 1848 at the latest, the main trial was regarded not only as more just but even as the exclusive location for establishing justice. It was this exclusivity and separateness that seemed to guarantee independence, as it were, and lent this location special legitimacy. Furthermore, the public trial above all legitimized the new process for establishing justice supposedly in effect since the mid-century. All the same, the notion of exclusivity proved to be mainly directed at the Early Modern Period practice of exercising influence behind the scenes and not at the decisions already made in the preliminary investigation.

The idea that the court was a separate, exclusive place for establishing justice where judges and procurators acted, having committed themselves to the search for truth in contrast to the emotionally driven attorneys, was underscored in various ways. The rituals of the courtroom, which were set down precisely in the new codes of criminal procedure, contributed significantly. Ultimately, as a result of the black robes, the rituals of rising and being seated, oath-taking, and the rhetoric of objectivity, the public trial was enveloped in an almost sacred aura, signaling that it was the only legitimate location for finding truth.

Moreover, important for the notion of a location sealed off from primarily secular influences, and especially whispered suggestions, was the public. Indeed, it was assigned central importance; the public, either as represented by the public audience in the courtroom or by the jurors, scrutinized and oversaw the independence of justice – according to the "common sense" of contemporaries. This common sense was produced by numerous elements: by the sharp symbolic separation of the preliminary investigation from the main trial, which in fact was constantly circumvented; by the supposedly elevated position of the jurors and their definition as part of the *Volk*, although in reality they only represented the exclusive circle of the male upper middle class; and the figure of the emotional defense attorney, who was cast as the adversary of the other legal personages and was supposed to defend his defendant like a lion, yet had scarcely any opportunity to speak in court.

Thus, at mid-century, not only did a new property concept and a new way of establishing justice develop, but the court itself changed its appearance. It was transformed into a location of objective and exclusive truth-finding, sealed off from all influences, endowed with the greatest possible legitimacy, and enhanced with attributes such as "palladium of freedom," "primevally German," "middle-class liberal," and "national."

The new legal system of the nineteenth century owes much of its form to theft and other crimes, of course in two respects clearly not as Foucault suggested when he stated that an "industrial class" created the disciplinary state as a reaction to theft. First, it was not a disciplinary state but a state of law, and second, the state of law did not arise from the fears of a propertied class. Foucault assumed that the need of a single social group for control would have been able to assert itself, that is, that the "industrial class" was as powerful as it always wanted to have us believe from its description of itself. This perspective disregards precisely what I took as the point of departure for my deliberations in using the concept "doing law." Law is a dynamic process that takes place, develops, and changes among many people; it cannot simply be established.[5]

The state of law was thus the product of a negotiation process that was not controlled by a single social group but because many people had a word to put in – jurists, gendarmes, witnesses, defendants, and also the new scientific fields – dynamics also came into play that could not be broken down into the specific goals of any one group among them.

JURISDICTIONAL POLITICS

At the same time, these conclusions are not meant to deny that the legal system in the nineteenth century assumed a specific new character. They should only raise doubt as to whether that character took the form claimed by the contemporary legal reformers, and in their wake, by traditional legal historians and early social historians, with their theories of class justice. Foucault's suppositions and Dirk Blasius' presumptions are also being called into question.

What was the nature of this specific new character, other than the factors already mentioned that closely interconnect new scientific fields and techniques for establishing justice in the preliminary investigation; aside from the tendency to automatically consider the jury court sacred; and beyond the actual focus of the legal proceeding on the preliminary investigation? The legal system at mid-century derived its specific character, among other things, from the new function of the public. The public's new importance did not, as the legal reformers had loudly proclaimed, come from its role in making certain that the rules of the procedural code were observed. Public openness cannot be defined in terms of one task, although the new codes of criminal procedure attempted to do so in their provisions regarding jurors and in their rules concerning the public. Public openness generated unanticipated dynamics, and those dynamics in particular gave rise to the specific new character of the nineteenth-century legal system.

In this context, it is not about either the public in the courtroom or the public as supposedly represented by the jurors, but rather the newspapers and their public. It is a matter of the people who created an image of the court events with their reports, and those who, by reading, were able to participate in the court events reported by the media and in the best case also learned why one offense was defined as serious while another was not even viewed as wrong. At the same time, the public was able on the basis of the court reports and other forms of court descriptions to form their own ideas about right and wrong. Drawing on such court reports or inspired by reading about the criminal activity often found in the "miscellaneous news items" column, readers could draw their own conclusions about relationship configurations, moral issues, and justice. The exact nature of those conclusions no doubt varied according to the case and the particular perspective. Discussion about whether the legal rules of decontextualization had been observed was rare because those rules played almost no role in the newspaper articles. According to the procedural codes and many participants in the legal debate, however, acting as guardian of the rules was regarded as the central task of the public, and precisely that was viewed as the specifically new character of the modern legal system that emerged at mid-century.

The public was not of crucial importance just because it ensured observance of the procedural code, but because it claimed the right to judge court events according to criteria that definitely did not have to be identical to those of the jurists. Instead of monitoring compliance with the procedural code and thus the decontextualization procedures, the public seized the opportunity to gain insights into how truth was found in court and compared these insights to parameters for right and wrong in keeping with logic beyond the procedural codes. It was thus less a matter of the public scrutinizing the court proceedings than of its observing court events and judging on its own whether truth was differentiated from untruth there according to reasonable criteria.

The discrepancy between a trial based on deduction and decontextualization, and a view of a crime that considered crime to be the expression of more or less existential problems gave rise to criticism of what was happening legally. That criticism – I am talking about the dynamics that grew out of the new character of the public – became the motor for demanding changes in the legal system.[6] Jurisdictional politics therefore became the topic of public discussion.

What are "jurisdictional politics?" Lauren Benton defines the term as "conflicts over the preservation, creation, nature, and extent of different legal forums and authorities"[7] which could only be discussed publicly if people knew about them and were furthermore authorized to do so. In the legal public, and after 1848 at the latest on the street, there was intense discussion about who could and should establish justice using which instruments, and about what was right and what wrong. These questions were discussed in the nineteenth century in Electoral Hesse, the German region, Europe, and areas outside Europe at least as vigorously as questions regarding the property system – not only in legal journals and essays, in the Frankfurt National Assembly at St. Paul's Church, and the parliaments of the individual federal states, but also in the press. This new option for debating "jurisdictional politics" openly and with great legitimacy, not secretly with caricatures or lampoons as undoubtedly had already been the case in the Early Modern Period, is perhaps the greatest innovation of all that can be observed in these decades. Just how intensively this new right was exercised is evident from the enormous interest – returning full circle to my observations at the beginning – generated by crime in general and property crime in particular.

Notes

1 Karl Marx, 1965, 365f.

2 Dirk Blasius, 1975; Michel Foucault, 2003.

3 Michel Foucault, 2003, 100ff: "Primarily in France, the fear of estates being plundered was an outright obsession; the fear of vagabonds and often of unemployed agricultural laborers who, in great poverty, lived hand to mouth and stole horses, fruit, and vegetables. One of the greatest problems of the French Revolution was the question of how to put an end to theft in the countryside. The great political uprisings which occurred during the second half of the Revolution in the Vendée and Provence were in part the result of the poverty and misery of the smallholders and agricultural laborers who in this new system of dividing up real property no longer had the income that the country estates of the Ancien Régime had provided. Because of this new geographical and social distribution of the industrial and agricultural wealth, new forms of social control became necessary at the end of the eighteenth century. The political power, the industrial class, the ownership class took over the new systems of social control from the *Volk* or the petite bourgeoisie and nationalized them. In my view, this is the origin of the disciplinary society."

4 Dirk Blasius, 1975, 125, names here the "humanizing of the penal system, equality before the law ... [and] abolishment of corporal punishment." His study relates to Prussia.

5 This perspective inexplicably equates possible intentions with actual consequences, completely leaving out the suspenseful dynamics of unintended consequences. Furthermore, proof is required that thefts – assuming that they had appreciably increased – were actually interpreted as a threat and not as an appeal for benevolent initiatives or other forms of paternalistic welfare. At least for Electoral Hesse, we have a great deal of evidence that in the middle class economic hardship was also taken as a reason to work on the moral and ethical education of the lower classes, but not by establishing a disciplinary society.

6 Of course, such a discrepancy also existed in the Early Modern Period. The thoughts of Martin Dinges on "justice phantasies" indicate that; see Martin Dinges, 1993. The studies of Michel Foucault and Arlette Farge on the *lettres de cachets* also show how very divergent notions of justice were. Likewise, the distinction between the first and second codes made by criminology calls attention to differences. However, the public imparted a new quality to the differences; Michel Foucault and Arlette Farge, 1982.

7 Lauren A. Benton, 2002, 11. The "confrontation" between colonial forces and the population of various colonies in the nineteenth century is the central focus of her study. Benton (also) analyzes the legal forms emerging from this "contact" using the concept of "jurisdictional politics" beyond the categories of "ruler" and "ruled." While I do not want to project this specific situation on the European social situation in the nineteenth century, the concept suggests an approach for determining the processes that also played a role within Europe in this important phase of establishing new legal reforms. The concept also facilitates bypassing the usual history-of-ideas approach of traditional legal historiography. On this topic, see the critique in Rebekka Habermas, 2003.

Relevant Laws

AUFHEBUNGSGESETZ GRUNDHERRLICHER RECHTE (LAW REPEALING SEIGNIORIAL RIGHTS)

Law of November 13, 1849, relating to repeal of the jurisdiction exercised by the mediatized princes and seigneurs, and of other sovereign and seigniorial rights, in: *Sammlung von Gesetzen, Verordnungen, Ausschreiben und anderen allgemeinen Verfügungen für Kurhessen*, Vol.12, 1849–1851 (Cassel, 1851), 125.

AUFLÖSUNGSVERORDNUNG 1850 (1850 DISSOLUTION REGULATION)

Regulation of March 21, 1850, relating to dissolution of the regional courts and formation of the justice offices, in: *Sammlung von Gesetzen, Verordnungen, Ausschreiben und anderen allgemeinen Verfügungen für Kurhessen*, Vol.12, 1849–1851 (Cassel, 1851), 15–18.

GERICHTSEINSETZUNGSGESETZ 1848 (1848 LAW ON ESTABLISHING COURTS)

Law of October 31, 1848, on establishing courts and state agencies at the courts, in: *Sammlung von Gesetzen, Verordnungen, Ausschreiben und anderen allgemeinen Verfügungen für Kurhessen*, Vol.11, 1846–1848 (Cassel, 1848), 163–176.

GERICHTSVERFASSUNGSGESETZ 1863 (1863 LAW ON THE CONSTITUTION OF THE COURTS)

Law of October 28, 1863, relating to constitution of the courts, in: *Sammlung von Gesetzen, Verordnungen, Ausschreiben und anderen allgemeinen Verfügungen für Kurhessen*, Vol.16, 1861–1863 (Cassel, 1863), 97–106.

ORGANISATIONSEDIKT 1821 (1821 EDICT ON ORGANIZATION)

Regulation of September 29, 1821, relating to reorganization of the previous state administrations, in: *Sammlung von Gesetzen, Verordnungen, Ausschreiben und anderen allgemeinen Verfügungen für Kurhessen*, Vol. 3, 1820–1822 (Cassel, 1822), 29–62.

POLIZEIVERWALTUNGSGESETZ 1848 (1848 LAW REGARDING POLICE ADMINISTRATION)

Law of July 22, 1851, relating to police administration, police and guild jurisdictions, and transfer to police supervision, in: *Sammlung von Gesetzen, Verordnungen, Ausschreiben und anderen allgemeinen Verfügungen für Kurhessen*, Vol.11, 1846–1848 (Cassel, 1848), 139f.

RECHTSPFLEGEGESETZ 1851 (1851 LAW ON THE ADMINISTRATION OF JUSTICE)

Provisional law of July 22, 1851, containing provisions altering the organization of the administration of justice and procedure in criminal matters, as well as in middle class legal disputes, in: *Sammlung von Gesetzen, Verordnungen, Ausschreiben und anderen allgemeinen Verfügungen für Kurhessen*, Vol.12, 1849–1851 (Cassel, 1851), 59–72.

STRAFPROZESSGESETZ 1848 (1848 LAW ON CRIMINAL PROCEDURE)

Law of October 31, 1848, relating to reorganization of the criminal trial, in: *Sammlung von Gesetzen, Verordnungen, Ausschreiben und anderen allgemeinen Verfügungen für Kurhessen*, Vol.11, 1846–1848 (Cassel, 1848), 177–236.

STRAFRECHTS- UND STRAFVERFAHRENSVERORDNUNG 1867 (1867 REGULATION ON CRIMINAL LAW AND CRIMINAL PROCEDURE)

Regulation of June 6, 1867, relating to criminal law and criminal procedure in the parts of the country that joined the monarchy under the law of September 20, 1866, and the two laws of December 24, 1866, with the exception of the former Meisenheim Upper Administrative District and the Kaulsdorf Enclave, in: Beamte des Königlichen Ober-Appellationsgerichtes, (Ed.), *Die Justizverwaltung in den neuen Preußischen Landestheilen* (Berlin, 1867), 730–743.

STRAFPROZESSORDNUNG UND EINFÜHRUNGSGESETZ 1877 (1877 CODE OF CRIMINAL PROCEDURE AND IMPLEMENTATION LAW)

Code of criminal procedure and implementation law, including references to the passages and materials related to the individual provisions, in: Werner Schubert and Jürgen Regge (Eds.), *Entstehung und Quellen der Strafprozeßordnung von 1877* (Frankfurt on the Main, 1989), 667–745.

STRAFVERFAHRENSGESETZ 1863 (1863 LAW ON CRIMINAL PROCEDURE)

Law of October 28, 1863, relating to the criminal trial, in: *Sammlung von Gesetzen, Verordnungen, Ausschreiben und anderen allgemeinen Verfügungen für Kurhessen*, Vol.16, 1861–1863 (Cassel, 1863), 124–179.

VERFAHRENSMÄNGELGESETZ 1834 (1834 LAW ON PROCEDURAL DEFICIENCIES)

Law of September 16, 1834, relating to remedying several deficiencies perceived in trial procedure, in: *Sammlung von Gesetzen, Verordnungen, Ausschreiben und anderen allgemeinen Verfügungen für Kurhessen*, Vol.7, 1834–1836 (Cassel, 1836), 75–82.

VERFAHRENSMÄNGELVERORDNUNG 1834 (1834 REGULATION ON PROCEDURAL DEFICIENCIES)

Regulation of November 6, 1834, relating to implementation of the law of September 16, 1834, enacted to remedy several deficiencies perceived in trial procedure, in: *Sammlung von Gesetzen, Verordnungen, Ausschreiben und anderen allgemeinen Verfügungen für Kurhessen*, Vol.7, 1834–1836 (Cassel, 1836), 169–175.

VERFASSUNGSURKUNDE 1831 (1831 CONSTITUTIONAL CHARTER)

Constitutional charter for the Electorate of Hesse, dated January 5, 1831, in: Ernst R. Huber (Ed.), *Dokumente zur deutschen Verfassungsgeschichte*, Vol. 1, *Deutsche Verfassungsdokumente 1803–1850*, 3rd Edn. (Stuttgart, 1978) 238–262.

VERFASSUNGSURKUNDE 1852 (1852 CONSTITUTIONAL CHARTER)

Constitutional charter for the Electorate of Hesse, dated April 13, 1852, in: *Sammlung von Gesetzen, Verordnungen, Ausschreiben und anderen allgemeinen Verfügungen für Kurhessen*, Vol.13, 1852–1854 (Cassel, 1852), 4–23.

Bibliography

UNPUBLISHED SOURCES

A Holdings of the Marburg State Archives (StAM)

Collection H 3 Locality description of Electoral Hesse

H 3 No. 3 Locality description of Amöneburg

H 3 No. 36 Locality description of Kirchhain

H 3 No. 39 Locality description of Marburg I

H 3 No. 40 Locality description of Marburg II

250 Kurhessisches Justizministerium 349 (1857–1858), Verbot des Barttragens der Justizdiener und Gesuche um Ausnahmeregelungen

250 Kurhessisches Justizministerium 563 (1850–1859), Die bei Gelegenheit des Geburtstags der Königl. Hoheit des Kurfürsten zur Begnadigung empfohlenen Sträflinge

250 Kurhessisches Justizministerium 565, Begnadigungsgesuche aus den Jahren 1858–1862

250 Kurhessisches Justizministerium 569, Die von Verübung bedeutender Verbrechen und der Einleitung deshalbiger Untersuchungen zu bewirkender Anzeigen

250 Kurhessisches Justizministerium 607 (1845–1856), Meinungsäußerungen vom Ministerium

250 Kurhessisches Justizministerium 608 (1857–1866), Meinungsäußerungen vom Ministerium

250 Kurhessisches Justizministerium 806

261 Oberappellationsgericht Verz. 7 Kriminalakten III (1849), Blum Georg, aus Wickersrode wegen Diebstahls

266 Obergericht Hanau 26, Acta generalia. Die Auslegung des Gesetzes vom 16. Sept. mit der Verordnung vom 6. [...] 1834 betr.

266 Obergericht Hanau 31, Die Vollziehung der Verordnung vom 16. November 1834 betr.
266 Obergericht Hanau 145 (1850), Untersuchungsacten wider den Schulknaben Johann Heinrich Bloh von Praunheim wegen Diebstahls
266 Obergericht Hanau 195 (1850), Untersuchungsacten wider den Goldarbeiter Jakob Golde, dahier, und den Goldarbeiter Johann Ludwig Wiedersum, von hier wegen Verleitung zu Fabrikdiebstählen
266 Obergericht Hanau 203 (1850), Untersuchungsacten wider den Handlungs-Commis Peter Hartenstein aus Dorndorf, Amts Hadamar, wegen Diebstahls
266 Obergericht Hanau 236 (1849), Untersuchungsacten wider die Gebrüder Johannes, Heinrich und Peter Kaufmann von der Loosemühle bei Hettersroth wegen Diebstahls
266 Obergericht Hanau 297 (1850), Untersuchungsacten wider Conrad Raab, von Rothenbergen wegen Anstiftung zum Familiendiebstahl
266 Obergericht Hanau 302 (1849), Untersuchungsacten wider Georg Richter und 2 Johannes Zinkhan Maurer zu Oberzell, Johannes Richter wegen Bleichdiebstahls
266 Obergericht Hanau 303 (1862–1863), Untersuchung gegen Nicolaus Fröhlich et al.
266 Obergericht Marburg 67 Tabelle, Berichte über Qualifikation der Referendare und Rechtspractikanten
266 Obergericht Marburg 72 (1849), Untersuchungsacten wider Balthasar Mengel von hier, wegen Diebstahls
266 Obergericht Marburg 98 (1864), Untersuchungsacten wider den Eisensträfling Wilhelm Schade aus Braach wegen Kirchendiebstahls, und Diebstahls mittels Einbruchs und Einsteigens zum Nachtheile des p. Freund hier
266 Obergericht Marburg 123 (1866), Untersuchungsakten die Spoliirung des Postwagens auf dem Weg von Treysa nach Kirchhain betreffend
268 Kurhessische Kriminalgerichte Hanau 8 (1853), Untersuchungsakten wider Charlotte Birk u.a. [wegen Diebstahls, Teilnahme daran und Unterschlagung]
268 Kurhessische Kriminalgerichte Hanau 29 (1859), Untersuchungsakten wider Johannes Bernstein jetzt zu Weichersbach [...] wegen Diebstahls und Vermittlung von falschen Zeugnissen
268 Kurhessische Kriminalgerichte Hanau 111 (1857), Untersuchungsakten gegen Friederike Ebert und Friedrich Ebert wegen versuchten Raubes von Eßwaren
268 Kurhessische Kriminalgerichte Hanau 301 (1862), Untersuchungsakten wider die Ehefrau des Weißbinders Johannes Blum, Maria geb. Kling [...] wegen Diebstahls
268 Kurhessische Kriminalgerichte Marburg 11 (1852), Untersuchung gegen Daniel Fischer et al.
268 Kurhessische Kriminalgerichte Marburg 14 (1855), Untersuchung gegen Heinrich von Schröder

268 Kurhessische Kriminalgerichte Marburg 50 (1854–1856), General Untersuchungsprotocoll gegen Ludwig Loos aus Treisbach wegen verschiedener Diebstähle

268 Kurhessische Kriminalgerichte Marburg 62 (1856–1857) Untersuchung wider den Tagelöhner Georg Quechel wegen Diebstahls

268 Kurhessische Kriminalgerichte Marburg 91 (1854, 1858), Untersuchungsacten wider Anton Zimmermann von Cÿriaxweimar wegen Raubs

268 Kurhessische Kriminalgerichte Marburg 96 (1849–1856), Repertorium über die Strafen in schwurgerichtlichen Strafsachen

268 Kurhessische Kriminalgerichte Marburg 97 (1849–1863), Criminalgericht zu Marburg. Repertorium über die Untersuchungsacten aus den Jahren 1840 bis einschließlich 1863

268 Kurhessische Kriminalgerichte Marburg 99, Acten die Bildung des Criminalgerichts betreffend

268 Kurhessische Kriminalgerichte Marburg 103, Acten die Rechtsprechung betreffend [Durchführungsbestimmungen in Bezug auf die Rechtsprechung 1852–1859]

269 Kreisgerichte Preußische, Marburg 16 (1874), Untersuchungssachen wegen Vergehens wider den Schulknaben Christian Euler wegen Diebstahls

269 Kreisgerichte Preußische, Marburg 171 (1874), Untersuchungssachen wegen Verbrechens wider den Studiosus pharm. Friedrich Arnold von Eschwege wegen Diebstahls

269 Kreisgerichte Preußische, Marburg 196 (1876), Untersuchungssachen wegen Verbrechens wider Wilhelm Hißerich, Friedr. Sohn, 14 ½ Jahre alt, in Neustadt wegen Verbrechens aus § 243^{2} St.G.B. (Diebstahls mittelst Einsteigens)

269 Kreisgerichte Preußische, Marburg 198 (1877), Untersuchungssachen wegen Verbrechens wider den Holzhauer Lorenz Ibach in Treysa wegen Diebstahls im Rückfall

269 Kreisgerichte Preußische, Marburg 200 (1873), Untersuchungssachen wegen Vergehens wider 1) den Tagelöhner Friedrich Kappauf; 2) Daniel Lanz; 3) Christian Kappauf sämmtlich von Treysa wegen Diebstahls

269 Kreisgerichte Preußische, Marburg 218 (1877), Untersuchungssachen wegen Verbrechens wider den Commis Erich v Lippe in Berlin wegen Diebstahls

273 Marburg 324 (1867), [Repertorium]

274 Marburg Staatsanwaltschaft 7 1871 Anzeige über einen Diebstahl gegen Heinrich Benzel

274 Marburg Staatsanwaltschaft 7, 1871 Anzeige über einen Diebstahl gegen Peter Fach

B Holdings of the Secret State Archives of the Prussian Cultural Heritage

GStA PK HA I Rep. 77, Ministry of Internal Affairs, Tit 114 No. 277

PUBLISHED SOURCES

Laws, Regulations, Law Collections, and Parliamentary Materials

Chronologisch geordnete Sammlung aller Gesetze, Verordnungen, Cabinetsordres, Erlasse, Ministerialverfügungen, Anweisungen, Instructionen und Bekanntmachungen, welche vom 20. September 1866 bis 1. October 1867 für die Neuen Preußischen Landestheile ergangen sind, Berlin 1867.

Sammlung von Gesetzen, Verordnungen, Ausschreiben und anderen allgemeinen Verfügungen für Kurhessen, Vols. 1–19, Cassel 1813–1866.

Verhandlungen des Kurhessischen Landtages, nebst Beilagen, Kassel 1830–1866.

Hattenhauer, Hans/Bernert, Günther (Eds.), *Allgemeines Landrecht für die preußischen Staaten von 1794*, Frankfurt a.M. 1970, cited as: ALR.

Huber, Ernst R. (Ed.), *Dokumente zur Deutschen Verfassungsgeschichte,* Vol. *1: Deutsche Verfassungsdokumente 1803–1850*, 2nd edition, Stuttgart 1961.

Dokumente zur deutschen Verfassungsgeschichte, Vol. *1: Deutsche Verfassungsdokumente 1803–850*, 3rd revised and expanded edition, Stuttgart 1978.

Limbach, Jutta, Die Frankfurter Reichsverfassung vom 28. März 1849, in: Jutta Limbach/Roman Herzog/Dieter Grimm (Eds.), *Die Deutschen Verfassungen. Reproduktion der Verfassungsoriginale von 1849, 1871, 1919 sowie des Grundgesetzes von 1949*, München 1999, 89–116.

Radbruch, Gustav (Ed.), *Die Peinliche Gerichtsordnung Kaiser Karls V. von 1532 (Carolina)*, 5th improved and expanded edition, edited by Arthur Kaufmann, Stuttgart 1975, cited as: Carolina.

Schubert, Ernst (Ed.), *Entwurf eines Strafgesetzbuchs für Kurhessen von 1849 mit Motiven*, Goldbach 1993.

Schubert, Werner, *Die deutsche Gerichtsverfassung (1869–1877): Entstehung und Quellen*, Frankfurt a.M. 1981.

Die Quellen zum Strafrecht von 1870/71, in: *Goltdammer's Archiv für Strafrecht* **129** (1982), 191–218.

Schubert, Werner/Regge, Jürgen (Eds.), *Entstehung und Quellen der Strafprozeßordnung von 1877*, Frankfurt a.M. 1989.

Seier, Hellmut (Ed.), *Akten und Dokumente zur kurhessischen Parlaments- und Verfassungsgeschichte 1848–1866*, Marburg 1987.

Stenglein, Melchior (Ed.), *Strafgesetzbuch für das deutsche Reich*, Berlin 1892.

(Ed.), *Sammlung der deutschen Strafgesetzbücher: Hannover, Großherzogtum Hessen und Frankfurt, Baden, Nassau*, Vol. 2, München 1858.

Stoepel, Paul, *Preußisch-Deutscher Gesetz-Codex. Ein chronologisch geordneter Abdruck der in der Gesetzsammlung für die Königlich Preußischen Staaten von 1806 im Bundes-Gesetzblatt und im Reichs-Gesetzblatt von 1871 an bis auf die neueste Zeit enthaltenen Gesetze, Verordnungen, Kabinettsordres, Erlasse etc. mit Rücksicht auf ihre noch jetzige Gültigkeit und praktische Bedeutung*, Vol. 3, Frankfurt a.M. 1908.

Verordnung vom 29sten September 1821. Die Umbildung der bisherigen Staatsverwaltungen betreffend, in: *Sammlung von Gesetzen, Verordnungen,*

Ausschreiben und anderen allgemeinen Verfügungen für Kurhessen, Vol. *3: Jahre 1820–22*, Cassel 1822, 29–62, cited as: Organisationsedikt 1821.

Verfassungsurkunde für das Kurfürstentum Hessen vom 5. Januar 1831, in: Ernst R. Huber (Ed.), *Dokumente zur deutschen Verfassungsgeschichte*, Vol. *1: Deutsche Verfassungsdokumente 1803–1850*, 3rd edition, Stuttgart 1978, 238–262, cited as: Verfassungsurkunde 1831.

Gesetz vom 16. September 1834. Die Abstellung mehrerer im prozessualischen Verfahren wahrgenommenen Mängel betreffend, in: *Sammlung von Gesetzen, Verordnungen, Ausschreiben und anderen allgemeinen Verfügungen für Kurhessen*, Vol. 7: *Jahre 1834–1836*, Cassel 1836, 75–82, cited as: Verfahrensmängelgesetz 1834.

Verordnung vom 6. November 1834. Betreffend die Vollziehung des zur Abstellung mehrerer im prozessualen Verfahren wahrgenommenen Mängel unter dem 16ten September 1834 erlassenen Gesetzes, in: *Sammlung von Gesetzen, Verordnungen, Ausschreiben und anderen allgemeinen Verfügungen für Kurhessen*, Vol. 7: *Jahre 1834–1836*, Cassel 1836, 169–175, cited as: Verfahrensmängelverordnung 1834.

Verordnung vom 7ten November 1834, betreffend die Vollziehung des über das in minderwichtigen oder ihrer Beschaffenheit nach einfachen Rechtsstreitigkeiten zu beobachtende prozessualische Verfahren unter dem 18ten October 1834 erlassenen Gesetzes, in: *Sammlung von Gesetzen, Verordnungen, Ausschreiben und anderen allgemeinen Verfügungen für Kurhessen*, Vol. 7: *Jahre 1834–1836*, Cassel 1836, 177–178.

Criminalgesetzbuch für das Königreich Hannover vom 8. April 1840, in: Melchior Stenglein (Ed.), *Sammlung der deutschen Strafgesetzbücher*, Vol. 2: *Hannover, Großherzogthum Hessen und Frankfurt, Baden, Nassau*, München 1858.

Gesetz vom 29. October 1848. Die Polizeiverwaltung, Polizei- und Zunft-Gerichtsbarkeit, sowie die Stellung unter polizeiliche Aufsicht betreffend, in: *Sammlung von Gesetzen, Verordnungen, Ausschreiben und anderen allgemeinen Verfügungen für Kurhessen*, Vol. 11: *Jahre 1846–1848*, Cassel 1848, 139f, cited as: Polizei-verwaltungsgesetz 1848.

Gesetz vom 31. October 1848. Über die Einrichtung der Gerichte und der Staatsbehörde bei den Gerichten, in: *Sammlung von Gesetzen, Verordnungen, Ausschreiben und anderen allgemeinen Verfügungen für Kurhessen*, Vol. 11: *Jahre: 1846–1848*, Cassel 1848, 163–176, cited as: Gerichtseinsetzungsgesetz 1848.

Gesetz vom 31sten October 1848, die Umbildung des Strafverfahrens betreffend, in: *Sammlung von Gesetzen, Verordnungen, Ausschreiben und anderen allgemeinen Verfügungen für Kurhessen*, Vol. 11: *Jahre 1846–1848*, Cassel 1848, 177–236, cited as: Strafprozessgesetz 1848.

Gesetz vom 13ten November 1849, die Aufhebung der von den Standes- und Grundherrren ausgeübten Gerichtsbarkeit und anderen Hoheits- oder grundherrlichen Rechte betreffend, in: *Sammlung von Gesetzen, Verordnungen, Ausschreiben und anderen allgemeinen Verfügungen für Kurhessen*, Vol. 12: *Jahre 1849–1851*, Cassel 1851, 125, cited as: Aufhebungsgesetz grundherrlicher Rechte.

Verordnung vom 21ten März 1850, die Auflösung der Landgerichte in Justizämter betreffend, in: *Sammlung von Gesetzen, Verordnungen, Ausschreiben und anderen allgemeinen Verfügungen für Kurhessen*, Vol. 12: *Jahre 1849–1851*, Cassel 1851, 15–18, cited as: Auflösungsverordnung 1850.

Das Preußische Strafgesetzbuch nebst dem Einführungsgesetz, Berlin 1851.

Ausschreiben des Ministeriums des Innern, vom 7ten Juli 1851, die Verwaltung Landespolizei in den Provinzial-Hauptstädten betreffend, in: *Sammlung von Gesetzen, Verordnungen, Ausschreiben und anderen allgemeinen Verfügungen für Kurhessen*, Vol. 12: *Jahre 1849–1851*, Cassel 1851, 37.

Verordnung vom 7ten Juli 1851, die Umbildung der inneren Landesverwaltung betreffend, in: *Sammlung von Gesetzen, Verordnungen, Ausschreiben und anderen allgemeinen Verfügungen für Kurhessen*, Vol. 12: *Jahre 1849–1851*, Cassel 1851, 27–31.

Provisorisches Gesetz vom 7ten Juli 1851, die Vollziehung der Verwaltungsbehörden, sowie die Bezirksräthe betreffend, in: *Sammlung von Gesetzen, Verordnungen, Ausschreiben und anderen allgemeinen Verfügungen für Kurhessen*, Vol. 12: *Jahre 1849–1851*, Cassel 1851, 31–37.

Provisorisches Gesetz vom 22. Juli 1851. Abändernde Bestimmungen über die Organisation der Rechtspflege und das Verfahren in Strafsachen sowie in bürgerlichen Rechtsstreiten enthaltend, in: *Sammlung von Gesetzen, Verordnungen, Ausschreiben und anderen allgemeinen Verfügungen für Kurhessen*, Vol. 12: *Jahre 1849–1851*, Cassel 1851, 59–72, cited as: Rechtspflegegesetz 1851.

Präambel zur Verfassungsurkunde für das Kurfürstentum Hessen vom 13. April 1852, in: Ernst R. Huber (Ed.), *Dokumente zur deutschen Verfassungsgeschichte*, Vol. 1: *Deutsche Verfassungsdokumente 1803–1850*, 2nd edition, Stuttgart 1978, 637.

Verfassungsurkunde für das Kurfüstenthum Hessen vom 13. April 1852, in: *Sammlung von Gesetzen, Verordnungen, Ausschreiben und anderen allgemeinen Verfügungen für Kurhessen*, Vol. 13: *Jahre 1852–1854*, Cassel 1852, 4–23, cited as: Verfassungsurkunde 1852.

Strafgesetzbuch für die preußischen Staaten nebst dem Gesetze über die Einführung desselben, und einigen neueren Strafgesetzen, 3rd edition, Berlin 1859.

Gesetz vom 28sten October 1863, die Gerichtsverfassung betreffend, in: *Sammlung von Gesetzen, Verordnungen, Ausschreiben und anderen allgemeinen Verfügungen für Kurhessen*, Vol. 16: *Jahre 1861–1863*, Cassel 1863, 97–106, cited as: Gerichtsverfassungsgesetz 1863.

Vorschriften, betreffend die Zuziehung von Gerichtsschöffen bei der untergerichtlichen Strafrechtspflege, in: *Sammlung von Gesetzen, Verordnungen, Ausschreiben und anderen allgemeinen Verfügungen für Kurhessen*, Vol. 16: *Jahre 1861–1863*, Cassel 1863, 107–109.

Der Gerichtsschöffe in Kurhessen. Nach den Bestimmungen der Justiz-Gesetze vom 28. Oktober 1863, Kassel 1864.

Gesetz vom 28sten October 1863, das Verfahren in bürgerlichen Rechtsstreitigkeiten betreffend, in: *Sammlung von Gesetzen, Verordnungen, Ausschreiben und anderen allgemeinen Verfügungen für Kurhessen*, Vol. 16: *Jahre 1861–1863*, Cassel 1863, 110–123.

Gesetz vom 28sten October 1863, das Strafverfahren betreffend, in: *Sammlung von Gesetzen, Verordnungen, Ausschreiben und anderen allgemeinen Verfügungen für Kurhessen,* Vol. 16: *Jahre 1861–1863*, Cassel 1863, 124–179, cited as: Strafverfahrensgesetz 1863.

Verordnung vom 25.6.1867 betreffend das Strafrecht und das Strafverfahren in den durch das Gesetz vom 20. September 1866 und die beiden Gesetze vom 24. Dezember 1866 mit der Monarchie vereinigten Landestheilen, mit Ausnahme des vormaligen Oberamtsbezirks Meisenheim und der Enklave Kaulsdorf, in: Beamte des Königlichen Ober-Appellationsgerichtes (Ed.), *Die Justizverwaltung in den neuen Preußischen Landestheilen*, Berlin 1867, 730–743, cited as: Strafrechts- und Strafverfahrensverordnung 1867.

Gerichtsverfassung in Schleswig-Holstein, Kurhessen, Nassau und den vormals Bayerischen und Großherzoglich Hessischen Gebietstheilen, in: *Jahrbuch der Preußischen Gerichtsverfassung* 8 (1868), 36–48.

Diebstahl und Unterschlagung, §242–247, in: Hans Rüdorff (Ed.), *Strafgesetzbuch für das Deutsche Reich*. (Issued in Berlin, May 15, 1871), text edition with notes and a complete index, Berlin 1871, 77–81.

Strafprozeßordnung und Einführungsgesetz nebst einer Nachweisung der auf die einzelnen Bestimmungen bezüglichen Stellen und Materialien, in: Werner Schubert/Jürgen Regge (Eds.), *Entstehung und Quellen der Strafprozeßordnung von 1877*, Frankfurt a.M. 1989, 667–745, cited as: Strafprozessordnung und Einführungsgesetz 1877.

Daily and Weekly Newspapers

Baierische Landtags-Zeitung, München 1818–1819.

Berliner Gerichtszeitung. Zeitschrift für Civil-, Criminal- und Polizei-Gerichtspflege des In- und Auslandes, 1857.

Eberhardt's Allgemeiner Polizei-Anzeiger, Dresden 1853–1900.

Illustrierte Zeitung, Leipzig 1843–1844.

Kreisblatt für die Kreise Marburg, Frankenberg-Böhl und Kirchhain, Marburg 1869–1890, cited as: *Kreisblatt.*

Marburger Tageblatt für Stadt und Land, Marburg 1874–1886, cited as: *Marburger Tageblatt.*

Marburger Wochenblatt. Zeitung für öffentliche Bekanntmachungen, Unterhaltung und Politik, Marburg 1869–70.

Wochenblatt für die Provinz Oberhessen, Marburg 1827–1841 and 1843–1850, cited as: *Wochenblatt Oberhessen.*

Unterhaltungsblatt. Beilage zum Hanauer Anzeiger [zuvor Hanauer Kreisblatt], Hanau 1872–1949, cited as: *Unterhaltungsblatt.*

Allgemeines Intelligenzblatt für den Kreis Alsfeld und die angrenzenden Bezirke. Amts- und Anzeigeblatt, Alsfeld 1847–1875.

Vossische Zeitung, Berlin 1911–1934. Vorgänger: *Königlich privilegirte Berlinische Zeitung von Staats- und gelehrten Sachen*, Berlin 1785–1911.

Frankfurter Zeitung und Handelsblatt: *Frankfurter Handelszeitung, Neue Frankfurter Zeitung*, Frankfurt a.M. 1866–1943.

Journals and Series

Handbuch des kurhessischen Militair-, Hof- und Civil-Staats auf das Jahr 1821, Cassel 1821.

Königlich Preussischer Staatsdiener Kalender für den Regierungsbezirk Cassel auf das Jahr 1869, Cassel 1869.

Kurfürstlich-Hessisches Hof- und Staatshandbuch, Cassel 1835–1866.

Kurhessisches Staats- und Adress-Handbuch, Cassel 1822–1834.

Annalen der Justizpflege und Verwaltung in Kurhessen, Cassel 1854–1866.

Hitzigs Annalen der deutschen und ausländischen Criminalrechtspflege, Leipzig 1845–1855.

Archiv des Criminalrechts, Halle 1799–1857.

Öffentlicher Anzeiger zum Amtsblatt der königlichen Regierung zu Cassel, 1877.

Zeitschrift des Königlich-Preussischen Statistischen Bureaus, Berlin 1864–1905.

Allgemeine Schwurgerichtszeitung für Deutschland und die Schweiz. Augsburg 1857–1860.

Königlich Preußische Commission für statistische Angelegenheiten (Ed.), *Beiträge zur Statistik des vormaligen Kurfürstentums Hessen*, Nos. 1-3, Kassel 1866–1867.

Jahrbücher für Nationalökonomie und Statistik, Stuttgart 1863–1875.

Preußischen Statistischen Landesamt (Ed.), *Statistische Correspondenz* 1874–1935.

Holtzendorf, Franz von (Ed.), *Allgemeine deutsche Strafrechtszeitung zur Förderung einheitlicher Entwicklung auf den Gebieten des Strafrechts, des Strafprocesses und des Gefängniswesens sowie für strafgerichtliche Medizin*, Leipzig 1861–1873.

"Anonymous Publications"

Besprechung von W. Drobisch der "Beiträge zur Statistik des vormaligen Kurfürstenthums Hessen 1. Heft Kassel 1866," in: *Jahrbuch für Nationalökonomie und Statistik* (1867), 176–179, cited as: Review of W. Drobisch, *Beiträge zur Statistik des vormaligen Kurfürstenhums Hessen*, 1867.

Der Bruch des Rechts in Kurhessen. Ein Beitrag zur Information der hohen deutschen Bundesversammlung, Berlin 1859.

Drei und zwanzig Jahre im Kerker und dennoch immer ein Gewohnheitsdieb, in: *Hitzigs Annalen der deutschen und ausländischen Criminalrechtspflege* 26, N.S. [Old 56] (1851), 94–97, cited as: Gewohnheitsdieb, in: *Hitzigs Annalen* 26, N.S. (1851).

Statistics

Uebersicht der im Justizjahre vom 1. Juli 1853 bis dahin 1854 bei den Gerichten des Herzogthums Braunschweig verhandelten Strafsachen. Nach der officiellen Veröffentlichung des Herrn Oberstaatsanwalts Breymann in Wolfenbüttel, in: *Hitzigs Annalen der deutschen und ausländischen*

Criminalrechtspflege 38, N.S. (1854), No. 2, 170–176, cited as: Uebersicht Herzogthums Braunschweig Strafsachen, in: *Hitzigs Annalen* 38, N.S. (1854).

Criminalstatistik, I. Zur Statistik der Todesstrafen, in: *Hitzigs Annalen der deutschen und ausländischen Criminalrechtspflege* 31, N.S. [Old 61] (1852), 202–204, cited as: Zur Statistik der Todesstrafen, in: *Hitzigs Annalen* 31, N.S. (1852).

Ergebnisse der Strafrechtspflege im Königreiche Preußen, einschließlich der zu den preussischen Oberlandesgerichts-Bezirken Naumburg, Kassel, Celle, Köln und Hamm gehörigen nicht preussischen Gebietstheile, und im Bezirke des gemeinschaftlichen thüringischen Oberlandesgerichtes in Jena während des Jahres 1881, in: *Zeitschrift des Preussischen Statistischen Bureaus* (1883) H. Ergänzungsheft XIV.

Ueber die Thätigkeit und Wirksamkeit der Schwurgerichte im Seekreise des Großherzogtums Baden 1851–53, in: *Hitzigs Annalen der deutschen und ausländischen Criminalrechtspflege* 40, N.S. (1855), No. 2, 184–193, cited as: Schwurgerichte des Großherzogtums Baden, in: *Hitzigs Annalen* 40, N.S. (1855).

Übersicht der von sämmtlichen Civil-Strafgerichten des Großherzogtums Hessen im Jahr 1851 abgeurtheilten Verbrechen und Vergehen, mit Rückblicken auf die Jahre 1847–1850, in: *Hitzigs Annalen der deutschen und ausländischen Criminalrechtspflege* 35, N.S. (1853), 204–213, cited as: Civil-Strafgerichte des Großherzogtums Hessen, in: *Hitzigs Annalen* 35, N.S. (1853).

Criminalstatistik, I. Ergebnis der Criminalrechtspflege in Berlin im Jahre 1845, in: *Hitzigs Annalen der deutschen und ausländischen Criminalrechtspflege* 6, N.S. [Old 36] (1846), 97–103, cited as: Criminalstatistik Berlin, in: *Hitzigs Annalen* 6, N.S. (1846).

Zur Criminalstatistik des Großherzogtums Hessen in den Jahren 1847–1851, in: *Hitzigs Annalen der deutschen und ausländischen Criminalrechtspflege* 36, N.S. (1854), No. 2, 183–187, cited as: Criminalstatistik des Großherzogtums Hessen, in: *Hitzigs Annalen* 36, N.S. (1854).

Criminalstatistik, III. Fürstenthum Schaumburg-Lippe. Uebersicht der im Laufe des Jahres 1845 daselbst von fürstlicher Justizkanzlei erkannten Criminalstrafen, in: *Hitzigs Annalen der deutschen und ausländischen Criminalrechtspflege* 5, N.S. [Old 35] (1846), 229–230, cited as: Criminalstatistik Fürstenthum Schaumburg-Lippe, in: *Hitzigs Annalen* 5, N.S. (1846).

Criminalstatistik, II. Königreich Bayern, Strafrechtspflege der Pfalz in den Etatsjahren 1843/44 und 1844/45. Nach den vom königlichen Generalstaatsprocurator Korbach erstatteten amtlichen Berichten, in: *Hitzigs Annalen der deutschen und ausländischen Criminalrechtspflege* 6, N.S. [Old 36] (1846), 190–195, cited as: Criminalstatistik Königreich Bayern, in: *Hitzigs Annalen* 6, N.S. (1846).

Criminalstatistik, Königreich Hannover 1852–1853. Fortsetzung, in: *Hitzigs Annalen der deutschen und ausländischen Criminalrechtspflege* 43, N.S. [Old 73] (1855), 71–82, cited as: Criminalstatistik Königreich Hannover, Fortsetzung, in: *Hitzigs* Annalen 43, N.S. (1855).

Criminalstatistik, Königreich Hannover 1852–1853, in: *Hitzigs Annalen der deutschen und ausländischen Criminalrechtspflege* 42, N.S. [Old 72]

(1855), 73–82, cited as: Criminalstatistik Königreich Hannover, in: *Hitzigs Annalen* 42, N.S. (1855).

Criminalstatistik, I. Königreich Sachsen. Übersicht der Geschäftsthätigkeit der höheren Gerichte in Criminalsachen von 1835–1849, in: *Hitzigs Annalen der deutschen und ausländischen Criminalrechtspflege* 24, N.S. [Old 54] (1851), 282–284, cited as: Criminalstatistik Königreich Sachsen, in: *Hitzigs Annalen* 24, N.S. (1851).

Criminalstatistik, I. Königreich Würtemberg. Ergebnisse der statistischen Berichte über die Etatsjahre 1843/44 und 1844/45, in: *Hitzigs Annalen der deutschen und ausländischen Criminalrechtspflege* 5, N.S. [Old 35] (1846), 214–228, cited as: Criminalstatistik Königreich Würtemberg, in: *Hitzigs Annalen* 5, N.S. (1846).

Criminalstatistik, Das Strafsystem und die Ergebnisse der Strafrechtspflege in St. Gallen, in: *Hitzigs Annalen der deutschen und ausländischen Criminalrechtspflege* 25, N.S. [Old 55] (1851), 173–180, cited as: Criminalstatistik St. Gallen, in: *Hitzigs Annalen* 25, N.S. (1851).

Die Ehrenstrafen, nach dem preußischen Strafgesetzbuche, beleuchtet von einem practischen Juristen, in: *Hitzigs Annalen der deutschen und ausländischen Criminalrechtspflege* 27, N.S. [Old 57] (1851), 1–23, cited as: Ehrenstrafen, nach dem preußischen Strafgesetzbuche, in: *Hitzigs Annalen* 27, N.S. (1851).

Statistische Nachrichten über die in den Jahren 1862 bis 1866 in den Straf-Anstalten Kurhessens detinirten Gefangenen, in: *Beiträge zur Statistik des vormaligen Kurfürstentums Hessen, hg. von der königlichen Commission für Statistische Angelegenheiten* 3 (1867), 1–54, cited as: Kurhessens detinirte Gefangene, in: *Beiträge zur Statistik des vormaligen Kurfürstentums Hessen* 3 (1867).

Articles and Monographs

Abegg, Julius F. H., Beitrag zur Geschichte der älteren einheimischen Strafrechtspflege mit Rücksicht auf sogenannte Malefizbücher, in: *Zeitschrift für Rechtsgeschichte* 3 (1864), 90–124.

Verordnung betreffend die Einführung des mündlichen und öffentlichen Verfahrens mit Geschwornen in Untersuchungssachen im Königreich Preußen, vom 3. Januar 1849. Präjudicien des Ober-Tribunals zu Berlin, in: *Archiv des Criminalrechts*. N.S. (1851), No. 2, 163–190.

Von der Bestrafung der Verbrechen und Vergehen im Allgemeinen, in: *Archiv des Criminalrechts*. N.S. Second supplemental number for 1851 (1851), 14–44.

Der Entwurf des Strafgesetzbuches für die Preußischen Staaten vom 10. December 1850 kritisch betrachtet in Vergleichung mit den Entwürfen von den Jahren 1843 und 1847, in: *Archiv des Criminalrechts*. N.S., Second supplemental number for 1851 (1851), 1–132.

Von den einzelnen Verbrechen und Vergehen und deren Bestrafung, in: *Archiv des Criminalrechts*. N.S. Second supplemental number for 1851 (1851), 44–126.

Von den Uebertretungen, in: *Archiv des Criminalrechts.*, N.S. Second supplemental number for 1851, 126–132.
Arnd, Karl, *Geschichte der Provinz Hanau und der unteren Maingegend*, Hanau 1858.
Avé-Lallemant, Friedrich C. B., *Das deutsche Gaunertum in seiner sozialpolitischen, literarischen und linguistischen Ausbildung zu seinem heutigen Bestande.* Two parts in one volume. New edition in one volume according to the revised Munich-Berlin 1914 edition in two volumes, Wiesbaden 1998.
Bähr, Otto, *Das frühere Kurhessen. Ein Geschichtsbild*, Kassel 1895.
Erinnerungen aus meinem Leben 1817–1878. Published as a manuscript. Reprint, Lauterbach 1993 [FE Kassel 1898].
Barth, Karl, Indizien-Beweis, in: *Allgemeine Schwurgerichtszeitung* 2 (1858), 359–365.
Bauer, Anton (Ed.), *Strafrechtsfälle*, Vol. 3, Göttingen 1837.
(Revision), Untersuchungssache wider Martin Friedrich Petersen aus Neuenkirchen. Inquisiten Diebstähle betreffend, in: Anton Bauer (Ed.), *Strafrechtsfälle*, Vol. 4, Göttingen 1839, 273–298, cited as: Anton Bauer, 1839b.
(Revision), Untersuchungssache wider den vormaligen Sergeanten Johann Friedrich Mohr und den Friseurgesellen Anton Beck. Inquisiten wegen Diebstahls, in: Anton Bauer (Ed.), *Strafrechtsfälle*, Vol. 4, Göttingen 1839, 299–334, cited as: Anton Bauer, 1839c.
(Revision), Untersuchungssache wider Anton Herfort aus Hameln. Inquisiten Diebstähle betreffend, in: Anton Bauer (Ed.), *Strafrechtsfälle*, Vol. 4, Göttingen 1839, 257–272, cited as: Anton Bauer, 1839d.
(Revision), Untersuchungssache wider Wilhelm Ahrens aus Altendonop wegen wiederholter Diebstähle, in: Anton Bauer (Ed.), *Strafrechtsfälle*, Vol. 4, Göttingen 1839, 233–256, cited as: Anton Bauer, 1839a.
Baumbach-Nassenerfurth, Karl von, *Stammtafeln der Althessischen Ritterschaft aus neuerer Zeit, als Fortsetzung des Rudolf von Buttlar'schen Stammbuchs. Bearbeitet unter Beifügung von Stammtafeln der ritterschaftl. Geschlechter im ehemaligen Großherzogtum Hessen; zum 400jährigen Jubiläum des ritterschaftlichen Stiftes Kaufungen mit Wetter*, Rudolstadt 1932.
Beamte des Königlichen Ober-Appellationsgerichts (Ed.), *Die Justizverwaltung in den neuen Preußischen Landestheilen*, Berlin 1867.
Beccaria, Cesare, *Über Verbrechen und Strafen. Nach der Ausgabe von 1766 übersetzt und hg. von Wilhelm Alff*, Frankfurt a.M. 1966.
Berlein, Ist durch die Verordnung vom 25. Juni 1867, betreffend das *Strafrecht und das Strafverfahren in Kurhessen die Civilklage wegen Injurien ausgeschlossen?, in: Zeitschrift für Gesetzgebung und Rechtspflege in Preußen* 1 (1867), 698–728.
Bernhardi, H. [Procurator], *Anleitung des Referendars beim Eintritt in die preußische Gerichtspraxis*, Berlin 1887.
Biener, Friedrich A., *Beiträge zur Geschichte des Inquisitionsprozesses und der Geschworenengerichte*, Aalen 1827.
Binding, Karl, *Die Ehre im Rechtssinn und ihre Verletzbarkeit. Rektoratsreden an der Universität Leipzig am 31. Oktober 1890, II. Rede des antretenden Rektors*, Leipzig 1892.

Grundriss des Deutschen Strafprocessrechts, Leipzig 1893.
Bopp, Art. Diebstahl, in: Karl Welcker/Karl von Rotteck (Eds.), *Das Staats-Lexikon. Encyklopädie der sämtlichen Staatswisenschaften für alle Stände*, Vol. 4, 3rd edition, Leipzig 1860, 541–545.
Die Praxis hinsichtlich der Todesstrafe bei dem Verbrechen des Raubs, nach dem Art. 126 der Carolina, in: *Zeitschrift für Gesetzgebung und Rechtspflege des Kurfürstenthums und Großherzogthums Hessen und der freien Stadt Frankfurt* 1 (1832), 189–197.
Der Diebstahl als Handwerk, in: *Hitzigs Annalen der deutschen und ausländischen Criminalrechtspflege* 11, N.S. [Old 41] (1847), 144–184.
Variae causarum criminalicum figurae. Mittheilungen aus der Praxis des gemeinen deutschen Strafrechts. Vom Herrn Advocat Bopp in Darmstadt, in: *Hitzigs Annalen der deutschen und ausländischen Criminalrechtspflege* 15, N.S. [Old 45] (1848), 69–83.
Rechtsfälle, II Beiträge zur Geschichte der deutschen Strafrechtspflege. Mitgetheilt von Hrn. Adv. Bopp in Darmstad, in: *Hitzigs Annalen der deutschen und ausländischen Criminalrechtspflege* 18, N.S. [Old 48] (1849), 36–48.
Meine Anfänge in der öffentlichen Vertheidigung, in: *Der Gerichtssaal* 2 (1850), No. 2, 331–347, cited as: Bopp, 1850a.
Ein Strafurtheil wegen Diebstahl aus dem ersten Jahre des 19. Jahrhunderts. Zur Geschichte der Bestrafung des Diebstahls, insbesondere der Praxis des Art. 162 der Carolina. Mittheilungen des Hrn. Adv. Bopp in Darmstadt, in: *Hitzigs Annalen der deutschen und ausländischen Criminalrechtspflege* 22, N.S. [Old 52] (1850), 165–180, cited as: Bopp, 1850b.
Ein Geschworener über das Schwurgericht, in: *Der Gerichtssaal* 3 (1851), No. 2, 176–182, cited as: Bopp, 1851a.
Die Beschränkung der Oeffentlichkeit des Strafverfahrens vor dem Publicum wegen Gefahr der Verletzung der Sittlichkeit. Darlegung von Erfahrungen, in: *Archiv des Criminalrechts*. N.S. (1851), 91–101, cited as: Bopp, 1851b.
Brauer, Eduard, *Die deutschen Schwurgerichtsgesetze in ihren Hauptbestimmungen übersichtlich zusammengestellt mit kurzem Hinweis auf fremdes, insbesondere französisches und englisches, auch schottisches und nordamerikanisches Recht*, Erlangen 1856.
Brauer, W[ilhelm], Ueber die Bildung der Geschwornenlisten. Vom Geheimrathe W. Brauer in Karlsruhe, in: *Der Gerichtssaal* 2 (1850), No. 2, 136–145.
Buddeus, Aurelio, Zur Criminalstatistik der Ostseeprovinzen Rußlands, in: *Hitzigs Annalen der deutschen und ausländischen Criminalrechtspflege* 2, N.S. (1846), 216–231.
Caspari, Lorenz, *Die Entstehung des Hanauer Edelmetallgewerbes von seiner Entstehung im Jahre 1597 bis zum Jahre 1873*, Elberfeld 1916.
Demme, Wilhelm Ludwig, *Das Buch der Verbrechen – das Interessanteste aus älterer, neuerer und neuester Zeit dies- und jenseits des Oceans. Ein Volksbuch*, Leipzig ab 1852.
Diezmann, A./Jordan, W./Meyer, L. (Eds.), *Nachtseiten der Gesellschaft. Eine Gallerie merkwürdiger Verbrechen und Rechtsfälle*, Leipzig 1844.

Dr. Giesecke, Der unverbesserliche Dieb, in: *Hitzigs Annalen der Criminalrechtspflege* 21, N.S. (1850), 113–157.
Dronke, Ernst, *Polizei-Geschichten*, Leipzig 1846.
Endemann, Wilhelm, Ueber den Karakter der kurhessischen Rechtspflege. Von Herrn Ober-Appellationsgerichts-Rath Professor Dr. Endemann zu Jena, in: *Zeitschrift für Gesetzgebung und Rechtspflege in Preußen* 1 (1867), 29–47, cited as: Wilhelm Endemann, 1867a.
Die Lage des Anwaltstandes in dem ehemaligen Kurhessen. Von Herrn Ober-Appellationsgerichts-Rath Professor Dr. Endemann zu Jena, in: *Zeitschrift für Gesetzgebung und Rechtspflege in Preußen* 1 (1867), 264–289, cited as: Wilhelm Endemann, 1867b.
Engels, Friedrich, *Die Lage der arbeitenden Klasse in England. Nach eigener Anschauung und authentischen Quellen*, Leipzig 1845, published in: Karl Marx, Friedrich Engels, *Werke*, Vol. 2, Berlin 1969, 225–506.
Feuerbach, Paul J. A. Ritter von, *Aktenmäßige Darstellung merkwürdiger Verbrechen. Dritte Auflage mit einer Einleitung von Dr. C. A. Mittermaier*, Frankfurt a.M. 1849.
Betrachtungen über die Öffentlichkeit und Mündlichkeit der Gerechtigkeitspflege, 2 vols., Neudruck Aalen 1969 [FE 1821–1825].
Feuerbach, Paul J. A. Ritter von /Mittermaier, Carl J. A. (Eds.), *Lehrbuch des gemeinen in Deutschland gültigen peinlichen Rechts*, Gießen 1836.
Fischer, Christian A. (Ed.), *Taschenbibliothek der neuesten unterhaltendsten Reisebeschreibungen. Nach ausländischen Originalen*, 1st Year, 4th Vol., Frankfurt a.M. 1827.
(Ed.), *Taschenbibliothek der neuesten unterhaltendsten Reisebeschreibungen. Nach ausländischen Originalen*, 3rd Year, 4th Vol., Frankfurt a.M. 1829.
Freygang, Wilhelm von/Freygang, Frederika von, *Wilhelm von Freygangs Briefe über den Kaukasus und Georgien, nebst angehängtem über Persien vom Jahre 1812*, Hamburg 1817.
Frledländer, Hugo, Manolenco, der König der Diebe, in: *Interessante Kriminal-Prozesse von kulturbistorischer Bedeutung*, Vol. IX, Berlin 1920, 5–12.
Genzmer, Stephan, *Die Polizei. Polizeiverwaltung – Strafpolizei – Sicherheitspolizei – Ordnungspolizei, Handbuch der Gesetzgebung in Preußen und dem Deutschen Reiche*, Vol. 7, ed. by Hue de Grais, Berlin 1905.
Gundelin, Ein Wort zur Berichtigung der Vorstellungen über den Beruf des Vertheidigers vor dem Schwurgerichte. Von Herrn Gerichtsassessor Gundelin, Staatsanwaltsgehülfe zu Anclam, in: *Allgemeine Schwurgerichtszeitung für Deutschland und die Schweiz* 2 (1858), 1–28.
Hassenpflug, Aus den Sitzungen des Schwurgerichts zu Eschwege. Mittheilungen des Hrn. Staatsprocurator Hassenpflug, in: *Allgemeine Schwurgerichtszeitung für Deutschland und die Schweiz* 2 (1858), 151–154.
Haynau, Victor von, *Blätter aus der Mappe eines Kriminalisten.* No. 1, Marburg 1852.
Heinrichs, Emilie, Begraben und auferstanden. Kriminalnovelle aus der Gegenwart, in: *Unterhaltungs-Blatt*, 2. Juni 1877–26. Juni 1877.
Henkel, Heinrich, *Bemerkenswerte Rechtsfälle, Entscheidungen und andere Mitteilungen aus der kurhessischen Rechtspflege*, Vol. 1, Kassel 1838.

Hepp, Rückblick auf die Strafproceßgesetzgebung der letzten fünf Jahre vor Einführung der Geschworenengerichte in Deutschland. Vom weiland Professor Dr. Hepp, in: *Der Gerichtssaal* 3 (1851), No. 2, 271–295; 507–543.

Heuser, Otto L. (Ed.), *Bemerkenswerthe Entscheidungen des Criminal-Senats des Ober-Appelationsgerichts zu Cassel*, Vols. 1–6, Cassel 1845–1853.

Bemerkenswerthe Entscheidungen aus dem Criminalprozesse, in: Otto L. Heuser (Ed.), *Bemerkenswerthe Entscheidungen des Criminal-Senates des Ober-Appellations-Gerichtes zu Cassel*, Vol. 4, Cassel 1849, 173–333.

Systematisches Handbuch des Kurhessischen Straf- und Polizei-Rechtes. Mit Einschluß der noch gültigen Strafbestimmungen des älteren Fuldaer, Hanauer, Mainzer, Isenburger und Schaumburger Rechtes und der Praxis des Ober-Appellations-Gerichtes u.s.w., Cassel 1853.

Hildebrandt, Bruno, *Statistische Mittheilungen über die volkwirtschaftichen Zustände Kurhessens nach amtlichen Quellen*, Berlin 1853.

Hinchius, Paul, Uebersicht über die Justizgesetzgebung in den neuen Provinzen, in: *Zeitschrift für Gesetzgebung und Rechtspflege in Preußen* (1867), 620–628.

Hoegel, Hugo, Die Straffälligkeit des Weibes, in: *Archiv für Kriminal-Anthropologie und Kriminalistik* 5 (1900), 231–289.

Imhof, Arthur E., *Historische Demographie als Sozialgeschichte. Gießen und Umgebung vom 17. zum 19. Jahrhundert*, Vol. 2, Darmstadt 1975.

Jagemann, Ludwig von, *Handbuch der gerichtlichen Untersuchungskunde*, Vol. 1: *Die Theorie der Untersuchungskunde*, Frankfurt a.M. 1838.

Handbuch der gerichtlichen Untersuchungskunde, Vol. 2: *Die Pragmatik der Untersuchungskunde in 344 actenmäßigen Beispielen: nebst drei Steindrucktafeln*, Frankfurt a.M. 1841.

Der Uebergang vom alten zum neuen Rechte. Zugleich als Prospect der Zeitschrift, in: *Der Gerichtssaal* 1 (1849), No. 1, 3–16.

Die Anforderungen der Neuzeit an den Richterstand, in: *Der Gerichtssaal* 2 (1850), No. 1, 45–63.

Jagemann, Ludwig von /Brauer, Wilhelm (Eds.), *Criminallexikon. Nach dem neuesten Stande der Gesetzgebung in Deutschland*, Erlangen 1854.

Jäger, Bemerkungen für die Gesetzgebung und Praxis des Strafverfahrens. Vom Herrn Kanzleirath Jäger in Tübingen, in: *Hitzigs Annalen der deutschen und ausländischen Criminalrechtspflege,* N.S. 40 (1855), No. 1, 1–14; 101–116.

Jäger, Markus, Ueber die Bestrafung des dritten Diebstahl in Kurhessen, in: *Zeitschrift für Gesetzgebung und Rechtspflege des Kurfürstenthums und Großherzogthums Hessen und der freien Stadt Frankfurt* 1 (1834), 311–326.

Criminalrechtsfälle, das Verbrechen der Blutschande betr., in: *Zeitschrift für Gesetzgebung und Rechtspflege* 1 (1834), 507–512.

Jannasch, (Gemeinrechtliche) Practische Erörterung einiger Doctrinen aus dem Kapitel vom Diebstahl. Vertheidigungsschrift vom Reg.-Adv. Dr. jur. Jannasch zu Köthen, in: *Hitzigs Annalen der deutschen und ausländischen Criminalrechtspflege* 1, N.S. [Old 31] (1845), 288–300.

Jannasch, Vertheidigungsschrift für die Dienstmagd Sophie Lehmann von hier, wegen verübten Diebstahls. Vom Regierungsadvocaten Herrn Dr. jur. Jannasch zu Köthen, in: *Hitzigs Annalen der deutschen und ausländischen Criminalrechtspflege* 15, N.S. [Old 45] (1848), 146–161.

Friedreich, Johann B., *System der gerichtlichen Psychologie für Gerichtsärzte, Richter und Vertheidiger*, 3rd edition, Regensburg 1852.

Kersting, Hermann, *Das Strafrecht und das Strafverfahren in Kurhessen. Das Strafrecht in Kurhessen*, Vol. 1, Rinteln 1853.

Kleist, Heinrich von, *Michael Kohlhaas. Historische Erzählung*, Berlin 1873.

Koch, Wilhelm, *Die Strafmaas-Praxis des Criminal- und des Schwurgerichts zu Cassel insbesondere in Diebstahlsfällen*, Cassel 1855.

Köhler, Manfred, *Die nationale Petitionsbewegung zu Beginn der Revolution 1848 in Hessen. Eingaben an das Vorparlament und an den Fünfzigerausschuß aus Hessen (März bis Mai 1848)*, Darmstadt 1985.

Krafft-Ebing, Richard von, *Lehrbuch der gerichtlichen Psychopathologie mit Berücksichtigung der Gesetzgebung von Oesterreich, Deutschland und Frankreich*, Stuttgart 1875.

Landau, Georg, *Beschreibung des Kurfürstenthums Hessen*, Kassel 1842.

Lichtenberg, Das schwurgerichtliche Verfahren im Königreich Hannover im Jahr 1851. Nach dem vom O.-J.-R. Lichtenberg an das f. hann. Justizministerium erstatteten Berichte, in: *Hitzigs Annalen der deutschen und ausländischen Criminalrechtspflege* 30 (1852), 94–104, cited as: Lichtenberg, 1852.

Hofrath und Justizamtmann Lucius, Grundzüge des königlich sächsischen Entwurfs einer Criminalproceß-Ordnung, in: *Zeitschrift für deutsches Strafverfahren* 3 (1843), 259–296.

Marx, Karl, *Das Kapital. Kritik der politischen Ökonomie*, Vol. 1, Buch 1: *Der Produktionsprozeß des Kapitals (*Karl Marx, Friedrich Engels, *Werke*, Vol. 23), Berlin 1962.

Das Kapital. Kritik der politischen Ökonomie, Vol. 4: *Theorien über den Mehrwert* (Karl Marx, Friedrich Engels, *Werke*, Vol. 26), Berlin 1965.

Verhandlungen des 6. Rheinischen Landtags. Von einem Rheinländer. Dritter Artikel. Debatten über das Holzdiebstahls-Gesetz. veröffentlicht in der Rheinischen Zeitung Nr. 298 vom 25. Oktober 1842, Beiblatt, in: Karl Marx, Friedrich Engels, *Werke*, Vol. 1, Berlin 1975, 199–236.

Mayr, Georg von, *Statistik der gerichtlichen Polizei im Königreiche Bayern und in einigen anderen Ländern*, München 1867.

Merkel, Adolf, *Lehrbuch des Deutschen Strafrechts*, Stuttgart 1889.

Metz, Ludwig (Ed.), *Statistische Beschreibungen des Regierungs-Bezirks Cassel. Unter Benutzung amtlicher Quellen*, Cassel 1871.

Meyer, Hugo, *Lehrbuch des Deutschen Strafrechts*, Erlangen 1877.

Mittermaier, Carl J. A., Beiträge zur Lehre vom Verbrechen des Kindermordes und der Verheimlichung der Schwangerschaft, in: *Neues Archiv des Criminalrechts* 7 (1824), 1–44.

Die Polizeistrafgesetzgebung nach den neuesten Erzeugnissen, in: *Archiv des Criminalrechts*. N.S. (1848), 181–208.

Die Schwurgerichte in Deutschland. Erfahrungen über die Wirksamkeit und Gebrechen derselben mit Prüfung der Ursachen und Verbesserungsvorschlägen, in: *Allgemeine Schwurgerichtszeitung* 2 (1858), 16–28.

Der Entwurf einer Strafproceß-Ordnung für das Königreich Sachsen vom 1842, in: *Zeitschrift für deutsches Strafverfahren* 3 (1843), 297–313.

Praktische Ergebnisse der Criminalstatistik zur Aufhellung wichtiger Fragen des Strafrechts und Strafverfahrens, in: *Der Gerichtssaal* 13 (1861), 23–42.

Möller, Wilhelm, Betrachtungen über die Kosten des Strafverfahrens, mit Berücksichtigung des Kurhessischen Rechts, in: *Archiv für praktische Rechtswissenschaft* 3 (1855), 359–377.

Das Volks- und Rechtsbewußtsein der Gegenwart über Bestrafung der Verbrecher, Kassel 1857.

Mühry, Uebersicht der 1846 im Königreich Hannover zur Entscheidung gekommenen Criminal-Untersuchungen, in: *Hitzigs Annalen der deutschen und ausländischen Criminalrechtspflege* 11, N.S. [Old 41] (1847), 209–211, cited as: Mühry, 1847.

Müller, Christian F. (Ed.), *Das preußische Straf-Gesetzbuch nebst dem Einführungs-Gesetz. Mit den Notizen des Hohen Justiz-Ministerii und der beiden Kammern, und Hinweisungen auf die ältere Gesetzgebung und die früheren Entwürfe. Ein praktisches Handbuch nach den amtlichen Quellen zusammengestellt für Richter, Staats- und Rechtsanwälte sowie zum Selbststudium für Referendarien und Auskultatoren*, Berlin 1851.

Noellner, Friedrich, Eine Erinnerung an das deutsche Strafverfahren zu Ende des vorigen Jahrhunderts, als Parallele zwischen Ehemals und Jetzt, in: *Zeitschrift für deutsches Strafverfahren* 3 (1846), 145–148.

Ueber die Art der Entstehung der Protokolle im Untersuchungsverfahren, in: *Zeitschrift für deutsches Strafverfahren* 3 (1843), 314–320, cited as: Friedrich Noellner, 1843b.

Die Verhandlungen auf dem letzten kurfürstlich hessischen Landtage zu Kassel über mehrere Theile des Strafverfahrens, im Wesentlichen dargestellt und mit Bemerkungen, in: *Zeitschrift für deutsches Strafverfahren* 3 (1843), 57–84, cited as: Friedrich Noellner, 1843a.

Oelzen, F., Uebersichtliche Darstellung der Rechtspflege in Kurhessen, in: *Zeitschrift für Gesetzgebung und Rechtspflege in Preußen* 1 (1867), 8–28.

Offenbrüggen, Die Berufung auf das Rechtsbewußtsein im Volke, in: *Archiv des Criminalrechts*. N.S. (1851), 152–170.

Ortloff, Hermann, *Methodologie oder Lehre des Studiums der Rechts- und Staatswissenschaft nebst deutschen Studien- und Examensordnungen*, Braunschweig 1863.

Ottwalt, Ernst, *Denn sie wissen was sie tun. Ein deutscher Justiz-Roman*, Berlin 1931.

Planck, Johann J. W. von, *Systematische Darstellung des deutschen Strafverfahrens auf Grundlage der neueren Strafprozessordnungen seit 1848*, Göttingen 1857.

Pressel, G., *Kurzgefaßte geschichtliche Darstellung der letzten politischen Ereignisse in der Stadt Hanau von ihrem ersten Entstehen bis zur Vollendung des großen Aktes am 12. März 1848*, Hanau 1848.

Probst, Karl, *Die Entwicklung der Gerichtsverfassung und des Zivilprozesses in Kurhessen. Dargestellt nach den Landesordnungen und Gesetzen*, Halle a. S. 1911.

Raabe, Wilhelm, *Horacker*, Berlin 1876.

Radbruch, Gustav (Ed.), *Die peinliche Gerichtsordnung Karls V. von 1532*, Stuttgart 1975, cited as: Carolina.

Schettler, Die Ergebnisse der criminalstatistischen Berichte über die Etatsjahre 1845/46, 1846/47 und 1847/48, vergleichend zusammengestellt und mit Bemerkungen begleitet vom Herausgeber, in: *Hitzigs Annalen der deutschen und ausländischen Criminalrechtspflege* 16, N.S. [Old 46] (1849), 165–175, cited as: Schettler, 1849.

Schiller, Friedrich, *Der Verbrecher aus verlorener Ehre und andere Erzählungen*, Stuttgart 1999 [EA 1786].

Schlink, Erfahrungen eines Assisenpräsidenten, in: *Der Gerichtssaal* 3 (1851), No. 1, 28–45.

Scholz, Julius, *Merkwürdige Strafrechtsfälle aus mehreren Ländern Deutschlands*, 2 vols., Braunschweig 1840.

Schwenken, Carl P. T., *Darstellung der Gerichtsbarkeit und des Verfahrens der kurhessischen Polizey-Commission als Polizey-Strafgerichte*, Schmalkalden 1828.

Die Rechtsmittel in Strafsachen und das Verfahren bei deren Anwendung. Nach den Grundsätzen des kurhessischen Strafprozesses, Hanau 1834.

Seelig, F. W., *Die Staatsbehörde bei den Strafgerichten. Nach Gesetzgebung und Praxis in Kurhessen. Ein Beitrag zur Entwickelungs-Geschichte der deutschen Staatsanwaltschaft*, Kassel 1864.

Starke, Wilhelm (Ed.), *Die Ergebnisse der Strafrechtspflege im Königreiche Preussen... während des Jahres 1881*, Berlin 1883.

Verbrechen und Verbrecher in Preußen 1854–1878. Eine kulturgeschichtliche Studie, Berlin 1884.

Steinert, Wilhelm, *Nordamerika vorzüglich Texas im Jahre 1849. Reisebericht. Ein Buch für Auswanderer besonders für Auswanderungslustige*, Berlin 1850.

Sundelin, Paul, Ein Wort zur Berichtigung der Vorstellungen über den Beruf des Vertheidigers vor dem Schwurgericht, in: *Allgemeine Schwurgerichtszeitung* 2 (1858), 1–28.

Die Staats-Anwaltschaft in Deutschland. Ihre jetzige Gestalt in den deutschen Gesetzen, ihre Prinzipien und Bedürfnißfragen, Anclam 1860.

Temme, Jodocus D. H., *Die Lehre vom Diebstahl nach preußischem Rechte. Mit einem Anhange enthaltend die Bestrafung des Diebstahls nach der Praxis des Königlichen Criminal-Gerichts der Residenz Berlin*, Berlin 1840.

Die Berufung auf das Rechtsbewußtsein im Volke, in: *Archiv des Criminalrechts*. N.S. (1851), 586–602.

Deutsche Criminalgeschichten, Vols. 1–3, Leipzig 1858.

Lehrbuch des Gemeinen Deutschen Strafrechts, Stuttgart 1876.

Vortmann, Jürgen (Ed.), *Die Lebenserinnerungen des Juristen Viktor Meibom (1821–1892). Ein Juristenleben zwischen Theorie und Praxis*, Marburg 1992.

Wagner, Johann G., *Grundzüge der Gerichtsverfassung und des untergerichtlichen Verfahrens, sowohl in streitigen Civil-Sachen, als bei den Handlungen der freiwilligen Gerichtsbarkeit, in Kurhessen*, Cassel 1843.

Weech, Joseph F. von, *Reise über England und Portugal nach Brasilien*, München 1831.

Weiske, Julius, *Rechtslexicon für Juristen aller teutschen Stände enthaltend die gesamte Rechtswissenschaft*, 15 vols., Leipzig 1839–1862.

Warnkönig, Art. Eigenthum, in: Carl Welcker/Karl von Rotteck (Eds.), *Das Staats-Lexikon. Encyklopädie der sämtlichen Staatswisenschaften für alle Stände*, Vol. 4, 3rd edition, Leipzig 1860, 741–768.

Welcker, Carl, Art. Jury, in: Carl Welcker/Karl von Rotteck (Eds.), *Das Staats-Lexikon. Encyklopädie der sämtlichen Staatswissenschaften für alle Stände*, Vol. 7, 2nd edition, Altona 1847, 687–793.

Werthauer, J[ohannes], *Moabitrium. Szenen aus der Großstadtstrafrechtspflege*, Berlin 1908.

Zachariae, Heinrich A., *Grundlinien des gemeinen deutschen Criminalprocesses*, Göttingen 1837.

Handbuch des deutschen Strafprozesses. Systematische Darstellung des auf den Quellen des gemeinen Rechts und der neuern deutschen Gesetzgebung beruhenden Criminal-Verfahrens, in wissenschaftlicher Begründung und Verbindung, Vol. 2, Göttingen 1868.

Zedler, Johann Heinrich, *Grosses vollständiges Universal-Lexikon*, Graz 1961–1964 [FE 1732 –1754].

Zimmermann, Carl W., *Die Diebe in Berlin oder Darstellung ihres Entstehens, ihrer Organisation ihrer Verbindungen, ihrer Taktik, ihrer Gewohnheiten und ihrer Sprache. Zur Belehrung für Polizeibeamte und zur Warnung für das Publikum*, 2 vols., Berlin 1847.

Zimmermann, Gustav, *Die deutsche Polizei im neunzehnten Jahrhundert*, Vol. 3, Hannover 1849.

Wesen, Geschichte, Literatur, characteristische Thätigkeiten und Organisation der modernen Polizei. Ein Leitfaden für Polizisten und Juristen, Hannover 1852.

Zola, Emile, *Therese Raquin*: Novel. Translated by Ernst Hardt. With an afterword by Hellmuth Petriconi, Frankfurt a.M. – Hamburg 1960 [FE 1867].

SECONDARY LITERATURE

Aleck, Jonathan/Sack, Peter (Eds.), *Law and Anthropology*, New York 1992.

Ambroise-Rendu, Anne-Claude, La délinquance mineure dans les récits de faits divers. Une spécialité de la presse provinciale?, in: Benoît Garnot (Ed.), *La petite délinquance du Moyen Age à l'époque contemporaine. Actes du colloque de Dijon 9 & 10 octobre 1997*, Dijon 1998, 91–100.

Amrhein, Fritz, *Die Entwicklung des hessischen Strafprozeßrechts im 18. und 19. Jahrhundert*, Würzburg 1955.

Appadurai, Arjun (Ed.), *The Social Life of Things. Commodities in Cultural Perspective*, Cambridge 1986.

Arends, Gerald/Klippel, Diethelm, Die juristischen Zeitschriften im 19. Jahrhundert. Beobachtungen zu den juristischen Periodika in der Zeitschriftenbibliographie von Joachim Kirchner, in: Michael Stolleis (Ed.), *Juristische*

Zeitschriften. Die neuen Medien des 18.–20. Jahrhunderts, Frankfurt a.M. 1999, 41–52.

Armbrüster, Klaus, *Die Entwicklung der Verteidigung in Strafsachen. Ein rechtsgeschichtlicher Beitrag von den Anfängen einer Verteidigertätigkeit in Deutschland bis zum Ende der Weimarer Zeit*, Berlin 1980.

Arnsberg, Paul, *Die jüdischen Gemeinden in Hessen*, Vol. 2: *Anfang, Untergang, Neubeginn*, Frankfurt a.M. 1972.

Artières, Philippe, *Le livre des vies coupables. Autobiographies de criminels (1896–1909)*, Paris 2000.

Barkai, Avraham, *Jüdische Minderheit und Industrialisierung. Demographie, Berufe und Einkommen der Juden in Westdeutschland 1850–1914*, Tübingen 1988.

Barthes, Roland, Structure du fait divers, in: Roland Barthes (Ed.), *Essais critiques*, Vol. 1, Paris 1964, 188–197.

Bausinger, Hermann, Sprachschranken vor Gericht, in: Konrad Köstlin/Kai D. Sievers (Eds.), *Das Recht der kleinen Leute. Beiträge zur rechtlichen Volkskunde, Festschrift für Karl-Sigismund Kramer zum 60. Geburtstag*, Berlin 1976, 12–27.

Beck, Gustav, *Hessen-Kassels Polizei und Gendarmerie 1331–1931*, Leipzig 1931.

Beck, Rainer, *Unterfinning. Ländliche Welt vor Anbruch der Moderne*, München 1993.

Becker, Peter, Randgruppen im Blickfeld der Polizei. Ein Versuch über die Perspektivität des »praktischen Blicks«, in: *Archiv für Sozialgeschichte* 32 (1992), 283–304, cited as: Peter Becker, 1992a.

Vom »Haltlosen« zur »Bestie«. Das polizeiliche Bild des »Verbrechers« im 19. Jahrhundert, in: Alf Lüdtke (Ed.), *»Sicherheit« und »Wohlfahrt«. Polizei, Gesellschaft und Herrschaft im 19. und 20. Jahrhundert*, Frankfurt a.M. 1992, 97–131, cited as: Peter Becker, 1992b.

Kriminelle Identitäten im 19. Jahrhundert. Neue Entwicklungen in der historischen Kriminalitätsforschung, in: *Historische Anthropologie* 2 (1994), No. 1, 142–157.

Von der Biographie zur Genealogie. Zur Vorgeschichte der Kriminologie als Wissenschaft und diskursive Praxis, in: Hans E. Bödeker/Peter H. Reill/Jürgen Schlumbohm (Eds.), *Wissenschaft als kulturelle Praxis 1750–1900*, Göttingen 1999, 335–375.

The Standardized Gaze. The Standardization of the Search Warrant in Nineteenth-Century Germany, in: Jane Caplan/John Torpey (Eds.), *Documenting Individual Identity. The Development of State Practices in the Modern World*, Princeton 2001, 139–163, cited as: Peter Becker, 2001b.

Überlegungen zu einer Kulturgeschichte der Verwaltung, in: *Jahrbuch für europäische Verwaltungsgeschichte* 15 (2001), 311–336, cited as: Peter Becker, 2001a.

Verderbnis und Entartung. Eine Geschichte der Kriminologie des 19. Jahrhunderts als Diskurs und Praxis, Göttingen 2002.

»Recht schreiben« – Disziplin, Sprachbeherrschung und Vernunft. Zur Kunst des Protokollierens im 18. und 19. Jahrhundert, in: Michael

Niehaus/Hans-Walter Schmidt-Hannisa (Eds.), *Das Protokoll. Kulturelle Funktionen einer Textsorte*, Frankfurt a.M. 2005, 50–76.

Becker, Peter /Clark, William (Eds.), *Little Tools of Knowledge. Historical Essays on Academic and Bureaucratic Practices*, Ann Arbor 2001, cited as: Peter Becker/William Clark, 2001a.

Introduction, in: Peter Becker/William Clark (Eds.), *Little Tools of Knowledge. Historical Essays on Academic and Bureaucratic Practices*, Ann Arbor 2001, 1–34, cited as: Peter Becker/William Clark, 2001b.

Below, Stefan von, Das Eigentum am Wald – ein Forschungsüberblick, in: Stefan von Below/Stefan Breit (Eds.), *Wald – Von der Gottesgabe zum Privateigentum. Gerichtliche Konflikte zwischen Landesherren und Untertanen um den Wald in der frühen Neuzeit*, Stuttgart 1998, 1–29.

Benton, Lauren A., *Law and Colonial Cultures. Legal Regimes in World History 1400–1900*, Cambridge 2002.

Bernstein, Basil, *Studien zur sprachlichen Sozialisation*, Düsseldorf 1972.

Bettenhäuser, Hermann, Die Entwicklung des Gerichtswesens in Hessen, in: *Justiz-Ministerial-Blatt für Hessen* 16 (1964), No. 7, 51–62.

Bildstein, Jakob G., Liste von wichtigeren Amtsblättern und Gesetzessammlungen der oberen Verwaltungsbehörden aus dem 18. und der ersten Hälfte des 19. Jahrhunderts, in: *Mitteilungen für die landschaftliche Archivpflege* 12 (1950), 291–301.

Björner, Ulf, *Die Verfassungsgerichtsbarkeit im Norddeutschen Bund und Deutschen Kaiserreich (1867–1918). Eine rechtshistorische Untersuchung über Gerichtsbarkeit im Spannungsfeld von Politik und Recht innerhalb der von Bismarck geschaffenen deutschen Bundesstaaten*, Frankfurt a.M. 2000.

Blaschke, Olaf (Ed.), *Konfessionen im Konflikt. Deutschland zwischen 1800 und 1970: ein zweites konfessionelles Zeitalter*, Göttingen 2002.

Blasius, Dirk, Der Kampf um die Geschworenengerichte im Vormärz, in: Hans-Ulrich Wehler (Ed.), *Sozialgeschichte heute. Festschrift für Hans Rosenberg zum 70. Geburtstag*, Göttingen 1974, 148–162.

Eigentum und Strafe. Probleme der preußischen Kriminalitäts- und Strafrechtsentwicklung im Vormärz, in: *Historische Zeitschrift* 220 (1975), 79–129.

Bürgerliche Gesellschaft und Kriminalität. Zur Sozialgeschichte Preußens im Vormärz, Göttingen 1976.

Kriminalität und Alltag. Zur Konfliktgeschichte des Alltagslebens im 19. Jahrhundert, Göttingen 1978.

»Diebeshandwerk« und »Widerspruchsgeist«. Motive des Verbrechens im 19. Jahrhundert, in: Richard van Dülmen (Ed.), *Verbrechen, Strafen und soziale Kontrolle. Studien zur historischen Kulturforschung*, Frankfurt a.M. 1990, 215–237.

Blauert, Andreas/Schwerhoff, Gerd (Eds.), *Kriminalitätsgeschichte. Beiträge zur Sozial- und Kulturgeschichte der Vormoderne*, Konstanz 2000.

Blauert, Andreas/Wiebel, Eva, *Gauner- und Diebslisten. Registrieren, Identifizieren und Fahnden im 18. Jahrhundert*, Frankfurt a.M. 2001.

Bleek, Wilhelm, *Von der Kameralausbildung zum Juristenprivileg. Studium, Prüfung und Ausbildung der höheren Beamten des allgemeinen Verwaltungsdienstes in Deutschland im 18. und 19. Jahrhundert*, Berlin 1972.

Bödeker, Hans E., On the Origins of the »Statistical Gaze«. Modes of Perception, Forms of Knowledge, and Ways of Writing in the Early Social Sciences, in: Peter Becker/William Clark (Eds.), *Little Tools of Knowledge. Historical Essays on Academic and Bureaucratic Practices*, Ann Arbor 2001, 169–195.

Bohmbach, Jürgen, Die Hungerjahre 1846/47 in *Oberhessen, in: Hessisches Jahrbuch für Landesgeschichte* 23 (1973), 333–365.

Bonß, Wolfgang, *Die Einübung des Tatsachenblicks. Zur Struktur und Veränderung empirischer Sozialforschung*, Frankfurt a.M. 1982.

Bösch, Frank, Zeitungsberichte im Alltagsgespräch. Mediennutzung, Medienwirkung und Kommunikation im Kaiserreich, in: *Publizistik. Vierteljahresheft für Kommunikationsforschung* 49 (2003), No. 3, 319–336.

Bourdieu, Pierre, La force du droit. Éléments pour une sociologie du champ juridique, in: *Actes de la recherche en sciences sociales* 64 (1986), 3–19.

Habitus, code et codification, in: *Actes de la recherche en sciences sociales* 64 (1986), 40–44.

Brakensiek, Stefan, *Fürstendiener – Staatsbeamte – Bürger. Amtsführung und Lebenswelt der Ortsbeamten in niederhessischen Kleinstädten (1750–1830)*, Göttingen 1999.

Brewer, John, Was können wir aus der Geschichte der frühen Neuzeit für die moderne Konsumgeschichte lernen?, in: Hannes Siegrist/Hartmut Kaelble/Jürgen Kocka (Eds.), *Europäische Konsumgeschichte. Zur Gesellschafts- und Kulturgeschichte des Konsums (18. bis 20. Jahrhundert)*, Frankfurt a. M. – New York 1997, 51–74.

Brewer, John/Staves, Susan (Eds.), *Early Modern Conceptions of Property*, London 1995, cited as: John Brewer/Susan Staves, 1995a.

Introduction, in: John Brewer/Susan Staves (Eds.), *Early Modern Conceptions of Property*, London 1995, 1–18, cited as: John Brewer/Susan Staves, 1995b.

Bullik, Manfred, *Staat und Gesellschaft im hessischen Vormärz. Wahlrecht, Wahlen und öffentliche Meinung in Kurhessen 1830–1848*, Köln – Wien 1972.

Burghartz, Susanna, Jungfräulichkeit oder Reinheit? Zur Änderung von Argumentationsmustern vor dem Baseler Ehegericht im 16. und 17. Jahrhundert, in: Richard van Dülmen (Ed.), *Dynamik der Tradition. Studien zur historischen Kulturforschung*, Frankfurt a.M. 1992, 13–40.

Castan, Yves, Dissuasion de violence et vol de rétorsion dans le Languedoc du XVIIIe siècle, in: Maria Pia di Bella (Ed.), *Vols et sanctions en Méditerranée*, Amsterdam 1998, 75–92.

Castells, Manuel/Portes, Alejandro, World Underneath. The Origins, Dynamics, and Effects of the Informal Economy, in: Lauren Benton/Manuel Castells/Alejandro Portes (Ed.), *The Informal Economy. Studies in Advanced and Less Developed Countries*, Baltimore 1991, 11–40.

Cerutti, Simona, Normes et pratiques, ou de la légitimité de leur opposition, in: Bernard Lepetit (Ed.), *Les formes de l'expérience. Une autre histoire sociale*, Paris 1995, 127–149.

Nature des choses et qualité des personnes. Le Consulat de commerce de Turin au XVIIIe siècle, in: *Annales* 57 (2002), No. 6, 1491–1520.

Chauvaud, Frédéric, La petite délinquance et La Gazette des Tribunaux. Le fait-chronique entre la farce et la fable, in: Benoît Garnot (Ed.), *La petite délinquance du Moyen Age à l'époque contemporaine. Actes du colloque de Dijon 9 & 10 octobre 1997*, Dijon 1998, 79–89.

Chauvaud, Frédéric /Yvorel, Jean-Jacques, *Histoire de la carte judiciaire [Texte imprimé]. L'organisation judiciaire entre les pouvoirs, les savoirs et les discours (1790–1930)*, Nanterre 1994.

Le juge, le tribun et le comptable. Histoire de l'organisation judiciaire entre les pouvoirs, les savoirs et les discours (1789–1930), Paris 1995.

avec la collaboration de Laurence Dumolín, *Experts et expertises judiciaires en France. France XIXe et XXe siècles*, Rennes 2003.

Chmielewski, Alexandra, Auf dem Weg zum Experten. Die Herausbildung des psychiatrischen Berufsstandes in Süddeutschland (1800 bis 1860), in: Helmut Berding/Diethelm Klippel/Günther Lottes (Eds.), *Kriminalität und abweichendes Verhalten. Deutschland im 18. und 19. Jahrhundert*, Göttingen 1999, 105–140.

Cole, Simon A., *Suspect Identities. A History of Fingerprinting and Criminal Identifikation*, Cambridge 2001.

Collier, Jane F./Starr, June (Eds.), *History and Power in the Study of Law. New Directions in Legal Anthropolgy*, Ithaca – London 1989.

Collin, Peter, Der Kampf gegen die Schwurgerichte – Preußen 1849–1853/54, in: *Zeitschrift für Neuere Rechtsgeschichte* 23 (2001), No. 3/4, 195–219.

Confino, Alon, *The Nation as a Local Metaphor. Württemberg, Imperial Germany and National Memory, 1871–1918*, Chapel Hill 1997.

Corbin, Alain, *Pesthauch und Blütenduft. Eine Geschichte des Geruchs*, Berlin 1984.

Cottereau, Alain, »Esprit Public« et Capacité de Juger. La stabilisation d'un espace public en France aux lendemains de la Révolution, in: Alain Cottereau/Paul Ladrière (Eds.), *Pouvoir et Légitimité. Figures de l'espace public*, Paris 1992, 239–272.

Cottereau, Alain /Ladrière, Paul (Eds.), *Pouvoir et Légitimité. Figures de l'espace public*, Paris 1992.

Dainat, Holger, Der unglückliche Mörder. Zur Kriminalgeschichte der deutschen Spätaufklärung, in: *Zeitschrift für deutsche Philologie* 107 (1988), 517–541.

Daston, Lorraine, *Wunder, Beweise und Tatsachen. Zur Geschichte der Rationalität*, Frankfurt a.M. 2001.

Demandt, Karl E., *Schrifttum zur Geschichte und geschichtlichen Landeskunde von Hessen*, Vol. 1, Wiesbaden 1965.

Descimon, Robert/Schaub, Jean-Frédéric/Vincent, Bernard, Avant-propos, in: Robert Descimon/Jean-Frédéric Schaub/Bernard Vincent (Eds.), *Les figures de l'Administrateur. Institutions, réseaux, pouvoirs en Espagne, en France et au Portugal 16e–19e siècle*, Paris 1997, 7–16.

Dietrich, Elisabeth, *Übeltäter, Bösewichter. Kriminalität und Kriminalisierung in Tirol und Vorarlberg im 19. Jahrhundert*, Innsbruck 1995.

Dilcher, Gerhard/Kern, Bernd-Rüdiger, Die juristische Germanistik des 19. Jahrhunderts und die Fachtradition der Deutschen Rechtsgeschichte, in: *Zeitschrift der Savigny-Stiftung für Rechtsgeschichte, Germanistische Abteilung* 100 (1984), 1–46.

Dinges, Martin, Frühneuzeitliche Justiz. Justizphantasien als Justiznutzung am Beispiel von Klagen bei der Pariser Polizei im 18. Jahrhundert, in: Heinz Mohnhaupt/Dieter Simon (Eds.), *Vorträge zur Justizforschung*, Vol. 1, Frankfurt a.M. 1992, 269–292.

Dinges, Martin Michel Foucault, Justizphantasien und die Macht, in: Andreas Blauert/Gerd Schwerhoff (Eds.), *Mit den Waffen der Justiz. Zur Kriminalitätsgeschichte des späten Mittelalters und der Frühen Neuzeit*, Frankfurt a.M. 1993, 189–212.

Ditte, Catherine, La mise en scène dans la plainte. Sa stratégie sociale. L'exemple de l'honneur populaire, in: *Droit et Cultures. Revue semestrielle d'anthropologie et d'histoire* 19 (1990), 23–48.

Döcker, Ulrike, Das gelebte Pathos. Bürgerliche Männlichkeitsideale und Männerpraktiken in der (Berufs-)Welt von Advokaten, in: Margret Friedrich/Peter Urbanitsch (Eds.), *Von Bürgern und ihren Frauen*, Wien 1996, 95–121.

Douglas, Mary/Isherwood, Baron, *The World of Goods*, New York 1979.

Edler, Erich, *Die Anfänge des sozialen Romans und der sozialen Novelle in Deutschland*, Frankfurt a.M. 1977.

Eibach, Joachim, *Der Staat vor Ort. Amtmänner und Bürger im 19. Jahrhundert am Beispiel Badens*, Frankfurt a.M.,New York 1994.

Kriminalitätsgeschichte zwischen Sozialgeschichte und historischer Kulturforschung, in: *Historische Zeitschrift* **263** (1996), 681–715.

Frankfurter Verhöre. Städtische Lebenswelten und Kriminalität im 18. Jahrhundert, Paderborn 2003.

Evans, Richard J. (Ed.), *Kneipengespräche im Kaiserreich. Stimmungsberichte der Hamburger Politischen Polizei 1892–1914*, Reinbek bei Hamburg 1989.

Rituale der Vergeltung. Die Todesstrafe in der deutschen Geschichte 1532–1987, Berlin 2001.

Evans, Richard J. /Lee, William R. (Eds.), *The German Peasantry. Conflict and Community in Rural Society from the Eighteenth to the Twentieth Centuries*, London 1986.

Farge, Arlette, *Dire et mal dire. L'opinion publique au XIIIe siècle*, Paris 1992.

Farge, Arlette /Foucault, Michel, *Le désordre des familles. Lettres de cachet des Archives de la Bastille*, Paris 1982.

Farr, Ian, Tradition and Peasantry: On the Modern Historiography of Rural Germany, in: Richard J. Evans/William R. Lee (Eds.), *The German Peasantry. Conflict and Community in Rural Society from the Eighteenth to the Twentieth Centuries*, London 1986, 1–36.

Fehrenbach, Elisabeth, *Der Kampf um die Einführung des Code Napoléon in den Rheinbundstaaten*, Wiesbaden 1973.

Felman, Shoshana, Forms of Judicial Blindness. Traumatic Narratives and Legal Repetitions, in: Austin Sarat/Thomas R. Kearns (Eds.), *History, Memory and the Law*, Michigan 1999, 25–94.

Fögen, Marie T., *Der Kampf um Gerichtsöffentlichkeit*, Berlin 1974.

Fontaine, Laurence/Schlumbohm, Jürgen (Eds.), *Household Strategies for Survival, 1600–2000. Fission, Faction and Cooperation*, Cambridge 2000.

Ford, Caroline, Story-Telling and the Social Imagery of Religious Conflict in Nineteenth-Century French Law Courts, in: Peter R. Coss (Ed.), *The*

Moral World of the Law, Cambridge – New York – Melbourne 2000, 161–177.

Formella, Eckhard, *Rechtsbruch und Rechtsdurchsetzung im Herzogtum Holstein um die Mitte des 19. Jahrhunderts. Ein Beitrag zum Verhältnis von Kriminalität, Gesellschaft und Staat*, Neumünster 1985.

Foucault, Michel (Ed.), *Der Fall Rivière. Materialien zum Verhältnis von Psychiatrie und Strafjustiz*, Frankfurt a.M. 1975.

Überwachen und Strafen. Die Geburt des Gefängnisses, Frankfurt a.M. 1976.

Die Wahrheit und die juristischen Formen, Frankfurt a.M. 2003.

Frank, Michael, Kriminalität, Strafrechtspflege und sozialer Wandel. Das Zuchthaus Detmold 1750–1801, in: *Westfälische Forschungen* **42** (1992), 273–308.

Ehre und Gewalt im Dorf der Frühen Neuzeit. Das Beispiel Heiden (Grafschaft Lippe) im 17. und 18. Jahrhundert, in: Klaus Schreiner/Gerd Schwerhoff (Eds.), *Verletzte Ehre. Ehrkonflikte in Gesellschaften des Mittelalters und der Frühen Neuzeit*, Köln 1995, 320–338, cited as: Michael Frank, 1995a.

Dörfliche Gesellschaft und Kriminalität. Das Fallbeispiel Lippe 1650–1800, Paderborn 1995, cited as: Michal Frank, 1995b.

Frevert, Ute, *Ehrenmänner. Das Duell in der bürgerlichen Gesellschaft*, München 1991.

Frey, Manuel, *Der reinliche Bürger. Entstehung und Verbreitung bürgerlicher Tugenden in Deutschland 1760–1860*, Göttingen 1997.

Frey, Dennis A., Jr., Industrious Households. Survival Strategies of Artisans in a Southwest German Town during the Eighteenth and Early Nineteenth Centuries, in: Laurence Fontaine/Jürgen Schlumbohm (Eds.), *Household Strategies for Survival, 1600–2000. Fission, Faction and Cooperation*, Cambridge 2000, 115–135.

Friedeburg, Robert von, *Ländliche Gesellschaft und Obrigkeit. Gemeindeprotest und politische Mobilisierung im 18. und 19. Jahrhundert*, Göttingen 1997.

Frommel, Monika, Strafjustiz und Polizei. Muß man die Strafrechtsgeschichte vom Kopf auf die Füße stellen?, in: Dieter Simon (Ed.), *Akten des 26. Deutschen Rechtshistorikertages*, Frankfurt a.M. 1987, 169–196.

Fuchs, Ralf-Peter, *Um die Ehre. Westfälische Beleidigungsprozesse vor dem Reichskammergericht 1525–1805*, Paderborn 1999.

Funk, Albrecht, *Polizei und Rechtsstaat. Die Entwicklung des staatlichen Gewaltmonopols in Preußen 1848–1918*, Frankfurt a.M. 1986.

Die Entstehung der modernen Polizei in Preußen 1870–1890. Bezugspunkte einer historischen Polizeianalyse, in: Herbert Reinke (Ed.), *»... nur für die Sicherheit da...«? Zur Geschichte der Polizei im 19. und 20. Jahrhundert*, Frankfurt a.M. 1993, 56–70.

Funk, Albrecht /Pütter, Norbert, Polizei und Miliz als »Bürgerorgane«, in: Alf Lüdtke (Ed.), *»Sicherheit« und »Wohlfahrt«. Polizei, Gesellschaft und Herrschaft im 19. und 20. Jahrhundert*, Frankfurt a.M. 1992, 37–64.

Galassi, Silviana, *Kriminologie im Deutschen Kaiserreich. Geschichte einer gebrochenen Verwissenschaftlichung*, Stuttgart 2004.

Garnot, Benoît, La perception des délinquants en France du XIVe aus XIXe siècle, in: *Revue historique* 120 (1996), No. 2, 349–363.

(Ed.), *Juges, notaires et policiers délinquants. XIVe–XXe siècle*, Bourgogne 1997.

(Ed.), *De la déviance à la délinquence (XVe–XXe siècle)*, Dijon 1999.

Geisel, Karl, Die kurhessischen Petitionen an die Frankfurter Nationalversammlung 1848/49, in: *Zeitschrift des Vereins für hessische Geschichte und Landeskunde* 81 (1970), 119–179.

Gerhard, Ute (Ed.), *Frauen in der Geschichte des Rechts. Von der Frühen Neuzeit bis zur Gegenwart*, München 1997.

Ginzburg, Carlo, *Der Käse und die Würmer. Die Welt eines Müllers um 1600*, Frankfurt a.M. 1979.

Gleixner, Ulrike, *»Das Mensch« und »der Kerl«. Die Konstruktion von Geschlecht in Unzuchtsverfahren der Frühen Neuzeit (1700–1760)*, Frankfurt a.M. 1994.

Geschlechterdifferenzen und die Faktizität des Fiktionalen. Zur Dekonstruktion frühneuzeitlicher Verhörprotokolle, in: *WerkstattGeschichte* 11 (1995), 65–70, cited as: Ulrike Gleixner, 1995a.

Das Gesamtgericht der Herrschaft Schulenburg im 18. Jahrhundert. Funktionsweise und Zugang von Frauen und Männern, in: Jan Peters (Ed.), *Gutsherrschaft als soziales Modell. Vergleichende Betrachtungen zur Funktionsweise frühneuzeitlicher Agrargesellschaften*, München 1995, 301–326, cited as: Ulrike Gleixner, 1995b.

Goldberg, Ann, Institutionalizing Female Sexual Deviancy. Women, Rural Society, and the Insane Asylum in Nassau, 1815–1849, in: Reinhard Blänkner/Bernhard Jussen (Eds.), *Institutionen und Ereignis. Über historische Praktiken und Vorstellungen gesellschaftlichen Ordnens*, Göttingen 1998, 275–293.

The Mellage Trial and the Politics of Insane Asylums in Wilhelmine Germany, in: *The Journal of Modern History* 74 (2002), No. 1, 1–33.

Göttsch, Silke, Zur Konstruktion schichtenspezifischer Wirklichkeitsstrategien und Taktiken ländlicher Unterschichten vor Gericht, in: Brigitte Bönisch-Brednich/Rolf Wilhelm Brednich/Helge Gerndt (Eds.), *Erinnern und Vergessen. Vorträge des 27. Deutschen Volkskundekongresses Göttingen 1989*, Göttingen 1991, 443–452.

»nachdem das Gerücht überall gegangen...«. Sprechen über Kriminalität in der ländlichen Gesellschaft des 18. Jahrhunderts, in: Burkhard Pöttler/Helmut Eberhart/Elisabeth Katschnig-Fasch (Eds.), *Innovation und Wandel. Festschrift für Oskar Moser zum 80. Geburtstag*, Graz 1994, 159–164.

Gowing, Laura, Gender and the Language of Insult in Early Modern London, in: *History Workshop Journal* 35 (1993), 1–21.

Graf, Klaus, Das leckt die Kuh nicht ab. »Zufällige Gedanken« zu Schriftlichkeit und Erinnerungskultur der Strafgerichtsbarkeit, in: Andreas Blauert/Gerd Schwerhoff (Eds.), *Kriminalitätsgeschichte. Beiträge zur Sozial- und Kulturgeschichte der Vormoderne*, Konstanz 2000, 245–288.

Graff, Helmut, *Die deutsche Kriminalstatistik. Geschichte und Gegenwart*, Stuttgart 1975.

Greve, Ylva, Richter und Sachverständige. Der Kompetenzstreit über die Beurteilung der Unzurechnungsfähigkeit im Strafprozeß des 19. Jahrhunderts, in: Helmut Berding/Diethelm Klippel/Günther Lottes (Eds.), *Kriminalität und abweichendes Verhalten. Deutschland im 18. und 19. Jahrhundert*, Göttingen 1999, 69–104.

Naturrecht und »Criminalpsychologie«, in: *Zeitschrift für Neuere Rechtsgeschichte* 22 (2000), No. 3/4, 69–94.

Griesebner, Andrea, *Konkurrierende Wahrheiten. Malefizprozesse vor dem Landgericht Perchtoldsdorf im 18. Jahrhundert*, Köln – Weimar – Wien 2000.

Grindel, Susanne, Disziplinierung und Integration. Zur öffentlichen Armenfürsorge im 19. Jahrhundert am Beispiel des Kurfürstentums Hessen, in: *Hessisches Jahrbuch für Landesgeschichte* 44 (1994), 91–113.

Armenpolitik und Staatlichkeit. Das öffentliche Armenwesen im Kurfürstentum Hessen (1803–1866), Darmstadt 2000.

Gugerli, David/Speich, Daniel, *Topografien der Nation. Politik, kartografische Ordnung und Landschaft im 19. Jahrhundert*, Zürich 2002.

Guillais, Joelle, *Crimes of Passion. Dramas of Private Life in Nineteenth Century France*, Cambridge 1990.

Haas, Stefan, *Die permanente Reform. Medialisierung von Herrschaft im Vollzug der preußischen Reformen in der ersten Hälfte des 19. Jahrhunderts*, Habilitationsschrift Münster 2004.

Die Kultur der Verwaltung. Die Umsetzung der preußischen Reformen 1800–1848, Münster 2005.

Haber, Günter, Probleme der Strafprozeßgeschichte im Vormärz, in: *Zeitschrift für die gesamte Strafrechtswissenschaft* 91 (1979), 590–638, cited as: Günter Haber, 1979a.

Strafgerichtliche Öffentlichkeit und öffentlicher Ankläger in der französischen Aufklärung mit einem Ausblick auf die Gesetzgebung der Konstituante, Berlin 1979, cited as: Günter Haber, 1979b.

Habermas, Rebekka, *Frauen und Männer des Bürgertums. Eine Familiengeschichte (1750–1850)*, Göttingen 2000.

Von Anselm von Feuerbach zu Jack the Ripper. Recht und Kriminalität im 19. Jahrhundert. Ein Literaturbericht, in: *Rechtsgeschichte. Zeitschrift des Max-Planck-Instituts für europäische Rechtsgeschichte* 3 (2003), 128–163.

Habermas, Rebekka/Hommen, Tanja (Eds.), *Das Frankfurter Gretchen. Der Prozeß gegen die Kindsmörderin Susanna Margaretha Brandt*, München 1999.

Habermas, Tilmann, *Geliebte Objekte. Symbole und Instrumente der Identitätsbildung*, Frankfurt a.M. 1999.

Hann, Christopher M., Introduction. The Embeddedness of Property, in: Christopher M. Hann (Ed.), *Property Relations. Renewing the Anthropological Tradition*, New York – Cambridge 1998, 1–47.

(Ed.), *Property Relations. Renewing the Anthropological Tradition*, New York – Cambridge 1998.

Harris, Ruth, Melodrama, Hysteria, and Feminine Crimes of Passion in the Fin de Siècle, in: *History Workshop Journal* 25 (1988), 31–63.

Murders and Madness. Medicine, Law and Society in the Fin de siècle, Oxford 1991.

Härter, Karl, Zum Verhältnis von »Rechtsquellen« und territorialen Rahmenbedingungen in der Strafgerichtsbarkeit des 18. Jahrhunderts. Vagabondage und Diebstahl in der Entscheidungspraxis der Kurmainzer Landesregierung, in: Harriet Rudolph/Helga Schnabel-Schüle (Eds.), *Justiz = Justice = Justicia? Rahmenbedingungen von Strafjustiz im frühneuzeitlichen Europa*, Trier 2003, 433–465.

Härter, Karl /Schilling, Lothar/Stolleis, Michael (Eds.), *Policey im Europa der Frühen Neuzeit*, Frankfurt a.M. 1996.

Haug, Helmut, *Die gerichtliche Voruntersuchung und die Frage ihrer Reformbedürftigkeit*, Stuttgart 1930.

Hauser, Andrea, *Dinge des Alltags. Studien zur historischen Sachkultur eines schwäbischen Dorfes*, Tübingen 1994.

Heidegger, Maria, *Soziale Dramen und Beziehungen im Dorf. Das Gericht Laudegg in der frühen Neuzeit – eine historische Ethnographie*, Innsbruck – Wien 1999.

Wir müssen es sagen, mit Freude vernahmen wir dieses gelinde Urteil. Inszenierung und Wahrnehmung von Justiz und »Gerechtigkeit« in Presseberichten über das Schwurgericht in Tirol 1850/51, in: Andrea Griesebner/Martin Scheutz/Herwig Weigl (Eds.), *Justiz und Gerechtigkeit. Historische Beiträge (16.–19. Jahrhundert)*, Innsbruck 2002, 449–467.

Hennig, Jörg, Gerichtsberichterstattung in deutschen Tageszeitungen 1850–1890, in: Jörg Schönert (Ed.), *Erzählte Kriminalität. Zur Typologie und Funktion von narrativen Darstellungen in Strafrechtspflege, Publizistik und Literatur zwischen 1770 und 1920*, Tübingen 1991, 349–367.

Henschel, Johann F., *Die Strafverteidigung im Inquisitionsprozeß des 18. und im Anklageprozeß des 19. Jahrhunderts*, Freiburg 1972.

Henze, Martina, Handlungsspielräume im Strafvollzug. Die Beschwerden von Gefangenen im hessen-darmstädtischen Zuchthaus Marienschloß 1830–1860, in: Helmut Berding/Diethelm Klippel/Günther Lottes (Eds.), *Kriminalität und abweichendes Verhalten. Deutschland im 18. und 19. Jahrhundert*, Göttingen 1999, 141–169.

Herzfeld, Michael, Le vol réciproque d'animaux en Crète. A l'intersection des idéologies, in: Maria Pia di Bella (Ed.), *Vols et sanctions en Méditerranée*, Amsterdam 1998, 199–218.

Hett, Benjamin C., *Death in the Tiergarten and Other Stories. Murder and Criminal Justice in Berlin, 1891–1933*, Diss. Phil. Harvard 2001.

The »Captain of Köpenick« and the Transformation of German Criminal Justice, 1891–1914, in: *Central European History* 36 (2003), No. 1, 1–43.

Death in the Tiergarten. Murder and Criminal Justice in the Kaiser's Berlin, Cambridge, Mass. – London 2004.

Hitzeroth, Heinz-Otto, *Die politische Presse Kurhessens 1833–1866*, München 1935.

Hobsbawm, Eric J., Social Criminality. Distinctions Between Socio-Political and other Forms of Crime, in: *Bulletin of the Society for the Study of Labour History* 25 (1972), 5–6.

Hobsbawm, Eric J. /Ranger, Terence (Eds.), *The Invention of Tradition*, Cambridge 1994.

Höck, Alfred, Gesindelöhne nach einem bäuerlichen Haus- und Rechnungsbuch, in: *Zeitschrift des Vereins für hessische Geschichte und Landeskunde* 77/78 (1966/67), 149–154.

Hodenberg, Christina von, *Die Partei der Unparteiischen. Der Liberalismus der preußischen Richterschaft 1815–1848/49*, Göttingen 1996.
Hoerner, Ludwig, »Ein königlich hannoversches ›Verbrecheralbum‹ von 1860/65«, in: *Hannoversche Geschichtsblätter*, N.S. 34 (1980), 177–182.
Hoffmann, Ludger, *Kommunikation vor Gericht*, Tübingen 1983.
Hohkamp, Michaela, *Herrschaft in der Herrschaft. Die vorderösterreichische Obervogtei Triberg von 1737 bis 1780*, Göttingen 1998.
Holenstein, André, Die Umstände der Normen – die Normen der Umstände. Policeyordnungen im kommunikativen Handeln von Verwaltung und lokaler Gesellschaft im Ancien Régime, in: Karl Härter (Ed.), *Policey und frühneuzeitliche Gesellschaft*, Frankfurt a.M. 2000, 1–46.
Holly, Günter, *Geschichte der Ehrengerichtsbarkeit der deutschen Rechtsanwälte*, Frankfurt a.M. – Bern – New York – Paris 1989.
Hörning, Karl H./Reuter, Julia (Eds.), *Doing Culture. Neue Positionen zum Verhältnis von Kultur und sozialer Praxis*, Bielefeld 2004.
Hufton, Olwen, *The Poor of Eighteenth-Century France 1750–1789*, Oxford 1974.
Hügel, Hans-Otto, *Untersuchungsrichter, Diebsfänger, Detektive. Theorie und Geschichte der deutschen Detektiverzählung im 19. Jahrhundert*, Stuttgart 1978.
Hull, Isabel, *Sexuality, State, and Civil Society in Germany, 1700–1815*, Ithaca – New York 1996.
Ignor, Alexander, *Geschichte des Strafprozesses in Deutschland 1532–1846. Von der Carolina Karls V. bis zu den Reformen des Vormärz*, Paderborn and others 2002.
Imm, Konstantin, Kaspar Hauser. Kriminalisierung und Historisierung, in: Jörg Schönert (Ed.), *Erzählte Kriminalität. Zur Typologie und Funktion von narrativen Darstellungen in Strafrechtspflege, Publizistik und Literatur zwischen 1770 und 1920*, Tübingen 1991, 449–464.
/Linder, Joachim, Verdächtige und Täter. Zuschreibung von Kriminalität in Texten der ›schönen Literatur‹ am Beispiel des Feuilletons der ›Berliner Gerichtszeitung‹, der Romanreihe ›Eisenbahn-Unterhaltungen‹ und Wilhelm Raabes ›Horacker‹ und ›Stopfkuchen‹, in: Günter Häntzschel/John Ormrod/Karl N. Renner (Eds.), *Zur Sozialgeschichte der deutschen Literatur von der Aufklärung bis zur Jahrhundertwende*. Individual studies, Tübingen 1985, 21–96.
Jäger, Jens, Photography. A Means of Surveillance? Judicial Photography, 1850 to 1900, in: *Crime, History & Societies* 5 (2001), 27–51.
Erkennungsdienstliche Behandlung. Zur Inszenierung polizeilicher Identifikationsmethoden um 1900, in: Jürgen Martschukat/Steffen Patzold (Eds.), *Geschichtswissenschaft und »performative turn«. Ritual, Inszenierung und Performanz vom Mittelalter bis zur Neuzeit*, Köln – Weimar – Wien 2003, 207–228.
Janßen, Heinrich, *Der Diebstahl in seiner Entwicklung von der Carolina bis zum Ausgang des 18. Jahrhunderts*, Göttingen 1969.
Jarausch, Konrad H., *The Unfree Professions. German Lawyers, Teachers, and Engineers 1900–1950*, New York 1990.

Jaun, Rudolf/Studer, Brigitte (Eds.), *Weiblich-männlich. Geschlechterverhältnisse in der Schweiz. Rechtsprechung, Diskurs, Praktiken – Féminin-masculin. Rapports sociaux de sexes en Suisse. Législation, discours, pratiques*, Zürich 1995.

Jauß, Hans R., *Ästhetische Erfahrung und literarische Hermeneutik*, Frankfurt a. M. 1982.

Jessen, Ralph, *Polizei im Industrierevier. Modernisierung und Herrschaftspraxis im westfälischen Ruhrgebiet 1848–1914*, Göttingen 1991.

Polizei, Wohlfahrt und die Anfänge des modernen Sozialstaates in Preußen während des Kaiserreichs, in: *Geschichte und Gesellschaft* 20 (1994), 157–180.

Preußische Polizei und Arbeiterschaft im Kaiserreich, in: Peter Nitschke (Ed.), *Die deutsche Polizei und ihre Geschichte. Beiträge zu einem distanzierten Verhältnis*, Hilden 1996, 46–71.

John, Michael, Between Estate and Profession. Lawyers and the Development of the Legal Profession in 19th Century Germany, in: David Blackbourn/Richard J. Evans (Eds.), *The German Bourgeoisie*, London 1991, 162–197.

Johnson, Eric A., Women as Victims and Criminals. Female Homicide and Criminality in Imperial Germany, 1873–1914, in: *Criminal Justice History* 6 (1985), 151–175.

Urbanisation and Crime. Germany 1871–1914, Cambridge 1995.

Joris, Elisabeth, Die geteilte Moderne. Individuelle Rechtsansprüche für Männer, ständische Abhängigkeit für Frauen, in: *Schweizerische Zeitschrift für Geschichte* 46 (1996), No. 3, 306–331.

Kalifa, Dominique, *L'encre et le sang. Récits de crimes et société à la Belle Epoque*, Paris 1995.

Karallus, Christine, Spuren, Täter, Orte. Das Berliner Verbrecheralbum von 1896 bis 1908, in: *Fotogeschichte* 18 (1998), No. 70, 45–54.

Kaschuba, Wolfgang/Lipp, Carola, *Dörfliches Überleben. Zur Geschichte materieller und sozialer Reproduktion ländlicher Gesellschaft im 19. und frühen 20. Jahrhundert*, Tübingen 1982.

Käthner, Martina, Frauen in Not. Diebstähle von Frauen und ihre Sanktionierung 1840–1850, in: Johannes Feest/Christian Marzahn (Eds.), *Criminalia. Bremer Strafjustiz 1810–1850*, Bremen 1988, 19–90.

Kaufmann, Doris, Psychiatrie und Strafjustiz im 19. Jahrhundert. Die gerichtsmedizinischen Gutachten der Medizinischen Fakultät der Universität Tübingen 1770–1860, in: *Medizin, Gesellschaft und Geschichte* 10 (1991), 23–39.

Aufklärung, bürgerliche Selbsterfahrung und die »Erfindung« der Psychiatrie in Deutschland, 1770–1850, Göttingen 1995.

Keller, Otfried, *Die Gerichtsorganisation des Raumes Marburg im 19. und 20. Jahrhundert*, Marburg 1982.

Kellner, Wolf E., Das Oberappellationsgericht zu Kassel als Kurhessischer Strafgerichtshof (1831–1866), in: *Justiz-Ministerial-Blatt für Hessen* 16 (1964), No. 7, 62–77.

Klemmer, Klemens/Wassermann, Rudolf/Wessel, Thomas Michael, *Deutsche Gerichtsgebäude. Von der Dorflinde über den Justizpalast zum Haus des Rechts*, München 1993.

Kesper-Biermann, Sylvia, *Staat und Schule in Kurhessen 1813–1866*, Göttingen 2001.

Die Kodifikation des Strafrechts. Ideen, Experten und Gesetzgebung in den deutschen Staaten des 19. Jahrhunderts, Habilitationsschrift, Gießen 2007.

Kesper-Biermann, Sylvia /Overath, Petra (Eds.), *Die Internationalisierung von Strafrechtswissenschaft und Kriminalpolitik (1870–1930). Deutschland im Vergleich*, Berlin 2007.

Kiefner, Hans, Species facti. Geschichtserzählung bei Kleist und in Relation bei preußischen Kollegialbehörden um 1800, in: *Kleistjahrbuch* (1988/89), 13–39.

Klaere, Helmut, Die Entstehung der Schwurgerichte im 19. Jahrhundert, in: *Zeitschrift für Rechtstheorie* 3 (2003); online-Ressource: http://jesz.ajk.elte.hu/klaere3.html (12.11.2007).

Klippel, Diethelm, Die juristischen Zeitschriften im Übergang vom 18. zum 19. Jahrhundert, in: Michael Stolleis (Ed.), *Juristische Zeitschriften. Die neuen Medien des 18.–20. Jahrhunderts*, Frankfurt a.M. 1999, 15–39.

Staat und Devianz. Zur Einführung, in: Helmut Berding/Diethelm Klippel/Günther Lottes (Eds.), *Kriminalität und abweichendes Verhalten. Deutschland im 18. und 19. Jahrhundert*, Göttingen 1999, 7–15.

Knöbl, Wolfgang, *Polizei und Herrschaft im Modernisierungsprozeß. Staatsbildung und innere Sicherheit in Preußen, England und Amerika 1700–1914*, Frankfurt a.M. 1998.

Koch, Elisabeth, Der Zeugenbeweis in der deutschen Strafprozeßreform des 19. Jahrhunderts, in: André Gouron/Laurent Mayali/Antonio P. Schioppa/Dieter Simon (Eds.), *Subjektivierung des justiziellen Beweisverfahrens. Beiträge zum Zeugenbeweis in Europa und den USA (18.–20. Jahrhundert)*, Frankfurt a. M. 1994, 245–263.

Kochheim, Hansjochen, *Die Haltung der kurhessischen Richterschaft im Verfassungsstreit, nebst Anhang: Die Mitglieder des Oberappellationsgerichts von 1831–1866*, Marburg 1966.

Kohser-Spohn, Christiane, Théories et pratiques de la dénonciation (1789–1793). Analyse d'un exemple, in: Friso Ross/Achim Landwehr (Eds.), *Denunziation und Justiz. Historische Dimension eines sozialen Phänomens*, Tübingen 2000, 77–94.

Kolling, Hubert, *Die kurhessischen »Straf- und Besserungsanstalten«. Institutionen des Strafvollzugs zwischen Fürsorge, Vergeltung und Abschreckung*, Frankfurt a.M. 1994.

König, Reinhard (Bearb.), *Repertorium zum Bestand 266 Obergericht Marburg*, Marburg 1999.

Kopytoff, Igor, The Cultural Biography of Things. Commodization as Process, in: Arjun Appadurai (Ed.), *The Social Life of Things. Commodities in Cultural Perspective*, Cambridge – New York 1988, 64–91.

Koselleck, Reinhart, *Preußen zwischen Reform und Revolution. Allgemeines Landrecht, Verwaltung und soziale Bewegung von 1791 bis 1848*, Stuttgart 1967.

Kraus, Kurt, *Die Frankfurter Polizei im Wandel der Zeiten. Von der Römerzeit bis zur Gegenwart*, Gockenbach 1997.

Krauss, Marita, *Herrschaftspraxis in Bayern und Preußen im 19. Jahrhundert. Ein historischer Vergleich*, Frankfurt a.M. 1997.

Krug-Richter, Barbara, Konfliktregulierung zwischen dörflicher Sozialkontrolle und patrimonialer Gerichtsbarkeit. Das Rügegericht in der westfälischen Gerichtsherrschaft Canstein 1718/19, in: *Historische Anthropologie* 5 (1997), 212–228.

Kukowski, Martin, *Pauperismus in Kurhessen. Ein Beitrag zur Entstehung und Entwicklung der Massenarmut in Deutschland*, Darmstadt 1995, cited as: Martin Kukowski, 1995a.

Proletarisierung vor der Industrialisierung. Ein Beitrag zur Wirtschaft und Sozialstatistik der kurhessischen Landbevölkerung um die Mitte des 19. Jahrhunderts, in: *Hessisches Jahrbuch für Landesgeschichte* 65 (1995), 193–203, cited as: Martin Kukowski, 1995b.

Kürschner, Walter, *Geschichte der Stadt Marburg*, Marburg 1934.

LaCapra, Dominick, Der Käse und die Würmer. Der Kosmos eines Historikers im 20. Jahrhundert, in: Dominick LaCapra (Ed.), *Geschichte und Kritik*, Frankfurt a.M. 1987, 38–63.

Landau, Peter, Die Reichsjustizgesetze von 1879 und die deutsche Rechtseinheit, in: Bundesministerium der Justiz (Ed.), *Vom Reichsjustizamt zum Bundesministerium der Justiz*, Köln 1977, 161–211.

Schwurgerichte und Schöffengerichte in Deutschland im 19. Jahrhundert bis 1870, in: Antonio P. Schioppa (Ed.), *The Trial Jury in England, France, Germany 1700–1900*, Berlin 1987, 241–304.

Landwehr, Achim, »Normdurchsetzung« in der Frühen Neuzeit? Kritik eines Begriffs, in: *Zeitschrift für Geschichtswissenschaft* 48 (2000), No. 2, 146–162, cited as: Achim Landwehr, 2000a.

Policey vor Ort. Die Implementation von Policeyordnungen in der ländlichen Gesellschaft der Frühen Neuzeit, in: Karl Härter (Ed.), *Policey und frühneuzeitliche Gesellschaft*, Frankfurt a.M. 2000, 47–70, cited as: Achim Landwehr, 2000b.

Langewiesche, Dieter, *Liberalismus in Deutschland*, Frankfurt a.M. 1988.

Föderativer Nationalismus als Erbe der deutschen Reichsnation. Über Föderalismus und Zentralismus in der deutschen Nationalgeschichte, in: Dieter Langewiesche/Georg Schmidt (Eds.), *Föderative Nation. Deutschlandkonzepte von der Reformation bis zum Ersten Weltkrieg*, München 2000, 215–243.

Ledford, Kenneth F., *From General Estate to Special Interest. German Lawyers 1878–1933*, Cambridge 1996.

Judicial Independence and Politial Representation: Prussian Judges as Parliamentary Deputies, 1849–1913, in: *Law and Social Inquiry* 25 (2000), 1049–1075.

Legband, Hans (Ed.), *Systematisches Inhaltsverzeichnis zur Zeitschrift des Vereins für hessische Geschichte und Landeskunde*, Vols. 1–45, Kassel 1912.

Lenger, Friedrich, *Zwischen Kleinbürgertum und Proletariat. Studien zur Sozialgeschichte der Düsseldorfer Handwerker 1816–1878*, Göttingen 1986.

Lepetit, Bernard (Ed.), *Les formes de l'expérience. Une autre histoire sociale*, Paris 1995.

Leps, Marie-Christine, *Apprehending the Criminal. The Production of Deviance in Nineteenth-Century Discourse*, Durham 1992.

Limbach, Anna C., *Das Strafrecht der Paulskirchenverfassung 1848/49*, Frankfurt a.M. 1995.

Lindenberg, Michael, Siegeszug der Winzigkeit. Die Fingerschau der Polizei, in: Trutz von Trotha (Ed.), *Politischer Wandel, Gesellschaft und Kriminalitätsdiskurse. Beiträge zur interdisziplinären wissenschaftlichen Kriminologie*, Baden-Baden 1996, 283–298.

Linder, Joachim, Deutsche Pitavalgeschichten in der Mitte des 19. Jahrhunderts, in: Jörg Schönert (Ed.), *Erzählte Kriminalität. Zur Typologie und Funktion von narrativen Darstellungen in Strafrechtspflege, Publizistik und Literatur zwischen 1770 und 1920. Vorträge zu einem interdisziplinären Kolloquium, Hamburg, 10.–12. April 1985*, Tübingen 1991, 313–348.

Linder, Joachim /Schönert, Jörg, Literarische Verständigung über »Kriminalität« in der deutschen Literatur 1850–1880. Vermittelnde Medien, leitende Normen, exemplarische Fälle, in: Jörg Schönert (Ed.), *Literatur und Kriminalität. Die gesellschaftliche Erfahrung von Verbrechen und Strafverfolgung als Gegenstand des Erzählens. Deutschland, England und Frankreich 1850–1880*, Tübingen 1983, 184–238, cited as: Joachim Linder/Jörg Schönert, 1983b.

Ein Beispiel: Der Mordprozeß gegen Christiane Ruthardt (1844/45). Prozeßakten, publizistische und literarische Darstellungen zum Giftmord, in: Jörg Schönert (Ed.), *Literatur und Kriminalität. Die gesellschaftliche Erfahrung von Verbrechen und Strafverfolgung als Gegenstand des Erzählens. Deutschland, England und Frankreich 1850–1880*, Tübingen 1983, 239–359, cited as: Joachim Linder/Jörg Schönert, 1983a.

Lindner, Rolf, *Walks on the Wild Side. Eine Geschichte der Stadtforschung*, Frankfurt a.M. – New York 2004.

Loetz, Francisca, L'infrajudiciaire. Facetten und Bedeutung eines Konzepts, in: Andreas Blauert/Gerd Schwerhoff (Eds.), *Kriminalitätsgeschichte. Beiträge zur Sozial- und Kulturgeschichte der Vormoderne*, Konstanz 2000, 545–562.

Löffler, Siegfried, Die Presse im preußischen Regierungsbezirk Kassel als Spiegelbild ihrer Zeit, in: *Zeitschrift des Vereins für Hessische Geschichte* 75/76 (1964/65), 601–610.

Losch, Philipp, *Die Abgeordneten der kurhessischen Ständeversammlungen von 1830 bis 1866*, Marburg i. H. 1909.

Ludi, Regula, *Die Fabrikation des Verbrechens. Zur Geschichte der modernen Kriminalpolitik 1750–1850*, Tübingen 1999.

Lüdtke, Alf, *»Gemeinwohl«, Polizei und »Festungspraxis«. Staatliche Gewaltsamkeit und innere Verwaltung in Preußen, 1815–1850*, Göttingen 1982.

Luhmann, Niklas, *Legitimation durch Verfahren*, Neuwied 1969.

Lüsebrink, Hans-Jürgen, *Kriminalität und Literatur im Frankreich des 18. Jahrhunderts. Literarische Formen, soziale Funktionen und Wissenskonstituenten von Kriminalitätsdarstellungen im Zeitalter der Aufklärung*, München 1983.

Martschukat, Jürgen, *Inszeniertes Töten. Eine Geschichte der Todesstrafe vom 17. bis zum 19. Jahrhundert*, Köln – Weimar – Wien 2000.

Marxen, Klaus, Zum Verhältnis von Strafrecht und Gerichtberichtserstattung in der zweiten Hälfte des 19. Jahrhunderts, in: Jörg Schönert (Ed.), *Erzählte Kriminalität. Zur Typologie und Funktion von narrativen Darstellungen in Strafrechtspflege, Publizistik und Literatur zwischen 1770 und 1920. Vorträge zu einem interdisziplinären Kolloquium, Hamburg, 10.–12. April 1985*, Tübingen 1991, 369–374.

Maset, Michael, Zur Relevanz von Michel Foucaults Machtanalyse für kriminalitätshistorische Forschungen, in: Andreas Blauert/Gerd Schwerhoff (Eds.), *Kriminalitätsgeschichte. Beiträge zur Sozial- und Kulturgeschichte der Vormoderne*, Konstanz 2000, 233–241.

Matyssek, Angela, Die Wissenschaft als Religion, das Präparat als Reliquie. Rudolf Virchow und das pathologische Museum der Friedrich-Wilhelms-Universität in Berlin, in: Anke te Heesen/Emma C. Spary (Eds.), *Sammeln als Wissen. Das Sammeln und seine wissenschaftsgeschichtliche Bedeutung*, Göttingen 2001, 142–168.

Mauss, Marcell, Essai sur le don. Forme et raison de l'échange dans les sociétés archaïques, in: Marcell Mauss (Ed.), *Sociologie et anthropologie*, Paris 1950, 143–279.

Mayer, Hans, *Die Entwicklung der Polizeigewalt in Hessen. Geschichtliche Entwicklung und geltendes Recht*, Gießen 1931.

McKendrick, Neil, Die Ursprünge der Konsumgesellschaft. Luxus, Neid und soziale Nachahmung in der englischen Literatur des 18. Jahrhunderts, in: Hannes Siegrist/Hartmut Kaelble/Jürgen Kocka (Eds.), *Europäische Konsumgeschichte. Zur Gesellschafts- und Kulturgeschichte des Konsums (18. bis 20. Jahrhundert)*, Frankfurt a.M. – New York 1997, 75–107.

McNeely, Ian F., *The Emancipation of Writing. German Civil Society in the Making, 1790s–1820s*, Berkeley – Los Angeles – London 2003.

Meiners, Otto, *Der Kampf um die gerichtliche Voruntersuchung*, Göttingen 1922.

Melchers, Alexander, *Kriminalstatistik im 19. Jahrhundert. Ein Beitrag zur Geschichte der Kriminalsoziologie und ihrer Methodik*, Frankfurt a.M. 1992.

Merry, Sally E., *Colonizing Hawai'i. The Cultural Power of Law*, Princeton 2000.

Meyer, Friederike, Zur Relation juristischer und moralischer Deutungsmuster von Kriminalität in den Kriminalgeschichten der ›Gartenlaube‹ 1855–1870, in: *Internationales Archiv für Sozialgeschichte der deutschen Literatur* 12 (1987), 156–189.

Meyer-Krentler, Eckhardt, »Die verkaufte Braut«. Juristische und literarische Wirklichkeitssicht im 18. und frühen 19. Jahrhundert, in: *Lessing-Yearbook* XVI (1984), 95–123.

»Geschichtserzählungen« und »Kriminalgeschichten«, »Sachverhaltsschilderungen« und »Phantasiekriminalität«. Überlagerungen und Abgrenzungen zwischen 1770 und 1830, in: Jörg Schönert (Ed.), *Erzählte Kriminalität. Zur Typologie und Funktion von narrativen Darstellungen in Strafrechtspflege, Publizistik und Literatur zwischen 1770 und 1920*, Tübingen 1991, 115–157.

Minkmar, Nils, *Ausgegossene Worte. Stadtbürgerlicher Ehrbegriff, Ehrenkonflikte und Habitus im Colmar des 16. Jahrhunderts in historisch-anthropologischer Perspektive*, Saarbrücken 1996.

Möhle, Sylvia, *Ehekonflikte und sozialer Wandel. Göttingen 1740–1840*, Frankfurt a.M. 1997.

Mommertz, Monika, »Ich. Lisa Thielen«. Text als Handlung und sprachliche Struktur – ein methodischer Vorschlag, in: *Historische Anthropologie* 4 (1996), 303–329.

Mooser, Josef, »Furcht bewahrt das Holz«. Holzdiebstahl und sozialer Konflikt in der ländlichen Gesellschaft 1800–1850 an westfälischen Beispielen, in: Heinz Reif (Ed.), *Räuber, Volk und Obrigkeit. Studien zur Geschichte der Kriminalität in Deutschland seit dem 18. Jahrhundert*, Frankfurt a.M. 1984, 43–99.

M'Sili, Marine, Le Recul de la petite délinquance dans la chronique des faits divers des débuts de la IIIe République à nos jours, in: Benoît Garnot (Ed.), *La petite délinquance du Moyen Age à l'époque contemporaine. Actes du colloque de Dijon 9 & 10 octobre 1997*, Dijon 1998, 101–111.

Müller, Christian, *Verbrechensbekämpfung im Anstaltsstaat. Psychiatrie, Kriminologie und Strafrechtsreform in Deutschland 1871–1933*, Göttingen 2004.

Müller, Philipp, Journalistische Vermittlung und ihre Aneignung. Die öffentlichen Verhandlungen über Wilhelm Voigt alias Hauptmann von Köpenick in Berlin 1906/08, in: *Österreichische Zeitschrift für Geschichtswissenschaften* 13 (2002), No. 2, 35–55.

Auf der Suche nach dem Täter. Die öffentliche Dramatisierung von Verbrechen im Berlin des Kaiserreichs, Frankfurt a.M. 2005.

Munter, Cameron, *»Das Land der armen Leute«. Poverty in the Marburg Region of Hesse in the Nineteenth Century*, Baltimore 1983.

Nader, Laura (Ed.), *Law in Culture and Society*, Chicago 1969.

Harmony Ideology. Justice and Control in a Zapotec Mountain Village, Stanford 1990.

(Ed.), *Law in Culture and Society*, Berkeley – London 1997.

Naucke, Wolfgang, ›Verfachlichung‹ des Strafrechts im 19. Jahrhundert, in: Jörg Schönert (Ed.), *Literatur und Kriminalität. Die gesellschaftliche Erfahrung von Verbrechen und Strafverfolgung als Gegenstand des Erzählens. Deutschland, England und Frankreich 1850–1880*, Tübingen 1983, 55–67.

Nagel, Lothar, *Die gerichtliche Voruntersuchung in der Geschichte des deutschen Strafprozesses bis zum Erlaß der Reichsstrafprozeßordnung*, Borna-Leipzig 1935.

Nebel, Adolf, *Die ländlichen Arbeiterverhältniße in Kurhessen*, Fulda 1909.

Nicke, Karl-Heinz, et al., Kurzbiographien, in: Georg Wannagat (Ed.), *Kassel als Stadt der Juristen (Juristinnen) und der Gerichte in ihrer tausendjährigen Geschichte*, Köln 1990, 367–537.

Niehaus, Michael, *Das Verhör. Geschichte – Theorie – Fiktion*, München 2003.

Wort für Wort. Zu Geschichte und Logik des Verhörprotokolls, in: Michael Niehaus/Hans-Walter Schmidt-Hannisa (Eds.), *Das Protokoll. Kulturelle Funktionen einer Textsorte*, Frankfurt a.M. and others 2005, 27–47.

Niehaus, Michael /Schmidt-Hannisa, Hans-Walter (Eds.), *Unzurechnungsfähigkeiten. Diskursivierungen unfreier Bewußtseinszustände seit dem 18. Jahrhundert*, Frankfurt a.M. 1998.

(Eds.), *Das Protokoll. Kulturelle Funktionen einer Textsorte*, Frankfurt a.M. and others 2005.

Nitschke, Peter, *Verbrechensbekämpfung und Verwaltung. Die Entstehung der Polizei in der Grafschaft Lippe (1700–1814)*, Münster 1990.

Nutz, Thomas, Gefängnisreformdiskurs und Kriminalpolitik in Preußen bis 1806, in: Helmut Berding/Diethelm Klippel/Günther Lottes (Eds.), *Kriminalität und abweichendes Verhalten. Deutschland im 18. und 19. Jahrhundert*, Göttingen 1999, 39–67.

Strafrechtsphilosophie und Gefängniskunde. Strategien diskursiver Legitimierung in der ersten Hälfte des 19. Jahrhunderts, in: *Zeitschrift für Neuere Rechtsgeschichte* 22 (2000), 95–110.

Strafanstalt als Besserungsmaschine. Reformdiskurs und Gefängniswissenschaft 1775–1848, München 2001.

Oberwittler, Dietrich, Jugendkriminalstatistiken und ihre Interpretation. Zur Entwicklung der Jugendkriminalität in Deutschland und England in der zweiten Hälfte des 19. und im frühen 20. Jahrhundert, in: *Historical Social Research* 22 (1997), 198–227.

Oermann, Nils O., The Law and the Colonial State. Legal Codification versus Practice in a German Colony, in: Geoff Eley/James Retallack (Eds.), *Wilhelminism and its Legacies. German Modernities, Imperialism, and the Meanings of Reform, 1890–1930*, New York – Oxford 2003, 171–185.

Ogorek, Regina, Zum politischen Selbstverständnis der Rechtsprechung am Vorabend des bürgerlichen Zeitalters – eine Fallstudie, in: *Ius commune* 10 (1983), 69–95.

Richterkönig oder Subsumtionsautomat. Zur Justiztheorie im 19. Jahrhundert, Frankfurt a.M. 1986.

Individueller Rechtsschutz gegenüber der Staatsgewalt. Zur Entwicklung der Verwaltungsgerichtsbarkeit, in: Jürgen Kocka (Ed.), *Bürgertum im 19. Jahrhundert*, Vol. 1, München 1988, 372–405.

Ormond, Thomas, *Richterwürde und Regierungstreue. Dienstrecht, politische Betätigung und Disziplinierung der Richter in Preußen, Baden und Hessen 1866–1918*, Frankfurt a.M. 1994.

Overath, Petra, Bayerische Schwurgerichte und die Todesstrafe. Handlungsspielräume von Laienrichtern in der zweiten Hälfte des 19. Jahrhunderts, in: Helmut Berding/Diethelm Klippel/Günther Lottes (Eds.), *Kriminalität und abweichendes Verhalten. Deutschland im 18. und 19. Jahrhundert*, Göttingen 1999, 171–197.

Tod und Gnade. Die Todesstrafe in Bayern im 19. Jahrhundert, Köln – Weimar – Wien 2001.

Park, Robert E., Natural History of the Newspaper, in: Everett C. Hughes (Ed.), *Completed Works*, Vol. III, Illinois 1955, 89–104.

Perrot, Michelle, Premières mésures des faits sonaux. Les débuts de la statistique criminelle en France (1780–1830), in: Michelle Perrot (Ed.), *Les ombres de l'histoire. Crime et châtiment au XIXe siècle*, Paris 2001, 257–270, cited as: Michelle Perrot, 2001a.

Faits divers et histoire au XIXe siècle, in: Michelle Perrot (Ed.), *Les ombres de l'histoire. Crime et châtiment au XIXe siècle*, Paris 2001, 271–281, cited as: Michelle Perrot, 2001b.

Philips, Susan U., *Ideology in Language of Judges. How Judges Practice Law, Politics, and Courtroom Control*, New York – Oxford 1998.

Platner, Thomas, Die Geschichte der Rechtsanwaltschaft aus Kasseler Sicht, in: Georg Wannagat (Ed.), *Kassel als Stadt der Juristen (Juristinnen) und der Gerichte in ihrer tausendjährigen Geschichte*, Köln 1990, 153–162.

Plaum, Bernd D., *Strafrecht, Kriminalpolitik und Kriminalität im Fürstentum Siegen 1750–1810*, St. Katharinen 1990.

Porret, Michel, *Le crime et ses circonstances. De l'esprit de l'arbitraire au siècle des Lumières selon les réquisitoires des procureurs généraux de Genève*, Genf 1995.

Rabe, Wilhelm, Die Pfarrer- und Beamtensippe Köster (Cöster) aus Niederlistingen, in: *Hessische Familienkunde* 3 (1955), 358–364.

Radbruch, Gustav, *Paul Johann Anselm Feuerbach. Ein Juristenleben*, Göttingen 1934.

Rappe, Susanne, Schelten, Drohen, Klagen. Frühneuzeitliche Gerichtsnutzung zwischen ›kommunikativer Vernunft‹ und ›falschem Zwang‹, in: *Werkstatt-Geschichte* 14 (1996), 87–94.

Regener, Susanne, *Fotografische Erfassung. Zur Geschichte medialer Konstruktionen des Kriminellen*, München 1999.

Reichling, Hartwig, *Die vollständige Protokollierung in der Hauptverhandlung in Strafsachen gemäß §273 Abs. 3 StPO*, Berlin 2003.

Reinke, Herbert, Kriminalität als »zweite« Wirklichkeit von Tätigkeitsnachweisen der Justizverwaltung. Bemerkungen zu Kriminalstatistiken des 19. Jahrhunderts als Materialien einer historisch orientierten Kriminologie, in: Helga Cremer-Schäfer (Ed.), *Kriminologie und Geschichte*, Weinheim 1987, 176–184.

Die »Liaison« des Strafrechts mit der Statistik. Zu den Anfängen kriminalstatistischer Zählungen im 18. und 19. Jahrhundert, in: *Zeitschrift für Neuere Rechtsgeschichte* 12 (1990), 169–179.

(Ed.), *»... nur für die Sicherheit da...«? Zur Geschichte der Polizei im 19. und 20. Jahrhundert*, Frankfurt a.M. 1993.

Polizeigeschichte in Deutschland. Ein Überblick, in: Peter Nitschke (Ed.), *Die deutsche Polizei und ihre Geschichte. Beiträge zu einem distanzierten Verhältnis*, Hilden 1996, 13–26.

»Großstadtpolizei«. Städtische Ordnung und Sicherheit und die Polizei in der Zeit des Deutschen Kaiserreiches (1871–1918), in: Martin Dinges/Sack Fritz (Eds.), *Unsichere Großstädte? Vom Mittelalter bis zur Postmoderne*, Konstanz 2000, 217–239.

Reulecke, Jürgen, Pauperismus, »social learning« und die Anfänge der Sozialstatistik in Deutschland, in: Hans Mommsen/Winfried Schulze (Eds.), *Vom Elend der Handarbeit. Probleme historischer Unterschichtenforschung*, Stuttgart 1981, 358–372.

Reuling, Ulrich, *Historisches Ortslexikon des Landes Hessen*, Vol. 3: *Marburg ehem. Landkreis und kreisfreie Stadt*, Marburg 1979.

Revel, Jacques, L'institution et le social, in: Bernard Lepetit (Ed.), *Les formes de l'expérience. Une autre histoire sociale*, Paris 1995, 63–84; 309–312.

Roper, Lyndal, Ödipus und der Teufel, in: Andreas Blauert/Gerd Schwerhoff (Eds.), *Mit den Waffen der Justiz. Zur Kriminalitätsgeschichte des Spätmittelalters und der frühen Neuzeit*, Frankfurt a.M. 1993, 32–53.

Blut und Latze. Männlichkeit in der Stadt der Frühen Neuzeit, in: Lyndal Roper (Ed.), *Ödipus und der Teufel. Männlichkeit in der Stadt der Frühen Neuzeit*, Frankfurt a.M. 1995, 109–126.

Roth, Andreas, *Kollektive Gewalt und Strafrecht. Die Geschichte der Massendelikte in Deutschland*, Berlin 1989.

Die Auswirkungen von Bevölkerungswachstum und polizeilicher Professionalisierung auf die registrierte Delinquenz im Kaiserreich, in: Jürgen Reulecke (Ed.), *Die Stadt als Dienstleistungszentrum. Beiträge zur Geschichte der »Sozialstadt« in Deutschland im 19. und frühen 20. Jahrhundert*, St. Katharinen 1995, 371–393.

Kriminalitätsbekämpfung in deutschen Großstädten 1850–1914. Ein Beitrag zur Geschichte des strafrechtlichen Ermittlungsverfahrens, Berlin 1997.

Strafrechtliche Zeitschriften im 19. Jahrhundert. Diskussionsforen oder Gesetzesinterpreten?, in: Michael Stolleis (Ed.), *Juristische Zeitschriften. Die neuen Medien des 18.–20. Jahrhunderts*, Frankfurt a.M. 1999, 303–329.

Rublack, Ulinka, *Magd, Metz' oder Mörderin. Frauen vor frühneuzeitlichen Gerichten*, Frankfurt a.M. 1998.

Rückert, Joachim, Zur Rolle der Fallgeschichte in Juristenausbildung und juristischer Praxis zwischen 1790 und 1880, in: Jörg Schönert (Ed.), *Erzählte Kriminalität. Zur Typologie und Funktion von narrativen Darstellungen in Strafrechtspflege, Publizistik und Literatur zwischen 1770 und 1920. Vorträge zu einem interdisziplinären Kolloquium, Hamburg, 10.–12. April 1985*, Tübingen 1991, 285–311, cited as: Joachim Rückert, 1991a.

Zur Verfachlichung der Verfachlichung, in: Jörg Schönert (Ed.), *Erzählte Kriminalität. Zur Typologie und Funktion von narrativen Darstellungen in Strafrechtspflege, Publizistik und Literatur zwischen 1770 und 1920*, Tübingen 1991, 635–650, cited as: Joachim Rückert, 1991b.

Geschichtlich, praktisch, deutsch. Die »Zeitschrift für geschichtliche Rechtswissenschaft« (1815–1850), das »Archiv für die civilistische Praxis« (1818–1867) und die »Zeitschrift für deutsches Recht und deutsche Rechtswissenschaft« (1839–1861), in: Michael Stolleis (Ed.), *Juristische Zeitschriften. Die neuen Medien des 18.–20. Jahrhunderts*, Frankfurt a.M. 1999, 107–257.

Rudé, George, *Criminal and Victim. Crime and Society in Early Nineteenth-Century England*, Oxford 1985.

Rudolph, Harriet, *»Eine gelinde Regierungsart«. Peinliche Strafjustiz im Geistlichen Territorium. Das Hochstift Osnabrück (1716–1803)*, Konstanz 2001.

Sabean, David W., Soziale Distanzierungen. Ritualisierte Gestik in deutscher bürokratischer Prosa der Frühen Neuzeit, in: *Historische Anthropologie* 4 (1996), No. 2, 216–233.

Sakai, Eihachiro, *Der kurhessische Bauer im 19. Jahrhundert und die Grundlastenablösung*, Melsungen 1967.

Sant Cassia, Paul, Vol, confiance et valeur, in: Maria Pia di Bella (Ed.), *Vols et sanctions en Méditerranée*, Amsterdam 1998, 151–198.

Saurer, Edith, Strafvollzug im 19. Jahrhundert, in: Erika Weinzierl/Karl R. Stadler (Eds.), *Justiz und Zeitgeschichte. Vorträge zum Symposium zur Geschichte des Strafvollzuges in Österreich*, Wien 1985, 11–34.

Schimpf, Dorothee, *Emanzipation und Bildungswesen der Juden im Kurfürstentum Hessen 1807–1866. Jüdische Identität zwischen Selbstbehauptung und Assimiliationsdruck*, Wiesbaden 1994.

Schindler, Norbert, *Wilderer im Zeitalter der Französischen Revolution. Ein Kapitel alpiner Sozialgeschichte*, München 2001.

Schioppa, Antonio Padoa (Ed.), *The Trial Jury in England, France, Germany 1700–1900*, Berlin 1987.

Schlumbohm, Jürgen (Ed.), *Familie und Familienlosigkeit. Fallstudien aus Niedersachsen und Bremen vom 15. bis 20. Jahrhundert*, Hannover 1993, cited as: Jürgen Schlumbohm, 1993a.

»Wilde Ehen«. Zusammenleben angesichts kirchlicher Sanktionen und staatlicher Sittenpolizei (Osnabrücker Land, ca. 1790–1870), in: Jürgen Schlumbohm (Ed.), *Familie und Familienlosigkeit. Fallstudien aus Niedersachsen und Bremen vom 15. bis 20. Jahrhundert*, Hannover 1993, 63–80, cited as: Jürgen Schlumbohm, 1993b.

Lebensläufe, Familien, Höfe. Die Bauern und Heuerleute des Osnabrückischen Kirchspiels Belm in proto-industrieller Zeit, 1650–1860, Göttingen 1994.

Gesetze, die nicht durchgesetzt werden – ein Strukturmerkmal des frühneuzeitlichen Staates?, in: *Geschichte und Gesellschaft* 23 (1997), 647–663.

Schmidt, Bruno, Geschichte der kommunalen Polizei in Marburg, in: *Marburger Almanach. Heimatjahrbuch für die Stadt Marburg* (1982), 81–84.

Schmölz-Häberlein, Michaela, Ehrverletzung als Strategie. Zum sozialen Kontext von Injurien in der badischen Kleinstadt Emmendingen 1650–1800, in: Mark Häberlein (Ed.), *Devianz, Widerstand und Herrschaftspraxis in der Vormoderne. Studien zu Konflikten im südwestdeutschen Raum (15.–18. Jahrhundert)*, Konstanz 1999, 137–163.

Schnyder-Burghartz, Albert, *Alltag und Lebensformen auf der Baseler Landschaft um 1700. Vorindustrielle, ländliche Kultur und Gesellschaft aus mikrohistorischer Perspektive; Bretzwil und das obere Waldenburger Amt von 1690 bis 1750*, Liestal 1992.

Schöler, Claudia, *Deutsche Rechtseinheit. Partikulare und nationale Gesetzgebung (1780–1866)*, Köln – Weimar – Wien 2004.

Scholz, Johannes-Michael, Zum modus operandi des Rechtshistorikers, in: *Ius commune* 21 (1994), 281–305.

Schönert, Jörg, Schauriges Behagen und distanzierender Schrecken. Zur Situation von Schauerromanen und Schauererzählungen im literarischen Leben der Biedermeierzeit, in: Alberto Martino (Ed.), *Literatur in der sozialen Bewegung. Aufsätze und Forschungsberichte zum 19. Jahrhundert*, Tübingen 1977, 27–92.

Kriminalgeschichten in der deutschen Literatur zwischen 1770 und 1890. Zur Entwicklung des Genres, in: *Geschichte und Gesellschaft* 9 (1983), 49–68, cited as: Jörg Schönert, 1983c.

(Ed.), *Literatur und Kriminalität. Die gesellschaftliche Erfahrung von Verbrechen und Strafverfolgung als Gegenstand des Erzählens. Deutschland, England und Frankreich 1850–1880*, Tübingen 1983, cited as: Jörg Schönert, 1983a.

Zur Ausdifferenzierung des Genres »Kriminalgeschichten« in der deutschen Literatur vom Ende des 18. bis zum Beginn des 20. Jahrhunderts, in: Jörg Schönert (Ed.), *Literatur und Kriminalität. Die gesellschaftliche Erfahrung von Verbrechen und Strafverfolgung als Gegenstand des Erzählens. Deutschland, England und Frankreich 1850–1880*, Tübingen 1983, 96–125, cited as: Jörg Schönert, 1983b.

Die Begleitstimme der ›schönen Literatur‹ zur Strafrechtsentwicklung, in: Dieter Simon (Ed.), *Akten des 26. Deutschen Rechtshistorikertages*, Frankfurt a.M. 1987, 211–230.

(Ed.), *Erzählte Kriminalität. Zur Typologie und Funktion von narrativen Darstellungen in Strafrechtspflege, Publizistik und Literatur zwischen 1770 und 1920*, Tübingen 1991, cited as: Jörg Schönert, 1991a.

Bilder vom »Verbrechermenschen« in den rechtskulturellen Diskursen um 1900. Zum Erzählen über Kriminalität und zum Status kriminologischen Wissens, in: Jörg Schönert (Ed.), *Erzählte Kriminalität. Zur Typologie und Funktion von narrativen Darstellungen in Strafrechtspflege, Publizistik und Literatur zwischen 1770 und 1920*, Tübingen 1991, 497–531, cited as: Jörg Schönert, 1991b.

Kriminalgeschichten (1815–1830) im Spektrum von »Aktenmäßiger Darstellung« bis zur »Historisch-Romantischen Manier«, in: Rainer Schöwerling/Hartmut Steinecke (Eds.), *Die Fürstliche Bibliothek Corvey. Ihre Bedeutung für eine neue Sicht der Literatur des frühen 19. Jahrhunderts*, München 1992, 147–162.

Schröder, Jan, *Wissenschaftstheorie und Lehre der ›praktischen Jurisprudenz‹ auf deutschen Universitäten an der Wende zum 19. Jahrhundert*, Frankfurt a.M. 1979.

Schuck, Gerhard, Die publizistisch-statistisch-staatswissenschaftlichen Zeitschriften um 1800, in: Michael Stolleis (Ed.), *Juristische Zeitschriften. Die neuen Medien des 18.–20. Jahrhunderts*, Frankfurt a.M. 1999, 53–66.

Schulte, Regina, *Das Dorf im Verhör. Brandstifter, Kindsmörderinnen und Wilderer vor den Schranken des bürgerlichen Gerichts. Oberbayern 1848–1910*, Hamburg 1989.

Bevor das Gerede zum Klatsch wird, in: Karin Hausen/Heide Wunder (Eds.), *Frauengeschichte – Geschlechtergeschichte*, Frankfurt a.M. – New York 1992, 67–73.

Semantische Konfliktlinien im Dorf des 19. Jahrhunderts im Spiegel bayerischer Gerichtsakten, in: Heinz Mohnhaupt/Dieter Simon (Eds.), *Vorträge zur Justizforschung. Geschichte und Theorie*, Vol. 2, Frankfurt a.M. 1993, 405–425.

Schulze, Reiner, Geschichte der neueren vorkonstitutionellen Gesetzgebung. Zu Forschungsstand und Methodenfragen eines rechtshistorischen Arbeitsgebiets, in: *Zeitschrift der Savigny-Stiftung für Rechtsgeschichte, Germanistische Abteilung* 98 (1981), 157–235.

Das Recht fremder Kulturen – Vom Nutzen der Rechtsethnologie für die Rechtsgeschichte, in: *Historisches Jahrbuch* 110 (1990), 446–469.

Schwaiger, Kajetan, *Die Stellung des Angeschuldigten in der Voruntersuchung*, Freising 1928.

Schwerhoff, Gerd, *Köln im Kreuzverhör. Kriminalität, Herrschaft und Gesellschaft in einer frühneuzeitlichen Stadt*, Bonn – Berlin 1991.

Aktenkundig und gerichtsnotorisch. Einführung in die Historische Kriminalitätsforschung, Tübingen 1999.

Kriminalitätsgeschichte im deutschen Sprachraum. Zum Profil eines »verspäteten« Forschungszweiges, in: Andreas Blauert/Gerd Schwerhoff (Eds.), *Kriminalitätsgeschichte. Beiträge zur Sozial- und Kulturgeschichte der Vormoderne*, Konstanz 2000, 21–67.

Seier, Hellmut, Liberalismus in Kurhessen 1815–1866. Stufen und Formen liberaler Willensbildung, in: Lothar Gall/Dieter Langewiesche (Eds.), *Liberalismus und Region. Zur Geschichte des deutschen Liberalismus im 19. Jahrhundert*, München 1995, 109–133.

Wahlrecht und Wahlen in Kurhessen 1807–1866. Grundzüge und Forschungsstand, in: *Hessisches Jahrbuch für Landesgeschichte* 51 (2001), 103–147.

Shaya, Gregory, The Flâneur, the Badaud, and the Making of a Mass Public in France, circa 1860–1919, in: *American Historical Review* 109 (2004), No. 1, 41–77.

Siegrist, Hannes, *Advokat, Bürger und Staat. Sozialgeschichte der Rechtsanwälte in Deutschland, Italien und der Schweiz*, 2 vols., Frankfurt a.M. 1996.

Siegrist, Hannes /Sugarman, David, Geschichte als historisch-vergleichende Eigentumswissenschaft. Rechts-, kultur- und gesellschaftsgeschichtliche Perspektiven, in: Hannes Siegrist/David Sugarman (Eds.), *Eigentum im internationalen Vergleich (18.–20. Jahrhundert)*, Göttingen 1999, 9–30, cited as: Hannes Siegrist/David Sugarman 1999b.

(Ed.), *Eigentum im internationalen Vergleich (18.–20. Jahrhundert)*, Göttingen 1999, cited as: Hannes Siegrist/David Sugarman 1999a.

Siemann, Wolfram, *»Deutschlands Ruhe, Sicherheit und Ordnung«. Die Anfänge der politischen Polizei 1806–1866*, Tübingen 1985.

Sievers, Kai D., Die Darstellung von Kriminalität und Strafvollzug in Schleswig-Holsteinischen Periodica zu Beginn des 19. Jahrhunderts, in: *Kieler Blätter zur Volkskunde* 7 (1975), 21–56.

Simon-Muscheid, Katharina, Reden und Schweigen vor Gericht. Klientelverhältnisse und Beziehungsgeflechte im Prozeßverlauf, in: Mark Häberlein (Ed.), *Devianz, Widerstand und Herrschaftspraxis in der Vormoderne. Studien zu Konflikten im südwestdeutschen Raum (15.–18. Jahrhundert)*, Konstanz 1999, 35–52.

Smaus, Gerlinda, Der Justizskandal Hilsner (1899/1900): Antisemitismus als ein Mittel zur Stärkung des tschechischen Nationalbewusstseins?, in: Joachim Linder/Claus-Michael Ort (Eds.) MichaelOrt (Eds.), *Verbrechen – Justiz – Medien. Konstellationen in Deutschland von 1900 bis zur Gegenwart*, Tübingen 1999, 171–192.

Snyder, Francis G., *Law and Anthropology. A Review*, Florenz 1993.

Speitkamp, Winfried, *Restauration als Transformation. Untersuchungen zur kurhessischen Verfassungsgeschichte 1813–1830*, Darmstadt – Marburg 1986.

Spencer, Elaine G., *Police and the Social Order in German Cities. The Düsseldorf District, 1848–1914*, DeKalb 1992.
Spiekermann, Uwe, Theft and Thieves in German Department Stores, 1895–1930. A Discourse on Morality, Crime and Gender, in: Geoffrey Crossick/Serge Jaumain (Eds.), *Cathedrals of Consumption. The European Department Stores, 1850–1939*, Aldershot 1999, 135–159.
Stagl, Justin, *Eine Geschichte der Neugier. Die Kunst des Reisens 1550–1800*, Wien – Weimar 2002.
Stebbings, Chantal (Ed.), *Law Reporting in England*, London 1995.
Steinmetz, Willibald, *Begegnungen vor Gericht. Eine Sozial- und Kulturgeschichte des englischen Arbeitsrechts (1850–1925)*, München 2002.
Stichweh, Rudolf, Zur Subjektivierung der Entscheidungsfindung im deutschen Strafprozeß des 19. Jahrhunderts, in: André Gouron, et al. (Eds.), *Subjektivierung des justiziellen Beweisverfahrens. Beiträge zum Zeugenbeweis in Europa und den USA (18.–20. Jahrhundert)*, Frankfurt a.M. 1994, 265–300.
Stingelin, Martin, Der Verbrecher ohnegleichen. Die Konstruktion ›anschaulicher Evidenz‹ in der Criminal-Psychologie, der forensischen Physiognomik, der Kriminalanthropometrie und der Kriminalanthropologie, in: Wolfram Groddeck/Ulrich Stadler (Eds.), *Physiognomie und Pathognomie. Zur literarischen Darstellung von Individualität [Festschrift für Karl Pestalozzi zum 65. Geburtstag]*, Berlin – New York 1994, 113–133.
Stolleis, Michael, Aufgaben der neueren Rechtsgeschichte oder: Hic sunt leones, in: *Rechtshistorisches Journal* 4 (1985), 251–264.
Geschichte des öffentlichen Rechts in Deutschland, Vol. 1: *Rechtspublizistik und Policey-wissenschaft 1600–1800*, München 1988.
Geschichte des öffentlichen Rechts in Deutschland, Vol. 2: *Staatsrechtslehre und Verwaltungswissenschaft 1800–1914*, München 1992.
Rechtsgeschichte als Kunstprodukt. Zur Entbehrlichkeit von »Begriff« und »Tatsache«, Baden-Baden 1997.
(Ed.), *Juristische Zeitschriften. Die neuen Medien des 18.–20. Jahrhunderts*, Frankfurt a.M. 1999.
Strathern, Marilyn, Divisions of Interest and Languages of Ownership, in: Christopher M. Hann (Ed.), *Property Relations. Renewing the Anthropological Tradition*, New York 1998, 214–232.
Suchy, Barbara, Zwischen Geborgenheit und Gefährdung. Jüdisches Leben in hessischen Kleinstädten und Dörfern, in: Uwe Schulz (Ed.), *Die Geschichte Hessens*, Stuttgart 1983, 145–159.
Sugarman, David, Writing »Law and Society« Histories, in: *Modern Law Review* 55 (1992), 292–308.
Summa, Rudolf, *Kasseler Unterschichten im Zeitalter der Industrialisierung. Ein Beitrag zur Sozialgeschichte der Stadt Kassel von der Mitte des 19. Jahrhunderts bis zum Beginn des Ersten Weltkriegs*, Darmstadt 1978.
Theisen, Frank, *Zwischen Machtspruch und Unabhängigkeit. Kurhessische Rechtsprechung von 1821–1848*, Köln – Weimar – Wien 1997.
Thompson, Edward P., The Moral Economy of the English Crowd in the Eighteenth Century, in: *Past and Present* 50 (1971), 76–136.

Die ›moralische‹ Ökonomie der englischen Unterschichten im 18. Jahrhundert, in: Dieter Groh (Ed.), *Plebeische Kultur und moralische Ökonomie*, Frankfurt a.M. 1980, 66–129.

Töngi, Claudia, *Um Leib und Leben. Gewalt, Konflikt, Geschlecht im Uri des 19. Jahrhunderts*, Zürich 2004.

Treichel, Eckhardt, *Der Primat der Bürokratie. Bürokratischer Staat und bürokratische Elite im Herzogtum Nassau 1806–1866*, Stuttgart 1991.

Trotha, Trutz von (Ed.), *Politischer Wandel, Gesellschaft und Kriminalitätsdiskurse. Beiträge zur interdisziplinären wissenschaftlichen Kriminologie. Festschrift für Fritz Sack zum 65. Geburtstag*, Baden-Baden 1996.

Ulbricht, Otto (Ed.), *Von Huren und Rabenmüttern. Weibliche Kriminalität in der frühen Neuzeit*, Köln – Weimar – Wien 1995.

Einleitung, in: Otto Ulbricht (Ed.), *Von Huren und Rabenmüttern. Weibliche Kriminalität in der Frühen Neuzeit*, Köln – Weimar – Wien 1995, 1–37, cited as: Otto Ulbricht, 1995a.

Zwischen Vergeltung und Zukunftsplanung. Hausdiebstahl von Mägden in Schleswig-Holstein vom 16. bis zum 19. Jahrhundert, in: Otto Ulbricht (Ed.), *Von Huren und Rabenmüttern. Weibliche Kriminalität in der Frühen Neuzeit*, Köln – Weimar – Wien 1995, 139–170, cited as: Otto Ulbricht, 1995b.

Unruh, Georg-Christoph von, Polizei, Polizeiwissenschaft und Kameralistik, in: Kurt G. A. Jeserich/Hans Pohl/Georg-Christoph von Unruh (Eds.), *Deutsche Verwaltungsgeschichte*, Vol 1: *Vom Spätmittelalter bis zum Ende des Reiches*, Stuttgart 1983, 388–426.

Vanja, Konrad, *Dörflicher Strukturwandel zwischen Übervölkerung und Auswanderung. Zur Sozialgeschichte des oberhessischen Postortes Halsdorf, 1785–1867*, Marburg 1978.

Vec, Miloš, *Die Spur des Täters. Methoden der Identifikation in der Kriminalistik (1879–1933)*, Baden-Baden 2002.

Verdenhalven, Fritz, Die Straffälligkeit in Lippe in der zweiten Hälfte des 18. Jahrhunderts, in: *Lippische Mitteilungen* 43 (1974), 62–144.

Vismann, Cornelia, *Akten. Medientechnik und Recht*, Frankfurt a.M. 2001.

Vits, Brigitta, *Hüfner, Kötter und Beisassen. Die Wirtschafts- und Sozialstruktur ländlicher Siedlungen in Nordhessen vom 16. bis zum 19. Jahrhundert*, Kassel 1993.

Vogel, Jakob, Moderner Traditionalismus. Mythos und Realität des Bergwerkseigentums im preußisch-deutschen Bergrecht des 19. Jahrhunderts, in: Hannes Siegrist/David Sugarman (Eds.), *Eigentum im internationalen Vergleich (18.–20. Jahrhundert)*, Göttingen 1999, 185–205.

Vogel, Ursula, Whose Property? The Double Standard of Adultery in Nineteenth-Century Law, in: Carol Smart (Eds.), *Regulating Womanhood. Historical Essays on Marriage, Motherhood and Sexuality*, London 1992, 147–165.

Wagner-Hasel, Beate, Egoistic Exchange and Altruistic Gift. On the Roots of Marcel Mauss' Theory of the Gift, in: Gadi Algazi/Valentin Groebner/Bernhard Jussen (Eds.), *Negotiating the Gift. Pre-Modern Figurations of Exchange*, Göttingen 2003, 141–171.

Walkowitz, Judith R., *City of Dreadful Delight. Narratives of Sexual Danger in Late-victorian London*, London – Chicago 1992.

Jack the Ripper und der Mythos von der männlichen Gewalt, in: Alain Corbin (Ed.), *Die sexuelle Gewalt in der Geschichte*, Frankfurt a.M. 1997, 107–135.

Wannagat, Georg (Ed.), *Kassel als Stadt der Juristen (Juristinnen) und der Gerichte in ihrer tausendjährigen Geschichte*, Köln 1990.

Weber, Wolfgang, Kriminalität, öffentliche Sicherheit und Industrialisierung in der ersten Hälfte des 19. Jahrhunderts. Bemerkungen zur Entwicklung in Augsburg, in: *Die Alte Stadt* 12 (1985), 251–275.

Wehler, Hans-Ulrich, Gesellschaftsgeschichte und Rechtsgeschichte, in: *Rechtshistorisches Journal* 8 (1989), 181–194.

Weigel, Sigrid, »*Und selbst im Kerker frei...!*« *Schreiben im Gefängnis. Zur Theorie und Gattungsgeschichte der Gefängnisliteratur (1750–1933)*, Marburg 1982.

Weiler, Inge, *Giftmordwissen und Giftmörderinnen. Eine diskursgeschichtliche Studie*, Tübingen 1998.

Wesel, Uwe, *Geschichte des Rechts von den Frühformen bis zum Vertrag von Maastricht*, München 1997.

West, Candace/Zimmerman, Don H., Doing Gender, in: *Gender and Society* 1 (1987), 125–151.

Wettmann-Jungblut, Peter, »Stelen inn rechter hungersnodt«. Diebstahl, Eigentumsschutz und strafrechtliche Kontrolle im vorindustriellen Baden 1600–1850, in: Richard van Dülmen (Ed.), *Verbrechen, Strafen, soziale Kontrolle. Studien zur historischen Kulturforschung*, Frankfurt a.M. 1990, 133–177.

Unordnung im Bürgerstaat. Kriminalität und strafrechtliche Repression im Großherzogtum Baden während der ersten Hälfte des 19. Jahrhunderts, in: Edwin Dillmann (Ed.), *Regionales Prisma der Vergangenheit. Perspektiven der modernen Regionalgeschichte (19./20. Jahrhundert)*, St. Ingbert 1996, 133–155.

Der nächste Weg zum Galgen? Studien zur Eigentumskriminalität in Südwestdeutschland, [unpublished dissertation], Saarbrücken 1997.

Rechtsanwälte an der Saar 1800–1960. Geschichte eines bürgerlichen Berufsstandes, Blieskastel 2004, 152–163.

Wetzell, Richard F., *Criminal Law Reform in Imperial Germany*, Stanford 1991.

Inventing the Criminal. A History of German Criminology, Chapel Hill 2000.

Wickham, Chris, Conclusion, in: Peter R. Coss (Ed.), *The Moral World of the Law*, Cambridge – New York – Melbourne 2000, 240–249.

Wiebel, Eva, Die ›Schleiferbärbel‹ und die ›schwarze Iris‹. Leben und Lebensbeschreibungen zweier berüchtigter Gaunerinnen des 18. Jahrhunderts, in: Andreas Blauert/Gerd Schwerhoff (Eds.), *Kriminalitätsgeschichte. Beiträge zur Sozial- und Kulturgeschichte der Vormoderne*, Konstanz 2000, 759–800.

/Blauert, Andreas, Gauner- und Diebslisten. Unterschichten und Randgruppenkriminalität in den Augen des absolutistischen Staats, in: Mark Häberlein (Ed.), *Devianz, Widerstand und Herrschaftspraxis in der Vormoderne. Studien zu Konflikten im südwestdeutschen Raum (15.–18. Jahrhundert)*, Konstanz 1999, 67–96.

Wiener, Martin J., *Reconstructing the Criminal. Culture, Law, and Policy in England, 1830–1914*, Cambridge – New York – Melbourne 1990.
Wienfort, Monika, Preußische Patrimonialrichter im Vormärz. Bildungsbürgertum auf dem Lande zwischen staatlichem Einfluß und gutsherrlichen Interessen, in: Klaus Tenfelde/Hans-Ulrich Wehler (Eds.), *Wege zur Geschichte des Bürgertums*, Göttingen 1991, 57–77.
Bildungsbürgertum und standesgemäße Lebensführung. Eine preußische Richterfamilie 1830–1863, in: Anja V. Hartmann (Ed.), *Eliten um 1800. Erfahrungshorizonte – Verhaltensweisen – Handlungsmöglichkeiten*, Mainz 2000, 85–101.
Patrimonialgerichte in Preußen. Ländliche Gesellschaft und bürgerliches Recht 1770–1848/49, Göttingen 2001.
Wiesner, Merry E., Frail, Weak, and Helpless. Women's Legal Position in Theory and Reality, in: Jerome Friedman (Ed.), *Regnum, Religio et Ratio. Essays presented to Robert M. Kingdom*, 1987, 161–169.
Winkelbauer, Thomas, »Und sollen sich die Parteien gütlich miteinander vertragen«. Zur Behandlung von Streitigkeiten und von »Injurien« vor den Patrimonialgerichten in Ober- und Niederösterreich in der frühen Neuzeit, in: *Zeitschrift der Savigny-Stiftung für Rechtsgeschichte. Germanistische Abteilung* 109 (1992), 129–158.
Wirsing, Bernd, *Die Geschichte der Gendarmeriekorps und deren Vorläuferorganisationen in Baden, Württemberg und Bayern 1750–1850*, Konstanz 1991.
»Gleichsam mit Soldatenstrenge«. Neue Polizei in süddeutschen Städten. Zu Polizeiverhalten und Bürger-Widersetzlichkeit im Vormärz, in: Alf Lüdtke (Ed.), *»Sicherheit« und »Wohlfahrt«. Polizei, Gesellschaft und Herrschaft im 19. und 20. Jahrhundert*, Frankfurt a.M. 1992, 65–94.
Wirthwein, Heike, Landjuden in Hessen im Vormärz, in: *Hessisches Jahrbuch für Landesgeschichte* 44 (1994), 71–90.
Wittstock, Jürgen (Ed.), *Bilder aus oberhessischen Dörfern. Zeichnungen und Aquarelle des Marburger Orientalisten Ferdinand Justi. Handbuch und Katalog zur Sonderausstellung vom 27.6.–16.8.1987*, Marburg 1987.
Wohlers, Wolfgang, *Entstehung und Funktion der Staatsanwaltschaft. Ein Beitrag zu den rechtshistorischen und strukturellen Grundlagen des reformierten Strafverfahrens*, Berlin 1994.
Wulfmeyer, Reinhard, Die Einführung der Bezirksräte und die Umbildung der inneren Landesverwaltung in Kurhessen 1821–1848, in: *Hessisches Jahrbuch für Landesgeschichte* 21 (1971), 160–213.
Wunder, Bernd, Vom Intelligenzblatt zum Gesetzblatt. Zur Zentralisierung inner- und außeradministrativer Normkommunikation in Deutschland (18./19. Jahrhundert), in: *Jahrbuch für europäische Verwaltungsgeschichte* 9 (1997), 29–82.
Zehr, Howard, The Modernization of Crime in Germany and France, 1830–1913, in: *Journal of Social History* 8 (1975), No. 2, 117–141.
Crime and the Development of Modern Society. Pattern of Criminality in Nineteenth-Century Germany and France, London 1976.
Zemon Davis, Natalie, *Fiction in the Archives. Pardon Tales and Their Tellers in the Sixteenth-Century France*, Stanford 1987.

Zimmermann, Bénédicte, Deux modes de construction statistique du chômage au tournant du siècle, in: Bénédicte Zimmermann (Ed.), *Le travail et la nation. Histoire croisée de la France et de l'Allemagne*, Paris 1999, 253–275.

Zimmermann, Clemens, Ländliche Gesellschaft und Agrarwirtschaft im 19. und 20. Jahrhundert. Transformationsprozesse als Thema der Agrargeschichte, in: Werner Trossbach/Clemens Zimmermann (Eds.), *Agrargeschichte. Positionen und Perspektiven*, Stuttgart 1998, 137–163.

Zucker, Alois, Soll die gerichtliche Voruntersuchung aufrechterhalten bleiben?, in: *Mittheilungen der culturpolitischen Gesellschaft* 1, Wien 1902.

Ein Wort zur Aufhabung der gerichtlichen Voruntersuchung, Berlin 1904.

Index